Causal Mapping for Research in Information Technology

V.K. Narayanan
Drexel University, USA

Deborah J. Armstrong
University of Arkansas, USA

IDEA GROUP PUBLISHING
Hershey • London • Melbourne • Singapore

Acquisitions Editor: Mehdi Khosrow-Pour
Senior Managing Editor: Jan Travers
Managing Editor: Amanda Appicello
Development Editor: Michele Rossi
Copy Editor: Bernard Kieklak, Jr.
Typesetter: Rachel Shepherd
Cover Design: Lisa Tosheff
Printed at: Yurchak Printing Inc.

Published in the United States of America by
Idea Group Publishing (an imprint of Idea Group Inc.)
701 E. Chocolate Avenue, Suite 200
Hershey PA 17033
Tel: 717-533-8845
Fax: 717-533-8661
E-mail: cust@idea-group.com
Web site: http://www.idea-group.com

and in the United Kingdom by
Idea Group Publishing (an imprint of Idea Group Inc.)
3 Henrietta Street
Covent Garden
London WC2E 8LU
Tel: 44 20 7240 0856
Fax: 44 20 7379 3313
Web site: http://www.eurospan.co.uk

Copyright © 2005 by Idea Group Inc. All rights reserved. No part of this book may be reproduced in any form or by any means, electronic or mechanical, including photocopying, without written permission from the publisher.

Library of Congress Cataloging-in-Publication Data

Causal mapping for research in information technology / V.K. Narayanan and Deborah J. Armstrong, editors.
   p. cm.
 Summary: "The causal mapping method has been used in a variety of research areas. The purpose of this book is to provide an introduction to causal mapping for IS researchers and practitioners, providing them everything they need to use causal mapping for both research and application"-- Provided by publisher.
 Includes bibliographical references.
 ISBN 1-59140-396-0 (hc) -- ISBN 1-59140-397-9 (sc) -- ISBN 1-59140-398-7 (ebook)
 1. Information technology--Data processing. 2. Causation--Research. 3. Causation--Economic aspects--Mathematical models. 4. Problem solving. 5. Thought and thinking. I. Narayanan, V. K. II. Armstrong, Deborah J.
 HD30.2.C3953 2005
 004'.072--dc22
                                              2004023605

British Cataloguing in Publication Data
A Cataloguing in Publication record for this book is available from the British Library.

All work contributed to this book is new, previously-unpublished material. The views expressed in this book are those of the authors, but not necessarily of the publisher.

Causal Mapping for Research in Information Technology

Table of Contents

Preface vi

Section I: Causal Mapping: An Overview of Approaches

Chapter I
Causal Mapping: An Historical Overview 1
    V.K. Narayanan, Drexel University, USA

Chapter II
Causal Mapping: A Discussion and Demonstration 20
    Deborah J. Armstrong, University of Arkansas, USA

Chapter III
What Have We Learned from Almost 30 Years of Research on Causal
Mapping? Methodological Lessons and Choices for the Information Systems and
Information Technology Communities 46
    Gerard P. Hodgkinson, The University of Leeds, UK
    Gail P. Clarkson, The University of Leeds, UK

Section II: Advances in Causal Mapping Methods

Chapter IV
Revealing Social Structure from Texts: Meta-Matrix Text Analysis as a Novel
Method for Network Text Analysis 81
    Jana Diesner, Carnegie Mellon University, USA
    Kathleen M. Carley, Carnegie Mellon University, USA

Chapter V
Belief Function Approach to Evidential Reasoning in Causal Maps 109
    Rajendra P. Srivastava, University of Kansas, USA
    Mari W. Buche, Michigan Technological University, USA
    Tom L. Roberts, University of Kansas, USA

Chapter VI
An Empirical Comparison of Collective Causal Mapping Approaches 142
    Huy V. Vo, Ho Chi Minh City University of Technology, Vietnam
    Marshall Scott Poole, Texas A&M University, USA
    James F. Courtney, University of Central Florida, USA

Chapter VII
Expanding Horizons: Juxtaposing Causal Mapping and Survey Techniques 174
    Deborah J. Armstrong, University of Arkansas, USA
    V.K. Narayanan, Drexel University, USA

Chapter VIII
Reflections on the Interview Process in Evocative Settings 195
    Kay M. Nelson, The Ohio State University, USA

Section III: Causal Mapping in IS/IT: Research and Applications

Chapter IX
Using Causal Mapping to Uncover Cognitive Diversity within a Top
Management Team 203
    David P. Tegarden, Virginia Tech, USA
    Linda F. Tegarden, Virginia Tech, USA
    Steven D. Sheetz, Virginia Tech, USA

Chapter X
Causal Mapping for the Investigation of the Adoption of UML in Information
Technology Project Development 233
    Tor J. Larsen, Norwegian School of Management, Norway
    Fred Niederman, Saint Louis University, USA

Chapter XI
Using Causal Mapping to Support Information Systems Development:
Some Considerations 263
    Fran Ackermann, Strathclyde Business School, UK
    Colin Eden, Strathclyde Business School, UK

Chapter XII
Strategic Implications of Causal Mapping in Strategy Analysis and Formulation 284
    Douglas L. Micklich, Illinois State University, USA

Chapter XIII
Knowledge at Work in Software Development: A Cognitive Approach for Sharing Knowledge and Creating Decision Support for Life-Cycle Selection 312
    Luca Iandoli, University of Naples Federico II, Italy
    Giuseppe Zollo, University of Naples Federico II, Italy

Section IV: Potential Directions

Chapter XIV
Object-Oriented Approaches to Causal Mapping: A Proposal 343
    Robert F. Otondo, The University of Memphis, USA

Chapter XV
An Outline of Approaches to Analyzing the Behavior of Causal Maps 368
    V.K. Narayanan, Drexel University, USA
    Jiali Liao, Drexel University, USA

About the Authors 378

Index 384

Preface

Causal maps represent cognition as a system of cause-effect relations for the purpose of capturing the structure of human cognition from texts, either archival or interview generated. Given the structure of causal maps, they can be represented pictorially, or as matrices. Once these cognitive structures have been represented, they can be examined for patterns, theory building or hypothesis testing. As you will see, the tool is *versatile* and can be used for policy making, exploratory, theoretical, and large scale empirical works.

Ever since Axelrod developed causal mapping as a tool for policy research its use has been increasing in frequency for research in various disciplines. IS researchers are just now discovering the power of causal mapping as a *research tool*, and its importance in *knowledge management*. Given the newness of the tool to the area, most researchers use other disciplines to learn about causal mapping, thus having to adapt the method for use in IT contexts.

The mission of the book is to bring together in a *single volume* both the necessary knowledge for using causal maps, recent advances yet to reach the professional IT community, and IS research works in progress employing causal mapping as a tool. Thus the primary mission of the book is to provide an *authoritative* source - a *one stop learning place*, if you will - for researchers interested in using causal mapping as a research or policy tool.

Contents of the Book

To accomplish this mission the chapters are clustered into four sections.

Section I lays out the context of the book, presenting the history and logic of causal mapping, and the mechanics of using it as a research or policy tool. Chapter I by Narayanan provides a historical perspective on the evolution of causal mapping into the IS/IT field. It sketches the diversity of perspectives, research contexts and foci within the causal mapping method. In Chapter II Armstrong explicates the choice points a researcher will face when conducting a causal mapping study and demonstrates the step-by-step process for conducting causal mapping research. Finally, in Chapter III, Hodgkinson and Clarkson review the major developments in the causal mapping method across a variety of domains so as to address the strengths and limitations of various approaches for the IS/IT community.

Section II includes five chapters that highlight the current advances in research (being made in related disciplines) using causal mapping to enrich the research of those currently employing causal mapping in IT research and policy making. Thus Chapter IV by Diesner and Carley details an approach to text based causal maps called the meta-matrix model, which lends a second level of organization to the networks of concepts found in a text. A tool for text analysis (AutoMap) is detailed in a demonstration of the approach. Chapter V by Srivastava, Buche and Roberts demonstrates the use of the evidential reasoning approach under the Dempster-Shafer theory of belief functions to analyze revealed causal maps in an IT organization example. Chapter VI by Vo, Poole and Courtney provides two studies that compare three approaches to building collective causal maps: aggregate mapping, congregate mapping and workshop mapping. The approaches are compared both conceptually and empirically to determine which approach performs best. In Chapter VII, Armstrong and Narayanan provide an extension of the causal mapping method in which casual maps derived from interviews are juxtaposed against causal maps developed from survey responses. Similarities and differences of the maps are discussed as well as the appropriateness of this validation technique. In Chapter VIII Nelson provides some reflections on the interactively elicited causal mapping process in a discovery (or exploratory) context. Issues in the interview process, identification procedure and coding scheme development are addressed.

Section III provides examples of papers in IS/IT using causal mapping techniques. Two chapters represent examples of causal mapping in IS/IT. Chapter IX by Tegarden, Tegarden and Sheetz details a study which focuses on the identification of cognitive diversity through causal mapping and cluster analysis. The study uncovered cognitive factions (diversity) within a top management team and details the various perceptions of the firm. Chapter X by Larsen and Niederman studies the use of UML and object-oriented analysis and design in software development. The remaining three studies illustrate the use of causal mapping inn applications. In Chapter XI, Ackermann and Eden focus on the use of causal mapping to facilitate the development of a shared meaning between business units and IS developers through a common platform which enables negotiated outcomes. Chapter XII by Micklich uses concept mapping, cognitive mapping and causal mapping to investigate factors in the demise of a telecommunications leader through a case study analysis. Finally, Chapter XIII by Luca Iandoli and Zollo presents a methodology based on causal mapping for the investigation and management of knowledge created by software development teams engaged in application development. A detailed application of the methodology to a case study in a software development firm is presented to demonstrate the methodological aspects.

The final section presents proposals for future causal mapping research to excite those whose research can be enriched by the use of causal mapping. Chapter XIV by Otondo presents a proposal to extend causal mapping research by representing linguistic and semantic nuances in associative, categorical and cognitive maps. Those maps are then used to link related elements to causal maps to create an integrated logical view of object-oriented design. In Chapter XV, Narayanan and Liao outline several methods for approaching the behavior of causal maps.

Acknowledgments

The chapters in this book were invited or solicited in a call for papers dispersed to the IS community via listserv and direct e-mail. Almost everyone invited participated in the development of the book. Out of those responding to the call, nearly half were picked up for further development. All chapters were involved in multiple rounds of reviews. Several individuals helped with the development of the book. We thank Mehdi Khosrow-Pour of Idea Group for encouraging us in developing the book, and Jan Travers, Michele Rossi, and Jennifer Sundstrom for keeping us on track. The authors would like to thank Paige Rutner, Christy Weer and other Ph.D. students at the University of Arkansas and Drexel University for their assistance and helpful comments. The authors would also like to thank Ken Armstrong for his creative input.

Section I

Causal Mapping: An Overview of Approaches

Chapter I

Causal Mapping:
An Historical Overview

V.K. Narayanan
Drexel University, USA

Abstract

In this chapter, I provide an historical overview of the use of causal mapping, and its migration from political science to organization theory, and more recently into research efforts in Information Technology (IT). Since this migration has brought in its wake a diversity of perspectives and approaches, a secondary objective of this chapter is to sketch this diversity. I discuss the diversity in perspectives, research contexts and focus. Three perspectives (social constructionist, objectivist, and expert-anchored), four research contexts (discovery, hypothesis testing, evocative and intervention) and three types of foci (content, structure and behavior) are summarized.

Introduction

A remarkable revolution is underway in the organization sciences: A new generation of scholars is enthusiastically bringing the role of the human mind back into the study of organizations. Unlike the deterministic views of man expounded by Skinner or of organizations promulgated by the early contingency theorists such as Lawrence and Lorsch, this new breed of scholars takes inspiration from the works of Barnard, Simon and Weick, and pays serious attention to human cognitive processes. Their cognitive

Copyright © 2005, Idea Group Inc. Copying or distributing in print or electronic forms without written permission of Idea Group Inc. is prohibited.

agenda is enabled by the availability of new research tools that have made possible the study of thought using "normal science" approaches. Indeed, these new tools have reached a level of maturity as witnessed by their increasingly frequent use in papers published in major management journals (Narayanan & Kemmerer, 2001).

One of these tools that has great potential for advancing research in managerial cognition is *causal mapping*. Causal maps represent thought as a network of causal relations, representing concepts through nodes and causality though links between nodes. They invoke the notion of causation, and users of the tool observe that causal analysis is built into our natural language, while side-stepping the philosophical challenges associated with the notion of causality. In recent years, this tool has been considered one of the most effective ways of representing thought (Mohammed, Klimoski & Rentsch, 2001).

This book is devoted exclusively to causal mapping. The primary objective of this chapter is to provide an historical overview of the use of causal mapping, and its migration from political science to organization theory, and more recently into research efforts in IT. This migration has brought in its wake a diversity of perspectives and approaches, and therefore, a secondary objective of this chapter is to sketch this diversity, so that readers can appreciate the subtle differences among the various users of the tool. Thus, this chapter is meant for those interested in an appreciation of the technique beyond its immediate application.

This chapter unfolds in two major sections. In the first section, I detail the migration of the causal mapping technique over five stages, identifying the milestones in its evolution, and the seminal works that punctuate this evolution. In the second, I summarize the diversity of approaches among users of causal mapping and, indeed, the discerning reader will notice this diversity in the contributions of this edited book.

Evolution of Causal Mapping

The term cognitive maps appeared in a paper written by Edward C. Tolman titled, "Cognitive Maps in Rats and Men," in the *Psychological Review* in 1948. Although he did not use the term in the sense known in organization sciences, Tolman extolled the virtues of reason, which were in contrast to the behavioral psychologist's view which focused on stimulus response mechanisms for explaining human behavior. The term was later used by Axelrod to name the methods he and his colleagues employed to represent the arguments of political elites. The term, "cognitive maps," however, conveyed the idea that the maps represented the actual workings of the mind. To avoid the claim that they were representing thought scholars following Axelrod began to employ the term "causal mapping." These scholars claimed that they focused only on causal assertions in a specific set of texts.

In addition to the evolution of the terminology, several streams of scholarship have contributed to the initial use of causal mapping as a tool for representing thought. These streams are varied and often not related to each other. Nonetheless, it is useful to reflect on this rich heritage, if only to discover opportunities that have not yet been exploited in the contemporary applications of this tool.

I discuss this evolution in five sections: (1) Early Precursors; (2) Immediate Precursors; (3) Axelrod's Seminal Work; (4) Causal Mapping in Organizational Sciences; and (5) Causal Mapping in IS. This is schematically presented in Figure 1.

Early Precursors

By early precursors, I refer to the streams of thought that are closely related to causal mapping, although they may not have been the sources of the original formulation of the tool. Although it is almost impossible to sketch *all* possible precursors, at least two distinct streams of thought have close affinity to the original causal mapping technique: structure of arguments, and industrial dynamics.

Structure of arguments. The idea that arguments can be represented has been well established in the philosophy of science for a quite a long time. A specific example was provided by Toulmin (1958): His analysis scheme is complex as it embraced a broader set of foci than the ones we find in contemporary causal mapping. The scheme responded directly to the need for a methodology that systematically probes the content, logic, and reasonableness of an argument, irrespective of the discipline or context and intent of the argument. The Toulmin framework was intended to achieve three purposes:

1) to enable the elements (and thus the structure) of any "argument" to be captured and delineated;
2) to allow any individual (whether the argument purveyor, opponent, or interested third party) to assess the quality of reasoning at the heart of the argument; and
3) to facilitate the comparison and assessment of two or more arguments, that is, to identify differences among arguments and to determine what these differences mean to both the reasoning and the outcomes.

The Toulmin framework consists of a number of elements: data, warrants, backing for each warrant, conclusion, and qualifiers including the conditions for rebuttal. The core of any argument is always woven around data to conclusions via warrants: some set of data allows a claim or conclusion (that is, an inference) to be drawn *because* a warrant enables a connection to be made between data and conclusions. Data can be simple, descriptive facts, historical statements, or projections about the future such as descriptions of the current conditions in the economy, its historic performance along multiple indicators, or judgments about the direction of emerging economic change. The overall intent of the framework is to test and establish the merit of, or justification for, the claim or conclusion.

From the 1950's onward, these ideas began to migrate into management circles. For example, the Toulmin method was employed by management scholars such as Mason &

Mitroff (1981) to facilitate strategic planning in organizations. More recently, this method has been used to deconstruct entire theories (Narayanan & Fahey, 2005). For empirically oriented scholars desirous of tracking social phenomena, this method was too complex and fuzzy since it required a large number of researcher-imposed judgments. For this reason, Toulmin was used mostly in the deconstruction of a theory or in interventions, not in empirical works. Nonetheless, Toulmin vividly underscored the idea that arguments can be examined as social facts.

Industrial dynamics. In many ways, the field of industrial dynamics that originated with Jay Forrester at MIT incorporated many of the central features of causal maps. Industrial dynamics aimed to describe the dynamics of a system (a firm, an industry, a city, a region, and even the world) with the aid of a mathematical representation of the system as nodes and flows. Using the power of computers, Forrester and his colleagues wanted to examine the behavior of the system under study. Forrester argued:

> "As industrial societies emerged, systems began to dominate life as they manifested themselves in economic cycles, political turmoil, recurring financial panics, fluctuating employment, and unstable prices. But these social systems became so complex and their behavior so confusing that no general theory seemed possible. A search for orderly structure, *for cause-effect relationships* (emphasis mine), and for a theory to explain system behavior gave way to a belief in random, irrational causes." (1968, pp.1-2)

The feedback and related principles developed in electrical engineering formed a basis on which to formulate a set of partial differential equations to capture system dynamics. A central facet of the system dynamics model is the incorporation of *two-way causality* that, in social sciences, was relatively less prevalent until the advent of the systems dynamic principles.

Unlike the Toulmin analysis, which was highly qualitative, system dynamics was highly quantitative, and hence, did not widely diffuse into organization sciences. The sheer mathematical sophistication required for its effective use, and the attendant information requirements, made it ill-suited for much of the social science work. Nonetheless the idea that system behavior can be depicted and analyzed can be traced to industrial dynamics.

Although the influence of Toulmin analysis and industrial dynamics were, at best, indirect, we can identify several immediate precursors to causal maps.

Immediate Precursors

Axelrod identifies five fields from which he has drawn inspiration to develop his cognitive mapping approach: (a) psycho-logic, (b) causal inference, (c) graph theory, (d) evaluative assertion analysis, and (e) decision theory.

Psycho-logic. Abelson and Rosenberg (1958) developed a mathematical system to deal with a person's cognitive processes called psycho-logic. Their system uses points and arrows, with points referring to "thing-like" concepts, and arrows expressing associations between concepts. As Axelrod notes, there are two major differences between cognitive maps and psycho-logic. First, nodes are variables that can have different values in a cognitive map, and not "things" as in psycho-logic. This makes cognitive mapping an algebraic system, not a logic system. Second, arrows in cognitive maps are representations of causal assertions, not attitudinal associations. Axelrod goes on to suggest, "Although the interpretations of the two systems are different, from a strictly mathematical point of view, a cognitive map can be regarded as a generalization of psycho-logic."

Causal inference. The statistical literature of causal inference was developed by Simon (1957) and Blalock (1964) to estimate the parameters appropriate to describe a given body of data. This literature is credited by Axelrod with the idea that points can be regarded as variables, and arrows can be regarded as causal connections between the points. However, cognitive mapping does not incorporate the complex calculations typically involved in the causal inference literature.

Graph theory. Graph theory and its mathematical ideas have been employed in both psycho-logic and cognitive mapping. It includes concepts such as paths, cycles, and components that are useful in the analysis of complex interconnections. Cognitive mapping uses graph theory, "but generalizes it by allowing the points as well as the arrows to take on different values."

Evaluative assertion analysis. Osgood, Saporta and Nunnally (1956) developed this analysis, which provides a method for systematically and reliably coding the structural relationships between pairs of concepts from a document. Axelrod's cognitive mapping method owes the coding process to evaluative assertion analysis.

Decision theory. This field, which has close affinity with the Operations Research discipline, was well developed by the time Axelrod formulated the cognitive mapping approach. The ideas of choice and utility from decision theory were transported by Axelrod to cognitive mapping, since one of the intended contributions of the cognitive mapping approach was to shed light on decision-making processes.

These five immediate pre-cursors, acknowledged as such by Axelrod, found their way to the original formulation of the cognitive mapping approach.

Axelrod's Seminal Work

In 1976, Axelrod published and edited his book, *Structure of Decision: The Cognitive Maps of Political Elites,* which heralded the advent of cognitive mapping in the literature.

In early 1970, while at the University of Berkeley, Axelrod along with his colleagues Matthew Bonham and Michael Shapiro turned their attention to the study of the beliefs of elite policy makers. Axelrod's initial work culminated in the development of a new approach to decision making based on the idea of a cognitive map of a person's stated values and causal beliefs. This approach was presented as a paper at the Conference on Mathematical Theories of Collective Decisions at the University of Pennsylvania, and published as a monograph (Axelrod, 1972a). Later, Axelrod used the verbatim transcripts of the British Eastern Committee to derive the cognitive maps of the committee members according to the coding rules he had developed, and the resulting analysis was presented to the Peace Research Society at their London Conference in 1971 (Axelrod, 1972b). Meanwhile Bonham and Shapiro collaborated to produce a preliminary report on their work (Shapiro & Bonham, 1973). To quote Axelrod:

> "By this time, the project seemed to have a life of its own, as different people found different uses for cognitive maps."

Axelrod pulled together the works of several of these people working on cognitive mapping to produce his classic, *Structure of Decision*.

Axelrod's work consisted of five major sections. The first section dealt with an introduction to cognitive mapping. The second section provided five empirical studies including Axelrod's study of the British Eastern Committee and Bonham and Shapiro's work. The remaining studies focused on Governor Morris in the Constitutional Convention, the Energy Crisis, and the politics of the international control of the oceans. The third section, which consisted of only one chapter, summarizes the conclusions of the empirical works, with particular emphasis on cognitive maps. The fourth section dealt with the limitations of the approach, and enumerated several projects for future work. The final section, the Appendix, contained the coding rules, and approaches to cognitive mapping including the questionnaire method, mathematics, simulation techniques, and a guide to source materials.

Axelrod's work thus provided several *methodological* ideas that are still with us today. Key among them are:

1) *Definition*. "A cognitive map is a specific way of representing a person's assertions about some limited domain such as a policy problem. It is designed to capture the structure of the person's causal assertions and to generate the consequences that follow from this structure."

2) *Method of coding*. Axelrod provided a detailed system by which a document may be coded. These rules have served the two following generations of researchers and will be covered in Chapter II.

3) *Sources of data*. Various sources of data from documents to interviews to questionnaires were illustrated by Axelrod.

4) *Analysis.* Although qualitative analysis is the most commonly used form of analysis in cognitive mapping, Axelrod presented several—even now infrequently used—analysis approaches, ranging from statistical analysis to simulations.

In short, the *Structure of Decision* was vast in its scope and profound in terms of the ideas it set forth. From the vantage point of this book, Axelrod's influence on the writings in organization sciences was immense. It is in this latter regard that I view this work as *seminal*. Indeed, almost all the contributors to the evolution of causal mapping owe a considerable debt to his work.

Causal Mapping in Organizational Sciences

During the last three decades, the use of causal mapping in organization sciences has increased, owing in no small extent to several developments in the field of managerial cognition. A comprehensive review of these developments is beyond the scope of this chapter (for a review, see Walsh, 1995). Instead, I will selectively cull out those developments that have facilitated the frequent use of causal mapping.

The first set of studies. Arguably the first effort to introduce causal mapping into organization sciences occurred with Bougon, Weick and Binkhorst's (1977) examination of the Utrecht Jazz Orchestra (UJO). Built around 14 variables obtained through naturalistic observation, discussion, and interviews, Bougon et al. first asked each UJO participant to indicate which variables influenced other variables, and whether the influence was positive or negative. Later they developed "etiographs" by unfolding the maps into content free graphs, which ranked variables into three clusters of givens, means, and ends. Their method was not a textual analysis of the kind proposed by Axelrod, but they made effective use of Axelrod's ideas to build a cybernetic theory of organizations. As the authors noted in the 1970's, their study represented a new approach to organizational analysis.

Next, following their footsteps, Hagerty and Ford (1984) used a modified version of causal mapping to examine the cause-effect beliefs about structure. In their study, the researchers presented a set of causes and effects and asked managers and students to create a causal map. Using metrics from graph theory, they found both agreement and disagreement between managers and MBA students.

The two studies invoked different methods of causal mapping. Bougon et al. (1977) used naturalistic observation and interviews to examine natural phenomena. Ford and Hagerty (1984) were primarily interested in theory testing, and therefore used an experimental approach in their use of causal mapping.

Influence of industrial dynamics. A second stream of work invoked industrial dynamics to examine organizational phenomena. Thus, Roos and Hall (1980) derived their inspiration from the industrial dynamics (system dynamics) tradition to better understand political processes within organizations. They conducted a case study of a new extended care facility connected to a hospital to highlight the advantages of influence diagrams by comparing the level of understanding before and after the technique was used. Roos and Hall acknowledged Axelrod, noting that the influence diagram represented their cognitive maps of factors influencing policies and budget levels for the extended care unit they studied. Thus, the mapping was not as systematic as in Bougon et al.'s study, since the primary objective of the authors was intervention-focused, or in their terms "to help integrate knowledge about decision-makers' values and the cause-effect of their pursuing these values."

Special issues. Two special issues gave a further boost to the users of the causal mapping technique. In 1987, a special conference convened in Boston to advance the cause of managerial and organizational cognition research. Several of the papers in this well attended conference were later published in a special issue of *Journal of Management Studies*. One of these papers featured causal mapping as a research tool. Building on earlier conceptual (Walsh & Fahey, 1986), and empirical works (Fahey & Narayanan, 1986), Fahey and Narayanan (1989) explicitly used the causal mapping technique to trace the evolution of Zenith, one of the then remaining US television manufacturers. They used annual reports to capture the thinking within Zenith, and used the term "revealed causal mapping" to distinguish what they did from cognitive mapping. Unlike Axelrod who had access to interviews, these authors, whose longitudinal study spanned over 20 years, were not able to access many of the players for interviews and, therefore, had to rely on archival sources of data. Fahey and Narayanan (1989) also noted that in many competitive situations, public statements represented *strategic* disclosure and may not have corresponded to the "true" cognitive maps held by the decision-makers. Unlike cognitive maps, which represented "true" thinking, these authors were content to study causal maps or the "assertions of causality."

A second special issue for *Organization Science* was organized by Meindl, Stubbart and Porac (1996), with the specific purpose of advancing the "cognition agenda." The editors noted that developments in a wide range of fields — from the sociology of knowledge to organization science — have called into question a strictly realist view of the world. In their opinion, even the environment should be viewed as partly contingent upon sense making by individuals. The causal mapping technique was featured in this collection, with Mauri Laukkanen (1994) articulating the steps involved in comparative causal mapping (i.e., comparing causal maps among individuals). According to him, all comparative projects have to address three critical tasks:

1) a need to acquire comparable natural data of several individuals or groups;
2) the problem of raw data conversion to achieve the necessary comparability and pragmatic compression; and
3) the need for a rigorous and efficient computerized platform for comparative analysis.

Laukkanen (1994) introduced the concept of "standard vocabularies" that can be used to capture concepts with similar meaning, but denoted by different words by different individuals. Laukkanen also provided a computer software called CMAP2 to mount the comparative analysis. Unlike Fahey and Narayanan (1989), who relied on manual techniques to create and compare causal maps, Laukkannen took the first steps in hypothesis testing studies.

Managerial and organizational cognition group in the academy of management. During the 1980's the move to advance a cognitive agenda was gathering strength. This culminated in the formation of the Managerial and Organization Cognition (MOC) interest group in 1989 in the Academy of Management, the premier professional association of management scholars. MOC was broadly based and focused on "how organizational members model reality and how such models interact with behavior."[2] The formation of the interest group, and its emergence as a division in 1999 within the Academy, signaled the arrival of cognition as a major area of inquiry in management literature, legitimizing this area within scholarly circles. For those individuals using or intending to use causal mapping as a research tool, this development gave them a big boost: It provided a forum to present their work, and with the competition for journal space, their work could no longer be as easily dismissed as inappropriate.

Mapping strategic thought. In 1990, Anne Huff published *Mapping Strategic Thought*, which laid the methodological foundations of the managerial cognition field. In retrospect, no book in recent years has had more influence on the methodological aspects of research in managerial cognition than this edited volume. Given the influence of this book, it is worthwhile quoting Huff about (one of) her reasons for putting the book together: "We are at the point in strategic management and other organization sciences that significant enthusiasm for cognitive studies is in danger of outreaching its methodological foundation. While a number of generally useful articles and books in management fields recommend a cognitive approach... little has been written about the technical aspects of specifying and studying cognition in organizations."

Although the book was not limited to causal mapping methods, causal statements were featured in four empirical studies (Huff & Schwenk, 1990; Bougon & Komocar, 1990; Boland et al., 1990; Narayanan & Fahey, 1990). Huff and Schwenk used causal mapping to study the attribution of success and failure by managers, raising two methodological issues: the validation and modification of causal maps and the constancy and variability of the maps. Bougon and Komocar drew attention to the importance of loops as the focus of change, highlighting the "circularity" of effects caused by a set of linear relationships. Boland et al. focused on the evolution of cognitive maps. Narayanan and Fahey extended the adaptation metaphor to the cognitive domain, by reexamining the 20-year history of the television receiver industry, focusing their attention on Zenith, and contrasting the results to their earlier study of Admiral (1989).

Most importantly, Huff's volume provided the technical details of causal mapping, and articulated for the first time the key methodological issues that needed to be tackled by serious researchers. These included: the purpose of a causal map, the map's territory, sources of data, and sampling, reliability, and validity. Huff and Fletcher (1990) concluded on a very optimistic note:

> "Cognitive maps, as artifacts of human reasoning can be used to study virtually any question raised by those who are interested in human activities... Our view is that...it is often most attractive as a method for studying topics that are intrinsically cognitive for explaining variance that is unexplained by other methods."

There is no doubt that Huff's book served to encourage hesitant researchers. It also became the textbook of choice for training a future generation of doctoral students.

Eden and Spender's Managerial and Organizational Cognition. Huff's volume was dominated by scholars of the U..S. tradition. By 1980, researchers in Europe were becoming increasingly interested in cognition. To showcase the European works, Eden and Spender (1998) edited a book based on the works initially presented at a Managerial and Organization Cognition research workshop held in Brussels in 1994. According to the authors,"In the past few years we have seen... *Organization Science's* special issue (1994), *Mapping Strategic Thought* (Huff, 1990) and new JAI series, Advances in Managerial Cognition and Organizational Information Processing. ... The present volume explores these questions, but unlike the works cited above, reflects a more European view — even though one European author appears in both places."

The book featured several chapters on causal mapping, three of which are noteworthy. First, Laukkanen succinctly summarized his ideas on comparative causal maps. Second, Jenkins summarized the key methodological challenges in comparing causal maps. Third, Eden and Ackerman described techniques used to analyze and compare idiographic causal maps. The book signaled the era of convergence and cross fertilization of ideas across the Atlantic.

Network studies. By 1990, the study of social networks had reached a level of maturity in sociology, with attendant analytical tools, software and particularly measures. Most researchers using causal maps understood that causal maps in the matrix representation form can benefit from the work done in social networks. They borrowed network measures because they were available, but initially did not pioneer the development of new measures. This task was left to scholars working at the intersection of social networks and computer science. Thus, following the quantitative tradition at Carnegie Mellon University, Carley and her colleagues developed numerous measures of causal maps at several levels of analyses, and created computer programs to analyze the maps. Although many of the network-based measures are underutilized at this time, the availability of computer software should facilitate the easy adoption of these measures.

In summary, as shown in Figure 1, over the last two decades, we have witnessed significant developments in the use of causal mapping. Three significant trends have

Figure 1. Causal mapping

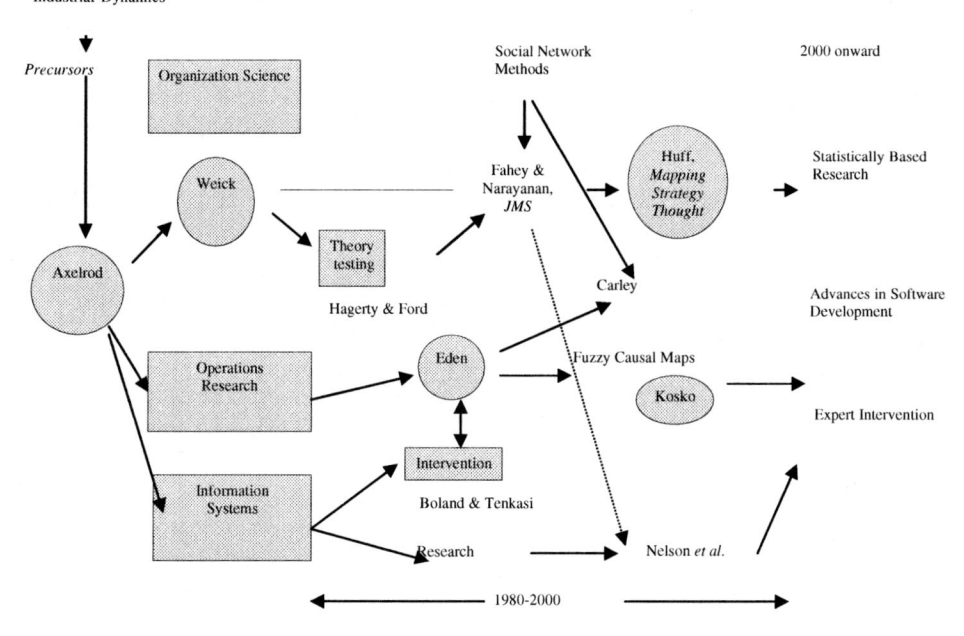

contributed to this progress. First, there has been a joining of three disciplines — the quantitative disciplines such as industrial dynamics, organization sciences and social sciences. Second, there has been greater international convergence, with U.S. and European researchers coming together under the auspices of the Academy of Management to push the frontiers of this method. Finally, computer software has proliferated, making it easier for researchers to use and analyze causal maps.

Causal Mapping in IS

In some ways, the use of causal mapping in the IS field is not new. Adherents to both the social science and operations research traditions in the organizational sciences sketched above have, over the last two decades, employed causal mapping in the IS field. These traditions respectively focused on two related problems:

- How do we use causal mapping to generate consensus, either in understanding or developing problem definitions?
- How do we use causal mapping to find solutions to specific technical problems?

In the first tradition, Boland et al. (1994) illustrated an intensive IT augmented approach to causal mapping to facilitate a hermeneutic process of inquiry. Causal maps then became a tool by which participants could glean and appreciate the logics in use by others in their organizations, and through a process of dialogue could develop a consensus of how to interpret their world. Similarly, Zmud et al. (1993) demonstrated the use of mental imagery in requirements analysis. Here, the focus was on developing a consensus in defining the problem — for example, the requirements of an IS system — so that the actual design would respond to the requirements and thus make the implementation less chaotic.

In the second tradition, causal mapping is used to arrive at solutions to specific, often technical, problems. As an example, Irani et al. (2002) used cognitive mapping to model various IT/IS factors, integrating strategic, tactical, operational, and investment considerations. The authors demonstrated how the causal mapping technique can capture the interrelationships between key dimensions identified in investment evaluation — something other more commonly used justification approaches cannot accomplish. Thus they claimed that causal mapping can be use as a complementary tool in project evaluations to highlight interdependencies between justificatory factors. I hasten to add that although this use of causal mapping has been less frequent in the literature, it offers great promise in the future.

During the early days, irrespective of tradition, the use of causal mapping in IS was application focused, i.e., to solve managerial problems in organizations. This began to change during the new millennium, with a special issue of *Management Information Science Quarterly* (MISQ) which dealt with qualitative methods of IS research. The issue featured causal mapping in a paper by Nelson et al. (2000). The paper not only provided a tutorial in causal mapping but demonstrated the possibility that in the IS field, causal mapping can be used in "evocative" research contexts. By "evocative," these authors referred to research contexts in which general theories were available to represent the phenomena under study, but the operationalization of theories to the respective contexts was not yet developed.

During the last four years, after the publication of the *MISQ* piece, there has been growing interest in the use of causal mapping in IS, not merely for qualitative studies, but for hypothesis testing studies as well. For example, Armstrong (2003) coupled causal mapping and survey data in a study of IS experts in Object Oriented and Procedural Programming. Similarly, a SIG-CPR3 workshop on causal mapping organized in 2003 in Philadelphia drew an audience of over 25 participants.

Above, I have sketched the evolution of causal mapping to highlight both the growing acceptance of this tool for research among scholars drawn from different disciplines, and also to segue to the diversity of approaches to using this technique. I now turn to this diversity.

Diversity of Approaches Among Users of Causal Mapping

Throughout the evolution of causal mapping, users have adopted diverse approaches, sometimes with different philosophical assumptions. So that we may appreciate this diversity, I will summarize the different approaches along three dimensions: a) Perspective, b) Research Contexts, and c) Focus. A fourth dimension, methodology, will be extensively dealt with in a later chapter (Chapter III) by Hodgkinson and Clarkson.

Perspective

Over the last three decades, researchers employing causal mapping as a methodological tool have invoked three different perspectives: (a) social constructionist, (b) objectivist, and (c) expert-anchored.

Social constructionist. In this perspective, the researcher is interested primarily in portraying the causal maps of the subjects — individuals or social systems — under study. The researcher is *intrinsically* interested in these maps, and expects the maps to have value in providing a cognitive explanation for the phenomena of his/her interest. The primary methodological challenge is establishing the accuracy of the researcher's representation of the subject's causal map. Most social constructionists deal with organizational and social psychological phenomena, where different individuals can hold different views of the world, and in most cases there is no single correct view. Barr et al. (1992) and Narayanan and Fahey (1990) exemplify this perspective.

Table 1. Social constructionist, objectivist and expert-anchored perspectives

	Social Constructionist	Objectivist	Expert-Anchored
Assumptions	Individual's causal maps shape their actions	Phenomena can be represented accurately as a causal map	Expert casual maps enable the cause-effect relations
Key Methodological Challenge	Accuracy of representation of individuals' causal map	Establishing the correct causal map	Locating the experts, and accurately representing their casual maps
Appropriate for	Social phenomena, uncertain theoretical contexts	Primarily for physical phenomena or deterministic social phenomena	Judgmental situations

Copyright © 2005, Idea Group Inc. Copying or distributing in print or electronic forms without written permission of Idea Group Inc. is prohibited.

Objectivist. Researchers adopting this perspective are typically interested in establishing the "true" causal representation of some phenomenon. For many, causal mapping is a simplified way to accomplish what industrial dynamics did for economic systems. A key methodological challenge is establishing not merely the accuracy of representation, but also an accurate description of the phenomenon. In the objectivist perspective, an individual's causal maps may be of interest largely to establish the degree to which the individual holds an accurate description of the phenomenon under study. The objectivist view is most applicable to the study of physical and technical subsystems, and is less prevalent in organizational sciences.

Expert-anchored. Researchers adopting this perspective are primarily interested in those phenomena where human judgment plays an important role. They acknowledge the social construction of many phenomena, but admit that individuals have varying levels of expertise within different knowledge domains. Thus, experts in their respective domains set a benchmark against which other individuals can be judged. Nadkarni and Narayanan (in press) exemplify this approach.

In the contemporary literature on causal mapping, discussions of the underlying perspective are often glossed over or left implicit. However, I will emphasize that researchers should be acutely aware of their perspective since it relates to key methodological challenges they may confront. For example, researchers representing a phenomenon as accurate — the objectivist perspective — should establish the accuracy of the causal map with respect to the phenomena, not merely the accuracy of the representation of an individual's causal map. Similarly, the expert-anchored perspective requires researchers to establish the credentials of the experts, and use the map of an expert (either a specific individual or a group of individuals in the case of complex phenomena) as a benchmark for evaluating the accuracy of others' maps.

Research Contexts

One of the great advantages of causal mapping is the versatility of its application. Indeed, it has been used in four distinct research contexts: (a) discovery, (b) hypothesis testing, (c) evocative, and (d) intervention.

Discovery. When utilized in ethno methodological inquiries, causal mapping provides a systematic approach to unearth phenomena. It is expected that two individuals following the causal mapping coding rules will arrive at congruent representations of the phenomena under discovery from the same set of interviews or archival materials. In this way, the use of causal mapping reduces the "subjective" component of data analysis that has been the *Achille's heel* of ethno methodological studies. However, this comes at a price — causal mapping reduces the role of human imagination in theory building. It also restricts researcher attention to phenomena that admit causal modeling. To date, causal mapping has been used predominantly in discovery contexts.

Hypothesis-testing. Increasingly, causal mapping is being used in "normal" science investigations, or more accurately, in studies that focus on hypothesis testing via statistical inference using large samples. The introduction of network methods of representation of causal maps and the derivative variables, which can be measured on interval or ratio scales, have enabled researchers of qualitative phenomena to operate in a hypothesis testing mode. Calori et al. (1994) and Marcozy (1997) exemplify this context. A significant barrier to large sample hypothesis testing studies has been the labor intensity of the causal mapping procedure. This may change as more sophisticated softwares enable us to automate the causal mapping procedure.

Evocative. In between discovery contexts with ill-defined theories and hypothesis testing contexts with clearly formulated theories, lies a context that Nelson et al. (2000) called "evocative." In evocative contexts, general theoretical frameworks are available, but specific operationalizations of concepts and linkages among them are undeveloped. In evocative contexts, experts who practice in a specific domain are available, but studies are needed to unearth their knowledge and examine it through available general theoretical frameworks to construct domain specific theories. Causal mapping evokes the concepts and causal linkages among them.

Intervention. Another popular use of causal mapping has been to assist management groups and organizations to make decisions. When complex IT systems are installed, the design phase may be enabled by the use of causal mapping to tease out implementation

Table 2. Causal mapping in four contexts

	Discovery	Evocative	Hypothesis testing	Intervention
State of Theory	Undeveloped	General theoretical framework available; No operationalization	Both theory and operationalization available	Can vary from undeveloped to fully developed
Applicability of Causal Mapping	Deriving concepts and establishing linkages	Operationalizing concepts	Obtaining relevant data	As an input to decision making
Source	Participants in the system	Experts	Relevant population sampling drawn by statistical consideration	Primary stakeholders and convenience sample
	Diverse sources to fully capture the phenomena			

challenges that could be addressed during the early phases. Alternately causal mapping can be used to get managers to reflect upon their reasoning processes. Eden (1992) and Boland et al. (1994) exemplify this research context.

Differing contexts pose different challenges to researchers using causal mapping. In the discovery and evocative contexts, validation of the derived causal maps by respondents is a key requirement in generating accurate representation of maps. In the intervention studies, derived causal maps can be used for further interpretation, or analysis, or even consensus building by exploring the differences among respondents. In hypothesis testing studies, reliability and construct validity assume greater importance.

Focus

Finally, researchers using causal maps as a methodological tool differ in terms of their focus on: (a) content, (b) structure, and (c) behavior.

Content. A focus on content leads the researcher to detail the concepts in the causal maps of respondents, and the cause-effect linkages among them. For example, Narayanan and Fahey (1990), in their longitudinal analysis of Admiral Corporation, attributed among other things, the absence of concepts pertaining to competition in Admiral's causal maps to the firm's eventual failure. Content-focused studies can be descriptive or comparative. In *descriptive* studies, the researcher may choose to describe a causal map in the respondent's own terms (a social constructionist perspective) or use concepts drawn from theory or from an expert. For example, in intervention contexts, the researcher will sometimes highlight the differences in content among individuals. In this case, the content categories derived from the individuals can be used without alteration. Alternately, the researchers may want to highlight the absence of significant content in a specific firm's causal map as a way of raising its awareness. In this case, they may recast the causal maps using a theory or an expert causal map. In *comparative analyses*, researchers compare concepts and linkages across different individuals. Here, researchers standardize the content so that comparisons can move forward (Laukkanen, 1994). The standardization involves the creation of a dictionary (i.e., a set of words to connote concepts that can be used across individuals).

Structure. Some researchers are interested in the structure of the causal map. For example, how comprehensive is the map? How focused is the map in terms of the cause-effect relationships? Are there feedback loops in the map? Indeed network measures are often used to operationalize the structural characteristics of the maps. For example, Calori et al. (1994) argued that the more diversified a corporation the more complex the firm's map would be and found empirical evidence to support their claim.

A critical consideration for structure-focused researchers is to demonstrate the validity of the measures they employ. Are they theoretically valid? Can one demonstrate acceptable construct validity and reliability for the measures? For example, Nadkarni and

Narayanan (in press) demonstrated the criterion-related validity of complexity and centrality, two network based measures of the structure of causal maps in an educational setting. However, in causal mapping research, efforts to establish the validity of the structural measures are still in the embryonic stages.

Behavior. Finally, some researchers are interested in the behavior of causal maps. They ask questions such as: Can you derive what decisions will flow from a causal map given a set of contingencies? Can you predict the decisions emanating from a causal map and check the predictions against actual decisions? Indeed analysis of the behavior of causal maps remains the Holy Grail for researchers using this tool in their work on managerial cognition.

Conclusion

Significant advances have been made in the refinement and application of causal mapping in several disciplines during the last three decades. The technique seems especially suited for empirical research in IS, as researchers deal with issues of representations of thought. The researchers now have a choice of perspectives (social constructionist, objectivist, and expert-anchored), research contexts (discovery, hypothesis testing, evocative, and intervention) and foci (content, structure, and behavior). I expect this diversity offered by causal mapping to stimulate the use of this technique. Indeed many empirical papers demonstrate the use and potential usability of this technique.

References

Abelson, R.P., & Rosenberg, M.J. (1958). Symbolic psycho-logic: A model of attitudinal cognition. *Behavioral Science,* 3, 1-13.

Armstrong, D.J. (2003). The quarks of object-oriented development. *University of Arkansas ITRC Working Paper WP034-0303.* Retrieved from the World Wide Web at: *http//itrc.uark.edu/display.asp?article=ITRC-WP034-0303*

Axelrod, R. (1976). *Structure of decision: The cognitive maps of political elites.* Princeton, NJ: Princeton University Press.

Barr, P.S., Stimpert, J.L., & Huff, A.S. (1992). Cognitive change, strategic action, and organizational renewal. *Strategic Management Journal,* 13, 15-36.

Blalock, H.M. (1964). *Causal inference in non-experimental research.* Glencoe, IL: Free Press.

Boland, R. J., Jr., Greenberg, R. H., Park, S. H., & Han, I. (1990). Mapping the process of problem reformulation: Implications for understanding strategic thought. In A. S. Huff (Ed.), *Mapping strategic thought* (pp. 195-226). Chichester, UK: Wiley.

Bougon, M.G., Baird, N., Komocar, J.M., & Ross, W. (1990). Identifying strategic loops: the self Q interviews. In A.S. Huff (Ed.), *Mapping strategic thought* (pp. 327-354). Chichester, UK: Wiley.

Bougon, M.G., Weick, K., & Binkhorst, D. (1977). Cognition in organizations: An analysis of the Utrecht jazz orchestra. *Administrative Science Quarterly*, 22, 606-639.

Calori, R., Johnson, G., & Sarnin, P. (1994). CEOs' cognitive maps and the scope of the organization. *Strategic Management Journal*, 15(6), 437-457.

Carley, K. (1997). Extracting team mental models through textual analysis. *Journal of Organizational Behavior*, 18, 183-213.

Eden, C. (1992). On the nature of cognitive maps. *Journal of Management Studies*, 29, 261-265.

Eden, C., & Spender, J.C. (1998). *Managerial and organizational cognition: Theory, methods and research.* Thousand Oaks, CA: Sage.

Fahey, L., & Narayanan, V.K. (1986). Organizational beliefs and strategic adaptation. *Proceedings of the Academy of Management Conference 1986*, Chicago, IL.

Fahey, L., & Narayanan, V.K. (1989). Linking changes in revealed causal maps and environmental change: An empirical study. *Journal of Management Studies,* 26, 361-378.

Ford, J.D., & Hegarty, W.H. (1984). Decision maker's beliefs abut the causes and effects of structure: An exploratory study. *Academy of Management Journal*, 27(2), 271-291.

Forrester, J.W. (1968). Market growth as influenced by capital investment. *Industrial Management,* 9(2), 83-105.

Huff, A.S. (1990). *Mapping strategic thought*. Chichester, UK: Wiley.

Huff, A.S., & Fletcher, K.E. (1990). Conclusion: Key mapping decisions. In A.S. Huff (Ed.), *Mapping strategic thought* (pp. 403-412). Chichester, UK: Wiley.

Huff, A. S., & Schwenk, C. (1990). Bias and sensemaking in good times and bad. In A. S. Huff (Ed.), *Mapping strategic thought* (pp. 81-108). Chichester, UK: Wiley.

Laukkanen, M. (1994). Comparative cause mapping of organizational cognitions. *Organization Science,* 5(3), 322-343.

Markoczy, L. (1997). Measuring beliefs: Accept no substitutes. *Academy of Management Journal*, 40(5), 1228-1242.

Mason, R.D., & Mitroff, I. (1981). *Challenging strategic planning assumptions.* New York: Wiley.

Meindl, J.R., Stubbart C., & Porac, J.F. (1996). *Cognition within and between organizations.* Thousand Oaks, CA: Sage Publications.

Mohammed, S., Klimoski, R., & Rentsch, J. (2001). The measurement of team mental models: We have no shared schema. *Organizational Research Methods*, 3/2, 123-165.

Nadkarni. S., & Narayanan, V.K. In press. Validity of the structural properties of text based causal maps: An empirical assessment. *Organizational Research Methods*.

Narayanan, V.K., & Fahey, L. (1990). Evolution of revealed causal maps during decline: A case study of admiral. In A.S. Huff (Ed.), *Mapping strategic thought* (pp. 107-131). Chichester, UK: Wiley.

Narayanan, V.K., & Fahey, L. (2005). The institutional underpinnings of Porter's model: a Toulmin analysis. *Journal of Management Studies*, in press.

Narayanan, V. K., & Kemmerer, B. (2001). A cognitive perspective on strategic management: Contributions, challenges, and implications. *Academy of Management Conference 2003*, Washington, DC.

Nelson, K.M., Nadkarni, S., Narayanan, V.K., & Ghods, M. (2000). Understanding software operations support expertise: A revealed causal mapping approach. *MIS Quarterly*, 24(3), 475-507.

Osgood, C.E., Saporta, S., & Nunnally, J.C. (1956). Evaluative assertion analysis. *Litera*, 3, 47-102.

Roos, L.L., & Hall, R.I. (1980). Influence diagrams and organizational power. *Administrative Science Quarterly*, 25(1), 57-71.

Shapiro, M.J., & Bonham, G.M. (1973). Cognitive processes and foreign policy decision-making. *International Studies Quarterly*, 17, 147-174.

Simon, H. (1957). *Models of man*. New York: Wiley.

Tolman, E.C. (1948). Cognitive maps in rats and men. *Psychological Review*, 55(4), 189-208.

Toulmin. S. E. (1958). *The uses of argument*. Cambridge, MA: University Press.

Walsh, J.P. (1995). Managerial and organizational cognition: Notes from a trip down memory lane. *Organization Science*, 6, 280-321.

Walsh, J.P., & Fahey, L. (1986). The role of negotiated belief structures in strategy making. *Journal of Management*, 12(3), 325-338.

Zmud, R.W., Anthony, W.P., & Stair, R.M. (1993). The use of mental imagery to facilitate information identification in requirements analysis. *Journal of Management Information Systems*, 9(4), 175-192.

Endnotes

[1] The author thanks Christy Weer, Drexel University, for her comments on an earlier version of this chapter.

[2] The statement in quotes is picked up from the domain statement of the Managerial and Organizational Cognition (MOC) division.

[3] Special Interest Group-Computer Personnel Research

Chapter II

Causal Mapping:
A Discussion and Demonstration

Deborah J. Armstrong
University of Arkansas, USA

Abstract

Causal mapping is a technique that can be used to represent cognition because it captures the structure of the causal assertions of an individual or group. As causal mapping becomes more prominent in the IS field, it is important that we understand the method, its strengths and limitations and its place within the spectrum of available research methods. Many researchers have made assumptions (both explicit and implicit) regarding causal mapping, without explicating the steps involved. This chapter details the causal mapping (CM) process and decisions that must be addressed so that researchers and practitioners can utilize this method to understand IS issues from a cognitive perspective, as well as provoke interest in expanding the boundaries of the CM method within the IS field.

Introduction

The growing interest in the cognitive foundations of behavior within the information systems (IS) field has led to a focus on representing and analyzing the cognitions of individuals and groups. Cognitive representations are created by eliciting the relevant cognitions of the participants and casting their cognitions into appropriate structural representations. Over the years there have been numerous methods of representing cognition that have been used, such as: argument mapping (Fletcher & Huff, 1990), context analysis (e.g., Birnhaum-More & Weiss, 1990), repertory grid (e.g., Tan & Hunter, 2002), and the Self-Q technique (e.g., Bougon, Weick & Binkhorst, 1977) to name a few.

Causal mapping is an additional technique that can be used to represent cognition. Causal mapping captures the structure of the *causal* assertions of an individual or group. Many believe that causal mapping holds great promise in addressing phenomena from a cognitive perspective, which is an under-utilized lens in the IS field. As we move causal mapping into the IS field, it is important that we understand the method, its strengths and limitations and place it within the spectrum of research methods. Many researchers have made assumptions (both explicit and implicit) regarding causal mapping, without explicating the steps involved. Thus buried in many of the studies found in the literature are the steps used to develop the cognitive representations of participants.

This chapter seeks to explicate the causal mapping (CM) process so that researchers and practitioners can utilize this method to address IS issues within organizations using a cognitive lens. The objectives of the chapter are two-fold:

- To demonstrate in detail how CM can be used to understand IS issues from a cognitive perspective
- To provoke interest in expanding the boundaries of the CM method within the IS field as we present advances and issues related to CM

In the remainder of the chapter, I provide the motivation behind causal mapping research and detail the causal mapping approach for both capturing individual maps and deriving collective causal maps. Next, I detail the representation and analysis of the maps, and discuss some key issues to address when reporting the results. I conclude the chapter with a summary of the key decision points researchers will face when conducting causal mapping research.

Selecting a Causal Mapping Approach

What are Causal Maps?

As Axelrod (1976) tells us, a *cognitive map* is a way of representing a person's assertions regarding a domain. A cognitive map is designed to capture the structure of the *causal* assertions of a person with respect to a particular domain. Over the years the concept of a cognitive map has been refined and is used here as a general class of representations of thoughts or beliefs. These maps can represent individual assertions, or those elicited from a group (Huff, 1990; Montazemi & Conrath, 1986).

Copyright © 2005, Idea Group Inc. Copying or distributing in print or electronic forms without written permission of Idea Group Inc. is prohibited.

A *causal map* is a sub-class of cognitive maps that focuses on the representation of causal beliefs; a network of causal relations embedded in an individual's statements, which is used to create an explicit cognitive representation (Huff, 1990; Nelson, Nadkarni, Narayanan & Ghods, 2000). A causal map is a collection of techniques used to explicate and assess the structure and content of mental models (Axelrod, 1976; Fiol & Huff, 1992). This allows the researcher to capture the cognitive structure of an individual by representing how domain knowledge is linked in his or her mind (Carley & Palmquist, 1992; Eden, Ackerman & Cropper, 1992).

A *revealed causal map* is the assertions of causality the participant *chooses* to reveal to the world (Narayanan & Fahey, 1990). With revealed causal mapping you are not assuming or implying that the representation elicited is in fact the "true" cognition of the individual. With revealed causal mapping you are explicitly stating that there is some gap between the representation evoked and the true cognition of the individual, because what has been captured is only what the participant was willing to reveal.

Why Use Causal Mapping?

Causal mapping (CM) is used to study cognition and the cognitive structure of individuals in a specific domain. Researchers employ CM to elicit a cognitive representation of interlinked concepts embedded in the knowledge and/or expertise of the participants around a domain. CM promotes understanding of the complexity of individuals' (and groups') knowledge base and belief structure (Kemmerer, Buche & Narayanan, 2001). The maps provide a frame of reference for understanding both what the participant knows and exhibits and the reasoning behind his or her actions.

As stated previously, there are several research contexts in which causal mapping can be utilized (see Chapter 1 for detailed discussion). In a discovery setting, the goal of using causal mapping is to discover commonalities in participants in search of possible patterns in the data elicited. In an evocative setting the goal is to develop mid-range theory to capture the cognitive aspects of expertise in the domain of interest. In a theory testing setting, the goal is to confirm, dispute, or expand existing theory. Lastly, in an intervention setting, the goal is often to create consensus around a course of action or issue at hand.

Types of Causal Maps

Mohammed, Klimoski and Rentsch (2000) have recently looked at four techniques for measuring mental models: Pathfinder Associative Networks, Multidimensional Scaling, Interactively Elicited Causal Maps and Text Based Causal Maps. The Pathfinder Associative Network (PAN) is a technique intended to produce a network structure in which the map nodes are the concepts and the linkages are the relatedness of the concepts (Schvaneveldt, 1990). Multidimensional Scaling (MDS) is a set of models that represents proximity data spatially (Carroll & Arabie, 1980, found in Mohammed et al., 2000). MDS uses geometric distance to identify the underlying dimensions of cognitive structure (Mohammed, et al., 2000). See Table 1 for a comparative summary of these methods.

Prior to creating revealed causal maps, a data source is selected and narratives are gathered. Although Mohammed et al. (2000) sees Interactively Elicited Causal Maps and Text Based Causal Maps as different techniques for measuring mental models, I see them as variants of the same technique. I argue that they are two data collection methods under the causal mapping technique. Data collection (elicitation of maps) can be accomplished in one of two ways: interviews (interactively elicited causal maps) or through archival texts such as annual reports (text-based causal maps). Interactively elicited causal maps (IECM) are developed from direct interaction with the participants to collect the data. Text-based causal maps (TBCM) are developed from documents or transcripts created for another purpose. The causal mapping data collection methods (IECM and TBCM) are detailed below.

Interview Method (IECM)

The researcher's goal is to gather participants' knowledge or beliefs and cast it into cognitive structures pertaining to a specific domain. The task is to access relevant participants and assist them in articulating their sometimes tacit knowledge or beliefs. Individuals serve as the data source and the narratives are gathered through interviews (ranging from unstructured to structured), which are discussed later in this section.

Sampling

One option is to use random sampling, which is particularly useful when engaging in studies from a social constructionist perspective. From this perspective, expertise is

Table 1. Mental model measurement techniques

Dimension	PAN	MDS	IECM	TBCM
Content	Fixed and supplied by the researcher, low emphasis	Fixed and supplied by the researcher, low emphasis	Variable and supplied by participant, high emphasis	Variable and supplied by participant, high emphasis
Structure	Associative explicit linkages, high emphasis	Associative explicit linkages, high emphasis	Causal explicit linkages, high emphasis	Causal inferred linkages, high emphasis
Researcher Skill	Low	Moderate	High	High
Participant Demands	Moderate	Moderate	High	None
Model Comparisons	Easy	Easy	Difficult	Difficult

Adapted from Mohammed, Klimoski and Rentsch (2000)
PAN = Pathfinder Associative Network; MDS = Multidimensional Scaling; IECM = Interactively Elicited Causal Map; TBCM = Text-Based Causal Map

uniformly distributed and therefore random sampling is an appropriate method of identifying participants in a study. In expert-anchored studies a snowball technique (Shanteau, 1987, 1992) with convenience sampling (Stone, 1978) is often used. Snowball sampling becomes necessary when experts of a domain cannot easily be located by random sampling or by screening, where domain knowledge (expertise) is important, and where the members of a domain are known to one another (Simon & Burstein, 1985). The snowball technique asserts that those individuals closest to a domain are appropriate to define the experts of that domain (Shanteau, 1987, 1992). An initial participant is chosen and additional participants are obtained from information provided by the initial participant. One expert identifies another and that expert identifies another, and so on. Once identified, each expert is interviewed (Axelrod, 1976; Huff, 1990).

Interview Protocol

The interview process may consist of fairly structured interviews (Bougon, 1983), semi-structured interviews, unstructured interviews depending on the research context. See Table 2 for a listing of appropriate data collection methods for each research context. An interview guide is developed by the researcher to facilitate the interview process. When developing the interview guide the researcher should be cognizant of several factors, such as the research context, the specific domain under study and the respondent pool. Readers wishing guidance in developing an interview guide may wish to see: Bradburn (1979); Kvale (1996); Payne (1951); and Rubin and Rubin (2004). Based on the participant's answer to the question, follow-up probes may be asked to elicit further details regarding the participants' thought process. The interviews are then transcribed verbatim into a document format (e.g., Microsoft Word).

Point of Redundancy

Within the CM method, the researcher should interview to the point of redundancy, which determines the adequacy of the sample size (Axelrod, 1976). In causal mapping research the point of redundancy, or saturation, represents the point at which further data collection would not lead to the identification of additional concepts. As the concepts emerge from the participants rather than being imposed by the researchers, this point serves as a way of establishing the adequacy of the sample. The point of redundancy

Table 2. IECM data collection methods

Research Context	Data Collection Methods
Discovery	Unstructured interviews
Evocative	Unstructured or semi-structured interviews
Hypothesis Testing	Semi-structured or structured interviews
Intervention	Structured interviews

is operationalized by aggregating the concepts mentioned by each participant (Nelson et al., 2000).

The participant's text (interview transcript) is reviewed and the number of concepts elicited is graphed (the X axis is the participant number and the Y axis is the *running total* of the number of concepts). The next participant text is reviewed, the number of additional concepts identified is added to the number from the first text, and the result is graphed. This process continues until all of the texts have been reviewed and the concepts elicited are identified. The difficulty is that the point of redundancy is not calculated until *after* the interviews have been completed and the classification scheme has been developed. If redundancy is not reached, additional interviews would have to be conducted. The same process would be used until redundancy is reached.

For example, if you identify ten concepts for the first participant, a point would be plotted on the graph at (1,10). If you identify an additional eight concepts for the second participant a point would be plotted on the graph at (2, 18), and so on. No additional concepts are elicited from participants 19 and 20, so the point of redundancy is reached by the 18th participant. See Figure 1 for a graphical representation.

Figure 1. Point of redundancy

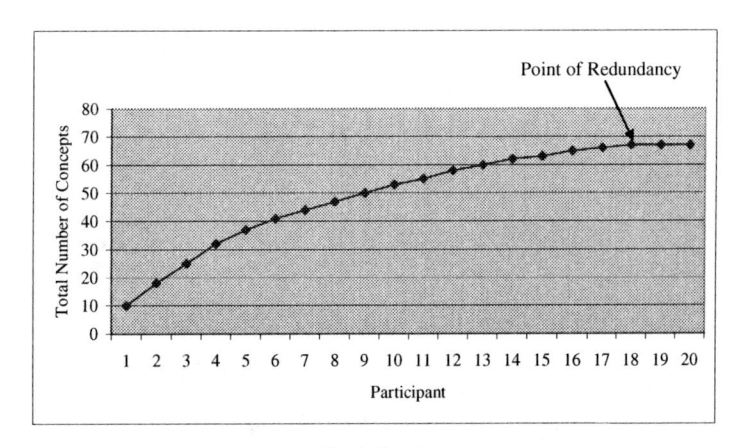

Data for Figure 1

Participant	Unique Concepts Identified	Total Concepts
1	10	10
2	8	18
3	7	25
4	7	32
5	5	37
...	...	...
15	1	63
16	2	65
17	1	66
18	1	67
19	0	67
20	0	67

Text-Based Method (TBCM)

Text-Based Causal Maps rely on non-invasive data collection techniques that avoid the recall biases of interviews (Axelrod, 1976). The researcher's goal is still to gather knowledge or beliefs and cast it into cognitive structure pertaining to a specific domain. The task with TBCMs is to determine the appropriate source of information and gather the data from that source. TBCMs have been found to be more economical in terms of time and effort required of researchers and subjects (Brown, 1992). Data sources for text-based causal mapping include any complex text (e.g., annual reports, case analysis, IS change request documentation, and legal decisions). TBCMs are particularly appropriate for longitudinal studies because they do not depend upon participants who may not be accessible, or whose memories may have faded with regard to the event under study (Narayanan & Fahey, 1990).

Sampling

The major challenge of using TBCM lies in defining the sample. There are several different sampling frames that may be used with TBCMs, including: (1) convenience, (2) random and (3) exhaustive.

1. The first type of sampling frame is the convenience sample. With a convenience sample, the researcher utilizes the statements/texts that are readily available to the researcher. For example, a researcher may be interested in the impact of a new product release, so he or she may use the press releases associated with the new product.
2. A second type of sampling frame is the random sample. Random sampling is useful when using public statements (e.g., annual reports), or when the universe of statements is quite vast and is difficult to specify with any degree of certainty. The researcher often must adopt some rules to determine which statements to sample. Although random sampling of statements may insure greater representativeness, problems of defining the universe render such sampling difficult. When using this method the researcher should try to explicate *a priori* decision rules regarding the choice of data sources. Examples of these decision rules include outlining a time unit to sample (e.g., month, year), number of data sources to utilize (if multiple sources are available).
3. A third type of sampling is exhaustive, in which the entire universe can be captured. This sampling frame is often used in a tightly controlled environment, such as a case study with a specified respondent pool (e.g., Nadkarni, 2003).

Point of Redundancy

The point of redundancy is only applicable to TBCM projects when using a convenience sample. If a convenience sample is used the point of redundancy should be calculated as previously indicated.

Deriving Causal Maps

There are several terms used in the causal mapping process that require explication and will help set the context for the following discussions. See Table 3 for a listing of the basic causal mapping terms and corresponding definitions.

Figure 2 provides a flow chart of a revealed causal mapping process based on the process developed by Narayanan and Fahey (1990) and Nelson et al. (2000). Each phase in the process is described in the following text.

Step 1: Identify Causal Statements

The first task is to identify the causal statements from the documents (e.g., interview transcripts or annual reports) (Axelrod, 1976). This process involves identifying the cause and effect phrases and the linkage between them. Causal statements are statements that imply a cause-effect relationship. Some of the key words used in identifying explicit causal statements are "if-then," "because," and "so" (Axelrod, 1976). In addition to explicit causal statements, according to Axelrod (1976), there are also implicit relationships found in causal statements. The phrase may not contain the traditional key words used to identify causal statements, but the causality of the sentence is clear within the context of the text. Some "key words" that have been used in identifying implicit causal statements are "think," "know," "use," and "believe". For example, the sentence "If I want to get beyond where I am today, then am I going to have to go outside of the business?" could be coded as an explicit statement since it contains the words "if" and "then." Additionally, the sentence "I don't think gender should be an issue, I would promote whoever is smartest" can be coded as an implicit statement. The statements in the form of concepts and cause-effect relationships are captured in the language of the

Table 3. Causal mapping definitions

Term	Definition
Causal Map	A network of causal assertions (cause/link/effect) that can be expressed in a matrix or diagram form.
Causal Statement	A statement (phrase or sentence) that contains a casual assertion, most generally of the form cause/link/effect.
Coding Scheme	A dictionary of terms (concepts or constructs) and definitions of those terms (concepts or constructs). The coding scheme is used to simplify the causal statements and corresponding maps.
Concept	A word or phrase that captures the meaning or essence of a participant's phrase.
Construct	A word or phrase that captures the meaning or essence of a group of concepts.
Link	The relationship or causal belief between two concepts (or constructs).
Raw Causal Map	A causal map in which the concepts (constructs) are represented in the language of the participant.
Raw Causal Statement	A causal statement that is captured in the language of the participant.
Revealed Causal Map	The assertions of causality the participant *chooses* to reveal to the world.

Figure 2. Revealed causal mapping process

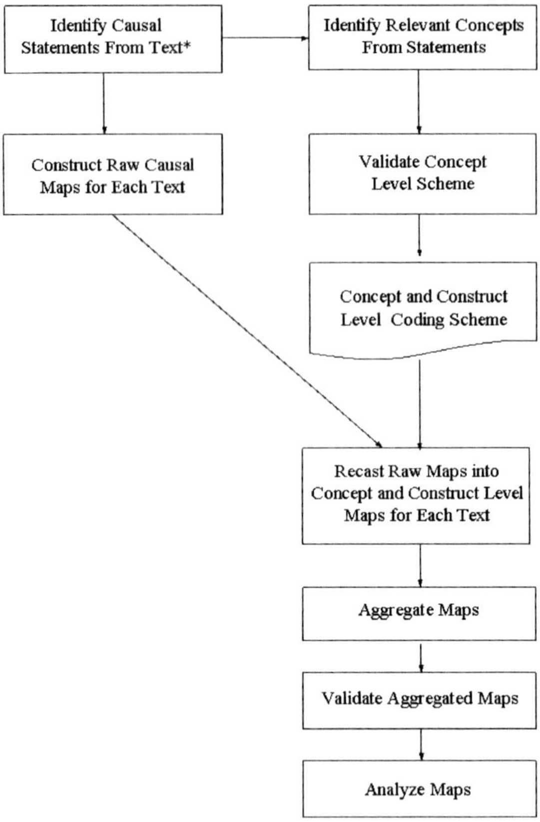
Identify Causal Statements From Text*
Identify Relevant Concepts From Statements
Construct Raw Causal Maps for Each Text
Validate Concept Level Scheme
Concept and Construct Level Coding Scheme
Recast Raw Maps into Concept and Construct Level Maps for Each Text
Aggregate Maps
Validate Aggregated Maps
Analyze Maps

**The term "text" is used to represent both IECM transcripts and TBCM texts.*

participants (Narayanan & Fahey, 1990). Other examples of causal statements would include:

1. Object-oriented development is easy *because* you think of everything as an object.
2. *If* I've got this object built up *then* I go back and actually try to write some of the methods.
3. Once I have all of the information I need I *think* about what are the objects that will be needed.

Depending on the type of data collection, IECM or TBCM, the coding process will differ. If you are using TBCM, generally you are using public documents (e.g., annual reports), which have been carefully crafted. The author of the document has (most likely) placed emphasis on the sentence construction, grammar and intended meaning of each sentence. In this context, the causal statements should be relatively clear and straightforward.

Copyright © 2005, Idea Group Inc. Copying or distributing in print or electronic forms without written permission of Idea Group Inc. is prohibited.

In contrast, if you are using IECM, the causal statements are often difficult to discern (Kemmerer, Buche & Narayanan, 2001). In this case the participant sample plays a large role in the ease (or difficulty) of coding. For example, if you are speaking to IS personnel regarding their current project, they are usually quite articulate. In contrast, if your research sample consists of IS students discussing a very technical topic, or respondents discussing a sensitive topic (e.g., layoffs) the participants may have difficulty expressing themselves. In addition, you will probably have several "starts and stops" within the transcript. By this I mean an individual will begin to speak, stop and then restart with the thought. This can present challenges when coding the transcript. In this case, it is up to the researcher to discern the causal statement (if any) in the text. It is often helpful to have an audio recording (if possible) to listen to the tone of the participant in addition to the words.

Identification Rules

The guidelines, which have been adapted from Axelrod (1976), are provided to show researchers how causal maps can be derived from texts. The coder must scrutinize the text to record all cause-effect relationships within the text. The sentences or phrases that are of interest to the coder are those that assert a causal relationship (A affects B). To appropriately identify the causal statements the researcher needs a set of decision rules to help guide the process. The rules are:

1. Some relationships are implicit in the phrase or sentence and a cause/effect relationship cannot be found in the structure of the phrase. In this case the coder should ask herself if the phrase implies a relationship between variables. If yes, then the phrase should be coded as a causal statement (be careful not to insert bias into coding implicit statements to create assertions).

2. It is important to maintain the original language of the participants as faithfully as possible.

3. It is important to reflect the speaker's statement in kind and number. If a speaker states a relationship more than once, the coder should note the relationship each time it is mentioned.

4. If a speaker agrees with an assertion made by someone else the coder should pay close attention to the speaker's wording. If the speaker is agreeing with the assertion then it is recorded as a causal statement. If the speaker is merely acknowledging the statement then it is not coded.

5. Assertions should be made within a sentence or two at most. Do not look for assertions by linking paragraphs.

In addition to these basic guidelines, Wrightson (1976) has provided a listing of the structural relationships that may be found within a text and how they should be coded. See Appendix A for an adapted (and abbreviated) sample of these structures.

Reliability

To establish the reliability of the identification procedure, interview texts are coded by multiple researchers/raters. The raters are deemed qualified to identify causal statements if they have a familiarity with the technique and the domain under study. If the sample is small, then complete sampling should be conducted. As the total number of pages of transcripts increases, it becomes impossible for each rater to code each text. There are usually two rounds of coding that cover a sample of the texts (5 - 10%). This subset of the texts should be chosen at random. Comparisons are made for agreement and disagreement between the researchers. Where disagreement occurred the discrepancies are resolved through discussion. The reliability between the researchers is calculated by measuring the level of agreement on the identification of causal statements and linkages. The level of agreement between the researchers should be at least 0.75, to have an acceptable level of reliability. For example, in her study of teaching methods, Nadkarni (2003) reported Kendall's coefficient of concordance (Siegel, 1956) to be 0.75 and argued this was an acceptable level of reliability. A reliability less than 0.75 indicates that the procedure is not robust enough for research purposes, and a modified identification procedure will need to be developed.

Step 2: Construct Raw Causal Maps

In the second step, the causal statements identified in the first step are then separated into "causes" and "effects" to construct the "raw causal maps." See Table 4 for sample causal statements.

A raw causal map is a map constructed using the language of the participants (See Figure 3).

Step 3: Develop Coding Scheme

In CM research developing a coding scheme is important for several reasons, which include: avoiding misclassification, interpretation and theory building. Carley and Palmquist (1992) argue that aggregating actual raw phrases in the text into generalized concepts can be used to move the coded text beyond explicitly articulated ideas to implied

Table 4. Sample causal statements

Cause	Link	Effect
You think of everything as an object	*Because*[1]	Object oriented development is easy
I've got this object built up	*If* then	I go back and actually try to write some of the methods
Once I have all of the information I need	I *think* about	What are the objects that will be needed

[1] *Note: When the keyword "because" is in the sentence the cause comes after the keyword. Refer to the sentences on page 28.*

Figure 3. Raw causal map

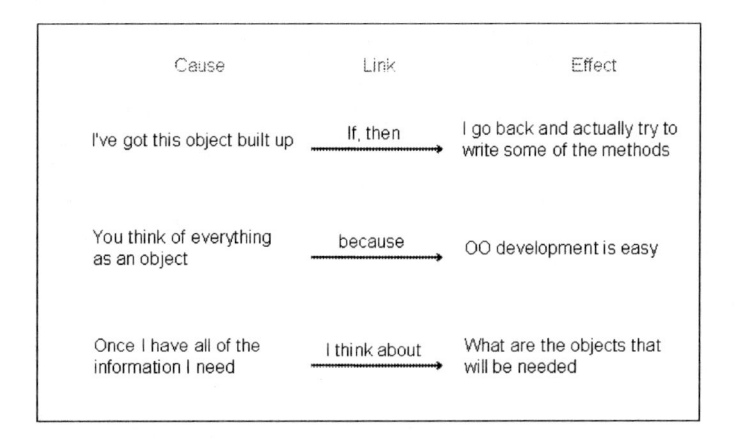

Cause	Link	Effect
I've got this object built up	If, then →	I go back and actually try to write some of the methods
You think of everything as an object	because →	OO development is easy
Once I have all of the information I need	I think about →	What are the objects that will be needed

or tacit ideas and to avoid misclassification of concepts due to peculiar wording on the part of individuals. In terms of interpretation, the coding scheme provides a mechanism to reduce the cognitive load for both the researcher and the end user of the causal map. For the researcher, a coding scheme is used to simplify the texts. Often the texts are numerous pages in length and can be cumbersome to work with. By developing a coding scheme, like terms can be combined and simplified into a standard format. This aids analysis and interpretation of the maps. For the end user, the readability of the maps is much improved when a word or short phrase can be substituted for a sentence. Again, this provides consistency and clarity for the end user. From a theory building perspective a coding scheme aids understanding of how the concepts (constructs) fit together into a cohesive unit.

The steps involved in developing a coding scheme are dependent on the research context of the study. Two different approaches have been employed to recast the content of causal maps into a common scheme: *benchmarking* and *theory-driven* (Nadkarni & Narayanan, in press). Each approach is described and associated with the appropriate research context.

Benchmarking

With the discovery and evocative approaches, the relevant concepts are identified from the participants' statements (Nadkarni & Narayanan, in press; Nelson et al., 2000). This process is referred to as benchmarking. In the benchmarking approach a list of ideal concepts and links between concepts emerges from the causal maps of one or a group of experts. This list is then used to compare the causal maps of other individuals. The benchmarking approach has been widely used in expert-novice comparison studies (e.g., Hong & O'Neil, 1992). In these studies a causal map is developed based on the concepts evoked from domain experts, with the expert map serving as the standard to which the novice maps are compared. The benchmarking approach is useful in discovery and evocative contexts and in particular studies linking causal maps to performance and learning.

Theory-Driven

With the hypothesis testing and intervention approaches, the relevant concepts are defined independent of, and prior to, coding from relevant literature. In the theory-driven approach, the content in the individual causal maps is recast into theoretical categories salient in the domain represented by the maps (e.g., Carley & Palmquist, 1992; Fahey & Narayanan, 1989). In taking this approach, the researchers should first review the relevant literature to determine if there are any theoretical classification schemes that would be appropriate. If no single classification scheme is available, a composite classification scheme encompassing the favorable aspects of the multiple schemes can be used. Tying emergent categories to extant theory has been recommended to develop standard categories (Carley & Palmquist, 1992) and build theory. See Table 5 for a summary of the decision process.

The coding process begins with grouping frequently mentioned words in the statements. A word or word group is created that captured the essence of the statement. For example, the sentence fragment "You group the requirements document items based on functions" could be labeled "Functions" or the fragment "bias on the part of management" could be labeled "Management Bias." Multiple researchers should review the statements and independently place them into conceptual categories. Comparisons are made for agreement and disagreement in the categorization of concepts. Where disagreement occurs the discrepancies are resolved through discussion. The level of agreement between the raters should be measured with the average no lower than 0.75. Once the conceptual level scheme is developed, all of the statements are placed into the appropriate concept category.

Once the concept-level coding is completed, a construct-level classification scheme can then developed. Again, the benchmarking or theory-driven process should be used.

Table 5. Coding scheme development

Research Context	Concepts	Theory Guidance
Discovery	Benchmarking from participants	No
Evocative	Benchmarking from participants	Minimal
Hypothesis Testing	From theory	Yes
Intervention	From theory	Yes

Table 6. Concept/construct level coding scheme

Raw Phrase	Coded Concept	Construct
You think of everything as an object	Object	Structure
Object-oriented development is easy	OO Development	Object-Oriented Development Systems
I've got this object built up	Object	Structure
I go back and actually try to write some methods	Method	Behavior
Once I have all of the information I need	OO Development	Object-Oriented Development Systems
What are the objects that will be needed	Identifying Objects	Object-Oriented Modeling / Analysis

Once the construct-level scheme is complete, the concepts can be aggregated into higher level (construct) categories. While some loss of information will be experienced, the ease of interpretation is greatly increased. Table 6 lists a sample of raw statements, the corresponding concept and construct-level categorization.

Validation of Concepts

Once the coding scheme has been developed the concepts should be validated to ensure reliability of the scheme. The coding scheme approach (benchmarking or theory-driven) will determine the most appropriate method of validation. When using the benchmarking approach validation of the coding scheme with individuals who have domain expertise but are not involved in a prior portion of the study is helpful. Validation can be accomplished in multiple ways (e.g., card sort, electronic card sort). With a card sort, the participants are provided the constructs and index cards with each concept. The reliability between the participants is calculated by measuring the level of agreement on the card sort. With the electronic card sort, participants are given an electronic spreadsheet with all of the concepts listed on one sheet and the statements on another sheet. The expert raters sort the concepts into the constructs. The results of each card sort are compared to determine reliability of the coding scheme.

When using the theory-driven approach, the coding scheme should be validated against the existing theoretical framework. When using the theory-driven approach validation of the coding scheme can be accomplished using researchers who have knowledge of the theoretical framework but are not involved in a prior portion of the study. The researchers can validate the scheme by comparing the coding scheme with the theoretical framework. Any discrepancies should be resolved through discussion.

Step 4: Recast "Raw" Maps into Revealed Causal Maps

Once the classification scheme is completed, the causal statements for each participant are placed into the appropriate concept (and construct level) categories. The result is a concept (and construct level) causal map for each participant. See Figures 4 and 5 for concept and construct level maps respectively.

Figure 4. Concept level causal map

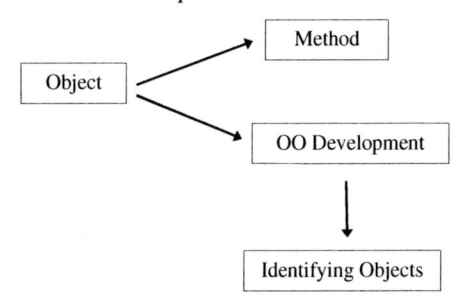

Figure 5. Construct level causal map

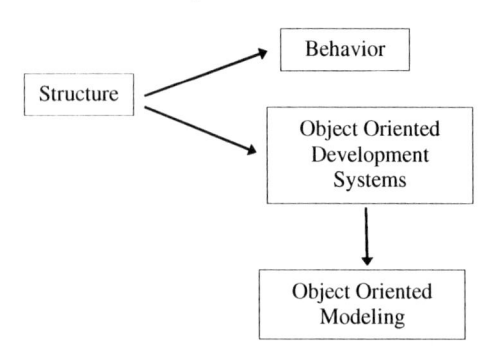

[Diagram: Structure → Behavior; Structure → Object Oriented Development Systems → Object Oriented Modeling]

The individual maps are then aggregated (Axelrod, 1976; Bougon et al., 1977). The aggregation is performed at both the concept level and the construct level. The aggregation process consists of combining the causal maps of each participant into a single aggregate map.[1]

Validation of Maps

Once the maps have been created, they should be validated. The validation method is determined by the data collection method (IECM or TBCM). As a source of validation for an IECM a member check may then be performed using the aggregated maps to ensure accurate and comprehensive representation (Lincoln & Guba, 1985). Each participant (or as many as you have access to) is shown the aggregated maps and asked if the maps accurately reflect the concepts, linkages and constructs. It should not be unexpected that as the participant walks through the map he or she will be surprised. The map reflects multiple causal relationships and most individuals do not consciously perceive the causality of concepts in terms of a network. The key is to engage the participant so he or she can reflect on the map you constructed based on the interviews. After a thorough discussion of the map with the participant, any discrepancies should be reported. For example, Nelson et al. (2000) fed the maps back to the organization to get feedback on maps.

When using TBCMs (e.g., archival data) validation becomes a more complicated process because there is no one to confirm your results. With TBCMs one commonly used method of validation is triangulation with other sources. For example, if the researcher is using change request data to track software development productivity, additional data may be gathered from departmental annual reports or individual annual reviews. In another example, Nadkarni and Narayanan (in press) validated the causal maps they constructed from annual reports of firms with the firms K-10 statements. Both internal and external sources can be used if available.

Representation of Maps

Causal maps may be represented in two main forms: via diagram or matrix. With the diagram method the concepts (constructs) are usually represented as a word or words enclosed in a box. The linkages are represented as lines with arrowheads. The lines originate from the cause concept (construct) with the arrowhead pointing to the effect concept (construct). Whenever possible, the map should be drawn so that the arrows flow from left to right with little or no crossing of the lines (Axelrod, 1976). In some instances there are mutually connected concepts. When two concepts are mutually connected the concepts are causally connected in both directions (the two concepts are both causes and effects of each other) (Knoke & Kuklinski, 1982). Mutually connected concepts are represented as a two-headed arrow.

With the matrix representation the two primary matrices utilized are the adjacency and reachability. An *adjacency matrix* is a matrix representing the association of direct linkages between two constructs (Knoke & Kuklinski, 1982). If you are interested in the presence or absence of a causal relationship between concepts, the adjacency matrix contains only "0's" and "1's" (Carley & Palmquist, 1992). In the matrix the in-degrees is the sum of all of the linkages flowing into the concept. Stated another way, it is the number of times that the concept is an effect concept in a causal statement. The out-degrees is the sum of all of the linkages flowing out of the concept. Again, stated another way, it is the number of times that the concept is a cause concept in a causal statement. Table 7 provides a sample adjacency matrix.

If you are interested in not only the presence or absence of a causal relationship between concepts but also the strength of the relationships, then the adjacency matrix contains "0" for no relationship and a whole number (e.g., "4") for the number of times that relationship is recorded (Carley & Palmquist, 1992). The method for calculating the frequency of linkages between two constructs is a percentage of the total linkages between all constructs (Ford & Hegarty, 1983).

The *reachability matrix* indicates both the direct and indirect effects of a variable on all other variables (Nelson, et al., 2000) and is calculated by the formula:

$$R = A + A^2 + A^3 + \ldots + A^{n-1}$$

where R is the reachability matrix, A is the adjacency matrix and n is the number of variables. Table 8 provides a sample reachability matrix.

It is important to note that while the diagram and matrix methods are both appropriate for causal mapping representation, as the maps become more complex researchers should carefully consider their choice. For example, in Figure 6 you can see that this is an extremely complex causal map (many concepts with many linkages). While possible, it may be easier to derive the structural properties using the matrix method (aided by computer analysis).

Table 7. Sample adjacency matrix from Figure 4 map

	1	2	3	4
Object	-	1	1	0
Method	0	-	0	0
OO Development	0	0	-	1
Identifying Objects	0	0	0	-

Table 8. Sample reachability matrix from Figure 4 map

	1	2	3	4
Object	-	1	1	1
Method	0	-	0	0
OO Development	0	0	-	1
Identifying Objects	0	0	0	-

Figure 6. Complex causal map

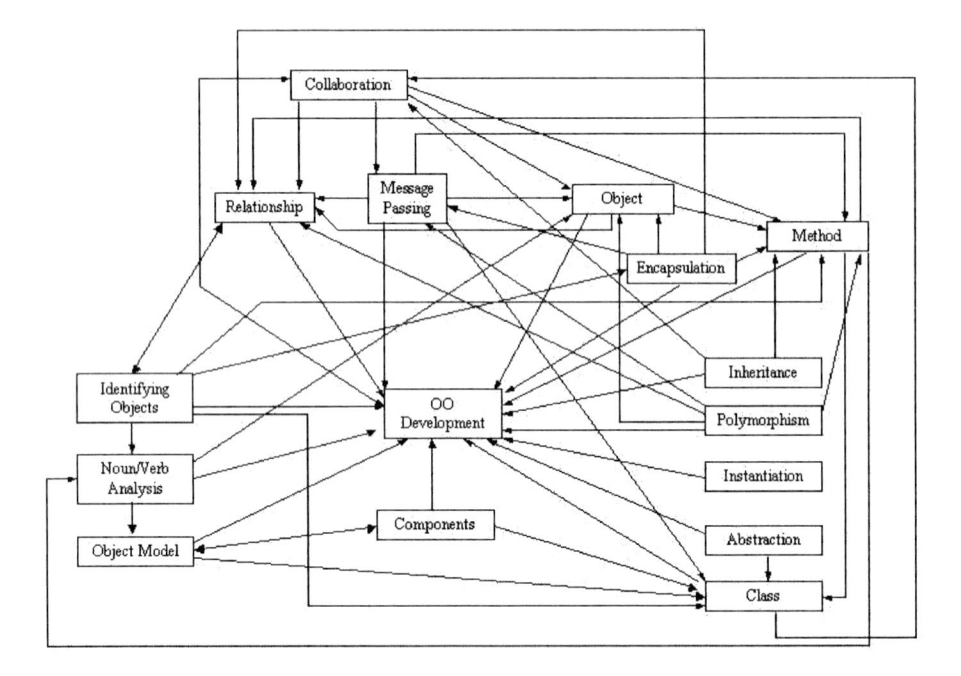

Analysis of Causal Maps

There are two aspects of causal mapping that have been consistently addressed in the literature on analysis: content and structure (Nadkarni & Narayanan, in press). The content refers to the meaning of specific concepts embedded in a causal map, and the structure reflects the organization of the concepts in a map. In addition to these two aspects, some researchers have begun to address the behavioral aspects of causal maps. Behavior (as defined in Chapter I) asks the question, once we understand what the map is telling us, can we use the map to make predictions? Toward the end of the book we propose approaches to study the behavior of causal maps. In this chapter I focus on the content and structural aspects only.

Content

The content of a causal map captures the meaning of specific concepts embedded in a causal map, and provides rich insights into the meaning embedded in the map. For example from Figure 4 we can see there are four concepts in the map. I could say that object-oriented software development is constituted by four concepts: objects, methods, object-oriented development and identifying objects. The definition of each of these concepts would be discussed in detail along with the implications of the causal connections. For example, the connection between object and method could be informed by quotes from the interviews and compared against existing theory (if applicable). In the discovery and evocative contexts, description of the content is of primary importance. In hypothesis testing and intervention, the content analysis plays a lesser role, because the analysis is strongly informed by existing theory.

Structure

The structure of a causal map reflects the organization of the concepts in a map. Since most techniques used to analyze content lack a quantitative mechanism for comparing causal maps, researchers have used structural measures of causal maps in comparative studies linking causal maps to other relevant constructs. Most of the measures focus on some aspect of the complexity of the map drawing on the assumption that the higher the complexity of the map, the higher the level of cognition of the individual.

From the map in Figure 4 you can see that there are four concepts (represented as a term enclosed in a box) and three linkages (lines with arrowheads) in the map. The three causal linkages are from object to method, object to object-oriented development and from object-oriented development to identifying objects. The concepts that have all arrows terminating into the concept are effect-only concepts (e.g., method), whereas the concepts with all arrows originating from the concept are cause-only concepts (e.g., object).

As mentioned previously, in some instances there are mutually connected concepts. When two concepts are mutually connected, the concepts are causally connected in both directions (the two concepts are both causes and effects of each other). Mutually connected concepts are represented as a two-headed arrow. This reciprocal relationship indicates that these concepts are closely intertwined and form a system within the map.

In addition to the concepts and linkages, measures are utilized to operationalize the structural properties of the causal maps. Many of the measures are adapted from the social network field (Knoke & Kulkinski, 1982) and the applicability of each measure is based on the research context used. The measures listed here are not exhaustive, but exemplars for researchers to contemplate using in their causal mapping endeavors. Table 9 lists the measures and a brief description.

Comprehensiveness is a characteristic of the overall map and is a measure of the number of concepts in the map (Carley & Palmquist, 1992). This measure can be used for comparisons between maps. The more comprehensive the map, the more complex the cognition (Nelson et al., 2000). *Density* is a characteristic of the overall maps and is a measure of how connected the concepts in the map are. *Density* is a proportion that is calculated as the number of linkages between the concepts divided by the number of

Table 9. Sample causal mapping measures

Measure	Definition
Comprehensiveness	Number of concepts included in the map (Carley and Palmquist, 1992); applicable at the overall map level
Density	Ratio of links between a concept and the total concepts in the map (Carley and Palmquist, 1992); applicable at the overall map level
Centrality	Reflects how central or involved the concept/construct is to the map; a ratio of the aggregate of linkages involving the concept/construct divided by the total linkages in the map (Knoke and Kuklinski, 1982); applicable at the concept/construct level

Note: These measures can be used at both the concept and construct level

Figure 7. Sample density measure

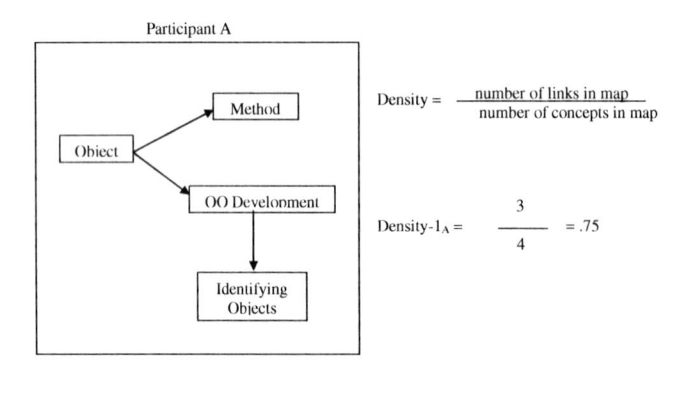

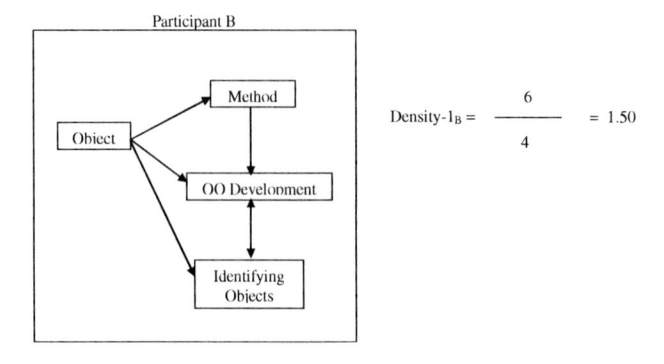

$$\text{Density} = \frac{\text{number of links in map}}{\text{number of concepts in map}}$$

$$\text{Density-1}_A = \frac{3}{4} = .75$$

$$\text{Density-1}_B = \frac{6}{4} = 1.50$$

concepts in the map. There is another density measure that has been used which is a proportion that is calculated as the number of all linkages occurring in the matrix divided by the number of all possible linkages (Knoke & Kuklinski, 1982). In both cases, the higher the ratio, the denser the map and the higher level of cognitive complexity (Nadkarni, 2003). Figure 7 provides a sample density calculation.

Centrality is a measure used for the individual concepts/constructs within a map. It is a measure of how central or involved the concept/construct is to the map, and reflects the degree of hierarchy characterizing the map. Centrality is a ratio of the aggregate of linkages involving the concept/construct divided by the total linkages in the matrix (Knoke & Kuklinski, 1982). Figure 8 provides a sample centrality calculation.

As stated previously, the structural analysis of causal maps differs for each of the research contexts. In the discovery context, the purpose of causal mapping is to identify patterns and describe aspects of the phenomenon. In an evocative setting, the goal is to develop domain specific theory. In theory testing the goal is to confirm/dispute/expand existing theory. Lastly, in an intervention setting, the goal is to create consensus around a course of action or issue at hand. With each research setting a different analysis protocol is appropriate. In a discovery setting, the analysis would take on the form of description, relying heavily on the content aspects and identifying which concepts are linked. In an evocative setting, the analysis would be concerned with both the content and the structural aspects. It is through understanding the linkages between the

Figure 8. Sample concept centrality measure

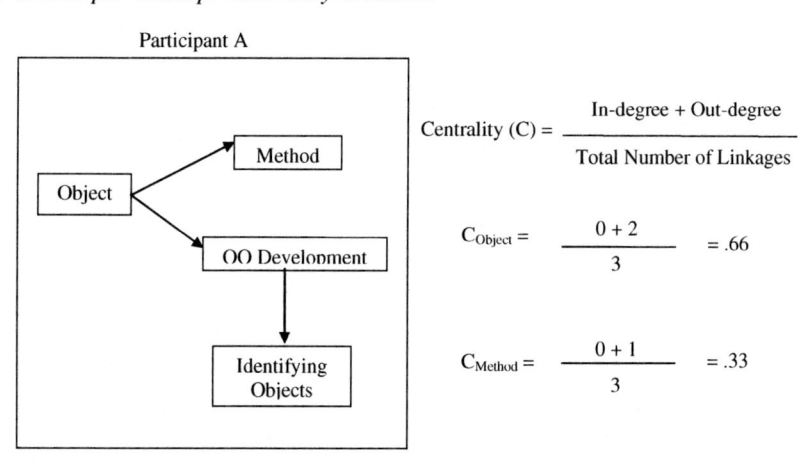

$$\text{Centrality (C)} = \frac{\text{In-degree} + \text{Out-degree}}{\text{Total Number of Linkages}}$$

$$C_{Object} = \frac{0 + 2}{3} = .66$$

$$C_{Method} = \frac{0 + 1}{3} = .33$$

	1	2	3	4	Out-degree
Object	-	1	1	0	2
Method	0	-	0	0	0
OO Development	0	0	-	1	1
Identifying Objects	0	0	0	-	0
In-degree	0	1	1	1	3

concepts (constructs) that theory can be developed. Basic measures such as density and centrality may be used to develop theory. In a hypothesis testing context, the measures would need to be much more robust and cover many aspects of the map's structure.

Reporting Results

While the standards in reporting CM results have not yet evolved, there are some key items that I have found reviewers will be looking for in your results. The first item is the sample design. Reviewers will want to know what sampling frame was used, was the sample population appropriate and was the sample adequate (point of redundancy). The second item that should be included is a discussion of the coding process. Reviewers will want to know what coding process was used as well as the reliability and validity of the process. One thing to keep in mind is that most IS reviewers are not yet familiar with the CM method. As with other research methods, you must prove that the research is well designed and rigorously undertaken. Similar to other qualitative methods, examples and quotes from the study are key to convincing the reviewer that what you report is an accurate (and rich) representation of the data. Over time, the need for clearly articulating the steps involved in CM research will diminish, but for now researchers may want you to include the steps provided in this chapter in an appendix to substantiate the CM process.

Summary of Key Decision Points

There are several issues discussed in this chapter that a researcher will want to consider when designing a CM study. There are nine key decision points that will be summarized here. See Table 10 for a listing of these decision points.

1. The first decision point is the selection of the research context (e.g., evocative, hypothesis testing). The research context should be selected based on the fit with the phenomenon under study and the research questions being addressed.
2. The second decision point is in the choice of data collection method (TBCM or IECM). This decision should be driven by which method is appropriate for the research question and the research context.
3. The third decision point is in the choice of which sampling method (e.g., random, snowball, exhaustive) to use. The sampling method should be chosen based on the data collection method (IECM versus TBCM) and in the IECM method also the sample (participants versus experts).
4. The fourth decision point is with regard to the reliability of the causal statement identification procedure. The level of agreement between the researchers should

be at least 0.75 to have an acceptable level of reliability. A reliability less than 0.75 indicates that the procedure is not robust enough for research purposes, and a modified identification procedure will need to be developed.

5. The fifth decision point is in the choice of coding scheme development method (benchmarking and theory-driven). This choice is primarily dependent on the research context of the study (discovery versus hypothesis testing).

6. The sixth decision point is with regard to validating the concepts. Once the coding scheme has been developed the concepts should be validated to ensure reliability of the scheme. The coding scheme approach (benchmarking or theory-driven) will determine the most appropriate method of validation.

7. The seventh decision point deals with the validation of the maps. The validation method is determined by the data collection method (IECM or TBCM). For IECMs one source of validation is a "member check," whereas using TBCMs validation is often accomplished via triangulation with other sources.

8. The eighth decision point deals with representation. Causal maps may be represented via diagram or matrix. The only limitation on the choice of representation may be in complexity of the map. The more complex the map, the more difficult to represent and analyze via diagrammatic methods.

9. The last decision point deals with the analysis of the maps. When analyzing a causal map the researcher should address both the content and structural aspects of the map. Within the structural analysis there are many possible measures that can be utilized to operationalize the structural properties of the causal maps (e.g., centrality). The applicability of each measure is based on the research context used and research questions addressed.

Table 10. Key decision points

Decision Point	Description
Research Context	The research context (e.g., evocative, hypothesis testing) should be selected based on the fit with the phenomenon under study and the research questions being addressed.
Data Collection Method	Choice of method (TBCM or IECM) is dependent on the research question and the research context.
Choice of Sampling Method	Choice of method (e.g., random, snowball, exhaustive) is dependent on data collection method and research context.
Causal Statement Identification Reliability	If reliability >= 0.80, then proceed with the study, if <= 0.80 the procedure will need to be modified.
Coding Scheme	Choice of method (benchmarking and theory-driven) is dependent on the research context of the study.
Concept Validation	The coding scheme approach (benchmarking or theory-driven) will determine the most appropriate method of validation.
Map Validation	The validation method is determined by the data collection method (IECM or TBCM). For IECMs a source of validation is a 'member check'. For TBCMs a source of validation is via triangulation with other sources.
Representation	Causal maps may be represented in two main forms: via diagram or matrix. The choice of representation is only limited by the complexity of the maps.
Analysis	Many measures can be utilized to operationalize the structural properties of the causal maps (e.g., centrality). The applicability of each measure is based on the research context used.

Conclusion

In this chapter I have explicated the CM process so that researchers and practitioners can utilize this method to address IS issues within organizations. While I have addressed the specific steps involved in the process there are issues that a researcher should be familiar with before engaging in CM research. As you have probably realized, the CM process is very labor intensive. Several software packages have been developed to aid the process (discussed in Chapter III), but there is still a significant amount of labor involved.

On the positive side, causal mapping is a versatile method on several fronts. As seen in this chapter, CM can be effectively used in several research contexts (discovery, evocative, hypotheses testing, and intervention). The CM method is also versatile with respect to the theories that can be used. With CM you can use multiple theories (lenses) to interpret the data collected (causal statements).

This chapter has detailed the process of conducting CM research. This book has a number of illustrations of how this method is employed. It is my hope that these techniques and examples will stimulate the use of causal mapping research within the IS field.

References

Axelrod, R. (Ed.) (1976). *Structure of decision: The Cognitive Maps of Political Elites*. Princeton, NJ: Princeton University Press.

Birnhaum-More, H., & Weiss, A.R. (1990). Discovering the basis of competition in 12 industries: Computerized content analysis of interview data from the US and Europe. In A. Huff (Ed.), *Mapping strategic thought*. London: John Wiley & Sons.

Bougon, M., Weick, K., & Binkhorst, D. (1977). Cognition in organizations: An analysis of the Utrecht jazz orchestra. *Administrative Science Quarterly*, 22(4), 606-639.

Bradburn, N.M. (1979). *Improving interview method and questionnaire design*. San Francisco: Jossey-Bass.

Carley, K., & Palmquist, M. (1992). Extracting, representing and analyzing mental models. *Social Forces*, 70, 215-225.

Caroll, J.D., & Arabie, P. (1980). Multidimensional scaling. *Annual Review of Psychology*, 31, 607-649.

Eden, C., Ackerman, F., & Cropper, S. (1992). On the nature of cause maps. *Journal of Management Studies*, 18, 37-47.

Fahey, L., & Narayanan, V. K. (1989). Linking changes in revealed causal maps and environment: An empirical study. *Journal of Management Studies*. 26(4), 361-378.

Fiol, C. M., & Huff, A. S. (1992). Maps for managers: Where are we? Where do we go from here? *Journal of Management Studies*, 29, 267-285.

Fletcher, K.E., & Huff, A. (1990). Strategic argument mapping: A study of strategy. In A. Huff (Ed.), *Mapping strategic thought*. London: John Wiley & Sons.

Ford, J.D., & Hegarty, W. (1984). Decision maker's beliefs about the causes and effects of structure: An exploratory study. *Academy of Management Journal*, 27(2), 271-291.

Hong, E., & O'Neil, H.F. (1992). Instructional strategies to help learners build relevant mental models in inferential statistics. *Journal of Educational Psychology*, 84(2), 150-160.

Huff, A. (Ed.) (1990). *Mapping strategic thought*. New York: John Wiley & Sons.

Kemmerer, B., Buche, M., & Narayanan, V.K. (2001). Deriving revealed causal maps from non-traditional source documents: Challenges and methodological extensions, *Academy of Management Conference*, Washington, DC, August 2001.

Knoke, D., & Kuklinski. J.H. (1982). *Network analysis*. Newbury Park, CA: Sage.

Kvale, S. (1996). *InterViews: An introduction to qualitative research interviewing*. Newbury Park, CA: Sage.

Lincoln, Y. S., & Guba, E. G. (1985). *Naturalistic Inquiry*. Newbury Park, CA: Sage.

Mohammed, S., Klimoski, R., & Rentsch, J. (2001). The measurement of team mental models: We have no shared schema. *Organizational Research Methods*, 3, 123-165.

Montazemi, A.R., & Conrath, D.W. (1986). The use of cognitive mapping for information requirements analysis. *MIS Quarterly*, 10(1), 45-57.

Nadkarni, S. (2003). Instructional methods and mental models of students: An empirical investigation. *Academy of Management Learning and Education*, 2(4), 335-351.

Nadkarni, S., & Narayanan, V.K. (2004). Validity of the structural measures of text-based causal maps: An empirical assessment. *Organizational Research Methods* (in press).

Narayanan, V.K., & Fahey, L. (1990). Evolution of revealed causal maps during decline: A case study of Admiral. In A. Huff (Ed.), *Mapping strategic thought* (pp. 109-133). London: John Wiley & Sons.

Nelson, K.M., Nadkarni, S., Narayanan, V.K., & Ghods, M. (2000). Understanding software operations support expertise: A causal mapping approach. *MIS Quarterly*, 24(3), 475-507.

Payne, S.L. (1951). *The art of asking questions*. Princeton, NJ: Princeton University Press.

Rubin, H.J., & Rubin, I.S. (2004). *Qualitative interviewing: The art of hearing data*. Newbury Park, CA: Sage.

Schvaneveldt, R.W. (1990). Proximities, networks, and schemata. In R.W. Schvaneveldt (Ed.), *Pathfinder associative networks: Studies in knowledge organization* (pp. 135-148). Norwood, NJ: Ablex.

Shanteau, J. (1987). Psychological characteristics of expert decision makers. In J. L. Mumpower, O. Renn, L. D. Phillips, & V. R. Uppuluri (Eds.), *Expert judgment and expert systems* (pp. 289-304). Berlin: Springer-Verlag.

Shanteau, J. (1992). Competence in experts: The role of task characteristics. *Organizational Behavior and Human Decision Processes*, 53, 252-266.

Siegel, S. (1956). *Nonparametric statistics for the behavioral sciences*. New York: McGraw-Hill.

Stone, E. (1978). *Research methods in organizational behavior*. Glenview: Scott and Foresman.

Tan, F.B., & Hunter, M.G. (2002). The repertory grid technique: A method for the study of cognition in information systems. *Management Information Systems Quarterly*, 26(1), 39-57.

Wrightson, M.T. (1976). The documentary coding method. In R. Axelrod (Ed.), *Structure of decision: The cognitive maps of political elites* (pp. 291-332). Princeton, NJ: Princeton University Press.

Endnotes

[1] Another approach that may be taken is to use group level mapping. If your text(s) capture a group situation (e.g., focus group) you could use the group as your level of analysis and develop a single map at the group level.

[2] Adapted from Wrightson (1976).

Appendix A: Coding Rules and Examples for Structural Relationships[2]

Linkage Codes

There are seven codes that can be applied to the linkages in a causal map. The codes and descriptions are provided.

Code	Description
+	Positive
-	Negative
⊕	Will not hurt, does not prevent, not harmful
⊖	Will not help, does not promote, no benefit
A	May or may not be related to
M	Effects in non-zero manner
0	No effect, no relation to

Structural Relationship Examples

1. Cause/Link/Effect

    "If there was on-site daycare then it would be easier for me to do my job."

    On-site daycare /+/ Easier for me to do my job.

2. Cause/Link/Complex Effect

    "It's visual so the programming is easier and the logic is easier too."

    It's visual /+/ programming is easier

    It's visual /+/ logic is easier

3. Complex Cause/Link/Simple Effect

    "If as a mother they know they have a place to take their children, they know they have a place for the kids to go after school, then I think there would be a lot less missed days."

    If as a mother they know they have a place to take their children /-/ missed days.

    If as a mother they know they ... for the kids to go after school /-/ missed days.

4. Either/Or Relationship

    "Either I'm going to get that promotion or I am going to move to a dot com company to get the money I deserve."

    Get that promotion /+/ get the money I deserve.

    Move to a dot com company /+/ get the money I deserve.

5. Probability

    "Hiring a new CIO might help with the lack of promotions for women."

    Hiring a new CIO /+/ lack of promotions for women.

6. Inverted

    "I'm just amazed because they are so into their children."

    They are so into their children /+/ I'm just amazed

7. Utility

    "The trend toward outsourcing will sure help India."

    Outsourcing /+/ India

8. Complex Cause/Link/Complex Effect

    "You have maintainability and robustness because you're using OO and you have a good number of classes."

    Using OO /+/ Maintainability

    Using OO /+/ Robustness

    Have a good number of classes /+/ Maintainability

    Have a good number of classes /+/ Robustness

Chapter III

What Have We Learned from Almost 30 Years of Research on Causal Mapping?
Methodological Lessons and Choices for the Information Systems and Information Technology Communities

Gerard P. Hodgkinson
The University of Leeds, UK

Gail P. Clarkson
The University of Leeds, UK

Abstract

In this chapter we review major developments that have occurred over the past 30 years or so in the philosophical underpinnings, elicitation, analysis, aggregation and comparison of causal maps (also known as cause maps) across a wide range of domains of application in the fields of management and organization studies, in order to distill vital lessons concerning the strengths and weaknesses of various approaches for the information systems (IS) and information technology (IT) research communities. We offer some general guidelines to aid the would-be user in making methodological choices appropriate to particular contexts of application. The importance of attending to measurement issues in respect to reliability and validity at all stages of the research

Copyright © 2005, Idea Group Inc. Copying or distributing in print or electronic forms without written permission of Idea Group Inc. is prohibited.

process, from initial data collection to final analysis and comparison, is highlighted and an accompanying appendix presents an overview of selected computer software systems supporting the full range of activities associated with causal mapping.

Introduction

The purpose of this chapter is to provide an overview of some of the key problems that researchers and policy makers using causal mapping techniques have wrestled with over the ensuing years, both in order to illustrate the range of choices confronting the would-be user of these techniques and to highlight the strengths and limitations of particular approaches. Despite the fact that causal and other forms of cognitive mapping techniques are generally more labor-intensive and time-consuming than other research methods, in recent years the emerging field of managerial and organizational cognition has developed dramatically (e.g., Eden & Spender, 1998; Hodgkinson & Thomas, 1997; Meindl, Stubbart & Porac, 1994; Narayanan & Kemmerer, 2001; Porac & Thomas, 1989), to the extent that its reach is now extending across virtually all of the major sub-fields of management and organization studies, including information technology-related applications (Nelson, Nadkarni, Narayanan & Ghods, 2000a; Swan, 1997). Researchers have employed a rich variety of methods in an attempt to gain insights into actors' belief systems, ranging from the relatively simple process of having participants list basic concepts (de Chernatony, Daniels & Johnson, 1993; Gripsrud & Gronhaug, 1985) to more sophisticated procedures such as the development and multivariate analysis of questionnaire items (Fombrun & Zajac, 1987) and repertory grid and related multidimensional scaling and related clustering techniques (Daniels, de Chernatony & Johnson, 1995; Daniels, Johnson & de Chernatony, 2002; Fournier, 1996; Ginsberg, 1989; Hodgkinson, 1997a; Hodgkinson, Padmore & Tomes, 1991; Hodgkinson, Tomes & Padmore, 1996; Reger & Huff, 1993). Fortunately, a number of comprehensive reviews of the many diverse methods for accessing thinking in organizational settings have been published elsewhere (e.g., Fiol & Huff, 1992; Hodgkinson, 2001; Hodgkinson & Sparrow, 2002; Huff, 1990; Jenkins, 1998; Lant & Shapira, 2001; Mohammed, Klimoski & Rentsch, 2000; J. Sparrow, 1998; Walsh, 1995).

In this chapter we shall confine our attention to a consideration of one particular class of cognitive mapping techniques — causal mapping — that has risen in popularity in research domains as diverse as strategic management (e.g., Fahey & Narayanan, 1989; Hodgkinson, Bown, Maule, Glaister & Pearman, 1999; Hodgkinson & Maule, 2002; Maule, Hodgkinson & Bown, 2003; Narayanan & Fahey, 1990), human resource management (Budhwar, 2000; Budhwar & Sparrow, 2002), and technological innovation (Swan, 1995; Swan & Newell, 1998). In the words of Huff (1990, p.16):

> "Causal maps allow the map maker to focus on action — for example, how the respondent explains the current situation in terms of previous events, and what changes he or she expects in the future."

It is the direct links to action implicit within this approach that make it such a powerful method, applicable across a wide range of contexts. However, as noted in this volume by Narayanan (2005), causal mapping techniques have been much under-utilized within the inter-related domains of information systems (IS) and information technology (IT). This is highly surprising, given the obvious parallels with general systems theory and the potential of these techniques to shed light on systems-designers' and users' understanding of a range of hardware and software capabilities and limitations (cf., Nelson et al., 2000a), thereby extending the repertoire of cognitive engineering tools and techniques available for use in these domains (Schraagen, Chipman & Shalin, 2000; Seamster, Redding & Kaempf, 1997). However, if this potential is to be realized, it is vital that important methodological insights already gained in the context of other domains, where causal mapping techniques have enjoyed widespread prominence, are brought to bear in the context of IS and IT applications. Since Axelrod (1976) produced his classic book that introduced causal mapping to the field of policy analysis, a number of significant methodological issues have risen to the fore across a range of fields, which in turn has stimulated much thinking and further advances.

In this chapter we map out some of the key methodological choices confronting the would-be user of causal mapping techniques, drawing upon the wider body of research that has been conducted using these techniques in other domains, over almost a 30-year period, both in order to illuminate the nature of those choices and to accelerate progress in these new, inter-related focal areas of application, by distilling the very valuable lessons that have emerged from extensive prior usage in these other domains. In so doing, our purpose is to accomplish three principal aims: (1) to illustrate the range of methodological choices associated with causal mapping techniques; (2) to highlight the strengths and limitations of the particular approaches identified; and (3) to offer some general guidelines to aid the would-be user of these techniques. Our recommendations are not intended to be prescriptive, but to assist potential users of causal mapping techniques in making methodological choices that are appropriate in particular contexts of application.

In Figure 1 we present a schematic overview of the principal stages involved in the causal mapping process, as discussed in this chapter. Undoubtedly, this representation oversimplifies the complex realities involved. (In practice, for example, the mapping process is often an iterative one, with feedback sought from participants during or soon after the construction and analysis stages.) Nevertheless, it serves as a useful framework to guide those new to the process of causal mapping and provides a clear overview of the organizing logic we have employed in structuring our chapter.

The chapter is organized in seven principal sections. Following this introduction, we alert the reader to ongoing philosophical debates concerning the ontological status of causal maps (also known as cause maps), outlining our own position in respect of these. In the third section, we identify a number of issues concerning knowledge elicitation that researchers need to address if they are to make well-informed mapping choices and we highlight a number of strengths and limitations associated with particular approaches. Next, we turn our attention to basic metrics for the analysis of individual cause maps. In the fifth section we discuss issues associated with the aggregation and comparative analysis of causal maps, while in section six we consider some measurement issues which

Figure 1. Schematic overview of the principal stages of the causal mapping process, as reviewed in the chapter

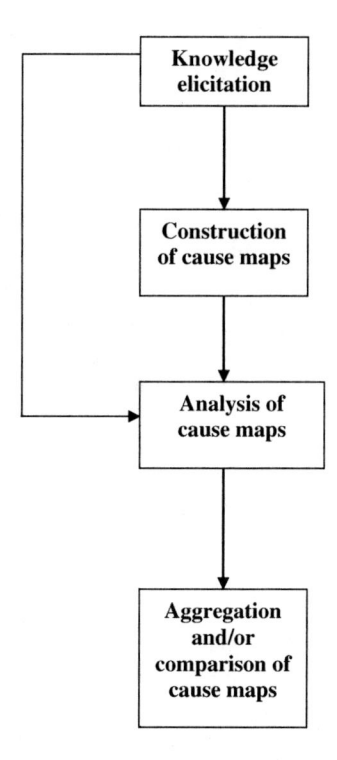

```
┌──────────────┐
│  Knowledge   │
│  elicitation │
└──────┬───────┘
       │
       ▼
┌──────────────┐
│ Construction │
│ of cause maps│
└──────┬───────┘
       │
       ▼
┌──────────────┐
│  Analysis of │◄────┐
│  cause maps  │     │
└──────┬───────┘     │
       │             │
       ▼             │
┌──────────────┐     │
│  Aggregation │     │
│    and/or    │     │
│ comparison of│     │
│  cause maps  │     │
└──────────────┘     │
```

are fundamental to the entire mapping process. Finally, we draw together our key recommendations and overall conclusions. In an accompanying appendix we provide a brief overview of some of the available computer software systems for supporting users throughout the various stages of the mapping process, from data collection/elicitation to analysis and comparison.

Philosophical Preamble

It is important to note at the outset that there is a wide spectrum of views concerning the ontological status of causal maps (and cognitive maps more generally). In this section we outline some of the main perspectives and clarify our own position.

In their attempts to capture information systems expertise, Nelson, Nelson and Armstrong (2000b, p.1) point out that it is not possible to literally "open the expert's head" and extract domain knowledge as represented directly in the human brain. To the extent that such a true one-to-one correspondence is unattainable, it follows that methods are required that can represent knowledge in ways that capture the *essence* of actors' thoughts and belief systems. This philosophical distinction between "causal maps" and "revealed causal maps" is an important one, reflecting fundamentally different schools of thought.

In the context of his work on political elites, Axelrod (1976, p.10) maintained that a valid map does not necessarily have to be consistent with a person's private beliefs. Indeed, the overall research strategy advocated by him in his seminal volume was "to base what is being measured on what is being asserted rather than what is being thought by a person." In keeping with this stance, a number of organizational researchers (e.g., Eden, 1992; Laukkanen, 1998) maintain that causal mapping need not necessarily be linked with the cognitive map construct — as developed in the field of psychology — to be a useful tool for summarizing and communicating information. Viewed from this perspective, causal maps are a meaningful way of representing elements of the thoughts (rather than the thinking) of an individual (or group), expressed in the form of a system of causal relations. For others, however, causal maps are viewed as more than a mere methodological tool and/or decision-aiding technique, being capable of representing an individual's literal beliefs concerning a particular domain at a given point in time (Langfield-Smith & Wirth, 1992), with the potential to have the same essential characteristics as thought itself (Huff, 1990).

Our own position falls somewhere between these philosophical extremes. We view causal mapping techniques (and other forms of cognitive mapping procedure) as one method for accessing the thinking of individuals in applied settings, adding to the general stock of knowledge elicitation and knowledge representation techniques — such as those discussed in Hodgkinson and Sparrow (2002), Shadbolt and Milton (1999), J. Sparrow (1998) and Schraagen et al. (2000) — more widely available for use in a variety of contexts. The overall degree of literal correspondence between the data generated by such procedures and the human information processing system that ultimately underpins cognition is of secondary importance, relative to the insights they yield into organizational life. As expressed by Nelson et al. (2000b, p.1): "Theory building is a cumulative rather than exhaustive process." To the extent that cognitive mapping procedures (of whatever form) give rise to findings as predicted by rigorously derived hypotheses grounded in well-supported management and organization theory, all well and good. To the extent that such predictions are also supported by theory and research from the cognitive sciences, even better (cf., Scheper & Faber, 1994).

Another important issue is that of how actors' *collective* belief systems might be captured most appropriately. To what extent is it meaningful to represent "shared beliefs" and how? Again, theorists and empirical researchers are divided on this issue, reflecting fundamental differences not only regarding the ontological status of cognitive maps but also the status of collective cognition. According to Scheper and Faber (1994), while certain forms of causal map are able to represent meaning at the individual level, this is not the case at the collective level. In respect to the latter, they advocate an alternative approach, based on semiotic analysis. In the words of Fiol (1989, p.278), citing Eco (1979):

"Semiotic analysis is a formal mode of analysis used to identify the rules that govern how signs convey meanings in a particular social system...semiotics assumes that diverse signs or expressions can convey shared meaning because they are grounded in a common set of underlying values."

We view Scheper and Faber's stance as premature at this stage in the development of the managerial and organizational cognition field. As noted by Cannon-Bowers and Salas (2001), in a discussion of shared cognition in the context of team functioning, there are a number of pressing issues upon which researchers have yet to reach basic agreement, not least questions concerning what it is that is actually shared, what sharing means, how sharing might most appropriately be measured and the nature of the outcomes that might be expected as a result of shared cognition.

In summary, contemporary theorists and empirical researchers are divided on two fundamental issues: (1) the nature and purpose of causal and other forms of cognitive mapping techniques, and (2) the nature of collective belief systems. Further consideration of these issues is beyond the scope of the present chapter, but sufficient detail has been provided to serve as a useful backdrop for understanding the range of alternative choices confronting would-be users of causal mapping techniques.

Over the years organizational researchers have devised a variety of alternative methods for the elicitation, analysis, and comparison of actors' individual and collective causal belief systems. We turn now to provide a summary of the many developments that have occurred in relation to these key, non-mutually-exclusive activities, each of which is fundamental to the mapping enterprise, commencing with the process of knowledge elicitation.

Approaches to Knowledge Elicitation

Despite the widespread popularity of causal mapping techniques, there is currently no consensus within the literature concerning the most appropriate way(s) to elicit actors' causal belief systems (Hodgkinson & Sparrow, 2002; Jenkins, 1998). Following Hodgkinson (2001) and Mohammed et al. (2000), we shall consider two broad classes of elicitation procedure: indirect and direct (see Figure 2).

Indirect elicitation techniques entail processes whereby maps are constructed from secondary data sources, typically extant written documents (including interview transcripts and letters to shareholders) derived initially for some other purpose then subsequently analyzed using causal mapping procedures (e.g., Barr & Huff, 1997; Barr, Stimpert & Huff, 1992), or primary sources in situations in which the data are elicited specifically for the research project but not in a manner that requires the participant to reflect on their causal beliefs in an explicit fashion. An example of the latter would the use of interview transcripts generated in narrative form by the researcher and subsequently converted into causal maps through a process of *post hoc* coding (for representative examples, see Calori, Johnson & Sarnin, 1992, 1994; Jenkins & Johnson, 1997a,

Figure 2. Taxonomy of principal methods for the elicitation and construction of cause maps

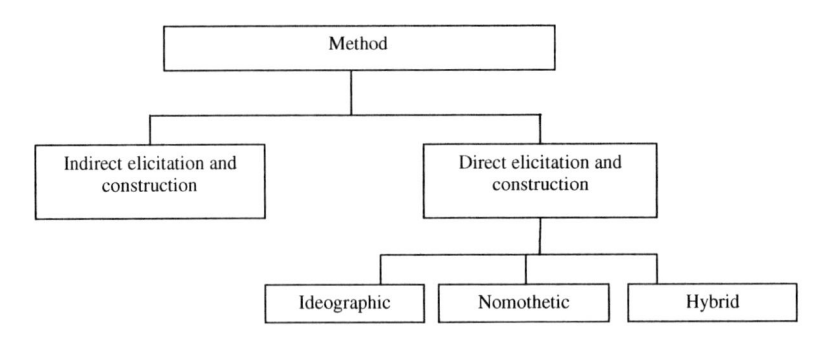

```
                        ┌─────────┐
                        │ Method  │
                        └────┬────┘
                   ┌─────────┴─────────┐
        ┌──────────┴──────────┐  ┌─────┴────────────────┐
        │ Indirect elicitation│  │ Direct elicitation and│
        │   and construction  │  │    construction       │
        └─────────────────────┘  └──────────┬───────────┘
                           ┌────────────────┼────────────────┐
                    ┌──────┴─────┐  ┌───────┴──────┐  ┌──────┴─────┐
                    │ Ideographic│  │  Nomothetic  │  │   Hybrid   │
                    └────────────┘  └──────────────┘  └────────────┘
```

1997b; and Nelson et al., 2000a). The common defining feature of indirect approaches to knowledge elicitation, regardless of whether the data is gathered from primary or secondary sources, is that the process of map construction is undertaken without the active involvement of the research participant. In contrast, direct elicitation methods require the active involvement of participants in the map construction process from the outset. Direct elicitation methods include structured questionnaires requiring participants to evaluate causal relations among predefined sets of variables — also referred to as elements or nodes[1] (e.g., Roberts, 1976; Swan & Newell, 1998) — and the use of computerized systems such as Decision Explorer® (Eden, Ackermann & Cropper, 1992) that enable maps to be constructed dynamically, in real time, through an iterative interview process. As we shall see, there is no such thing as a perfect method. Each approach is characterized by particular strengths and weaknesses.

Indirect Elicitation Procedures

In point of fact, the initial approach to causal mapping entailed the use of secondary data in conjunction with indirect methods of elicitation. (By definition it is impossible to combine direct elicitation methods with secondary data, unless the researcher is re-analyzing pre-existing maps from earlier studies.) Axelrod's (1976) preference was that cognitive maps be derived from whatever materials are left behind in the normal course of the decision-making process, on the grounds that although this was potentially problematic in terms of issues of authenticating the researcher's interpretation, documentary evidence is non-intrusive and therefore unlikely to influence participants' thought processes. Working with documentary evidence also allows the investigator to gain access to busy individuals who might otherwise be unwilling to participate using more intrusive, interactive forms of data generation procedures (Huff, 1990). However, documentary sources are beset with a number of potentially severe limitations in that the data contained within them is often only of tangential relevance to the investigator's purpose(s). Moreover, the fact that secondary source documents, such as letters to shareholders, by definition, are prepared for particular audiences renders it difficult if not impossible for the researcher to ascertain the extent to which any biases contained within them are genuinely a product of the originator's sensemaking processes and/or a deliberate attempt to influence the perceptions of the stakeholders to whom they were initially directed, a problem which is compounded by the fact that the data emerging from the use of causal mapping in this way can rarely be checked for "accuracy" and validated against comparable data from objective, independent sources (Hodgkinson & Sparrow, 2002).

In a number of respects, the tasks associated with the coding of primary data originating from interview transcripts in narrative form using causal mapping techniques are similar in nature to the process of coding secondary documents. However, a major advantage of the former is that the data are obtained specifically for the researcher's own purposes, thus circumventing, to a certain extent at least, the authenticity problem alluded to above. Nevertheless, there are still significant risks of bias, not least due to the potential influence of demand characteristics arising from the research situation during the elicitation process (cf., Hodgkinson, 1997b). Moreover, as with maps derived from secondary source documents, when using primary interview transcripts the researcher must face the vexed question as to how the maps so derived are to be subsequently validated. This validation problem is compounded in the case of unstructured documents, including unstructured interview transcripts, by the associated problems of poor data quality that often result from using such sources, not least the fact that these documents typically contain sentence fragments, incomplete thoughts, and over-elaborate explanations (Kemmerer, Buche & Narayanan, 2001).[2]

Direct Elicitation Procedures

Increasingly, direct methods of knowledge elicitation are being employed by organizational researchers in the field, both prescriptively, as a basis of intervention through 'action research' (Cropper, Eden & Ackermann, 1990; Eden & Ackermann, 1998a; Eden et al., 1992), and for descriptive purposes, where the object of the exercise is to better understand the extent to which and in what ways actors' mental representations of organizational phenomena are similar to and/or different from one another and isolate the correlates of such similarities and differences (Markóczy, 1995, 1997, 2001; Markóczy & Goldberg, 1995). A primary advantage of direct methods over their indirect counterparts is that they obviate the need for cumbersome coding procedures for map construction — the maps being constructed *in situ*, directly from the raw data — and enable the researcher to focus the data collection on issues of immediate concern to the investigation. Used in this fashion, causal mapping techniques are akin to knowledge elicitation techniques employed more generally within the cognitive and organizational sciences.

Direct elicitation procedures can usefully be sub-divided in terms of the extent to which the elicitation process requires participants to identify the variables to be causally mapped, using their own everyday natural language, or whether the subject matter is supplied by the researcher, on the basis of extant theory and research or an *a priori* conceptual analysis of the domain to be mapped. In the case of the first approach, known as *ideographic elicitation*, the primary concern of the researcher is to ensure that valuable richness and detail in individual cognition are not lost or threatened by researcher bias. This approach can be traced to the personal construct theory of George Kelly (1955), which asserts that individuals are inherently unique in the ways in which they construe their worlds. Accordingly, if we are to gain insights into participants' beliefs, it is vital that the elicitation process does not impose concepts that are alien in meaning. In Kellyian terms the elements involved in any mapping exercise must fall within the participants' "range of convenience." Kelly devised a particular approach to cognitive mapping, the repertory grid technique, which lies beyond the scope of this chapter (for details and applications, see Daniels et al., 2002; Fournier, 1996; Huff, 1990; Reger & Huff, 1993). Within the realm of causal mapping, Eden and his colleagues (e.g., Eden & Ackermann, 1998a, 1998b; Eden, Jones & Sims, 1979, 1983) have devised a system of elicitation that is derived ultimately from personal construct theory. Laukkanen (1994, 1998) also strongly advocates that causal maps should be elicited in a manner that enables participants to express their thoughts using their natural language. In this connection, a prime strength of documentary sources, particularly interview transcripts gathered *in situ*, is that they are expressed in their natural language form. The same is true of certain archival sources. While it is undoubtedly the case that maps in their natural language form are inherently more meaningful to the individual participants, a major drawback of this approach is the problems this poses for comparative analysis purposes, an issue to which we shall return in due course.

The second approach to direct elicitation, *nomothetic elicitation*, entails the use of standardized lists of variables supplied by the researcher. A variety of approaches to the basic task of map construction have been adopted by researchers using this type of procedure, ranging from highly structured questionnaires involving the pairwise evaluation of all possible combinations of causal relations (Roberts, 1976; Swan, 1995; Swan & Newell, 1998) to more basic methods, entailing the hand-drawing of causal maps (Green & McManus, 1995). Systematically considering all pairwise effects (Swan & Newell, 1998) involves assessing causality by reviewing every possible combination of variables and should significantly diminish the possibility that important effects are omitted (Hart, 1976). Pairwise comparison is also seen as being particularly helpful in overcoming the potential problem of coding errors with respect to loops, which tend to be common with causal maps because of the problematic nature of determining the interviewee's view about what is cause and what is effect (Eden et al., 1992).

A major criticism leveled against researcher-standardization of variables for elicitation purposes by the advocates of ideographic approaches (e.g., Eden & Ackermann, 1998b) is that researchers run the risk that the basic map construction task might prove meaningless for participants. However, as we shall see later, there are also some major advantages to nomothetic approaches, particularly in relation to comparative analysis in situations involving large numbers of participants, where the aim is to statistically analyze the maps in order to identify patterns of belief similarities and differences and/ or identify factors that explain such patterns. Moreover, there are a number of strategies that can be readily adopted to minimize the dangers of lack of meaning alluded to by those favoring ideographic approaches to elicitation, not the least of which is ensuring that the final list of variables forming the focus of the mapping exercise are carefully formulated by recourse to relevant literature and/or the use of expert panels, the members of which are highly representative of the participant sample involved in the main mapping exercise. Careful piloting of the requisite elicitation task is also invaluable in this respect. Use of standardized variables for elicitation purposes not only overcomes difficulties associated with *post hoc* coding schemes (which are considered in further detail later in this chapter), but also minimizes the impact of demand characteristics associated with semi-structured interviews, as discussed above. Ultimately, however, the use of fixed sets of variables, by definition, limits the extent to which the resulting maps can capture individual differences in terms of both map content and map structure. The requirement that participants work with a common set of variables eliminates the possibility of the detection of individual differences in terms of what is considered to be sufficiently salient to warrant incorporation into the maps, the inclusion or exclusion of particular variables not being permitted. Clearly this type of approach suppresses a potential source of significant variation.

Fortunately, in recent years researchers have begun to develop new approaches that seek to combine the major strengths of ideographic and nomothetic approaches to knowledge elicitation, while dispensing with their associated weaknesses (e.g., Hodgkinson, 2002; Hodgkinson et al., 1999; Hodgkinson & Maule, 2002; Markóczy & Goldberg, 1995). We shall consider these developments in detail in a later section when we review 'Recent Advances in the Large-Scale Comparative Analysis of Cause Maps' (pp.59-60).

Basic Metrics for the Analysis of Individual Cause Maps

The previous section identified the principal methods for eliciting data for the construction of causal maps and considered their relative strengths and limitations. Having acquired such data, the researcher must then set about the task of map construction and analysis. In this section we consider some of the major approaches that have been devised for these purposes. We shall confine our discussion to a brief consideration of the various indices that have been derived over the years for analyzing the structure and content of individual causal maps, as a precursor to a more detailed treatment of issues concerning the aggregation and comparative analysis of such maps.

In their most basic form, causal maps can be depicted graphically, using the medium of the influence diagram (Diffenbach, 1982). Adopting this approach, variables are depicted as nodes in a network, interconnected by a series of arrow-headed pathways, terminating in each case on the dependent variable(s). The simplest forms are restricted to a consideration of positive (increases in one variable cause corresponding increases in one or more other variables), negative (increases in one variable cause corresponding decreases in one or more other variable(s)), and neutral (no causality implied) relationships. More sophisticated variants of the technique enable these relationships to be differentially weighted, on the basis of the participant's belief strength, for example, or the degree of certainty/uncertainty surrounding each causal assertion.

As noted earlier, the focus of Axelrod's (1976) initial work was to explore in detail the causal influences *within* individual participants' maps. As his basis of analysis, Axelrod used the theory of directed graphs (Harary, Norman & Cartwright, 1965) and represented each cognitive map as a valency or adjacency matrix. Building on these foundations, researchers over the years have devised a great many indices for the assessment of map structure and content and a detailed consideration of these is not possible within the confines of the present chapter. Given Diesner and Carley's (2005) extended treatment in this volume of the relative strengths and weaknesses of particular causal map indices, we confine our discussion to a highly selective overview of some of the more commonly employed structure and content measures applicable to most, if not all, forms of causal maps, as widely used by researchers in an attempt to capture the essence of actors' causal belief systems.

Basic measures to assess the content and structure of causal maps have ranged from simply counting the number of occurrences of particular variables and associated links (i.e., arrows connecting constructs), through the link-to-node ratio (i.e., number of links/number of nodes), to map density (i.e., the number of observed links/total number of links theoretically possible, given the number of variables in the participant's map). As shown in Table 1, each of these measures is characterized by particular strengths and weaknesses of which the would-be user needs to be aware. These measures are foundational to the comparative analysis of causal maps, to which we turn in the next section.

Aggregation and Comparative Analysis of Cause Maps

We noted at the outset that theorists and empirical researchers are divided not only regarding the ontological status of cognitive maps at the individual level analysis, but are also divided as to the nature and significance of collective beliefs and cognition. Given the lack of basic agreement concerning the extent to which collective beliefs are theoretically meaningful as a construct, it will come as no surprise to learn that researchers are also divided as to how such beliefs might best be elicited and represented (Mohammed et al., 2000). At the risk of over-simplification, in the present context the faultline in respect of this issue centers broadly on the relative merits of the aggregation of actors' causal belief statements and/or evaluative judgments of causality versus the systematic, comparative analysis of individuals' causal maps in the search for patterns of homogeneity and/or heterogeneity.

As observed in the previous section, individual causal maps can be analyzed along two principal dimensions: content and structure. Content measures when used for the purpose of comparative analysis capture key differences in terms of which constructs individuals perceive as more or less relevant to a given domain and the ways in which these constructs are perceived to relate to one another. Structural differences, in contrast, are used to ascertain the relative complexity of the various maps under consideration. The four basic types of difference that can be identified in the comparison of cause maps are shown in Table 2.

Table 1. Nature and purpose of some commonly used metrics for the assessment of cause maps

	Measure	Description	Purpose
Measures of Map Content	Indegrees (Axelrod, 1976)	The number of links *to* a given node/variable.	Reveal the extent to which the construct in question is influenced directly by the other constructs in the actor's causal belief system.
	Outdegrees (Axelrod, 1976)	The number of links emanating *from* a given node/variable.	Indicate the extent to which a construct exerts a direct causal influence on those other constructs within the actor's causal belief system.
	Reachability (Harary et al., 1965)	The sum of all direct and indirect influences exerted by a given node/variable on the system of perceived causal relations as a whole.	Indicate the direct and indirect impact of a construct within the actor's causal belief system.
Measures of Map Structure	Link-to-node ratio (Eden et al., 1992)	The proportion of links to nodes ÷ variables within a given map. Higher scores denote greater structural complexity.	Provides some evidence of cognitive complexity, individuals whose maps are more interconnected having a greater understanding of the relationships impacting upon an issue.
	Map density (Hart, 1976)	The number of observed links ÷ total number of links theoretically possible, given the number of nodes/variables in a given map. Higher scores denote greater structural complexity.	As above.
	Average chain length (Jenkins & Johnson, 1997a)	A chain refers to a sequential set of perceived causal links. Average chain length is derived by calculating the mean length of all complete chains within a given map. For example, in the case of a map containing two chains, one comprising four links, the other two, the average chain length would be three.	The greater the average chain length, the greater the elaboration in terms of explanations for the patterns of events or actions depicted in the map.

Table 2. Four indicators reflecting potentially significant differences between cause maps (after Langfield-Smith & Wirth, 1992)

	Difference	Meaning
1	The existence vs. non-existence of particular variables	One individual or group believes that a particular variable is important, whereas a second individual or group does not
2	The existence vs. non-existence of relationships between particular variables	One individual or group believes a given variable has an influence upon or is influenced by another variable, whereas a second individual or group does not
3	The polarity of relationships represented within the maps	One individual or group believes that the relationship between two given constructs is negative, whereas a second individual or group believes the relationship is positive
4	The polarity strength	Two individuals or groups hold the same belief about the polarity of a given relationship but one of them believes the relationship is stronger than the other

Aggregation Procedures for the Analysis of Collective Cognition

When maps have been elicited using highly structured rating scales common to each participant, it is possible to construct one or more aggregate maps by combining individual adjacency matrices. At the most basic level such aggregation can be accomplished by simply adding or averaging participants' judgments of common causal relations (e.g., Bougon, Weick & Binkhorst, 1977; Ford & Hegarty, 1984; Voyer & Faulkner, 1989).

Aggregated maps do not necessarily reflect the views of any one individual. However, they are potentially insightful insofar as they enable the detection of overall group tendencies, the possibility of widespread within-group variance notwithstanding (cf., Walsh, 1995). The latter, of course, is detectable by computing basic measures of spread, such as the semi-inter-quartile ranges or standard deviations associated with particular mean responses. Such aggregate analyses can be highly insightful, as, for example, in the identification of mean sub-group differences in the perception of how much a given construct influences, or is influenced by, other constructs, and its overall detrimental or beneficial effect. Aggregate causal mapping methods also permit the study of the overall structure of group-level mean perceptions of a given set of constructs, thus extending the analysis beyond such basic bivariate relationships.

The Comparative Analysis of Ideographic Cause Maps

In cases where individual maps have been elicited using ideographic techniques, the process of deriving 'shared maps' in an attempt to capture collective cognition is infinitely more complex. The aforementioned aggregation procedure, for example, by necessity must involve an additional, preliminary stage, in which the various constructs upon which causal judgments are to be combined are first pooled, prior to summation or averaging (e.g., Nelson et al., 2000). The procedure known as composite mapping (Eden et al., 1983) requires individuals to first describe their own (idiosyncratic) causal beliefs. Next, they are presented with the causal maps elicited from other participants, following which a (single) composite map, one that contains all the concepts and relations found within the individuals' maps is compiled. Finally, through a process of negotiation between the researcher(s) and participants, there is an attempt to build a 'team map,' that is, a map that reflects the views of the participants as a collective. In practice, the ability to derive maps that are acceptable to participants on a group basis has proven far from straightforward, to the extent that Huff and Fletcher (1990, p.405) find it necessary to advocate "decision rules for handling inevitable inconsistencies." However, as was well illustrated in Langfield-Smith's (1992) study, even gaining consensus with as few as six group members can prove to be impossible.

An alternative approach to the analysis of collective beliefs entails the identification of common elements among diverse causal maps that serve to link participants' beliefs (Hall, 1984). Laukkanen (1994), for example, operationalized collective cognition using a variant of this technique by first deriving separate causal maps for each individual, in similar vein to the earliest stages of the composite mapping procedure outlined above. Next, he assessed the overall level of commonality, i.e., agreement among the individual maps by identifying synonymous terms, which he then standardized prior to incorporating these within a higher-level map, depicting the collective view of his participants.

Recent Advances in the Large-Scale Comparative Analysis of Cause Maps

A potential criticism of nomothetic elicitation methods in the context of explorations of collective cognition is that, by constraining choice, they might potentially lead to a greater convergence of responses than free response methods, by virtue of the standardized variables employed in the elicitation process (Daniels et al., 2002). Conversely, as noted earlier, ideographic methods may increase the divergence among cognitive maps, this being an artifact of the demand characteristics of the elicitation processes, which tend to accentuate surface-level triviality in the resulting maps (Hodgkinson, 1997b, 2002), although it is by no means inevitable that they will do so (cf., Daniels & Johnson, 2002).

Within the past decade or so, a number of researchers have sought to capitalize on the strengths of ideographic and nomothetic elicitation procedures, while dispensing with some of their associated weaknesses, through the development and use of hybrid techniques (e.g., Hodgkinson, et al., 1999; Hodgkinson & Maule, 2002; Markóczy &

Goldberg, 1995). These techniques require participants to select from a comprehensive pool a subset of constructs to be mapped, ones that are personally salient, thereby satisfying the twin imperatives of meaningfulness of the research task and data comparability. By far the most comprehensive of such hybrid procedures to date is that devised by Markóczy and Goldberg (1995), which totally obviates the need for subjective researcher judgment in making such comparisons:

1. Develop a *pool of constructs* by conducting and analyzing interviews with [representative participants] and a review of relevant literature. This is done prior to the study so that each [participant] selects constructs from the same pool.
2. Have each [participant] select a fixed number of *constructs* by identifying items from a constant pool of constructs.
3. Construct the *causal map* of each individual [participant] by having her/him assess the influence of each of her/his selected constructs on her/his other selected constructs.
4. Calculate *distance ratios* between causal maps using a generalized version of Langfield-Smith and Wirth's (1992) formula.
5. Perform a variety of statistical tests on the distance ratios to identify what *characteristics* account for similarities in thinking.

The distance ratios derived from this procedure can be meaningfully employed in order to investigate patterns of similarity and difference among subgroups of participants, in addition to conducting correlational analyses (for substantive applications, see Markóczy, 1995, 1997, 2001). As discussed in the Appendix to this chapter, recent advances and ongoing developments in computerized systems for the elicitation and analysis of causal maps are placing this relatively sophisticated approach within easy reach of virtually any potential user.

Psychometric Issues

As with cognitive mapping techniques in general, users of causal mapping procedures have tended to downplay reliability and validity issues (Huff, 1990), a fundamental prerequisite for the advancement of any social scientific field. Hodgkinson (2001) has discussed the psychometric proprieties required of cognitive maps more generally (including causal maps), both those elicited directly from participants and those elicited from secondary data sources and interview transcripts. The material presented in this section develops and extends the arguments and recommendations put forward in that earlier publication. Our discussion in this section is necessarily technical, focusing on the statistical requirements for ascertaining the reliability and validity of causal maps. It is convenient to introduce this material at this juncture because it is highly relevant to all stages of the mapping process, not only the elicitation of raw data, but also the construction, analysis and comparison of causal maps.

As noted earlier, one of the major strengths of direct elicitation procedures is that they obviate the need for a two-stage approach to map construction, the maps emerging directly from the elicitation process. In contrast, indirect methods require a considerable amount of additional effort on the part of the researcher, in that the causal maps first have to be identified through elaborate coding procedures, prior to the computation of basic structural indicators and other metrics for capturing the characteristic features of the maps. In turn, this further complicates the process of establishing the reliability and validity of the resulting outputs. Accordingly, we begin this discussion of reliability and validity issues with a consideration of the more straightforward case of maps elicited by direct means.

Basic Requirements for Direct Elicitation Procedures

In contexts where the intended application of causal mapping is to access the relatively enduring features of actors' perceptions and beliefs, as a basic minimum requirement, the procedure(s) employed should exhibit acceptable test-retest reliability and construct validity. In this context, test-retest reliability refers to the degree of consistency in the content and structure of participants' causal maps assessed on multiple occasions. To the extent that similar maps emerge from one occasion to the next, they are said to possess test-retest reliability. Reliability statistics can be computed in a variety of ways, ranging from basic frequency analyses of map content (e.g., the percentage of variables incorporated in the maps on multiple occasions) to more sophisticated comparisons of structural indices, expressed in the form of a reliability coefficient (e.g., the Pearson product-moment or Spearman rank-order correlation), ranging between zero (no reliability) and unity (perfect reliability). In general, reliability coefficients should exceed 0.70 as a basic minimum indication of acceptable reliability (Nunnally, 1978).

Construct validity in this context concerns the extent to which indices of map structure and content correlate with one another in ways that are in line with *a priori* theoretical predictions. Sound theorizing should enable strong predictions concerning which particular indices will be significantly correlated with one another and in what direction(s). The greater the number of significant positive and negative relationships (and non-significant relationships) predicted on the basis of theory, in advance of measurement, the greater the construct validity of the mapping indices. Ultimately, it is also desirable that causal maps should exhibit acceptable levels of criterion-related validity, i.e., indices of map structure and content should correlate significantly in ways that are theoretically meaningful with a range of exogenous variables (i.e., variables measured outside the cognitive mapping exercise) including pertinent individual differences and group process and outcome variables.

In cases where the intended application is largely practical in nature, for example in the context of interventions designed to facilitate strategy debates among the top management team (TMT) with a view to challenging the assumptions of key decision makers (e.g., Eden & Ackermann, 1998a), arguably, it is still the case that the mapping procedures so employed should exhibit acceptable test-retest reliability, albeit over relatively shorter time-periods. If the aim of such interventions is to act as a catalyst for cognitive change, ultimately we need to ensure that the changes resulting from such applications are in fact non-trivial, deeper-level changes concerning actors' enduring thoughts (cf., Daniels, de Chernatony & Johnson, 1995; Hodgkinson, Maule & Bown, 2004; Stubbart & Ramaprasad, 1990).

Basic Requirements for the Construction of Maps from Indirect Sources

As pointed out by Jenkins (1998), there is a lack of consistency in the literature overall regarding how coding issues are dealt with and reported. As a basic minimum, the coding schemes employed should meet the dual requirements of acceptable test-retest and inter-coder reliability. In this context, test-retest reliability means that repeated coding exercises would yield more or less identical results (technically known as code-recode reliability) while inter-coder reliability requires that multiple coders reach acceptable levels of agreement (Miles & Huberman, 1994).

The degree of code-recode reliability ultimately has a bearing on the attainment or otherwise of acceptable levels of inter-coder reliability. Hence, as noted by Huff and Fletcher (1990) both of these forms of reliability are necessary prerequisites for a coding scheme to be deemed technically adequate. It is heartening, therefore, that the majority of researchers utilizing documentary and other indirect sources routinely take steps to ensure that their coding schemes exhibit acceptable inter-coder reliability. Typically, however, this merely takes the form of an analysis of the number of instances where two or more coders are in basic agreement with one another (i.e., percentage agreement) with regard to the assignment of the various elements of data to each of the predetermined categories within the coding scheme, which parts of the various assertions coded contain the causal concept and the sign of the causal assertion (for representative examples, see Barr, 1998; Barr & Huff, 1997; Calori et al., 1992, 1994; Jenkins & Johnson, 1997a, 1997b).

As discussed in the Appendix, Laukkanen (1994, 1998) has devised a computerized system for the analysis of causal maps derived from documentary sources, including interview transcripts, that seeks to simplify data in the form of "standardized natural language" in order to facilitate subsequent comparative analyses. Similarly, Nelson et al. (2000a) have devised procedures for standardizing the variables elicited from individual participants in order to undertake such comparisons. Laukkenan (1998) argues that some form of validation process should underpin the standardization of data. In this connection he advocates the involvement of experienced research colleagues and other knowledgeable individuals to independently assess the quality of the data coding. While the process of independent data coding can be extremely cumbersome and time consuming, multiple trained assessors can be employed, which alleviates the burden to a certain extent, providing of course that the assessors are able to do so reliably, as discussed above. In line with the "good practice guidelines" devised by Huff and Fletcher (1990), Laukkenan also suggests feeding back the findings to individual participants, in an attempt to validate the coding process. In keeping with this prescription, Nelson et al. (2000a) went back to their original expert respondents to validate the maps encoded by the research team.

Despite the popularity of participant validation as an approach to trying to safeguard factual and interpretive accuracy, there are some non-trivial problems and drawbacks associated with it, not least the fact that changes can occur very rapidly between that which is thought at the time a decision occurs and how those experiences come to be recounted subsequently. A recent study by Hodgkinson et al. (2004) illustrates just how marked the variations can be that emerge as a function of the type of elicitation procedure employed. Two direct elicitation procedures, a freehand approach and the pairwise evaluation of causal relations, were compared systematically. In keeping with their hypotheses, based largely on work conducted by experimental cognitive psychologists in the field of human memory, Hodgkinson and his colleagues found that the pairwise technique yielded significantly richer maps, but participants found the task more difficult, less engaging and less representative than the freehand approach. Hodgkinson et al. attributed these findings to key differences in the nature of the basic human memory mechanisms underpinning the two tasks. When one considers that the causal maps compared in this study were gathered very soon after the point of decision, using direct forms of elicitation procedure, it becomes clear that techniques relying on participant validation of researcher-derived coding schemes are more — not less — likely to introduce further sources of latent error, as participants reconstruct their thoughts not as they actually occurred but very much how they would like them to have been. In the words of J. Sparrow (1998, p.48):

"The way in which a person recollects an event changes over time, depending on the audience and circumstance as well as any reframing in the light of experience."

Given the politically sensitive nature of the organizational issues typically investigated using causal mapping techniques, it becomes clear that techniques requiring negotiation of the findings should be used sparingly, if the purpose is to try and capture in a manner that represents as accurately as possible the belief systems of actors at the moment of decision. Participant validation methods administered distally in time from the moment of decision are limited by virtue of their failure to control for the dynamic capabilities of the human memory system to distort reality, to say nothing of the demand characteristics introduced by the researcher during this subsequent process, however unwittingly (cf., Hodgkinson, 1997b, 2002).

In the final analysis, participant (and expert panel) validation does not go nearly far enough as a basis for ascertaining the validity of causal maps elicited by indirect procedures. As in the case of maps elicited using direct procedures, it is essential that the construct validity of structure and content indices are established and, wherever possible, researchers should attempt to demonstrate the criterion-related validity of maps derived in this way by correlating the various structural and content indices with key individual differences and/or process and/or outcome variables. Unfortunately, however, it has been rare indeed for researchers to take these vital steps.

In sum, when assessed by the psychometric standards outlined above, basic requirements in virtually any area of applied psychology, it is clear that the procedures adopted

Table 3. Minimum acceptable psychometric properties required of cause maps elicited by direct and indirect procedures

	Direct Procedures	Indirect Procedures	Overall Recommendations
Reliability Requirements	Test-retest, i.e., an acceptable degree of temporal consistency in map content and structure when assessed on multiple occasions	Inter-coder, i.e., an acceptable level of agreement among multiple coders concerning the structure and content of coded maps	All associated reliability coefficients should exceed 0.7.
		Test-retest, i.e., more or less identical results over repeated coding exercises	Where percentage agreement statistics are used at minimum agreement should be somewhere in the region of 70-80 percent.
Validity Requirements	Construct validity	Construct validity	Establish the nature and extent of theoretically meaningful correlations among indices of map content and structure, having specified in advance which relationships will be significant (convergent validity) and those that won't (divergent validity). Preferably, specify the direction of those relationships expected to be statistically significant, thereby enabling 1-tailed tests.
	Criterion-related validity	Criterion-related validity	Establish the degree of correlation of various structural and content indices with key exogenous individual differences and process and/or outcome variables.
		Participant validation	Participant validation, even when carried out as close as possible to the point in time when the cause maps were elicited or constructed, at best, should be regarded as nothing more than a basic first step in the validation process.

by many authors of published studies involving causal cognitive mapping fall a long way short of the mark, with little or no attention having been given to reliability and validity issues in the strict statistical sense of these terms. Indeed, several commentators, (e.g., Eden & Ackermann, 1998b), are openly hostile to the suggestion that there is a need for greater rigor in this domain. This is understandable, given the many practical difficulties in meeting these requirements, not the least of which is the laboriousness involved, which should not be underestimated, particularly in cases involving large numbers of data sources. Nevertheless, if significant inroads are to be made in the advancement of new and established substantive domains of application, including, but by no means restricted to, the IS and IT fields, it is vital that the standards of scientific rigor advocated in this chapter be adopted as a matter of course.

We have covered much territory in this section. In order to provide a clear sense of direction for the would-be user of causal mapping techniques, a summary of the main psychometric issues that need to be considered when making particular methodological choices and our recommended solutions to the problems identified is presented in Table 3.

Conclusions and Recommendations

The central message of this chapter is that, as with any other cognitive mapping/ knowledge elicitation technique, the would-be user of causal mapping procedures faces a series of inter-related issues and choices that have a direct bearing on the type of data that can be gathered, the sorts of analyses that can be conducted, and what inferences that can be drawn. These issues apply equally regardless of whether the work is being undertaken for policy-making/intervention purposes, or in an attempt to capture actors' beliefs in the context of theoretically driven empirical research.

The question as to what constitutes the most appropriate methodological choices in causal mapping research can only be answered by carefully considering the precise nature of the inquiry being undertaken and the context(s) in which the investigation is taking place (cf., Daniels & Johnson, 2002; Hodgkinson, 2002). As we have seen, causal mapping procedures have been adapted in a variety of ways over the years, particular approaches having evolved in response to demands for data in forms suitable for addressing particular sorts of research questions, taking due account of the practical constraints imposed by specific research settings. Clearly, however, these developments represent more than a set of mere pragmatic reactions to prevailing circumstantial contingencies. As noted at the outset, researchers are divided along clear ontological faultlines regarding the fundamental nature and status of causal maps (and other forms of cognitive map) and collective cognition. The particular approaches we have reviewed are as much a manifestation of the underlying ontological assumptions of their advocates, upon which they are predicated, as they are solutions to what are essentially mundane practical problems, such as the need to gain site access with minimal intrusion, the requirement for robust data, and so on. It is the combination of methodological differences in underlying ontology and the non-trivial pragmatic issues such as access requirements that are the main determinants of which particular research questions are pursued and how they come to be formulated in the first place (cf., Easterby-Smith, Thorpe & Lowe, 1991; Gill & Johnson, 1991; Jenkins, 1998). Given this complex state of affairs, what concrete recommendations are we able to make for the IS and IT research communities that might assist the potential user of causal mapping techniques?

In the final analysis, we ourselves are advocates of a Pragmatic Science approach to knowledge production, which entails the pursuit of research questions directed toward the development of insights that are both theoretically and methodologically robust on one hand, but also of high practical relevance on the other (Anderson, Herriot & Hodgkinson, 2001; Hodgkinson & Herriot, 2002; Hodgkinson, Herriot & Anderson, 2001). Skillfully adopted, this philosophy will yield *actionable knowledge* (Argyris, 1999), i.e., knowledge that is both academically rigorous *and* contributes directly to the enhancement of employee well-being and organizational effectiveness. Use of the term 'science' in this connection is not meant to imply that we are advocating the wholesale abandonment of in-depth, qualitative approaches in favor of larger-scale hypothetico-deductive ones. Nor should the 'pragmatic' element of our approach be taken to imply the adoption of sub-standard theory and methods in order to generate immediate solutions to the most pressing practical issues of the day. On the contrary, as explained by Anderson et al. (2001): "there is a need to broaden our search for, and the acceptance of, methodological alternatives that meet the twin imperatives of rigour and relevance." 'Scholarly consulting,' as advocated by Argyris (1999), major elements of which have been termed action research, fall within this definition of pragmatic science, as potentially do all of the approaches to causal mapping reviewed in this chapter.

The overriding necessity, from our point of view, is that researchers using causal mapping methods make choices that are both internally consistent with one another and commensurate with the requirements of the research question under investigation. As researchers we are trying to get as close to the worldviews of participants as our (imperfect) techniques will allow. Techniques that impose too much structure will stifle participants, whereas procedures that fail to provide sufficient structure will yield overly elaborated data. Both are potentially problematic, but the extent to which each is actually a problem in practice is a function of context and the nature of the research question to be addressed (Hodgkinson, 2002; Hodgkinson et al., 2004). For instance, if the aim of research were to try and capture the dynamics of cognition in real time, such as in applications seeking to sample the causal beliefs of IT users on the Internet, how would one set about studying this? One way would be to go down the ideographic route, as championed by Eden and his associates. This would require the researcher to take repeated snap shots of small numbers of participants as their maps evolved. Another approach would be to have them make decisions then immediately try and capture the complexity of their thinking as fully as possible, using highly structured elicitation techniques, such as the Pathfinder network approaches reviewed in Gillan and Schvaneveldt (1999). In this context, as with all applications of causal mapping (and any other knowledge elicitation and knowledge representation procedure), the adopted choices must depend on what one is trying to do with the data.

Ultimately, researchers must make a tradeoff between depth and richness of insight on one hand and comparability and generalizability on the other hand (Hodgkinson, 2002). In situations where there is a fundamental requirement for greater depth and richness of insight into the thoughts of individual participants, ideographic approaches to elicitation and map construction are the order of the day. Clearly, however, these are not suitable for use in situations where large-scale comparisons and generalizability of the findings are fundamental prerequisites, not least due to the unreasonable coding burdens placed on the researcher, leading in turn to fundamental concerns with regard to reliability and validity. While the nomothetic alternative of providing all participants with an *a priori* standardized list of variables has been criticized on the grounds that potentially this might yield less salient data (Eden et al., 1992), the implication being that the researcher's subjectivity rather than that of the participant overly determines the nature of the data obtained, it is clear that data transformation processes as employed by ideographic researchers also entail a considerable amount of researcher subjectivity, despite the development of techniques to enhance inter-coder reliability (c.f., Huff, Narapareddy & Fletcher, 1990).

In sum, as observed by Jenkins (1998), there needs to be some level of tradeoff between fully capturing data which is meaningful to participants and ensuring that data is elicited in such a manner as to ensure sufficient commonality, so that comparisons of causal maps are meaningful. Hybrid elicitation procedures, such as those devised by Hodgkinson et al. (1999) and Markóczy and Goldberg (1995), were developed in an effort to strike a balance between these competing requirements. As we have seen, they are especially promising in a number of research contexts, since by allowing choice within pre-specified limits (participants choose variables to be mapped from a menu) the data is not only more meaningful for the individual participants concerned, but also comparable across multiple levels of analysis, without the necessity for elaborate coding procedures of dubious reliability and validity (Hodgkinson, 2002).

While in principle the Markóczy and Goldberg (1995) procedure could prove highly suited to the collection and comparative analysis of much larger-scale datasets than has been possible hitherto, a number of software limitations have prevented its wider adoption and all applications within the extant literature having been authored by its originators (e.g., Markóczy, 1995, 1997, 2001). Fortunately, however, as discussed in the Appendix, software currently being evaluated by the present authors looks as if it will rectify these limitations. Repeated trials have shown that the Windows-based system is capable of performing all aspects of the Markóczy and Goldberg procedure — and the earlier approaches to the comparison of cause maps devised by Langfield-Smith and Wirth (1992) — in real time, within highly demanding workplace settings.

As this review of methodological advances in causal mapping has demonstrated, the study of managerial and organizational cognition is complex, but it is this very complexity that makes it such a challenging and exciting endeavor. The introduction of causal mapping techniques to the IS and IT communities at this particular juncture is highly fortuitous. The large volume of work that has been undertaken in the fields of strategic management, and management and organization studies more generally, means that IS and IT researchers are inheriting a rich legacy. The gathering and analysis of large-scale, multi-level longitudinal datasets — much needed for the scientific advancement of many areas of application, but which have thus far eluded all but a handful of scholars — is now within our wider methodological capabilities. Much has been accomplished, yet there is still much to do, and researchers in the IS and IT fields are eminently well placed to contribute to the advancement of cognitive mapping theory, method and practice.

Copyright © 2005, Idea Group Inc. Copying or distributing in print or electronic forms without written permission of Idea Group Inc. is prohibited.

Notes and Acknowledgments

The financial support of the UK ESRC/EPSRC Advanced Institute of Management Research (AIM) in the preparation of this chapter (under grant number RES-331-25-0028) is gratefully acknowledged. We are also grateful to V.K. Narayanan and two anonymous referees for their helpful and constructive comments on an earlier version of our manuscript.

1. This lack of agreement over basic nomenclature is unfortunate, leading to frequent confusion.
2. Recently, Maule et al. (2003) have reported a laboratory experiment in which participants were required to record their thoughts by writing free-text narratives immediately following a decision task. The narratives were subsequently coded into causal maps. While this approach shares the problems identified by Kemmerer et al. (2001) in respect to the coding of free-response source documents, it circumvents the potential problems associated with face-to-face interviews, arising from the demand characteristics of the social situation, which can result in overly elaborate or impoverished maps, as noted by Hodgkinson (1997b).

References

Ackermann, F., Eden, C., & Cropper, S. (1990). *Cognitive mapping: A user's guide*. Working Paper No. 12, Department of Management Science, University of Strathclyde, UK.

Anderson, N., Herriot, P., & Hodgkinson, G.P. (2001). The practitioner-researcher divide in industrial, work and organizational (IWO) psychology: Where are we now and where do we go from here? *Journal of Occupational and Organizational Psychology*, 74, 391-411.

Argyris, C. (1999). *On organizational learning* (2nd ed.). Oxford, UK: Blackwell.

Axelrod, R. (Ed.) (1976). *Structure of decisions: The cognitive maps of political elites*. Princeton, NJ: Princeton University Press.

Barr, P.S. (1998). Adapting to unfamiliar environmental events: A look at the evolution of interpretation and its role in strategic change. *Organization Science*, 9, 644-669.

Barr, P.S., & Huff, A.S. (1997). Seeing isn't believing: Understanding diversity in the timing of strategic response. *Journal of Management Studies*, 34, 337-370.

Barr, P.S., Stimpert, J.L., & Huff, A.S. (1992). Cognitive change, strategic action, and organizational renewal. *Strategic Management Journal*, 13(Special Issue), 15-36.

Borgatti, S.P., Everett, M.G., & Freeman, L.C. (1992). *UCINET IV version 1.0*. Columbia: Analytic Technologies.

Bougon, M., Weick, K., & Binkhorst, D. (1977). Cognition in organizations: An analysis of the utrecht jazz orchestra. *Administrative Science Quarterly*, 22, 606-639.

Budhwar, P.S. (2000). Strategic integration and devolvement of human resource management in the UK manufacturing sector. *British Journal of Management*, 11, 285-302.

Budhwar, P.S., & Sparrow, P.R. (2002). Strategic HRM through the cultural looking glass: Mapping the cognition of British and Indian managers. *Organization Studies*, 23, 599-638.

Calori, R., Johnson, G., & Sarnin, P. (1994). CEOs' cognitive maps and the scope of the organization. *Strategic Management Journal*, 15, 437-457.

Calori, R., Johnson, G., & Sarnin, P. (1992). French and British top managers' understanding of the structure and the dynamics of their industries: A cognitive analysis and comparison. *British Journal of Management*, 3, 61-78.

Cannon-Bowers, J.A., & Salas, E. (2001). Reflections on shared cognition. *Journal of Organizational Behavior*, 22, 195-202.

Clarke, I., & Mackaness, W. (2001). Management 'Intuition': An interpretive account of structure and content of decision schemas using cognitive maps. *Journal of Management Studies*, 38, 147-172.

Clarkson, G., Hodgkinson, G.P., & Fearfull, A. (2001). *A conceptual framework for the study of call centre environments from a sensemaking perspective.* Paper presented at the Annual Conference of the British Academy of Management, Cardiff, UK.

Cossette, P., & Audet, M. (1992). Mapping of an idiosyncratic schema. *Journal of Management Studies*, 29, 325-347.

Cropper, S., Eden, C., & Ackermann, F. (1990). Keeping sense of accounts using computer-based cognitive maps. *Social Science Computer Review*, 8, 345-366.

Daniels, K., de Chernatony, L., & Johnson, G. (1995). Validating a method for mapping managers' mental models of competitive industry structures. *Human Relations*, 48, 975-991.

Daniels, K., & Johnson. G. (2002). On trees and triviality traps: Locating the debate on the contribution of cognitive mapping to organizational research. *Organization Studies*, 23, 73-81.

Daniels, K., Johnson, G., & de Chernatony, L. (2002). Task and institutional influences on managers' mental models of competition. *Organization Studies*, 23, 31-62.

de Chernatony, L., Daniels, K., & Johnson, G. (1993). A cognitive perspective on managers' perceptions of competition. *Journal of Marketing Management*, 9, 373-381.

Diesner, J., & Carley, K.M. (2005). Revealing social structure from texts: Meta-matrix text analysis as a novel method for network text analysis. In V.K. Narayanan & D.J. Armstrong (Eds.), *Causal mapping for information systems and technology research: Approaches, advances and illustrations* (pp.81-108). Hershey, PA: Idea Group Publishing.

Diffenbach, J. (1982). Influence diagrams for complex strategic issues. *Strategic Management Journal*, 3, 133-146.

Easterby-Smith, M., Thorpe, R., & Lowe, A. (1991). *Management research: An introduction*. London: Sage.

Eco, U. (1979). *A theory of semiotics*. Bloomington, IN: University of Indiana Press.

Eden, C. (1992). On the nature of cognitive maps. *Journal of Management Studies*, 29(Special Issue), 261-265.

Eden, C., & Ackermann, F. (1998a). *Making strategy: The journey of strategic management*. London: Sage.

Eden, C., & Ackermann, F. (1998b). Analysing and comparing idiographic cause maps. In C. Eden & J. C. Spender (Eds.), *Managerial and organizational cognition: Theory, methods and research* (pp. 192-209). London: Sage.

Eden, C., Ackermann, F., & Cropper, S. (1992). The analysis of cause maps. *Journal of Management Studies*, 29, 309-324.

Eden, C., Jones, S., & Sims, D. (1983). *Messing about in problems: An informal structured approach to their identification and management*. Oxford: Pergamon Press.

Eden, C., Jones, S., & Sims, D. (1979). *Thinking in organizations*. London: Macmillan.

Eden, C., & Spender, J. C. (1998). *Managerial and organizational cognition: Theory, methods and research*. London: Sage.

Fahey, L., & Narayanan, V.K. (1989). Linking changes in revealed causal maps and environmental changes: An empirical study. *Journal of Management Studies*, 26(Special Issue), 361-378.

Fiol, C.M. (1989). A semiotic analysis of corporate language: Organizational boundaries and joint venturing. *Administrative Science Quarterly*, 34, 277-303.

Fiol, C.M., & Huff, A.S. (1992). Maps for managers: Where are we? Where do we go from here? *Journal of Management Studies*, 29, 267-286.

Fombrun, C. J., & Zajac, E. J. (1987). Structural and perceptual influences on intra-industry stratification. *Academy of Management Journal*, 30, 33-50.

Ford, J.D., & Hegarty, W.H. (1984). Decision makers' beliefs about the causes and effects of structure: An exploratory study. *Academy of Management Journal*, 27, 271-291.

Fournier, V. (1996). Cognitive maps in the analysis of personal change during work role transition. *British Journal of Management*, 7, 87-105.

Gill, J., & Johnson, P. (1991). *Research methods for managers*. London: Chapman.

Gillan, D.J., Breedin, S.D., & Cooke, N.M. (1992). Network and multidimensional representations of the declarative knowledge of human-computer interface design experts. *International Journal of Man-Machine Studies*, 36, 587-615.

Gillan, D.J., & Schvaneveldt, R.W. (1999). Applying cognitive psychology: Bridging the gulf between basic research and cognitive artefacts. In F.T. Durso, R.S. Nickerson, R.W. Schvaneveldt, S.T. Dumais, D.S. Lindsay & M.T.H. Chi (Eds.), *Handbook of applied cognition* (pp. 3-31). Chichester, UK: Wiley.

Ginsberg, A. (1989). Construing the business portfolio: A cognitive model of diversification. *Journal of Management Studies*, 26(Special Issue), 417-438.

Goldberg, J. (1996). *The Distrat/Askmap Suite of programs for cause map analysis: A user's guide.* Retrieved from the WWW at: *http://www.goldmark.org/jeff/programs/distrat/software/drdoclet.ps.gz*

Green, D.W., & McManus, I.C. (1995). Cognitive structural models: The perception of risk and prevention in coronary heart disease. *British Journal of Psychology*, 86, 321-336.

Gripsrud, G., & Gronhaug, K. (1985). Structure and strategy in grocery retailing: A sociometric approach. *Journal of Industrial Economics*, XXXIII, 339-347.

Harary, F., Norman, R.Z., & Cartwright, D. (1965). *Structural models: An introduction to the theory of directed graphs.* New York: Wiley.

Hart, J. (1976). Comparative cognition: Politics of international control of the oceans. In R. Axelrod (Ed.), *Structure of decision: The cognitive maps of political elites* (pp. 180-220). Princeton, NJ: Princeton University Press.

Hodgkinson, G.P. (2002). Comparing managers' mental models of competition: Why self-report measures of belief similarity won't do. *Organization Studies*, 23, 63-72.

Hodgkinson, G. P. (2001). The psychology of strategic management: Diversity and cognition revisited. In C.L. Cooper & I.T. Robertson (Eds.), *International review of industrial and organizational psychology*, vol. 16 (pp.65-119). Chichester, UK: Wiley.

Hodgkinson, G. P. (1997a). Cognitive inertia in a turbulent market: The case of UK residential estate agents. *Journal of Management Studies*, 34, 921-945.

Hodgkinson, G. P. (1997b). The cognitive analysis of competitive structures: A review and critique. *Human Relations*, 50, 625-654.

Hodgkinson, G. P., Bown, N.J., Maule, A. J., Glaister, K. W., & Pearman, A. D. (1999). Breaking the frame: An analysis of strategic cognition and decision making under uncertainty. *Strategic Management Journal*, 20, 977-985.

Hodgkinson, G.P., & Herriot, P. (2002). The role of psychologists in enhancing organizational effectiveness. In I. T. Robertson, M. Callinan & D. Bartram (Eds.), *Organizational effectiveness: The role of psychology* (pp. 45-60). Chichester, UK: Wiley.

Hodgkinson, G.P., Herriot, P., & Anderson, N. (2001). Re-aligning the stakeholders in management research: Lessons from industrial, work and organizational psychology. *British Journal of Management*, 12(Special Issue), S41-S48.

Hodgkinson, G.P., & Maule, A.J. (2002). The individual in the strategy process: Insights from behavioural decision research and cognitive mapping. In A.S. Huff & M. Jenkins (Eds.), *Mapping strategic knowledge* (pp.196-219). London: Sage.

Hodgkinson, G.P., Maule, A.J., & Bown, N.J. (2004). Causal cognitive mapping in the organizational strategy field: A comparison of alternative elicitation procedures. *Organizational Research Methods*, 7, 3-26.

Hodgkinson, G.P., Padmore, J., & Tomes, A.E. (1991). Mapping consumers' cognitive structures: A comparison of similarity trees with multidimensional scaling and cluster analysis. *European Journal of Marketing*, 25(7), 41-60.

Hodgkinson, G.P., & Sparrow, P.R. (2002). *The competent organization: A psychological analysis of the strategic management process*. Buckingham, UK: Open University Press.

Hodgkinson, G.P., & Thomas, A.B. (Eds.) (1997). Thinking in organizations. *Journal of Management Studies*, 34(Special issue), 845-952.

Hodgkinson, G.P., Tomes, A.E., & Padmore, J. (1996). Using consumers' perceptions for the cognitive analysis of corporate-level competitive structures. *Journal of Strategic Marketing*, 4, 1-22.

Huff, A.S. (Ed.) (1990). *Mapping strategic thought*. Chichester, UK: Wiley.

Huff, A.S., & Fletcher, K.E. (1990). Conclusion: Key mapping decisions. In A. S. Huff (Ed.), *Mapping strategic thought* (pp. 403-412). Chichester, UK: Wiley.

Huff, A.S., Narapareddy, V., & Fletcher, K.E. (1990). Coding the causal association of concepts. In A. S. Huff (Ed.), *Mapping strategic thought* (pp. 311-325). Chichester, UK: Wiley.

Jasinski, D.W., & Huff, A.S. (2002). Using as knowledge-based system to study strategic options. In A. S. Huff & M. Jenkins (Eds.), *Mapping strategic knowledge* (pp. 237-267). London: Sage.

Jenkins, M. (1998). The theory and practice of comparing causal maps. In C. Eden & J.C. Spender (Eds.), *Managerial and organizational cognition: Theory, methods and research* (pp. 231-249). London: Sage.

Jenkins, M., & Johnson, G. (1997a). Linking managerial cognition and organizational performance: A preliminary investigation using causal maps. *British Journal of Management*, 8(Special Issue), S77-S90.

Jenkins, M., & Johnson, G. (1997b). Entrepreneurial intentions and outcomes: A comparative causal mapping study. *Journal of Management Studies*, 34, 895-920.

Kelly, G.A. (1955). *The psychology of personal constructs* (in 2 volumes). New York: Norton.

Kemmerer, B., Buche, M., & Narayanan, V.K. (2001). *Deriving revealed causal maps from non-traditional source documents: Challenges and methodological extensions*. Paper presented at Annual Meeting of the Academy of Management, Washington, DC.

Langfield-Smith, K. (1992). Exploring the need for a shared cognitive map. *Journal of Management Studies*, 29, 349-368.

Langfield-Smith, K., & Wirth, A. (1992). Measuring differences between cognitive maps. *Journal of the Operational Research Society*, 43, 1135-1150.

Lant, T.K., & Shapira, Z. (Eds.) (2001). *Organizational cognition: Computation and interpretation*. Mahwah, NJ: Lawrence Erlbaum Associates.

Laukkanen, M. (1994). Comparative cause mapping of organizational cognitions. *Organization Science*, 5, 322-343.

Laukkanen, M. (1998). Conducting causal mapping research: Opportunities and challenges. In C. Eden & J.C. Spender (Eds.), *Managerial and organizational cognition: Theory, methods and research* (pp. 168-191). London: Sage.

Markóczy, L. (2001). Consensus formation during strategic change. *Strategic Management Journal*, 22, 1013-1031.

Markóczy, L. (1997). Measuring beliefs: Accept no substitutes. *Academy of Management Journal*, 40, 1228-1242.

Markóczy, L. (1995). States and belief states. *The International Journal of Human Resource Management*, 6, 249-270.

Markóczy, L., & Goldberg, J. (1995). A method for eliciting and comparing causal maps. *Journal of Management*, 21, 305-333.

Maule, A.J., Hodgkinson, G.P., & Bown, N.J. (2003). Cognitive mapping of causal reasoning in strategic decision making. In D. Hardman & L. Macchi (Eds.), *Thinking: Psychological perspectives on judgment and decision making* (pp. 253-272). Chichester, UK: Wiley.

Meindl, J.R., Stubbart, C., & Porac, J.F. (Eds.) (1994). Cognition. *Organization Science*, 5(Special Issue), 288-477.

Miles, M.B., & Huberman, A.M. (1994). *Qualitative data analysis* (2nd edition). Thousand Oaks, CA: Sage Publications.

Mohammed, S., Klimoski, R., & Rentsch, J.R. (2000). The measurement of team mental models: We have no shared schema. *Organizational Research Methods*, 3, 123-65.

Nayaranan, V. K. (2005). Causal mapping: An historical overview. In V.K. Narayanan & D.J. Armstrong (Eds.), *Causal mapping for research in information technology* (pp.1-19). Hershey, PA: Idea Group Publishing.

Narayanan, V.K., & Fahey, L. (1990). Evolution of revealed causal maps during decline: A case study of admiral. In A. S. Huff (Ed.), *Mapping strategic thought* (pp. 109-133). Chichester, UK: Wiley.

Narayanan, V.K., & Kemmerer, B. (2001). *A cognitive perspective on strategic management: contributions, challenges, and implications*. Paper presented at Annual Meeting of the Academy of Management, Washington, DC.

Nelson, K.M., Nadkarni, S., Narayanan, V.K., & Ghods, M. (2000a). Understanding software operations support expertise: A revealed causal mapping approach. *MIS Quarterly*, 24, 475-507.

Nelson, K.M., Nelson, H.J., & Armstrong, D. (2000b). Revealed causal mapping as an evocative method for information systems research. *Proceedings of the 33rd Hawaii International Conference on System Sciences.*

Nunnally, J.C. (1978). *Psychometric theory*. New York: McGraw Hill.

Porac, J. F., & Thomas, H. (Eds.) (1989). Managerial thinking in business environments. *Journal of Management Studies*, 26(Special Issue), 323-438.

Reger, R.K., & Huff, A.S. (1993). Strategic groups: A cognitive perspective. *Strategic Management Journal*, 14, 103-124.

Roberts, F.S. (1976). Strategy for the Energy Crisis: The Case of Commuter Transportation Policy. In R. Axelrod (Ed.), *Structure of decision: The cognitive maps of political elites* (pp. 142-179). Princeton, NJ: Princeton University Press.

Roske-Hofstrand, R.J., & Papp, K.R. (1986). Cognitive networks as a guide to menu organization: An application in the automated cockpit. *Ergonomics*, 29, 1301-1311.

Salancik, G.R., & Porac, J.F. (1986). Distilled ideologies: Values derived from causal reasoning in complex environments. In H. P. Sims Jr. & D. A. Gioia Associates (Eds.), *The thinking organization: Dynamics of organizational and social cognition* (pp. 75 - 101). San Francisco: Jossey Bass.

Scheper, W.J., & Faber, J. (1994). Do cognitive maps make sense? *Advances in Managerial Cognition and Organizational Information Processing*, 5, 165-185.

Schraagen, J.M., Chipman, S.F., & Shalin, V.L. (Eds.) (2000). *Cognitive task analysis*. Mahwah, NJ: Lawrence Erlbaum Associates.

Schvaneveldt, R.W. (1990). Proximities, networks, and schemata. In R.W. Schvaneveldt (Ed.), *Pathfinder associative networks: Studies in knowledge organization* (pp. 135-148). Norwood, NJ: Ablex Publishing.

Schvaneveldt, R.W., & Durso, F.T. (1981). *General semantic networks*. Paper presented at the annual meeting of the Psychonomic Society, Philadelphia.

Schvaneveldt, R.W., Dearholt, D.W., & Durso, F.T. (1989). Network structures in proximity data. In G. Bower (Ed.), *The psychology of learning and motivation: Advances in research and theory* (Vol. 24, pp. 249-84). New York: Academic Press.

Schvaneveldt, R.W., Dearholt, D.W., & Durso, F.T. (1988). Graph theoretic foundations of Pathfinder networks. *Computers and Mathematics with Applications*, 15, 337-45.

Seamster, T.L., Redding, R.E., & Kaempf, G.L. (1997). *Applied cognitive task analysis in aviation*. Avebury: Aldershot.

Shadbolt, N., & Milton, N. (1999). From knowledge engineering to knowledge management. *British Journal of Management*, 10, 309-322.

Sparrow, J. (1998). *Knowledge in organizations: Access to thinking at work*. London: Sage.

Stubbart, C. I., & Ramaprasad, A. (1990). Comments on the empirical articles and recommendations for future research. In A.S. Huff (Ed.), *Mapping strategic thought* (pp. 251-288). Chichester, UK: Wiley.

Swan, J.A. (1995). Exploring knowledge and cognitions in decisions about technological innovation: Mapping managerial cognitions. *Human Relations*, 48, 1241-70.

Swan, J. (1997). Using cognitive mapping in management research: Decisions about technical innovation. *British Journal of Management*, 8, 183-198.

Swan, J., & Newell, S. (1998). Making sense of technological innovations: The political and social dynamics of cognition. In C. Eden & J.C. Spender (Eds.), *Managerial and organizational cognition: Theory, methods and research* (pp. 108-129). London: Sage.

Voyer, J., & Faulkner, R. (1989). Organizational cognition in a jazz ensemble. *Empirical Studies of the Arts*, 7, 57-77.

Walsh, J.P. (1995). Managerial and organizational cognition: Notes from a trip down memory lane. *Organization Science*, 6, 280-321.

Weick, K.E., & Bougon, M.G. (1986). Organizations as cognitive maps: Charting ways to success and failure. In Sims, H.P., Gioia, D.A. and Associates (Eds.), *The thinking organization: Dynamics of organizational social cognition* (pp. 102-135). San Francisco: Jossey-Bass.

Appendix

Supporting Software for the Elicitation, Construction, Analysis and Comparision of Causal Maps

In all but the very simplest of applications, the use of computer software systems can greatly assist the researcher in all stages of the causal mapping process, from knowledge elicitation and map construction to individual and comparative analysis. This is equally true not only in the case of applications involving the detailed analysis of single (Cossette & Audet, 1992) or small numbers (Clarke & Mackaness, 2001) of maps, but also in much larger-scale comparative studies (Markóczy & Goldberg, 1995) of causal maps. Clearly there are times when small-scale, complex ideographic studies, exploratory and inductive in nature, conducted in the context of under-explored knowledge domains, are invaluable. In this type of application, which can result in maps containing as many as several hundred concepts (Eden & Ackermann, 1998a), it is impracticable to analyze the structure and content of the maps using basic manual procedures. However, much of the utility of causal mapping techniques in organizational research lies in their application to larger numbers of individuals and/or groups, comparing their similarities and differences in a range of contexts and/or over multiple points in time. As noted in the main body of the chapter, such comparisons are potentially unwieldy, but fortunately recent developments in mobile computing and associated software advances are paving the way for new support systems that will rapidly resolve these difficulties.

Generic computer software tools such as ATLAS/ti (Jasinski & Huff, 2002) are enabling ideographic researchers to tackle more demanding problems and extend their analyses considerably further than would have been possible using manual coding techniques. Moreover, software systems devised for the structural analysis of social networks, such as UCINET (Borgatti, Everett & Freeman, 1992), are potentially also suitable for the analysis of causal maps, having common mathematical roots in graph theory. Indeed, many of the structural indices commonly employed by network analysts and routinely available in software packages to support the analysis of social networks bear a strikingly close resemblance to those devised by Eden et al. (1992) specifically for the analysis of causal maps. There is no doubt that these software tools are extending the range of computer technology broadly capable of supporting causal mapping. One other system

Copyright © 2005, Idea Group Inc. Copying or distributing in print or electronic forms without written permission of Idea Group Inc. is prohibited.

Table A1. Selected software supporting causal mapping

Name of Program	Approach to Knowledge Elicitation/Map Construction	Output Statistics	Strengths	Limitations	Illustrative applications	Source of Software
ATLAS/ti	Though not developed specifically for causal mapping purposes, this knowledge-based computer system (KBS) has been used to support the construction of maps based on ideographic interview transcripts and could equally be applied to facilitate the construction of maps from other forms of documentary data.	Not Applicable (N/A)	The software assists researchers in identifying patterns among key concepts in documentary data, enabling them to be depicted graphically in the form of non-hierarchical network structures. Data are readily exportable to other software packages (e.g. SPSS™) suitable for performing quantitative analyses of the text patterns identified.	Data must take the form of plain ASCII or ANSI text, i.e. there is no recognition of word processor formats (though data can be internally translated). The reliability and validity problems associated with the coding of maps constructed from ideographic data gathered through indirect means (as detailed in the main body of this chapter) apply when using this software package.	Jasinski & Huff, (2002)	The package is available commercially from Scolari, Sage Publications. A demo version is downloadable from: http://www.scolari.com
CMAP2	This software was developed to support the construction of maps indirectly elicited from documentary sources, including interview transcripts. Documentary data is coded post hoc. In addition to modules for the inputting of raw data and the creation of a standard language vocabulary for coding natural language expressions and achieving comparability over research participants, the program also contains a variety of tools for editing the input data and the generation of analyzable databases.	Key numerical outputs from the program include measures of the distances between the maps of individual participants or clusters of participants.	CMAP2 is based on the observation that causal maps can be decomposed into causal units, i.e. concept-concept pairs assumed to be causally linked to one another. The computer can process these causal units as semi-independent data entries. The software links the computer's databases with the input data elements and thus with the source. As such, it promotes good organization of data, and enables an audit trail from the source to the final standardized concepts and causal units.	The software is currently written in DOS mode. As acknowledged by the author, this does not permit easy export of the various output data into better-developed user interface environments for supplementary statistical analysis, using standard software packages such as SPSS. Moreover, the absence of methods for direct raw data acquisition and input by the participants themselves, in conjunction with primary-level standardization facilities and opportunities for concurrent feedback, renders the whole process extremely labor intensive on the part of the researcher.	Laukkanen (1994, 1998)	This software is available on a non-commercial basis from the developer. For details, see Laukkanen (1998: 189)
Decision Explorer®	This software was developed to permit the direct elicitation and construction of cause maps. Typically, maps are constructed iteratively, in face-to-face meetings in situ.	This software enables the graphical representation of maps as well as the calculation of a variety of quantitative indices of a structural nature.	The software has proved to be of immense benefit in areas where interactively generated maps have helped to build up a comprehensive qualitative map or model, which is then explored and analysed to help develop strategy, decision making and business problems. Decision Explorer® allows researchers to manipulate the data and hence view it from a variety of perspectives. This is not only beneficial from an analytical standpoint, but enables the researcher to actively gain and maintain the interest of participants in the research process. Data can be readily imported from and exported to a number of standard software packages for supplementary qualitative and/or quantitative analysis (e.g. QSR NVivo and SPSS™).	Overly simplistic or complex and 'messy' maps may be constructed at the original stage of data input. As with ideographic methods more generally, the highly idiosyncratic nature of the data renders problematic the systematic comparison of maps, particularly where large numbers of maps are involved. There are no features to support the analysis of inter-coder and code-recode reliability. (For an explanation of these terms see the section entitled 'Psychometric Issues' in the main body of this chapter). The software does not permit the links between variables to be formally weighted numerically, although basic polarities (positive and negative) can be depicted through the use of contrasting color codes and/or variations in the relative thickness of the lines interconnecting the concept nodes.	Cropper, Eden & Ackermann (1990) Eden & Ackermann (1998a, 1998b).	This software package is available commercially from Banxia Software Ltd. A demonstration copy can be downloaded from: http://www.banxia.co

Table A1. Selected software supporting causal mapping (continued)

Name of Program	Approach to Knowledge Elicitation/ Map Construction	Output Statistics	Strengths	Limitations	Illustrative applications	Source of Software
Distral/ askmap suite of programs	Not applicable. This suite of programs was devised facilitate the comparative analysis of cause maps elicited using the hybrid procedures devised by Markóczy & Goldberg (1995)	The programs perform several of the analytical tasks associated with the Markóczy-Goldberg approach.		As stated in Goldberg's (1996) analysis guide, the software is inflexible and of little benefit to anyone not using the particular methods described. The input and output data are configured such that they are not readily transferable to and from other systems, especially of the larger, fully integrated, interactive variety.	Markóczy (1995, 1997, 2001) Markóczy & Goldberg (1995)	The complete collection of programs is available to researchers on a non-commercial basis. For details see Goldberg (1996), down loadable from: http://www.goldmark.org/jeff/programs/distral/software/index.list.ps.gz.
KNOT (Knowledge Network Organizing Tool)	Not applicable. This software package was not developed specifically for the purpose of causal mapping. Its purpose is to implement the Pathfinder network algorithm. The Pathfinder algorithm seeks to represent the information contained in the input proximity matrix in as few links as possible, consistent with the parametric values set by the investigator. The aim is data reduction to facilitate comprehension of the resulting network.	The software performs a similar range of functions to programs for the analysis of social network structures, i.e. the input distance measures are represented as nodes, with links representing the relations between objects. Weights associated with the links, derived from the original proximity data, reflect the strength of the relations.	The KNOT system includes several programs and utilities to facilitate Pathfinder network analyses of proximity data. The system is oriented around producing graphical representations of the solutions, but representations of networks and other information are also available in the form of text files, which can be used in conjunction with other software. Although it was designed for in DOS mode with minor modifications it runs in a Windows environment.	This software does not support the initial elicitation of data for the construction of cause maps.	For details of the general Pathfinder method and its application see Schvaneveldt (1990)	KNOT is a commercially distributed software package, available from Interlink. For details see http://www.interlinkinc.net/Pathfinder.html
UCINET	N/A. This package was devised for the analysis of social network data (typically questionnaires or documentary sources).	A number of basic output statistics for the identification of social network structures including, for example, centrality measures, predicated upon elementary graph theory are equally suited to causal mapping applications. In addition, the package has a number of matrix analysis routines useful in the context of cause map analysis.	The software program NetDraw is integrated with UCINET for drawing diagrams representing social networks, but is equally suitable for drawing networks of concepts, as in causal mapping applications.	This software does not support the initial elicitation of data for the construction of cause maps.	Borgatti, Everett, & Freeman (1992)	A demonstration copy of this commercially distributed software package is available at http://www.analytictech.com
Cognizer This software package is currently being developed by Mandrake Technology	This software enables direct elicitation of cause maps. Building on Markóczy & Goldberg (1995), data elicitation and map construction are achieved by participants first selecting from a predefined pool of variables shown on screen (randomised to minimize potential order effects in an individualized basis, so as to minimize potential order effects in variable selection and pairwise evaluation tasks). Participants then perform on-screen pairwise evaluations of their chosen variables (including explicitly detailing the strength of relationship between each pair of variables). The resulting cause map can next be immediately available for viewing and can be edited by direct manipulation of the on screen graphical outputs.	Many basic analytical functions are incorporated, including, a number of *map content measures* (e.g. indegree, outdegree and reachability values) and *structural measures* (e.g. link-to-node ratio and map density) (see Table 1 in the main body of the chapter for a description of these measures). Distance ratios, reflecting the degree of overall dissimilarity between pairs of cause maps (Langfield-Smith & Wirth, 1992; Markóczy & Goldberg, 1995) can be readily computed and employed in order to investigate patterns of similarity and difference among subgroups of participants.	Cognizer is essentially being developed to permit the elicitation of cause maps in a manner that is meaningful to participants and amenable to mass-comparison. However, the software also allows cause maps to be elicited in other ways, each of which may be more or less acceptable in particular contexts of application. For example, maps can be constructed directly, by drawing a weighted digraph (a sophisticated variant of the basic influence diagram, as discussed in the main body of this chapter under' basic metrics for the analysis of individual cause maps'). The results are easily exportable to other appropriate analytical packages, such as SPSS™.	The limitations of the software will depend upon the chosen method of elicitation and analysis (see the main body of the chapter for a detailed discussion regarding the pros and cons of each method).	Clarkson, Hodgkinson & Fearfull (2001)	For additional details and/or a demonstration copy of Cognizer, e-mail: mandrakeech@fsbusiness.co.uk

worthy of brief mention in this connection, before turning to consider more specialist software tools specifically devised for the analysis of cause maps, is the general approach known as Pathfinder (Schvaneveldt, 1990; Schvaneveldt & Durso, 1981; Schvaneveldt, Dearholt & Durso, 1988, 1989). In a similar vein to UCINET, the Pathfinder algorithms, as implemented in software systems such as KNOT (The Knowledge Network Organizing Tool) (http://www.interlinkinc.net/Pathfinder.html), are used to explore network structures derived from proximity data (i.e., distance matrices reflecting the degree of overall (dis)similarity, or some other proximity measure, between concepts). Within the specific domain of information technology, Pathfinder has been successfully applied to a variety of problems concerning the design of user interfaces (e.g., Gillan, Breedin & Cooke, 1992; Roske-Hofstrand & Paap, 1986). As observed by Gillan & Schvaneveldt (1999), in general, applications in this context (typically involving the analysis of relatedness ratings) have demonstrated that users are more effective in using interfaces derived from their revealed models of the system, as identified by the Pathfinder algorithm, in comparison with existing interfaces.

Although software systems such as ATLAS/ti, UCINET and the Pathfinder algorithm are proving generally useful as basic support mechanisms in the conduct of causal mapping research, fully integrated software systems, dedicated to the elicitation, construction, analysis and comparison of causal maps are ultimately required, if causal mapping is to fulfill its true methodological and substantive potential. To this end, there have been a number of advances over the past decade or so and in the remainder of this appendix we highlight what we consider to be the most significant of these. Due to space limitations we shall confine our attention to a brief consideration of just three of the more popular software packages presently available for the dedicated analysis of causal maps, namely, CMAP2 (Laukkanen, 1994), Decision Explorer® (Eden et al., 1992) and the suite of programs developed by Goldberg (1996), known as distrat/askmap, in addition to reporting some ongoing developments of our own. Clearly, all of these systems are constrained (albeit to varying degrees) by virtue of the underlying assumptions and concomitant choices that their developers have made in relation to the various issues discussed in the main sections of this chapter.

CMAP2 (Laukkanen, 1994, 1998) was developed for the comparative analysis of causal maps derived through interview transcripts and/or documentary sources. A data-based-orientated PC program, it is intended specifically for use in settings where the input data take the form of natural communication and key parameters such as the number of concepts explored, the number of mapped relationships and indeed the number of participants must be flexible (Laukkenan, 1998). Unfortunately, as observed by Jenkins (1998), CMAP2 is limited in several important respects. First, no research has been undertaken to assess the reliability of the processes by which the input data are transformed into comparable units of analysis. As noted in our discussion concerning the relative merits of direct vs. indirect elicitation procedures, this is clearly not a problem unique to CMAP2 but is common to a number of applications of causal mapping procedures more generally, where the maps have been inferred from interview transcripts and/or other indirect documentary sources. Clearly, however, if the practice of causal mapping and the associated application of particular procedures such as CMAP2 are to gain credence in terms of their scientific legitimacy, there is an urgent need to increase the volume and quality of research addressing these and other equally pressing issues concerning their psychometric efficacy.

Decision Explorer® (Eden et al., 1992), a re-launch of Graphics COPE, the system developed several years earlier by Eden and his colleagues for use in the context of group decision support (e.g., Ackermann, Eden & Cropper, 1990; Eden & Cropper, 1990), has proven to be of immense benefit in the context of building comprehensive cognitive maps of complex organizational problems. Decision Explorer® allows the researcher to manipulate data in ways that enable it to be viewed from a variety of perspectives (Eden & Ackermann, 1998b). This is helpful not only from an analytical standpoint, but also in enabling the researcher to actively gain and maintain the interest of participants in the research process. However, Decision Explorer®, as with Laukkanen's software package, was designed primarily for use in the context of local settings, where the focus of attention is on the intensive analysis of ideographic data, gathered from small numbers of individuals. It is less suitable for use in the context of larger-scale studies.

In contrast, Goldberg's (1996) computer programs were designed to perform several of the tasks associated with the Markóczy-Goldberg approach to causal mapping (Markóczy & Goldberg, 1995). As discussed in the main body of the chapter, this approach is potentially very useful in situations that demand the comparative analysis of large numbers of maps. Unfortunately, however, a number of the statistical procedures as devised and implemented by Markóczy and Goldberg (1995), including those building on the earlier work of Langfield-Smith and Wirth (1992), have no accompanying software provision within the distrat/askmap system, thus rendering their implementation difficult, if not impossible, using these programs. Nevertheless, the fact remains that the Markóczy-Goldberg approach to causal map elicitation, analysis and comparison – and the earlier work of Langfield-Smith and Wirth, which laid the foundations for these innovations – represents a major methodological breakthrough. However, if the ultimate potential of this approach is to be realized, there is an urgent need for further developments in the provision of user-friendly software, capable of readily implementing the full range of associated procedures, from elicitation through analysis to comparison, in real-time environments. At the time of writing, the present authors are in the advanced stages of actively evaluating such a system. To date, this Windows-based system, known as Cognizer, has been successfully implemented in the elicitation, analysis and comparison of well over 200 maps, all gathered in the context of face-to-face interviews, *in situ*, with busy employees. (Further details of all of the individual software systems discussed in this Appendix, including a summary of their main strengths and limitations, together with information concerning their availability, are presented in Table A1.)

Section II

Advances in Causal Mapping Methods

Chapter IV

Revealing Social Structure from Texts:
Meta-Matrix Text Analysis as a Novel Method for Network Text Analysis[i]

Jana Diesner
Carnegie Mellon University, USA

Kathleen M. Carley
Carnegie Mellon University, USA

Abstract

Texts can be coded and analyzed as networks of concepts often referred to as maps or semantic networks. In such networks, for many texts there are elements of social structure — the connections among people, organizations, and events. Within organizational and social network theory an approach called the meta-matrix is used to describe social structure in terms of the network of connections among people, organizations, knowledge, resources, and tasks. We propose a combined approach using the meta-matrix model, as an ontology, to lend a second level of organization to the networks of concepts recovered from texts. We have formalized and operationalized this approach in an automated tool for text analysis. We demonstrate how this approach enables not only meaning but also social structure to be revealed through text analysis. We illustrate this approach by showing how it can be used to discover the social structure of covert networks — the terrorist groups operating in the West Bank.

Copyright © 2005, Idea Group Inc. Copying or distributing in print or electronic forms without written permission of Idea Group Inc. is prohibited.

Introduction

Texts are a typical source of information about meaning, organizations, and society. Today, a large and growing number of texts are available in an electronic form that describes, discusses, or displays information about people, the groups to which they belong, the activities in which they engage, and the resources at their disposal. This data and its accessibility motivate the development and investigation of automated techniques for extracting the underlying social and organizational structure from such texts in an effective and efficient way.

In this chapter, we present an automated approach to text analysis that can be used to extract the underlying social and organizational structure contained in texts. This approach is based on the following insights. First, texts can be represented as networks of concepts and the connections between them. These concepts refer to ideas, people, resources, organizations, events, etc. Second, many of the items referred to, such as people, are core entities in the structure of groups and organizations. Hence, the extracted networks contain representations of the social structure — the entities and relations among them that comprise a group, organization, or society. By classifying the concepts into entity classes used in defining social structures and partitioning the extracted network into sub-networks, we have effectively used network analysis of texts to reveal the social structure represented in texts.

Herein, we describe this approach in detail and explain how we operationalized, formalized, and implemented it into a software called AutoMap that enables analysts to extract social structure from texts. As part of this work, we have operationalized an ontological scheme based on the meta-matrix proposed by Carley (2002) for describing social and organizational structure. This ontology is utilized as part of a hierarchical scheme for cross categorizing concepts. In this chapter we furthermore demonstrate how analysts can use AutoMap to automatically extract not just networks of concepts and the relations among them, but also classify the concepts and relations between them according to this ontology. This enables the automatic extraction of views of the social structure.

The chapter begins with a brief overview on the model and methods involved. We then describe how we formalized and implemented the combination of the meta-matrix model and the network text analysis technique. This is followed by a substantive example that we provide in order to illustrate this approach for revealing social structure through the analysis of texts by extracting an image of the social structure of the terrorists groups in the West Bank. We conclude with a discussion of the potentials and limitations of our approach.

Note, this chapter should not be viewed as a description of the West Bank terrorist groups. We have coded for this chapter only a small sample of texts to illustrate the technique. No conclusions for this group should be drawn from the results reported herein.

Using Network Text Analysis to Code Texts

In the area of network text analysis, previous research and development have provided computer-supported solutions that enable analysts to gain a window into social structure and meaning as represented in texts. Collectively these approaches enable the analyst to extract networks of concepts and the connections between them from the texts. These networks are sometimes referred to as maps (Carley, 1997b), networks of centering words (Corman, Kuhn, Mcphee & Dooley, 2002), semantic nets (Reimer, 1997), semantic networks (Monge & Contractor, 2001, 2003; Popping, 2003; Ryan & Bernard, 2000), networks of concepts (Popping, 2000), or networks of words (Danowski, 1993). Herein, we refer to such techniques using the general term — network text analysis (NTA) (Carley, 1997b; Popping, 2000). NTA approaches vary on a number of dimensions such as the level of automation, a focus on verbs or nouns, the level of concept generalization, and so on. Nevertheless, in all cases, networks of relations among concepts are used to reveal the structure of the text, meaning, and the views of the authors. Further, these networks are windows into the structure of the groups, organizations and societies discussed in these texts. This structure is implicit in the connections among people, groups, organizations, resources, knowledge tasks, events, and places.

NTA is a specific text analysis method that encodes the links between words in a text and constructs a network of the linked words (Popping, 2000). The method is based on the assumption that language and knowledge can be modeled as networks of words and the relations between them (Sowa, 1984). NTA methodologically originates from traditional techniques for indexing the relations between words, syntactic grouping of words, and the hierarchical and non-hierarchical linking of words (Kelle, 1997). The method of NTA enables the extraction, analysis, and concise representation of the complex network structure that can be represented in texts. Furthermore, NTA covers the analytic spectrum of classical content analysis by supporting the analysis of the existence, frequencies, and covariance of words and themes (Alexa, 1997; Popping, 2000). Given these functionalities, computer-supported NTA is a suitable method for analyzing large collections of texts effectively and efficiently. Several NTA methods exist (see bullet items listed below; for more details on methods, see Popping, 2000; Popping & Roberts, 1997). Many have been applied in empirical settings (see discussion by Monge & Contractor, 2003) such as:

- Centering Resonance Analysis (Corman et al., 2002)
- Functional Depiction (Popping & Roberts, 1997)
- Knowledge Graphing (Bakker, 1987; James, 1992; Popping, 2003)
- Map Analysis (Carley, 1988, 1997b; Carley & Palmquist, 1992)
- Network Evaluation (Kleinnijenhuis, Ridder & Rietberg, 1996)
- Word Network Analysis (Danowksi, 1982).

Copyright © 2005, Idea Group Inc. Copying or distributing in print or electronic forms without written permission of Idea Group Inc. is prohibited.

Besides the analysis of textual data, current work also focuses on the visualization of networks extracted from texts (Batagelj, Mrvar & Zaveršnik, 2002).

In this research we concentrate on map analysis. Map analysis systematically extracts and analyzes the links between words in texts in order to model the authors "mental maps" as networks of linked words. Coding texts as maps focuses analysts on investigating the meaning of texts by detecting the relationships between and among words and themes (Alexa, 1997; Carley, 1997a). Maps are a cognitively motivated representation of knowledge (Carley, 1988). In map analysis, a concept is a single idea represented by a single word or a phrase. A statement is two concepts and the relation between them. A map is the network of the statements (Carley, 1997b).

Before continuing, it is worth noting that the terminology in this area is very diverse, having come from a variety of disciplines. Thus to orient the reader and help avoid confusion, we provide some basic terminology as we will use it herein in Table 1. This will foreshadow the discussion of the procedure we are proposing in this chapter.

Table 1. Terminology and associated symbols

Term	Definition	Alternative Terms	Examples
Text	A written work.	Sample	Newspaper article, abstract, Web site, interview
Text-level concept	Words that appear in text	Word, concept, phrase, named-entity	Rantissi, Palestine, Hamas, terrorism, captured
Higher-level concept	A word or phrase chosen by the analyst into which other words or phrases are generalized	Concept, node	Terrorist, Osama bin Laden
Concept	Single ideational kernel	Node	Terrorism, terrorist, Friday, 9-11
Entity class	Objective category that can be used for classifying concepts; Top level in the ontology	Meta-node, entity, category, concept type, node type	People, Organizations
Relation	Connection between concepts	Link, tie, edge, connection	Rantissi is in the Hamas
Relation class	Objective category that can be used for classifying relations connecting concepts in entity class "a" to concepts in entity class "b," such that "a" and "b" may or may not be distinct.	Relation type, Edge type, Tie type, sub-network	Social network, is a member of
Map	The network formed by the set of statements (two concepts and the relation between them) in a text.	Network, concept network, semantic network, network of concepts	See Figures 3 and 4
Meta-matrix	Conceptual organization of concept networks into a set of networks defined by entity classes and relation classes	Ontology, classification scheme, meta-network	See Tables 2 and 3

Using the Meta-Matrix as an Ontology

Since NTA can be used to extract networks of concepts, we can leverage the methods of social network analysis (SNA) to analyze, compare and combine the network of concepts extracted from the texts (see e.g., Scott, 2000; Wasserman & Faust, 1994 for SNA techniques). This provides the analyst with tremendous analytical power (see Hill & Carley, 1999 for illustrative study). If in addition, we cross classify the extracted concepts into an ontology, particularly one designed to capture the core elements of social and organizational structure, we gain the added theoretical power of extracting in a systematic fashion an empirical description of the social and organizational structure. The key would be to design a useful ontology.

Such an ontology is implicit in the meta-matrix approach (Carley 2003, 2002; Krackhardt & Carley 1998) to organizational design. Krackhardt and Carley defined an approach to represent the state of an organizational structure at a particular point in time as the set of entities (people, resources, and tasks) and the relations among them. The meta-matrix approach is a representational framework and a set of derived methods for the computational analysis of multi-dimensional data that represents social and organizational systems. The concept of the meta-matrix originates from the combination of:

1. Information processing and knowledge management (Carley & Hill, 2001; Galbraight, 1977; March & Simon, 1973).
2. The PCANS approach (Krackhardt & Carley, 1998), which was later generalized by Carley and Hill to include knowledge, events, and organizations (Carley, 2002; Carley & Hill, 2001).
3. Operations research (Carley & Krackhardt, 1999; Carley, Ren & Krackhardt, 2000).
4. Social network analytic techniques and measures (see e.g., Scott, 2000; Wasserman & Faust, 1994).

The meta-matrix enables the representation of team or organizational structure in terms of entity classes and relations. In principle, this is an extensible ontology such that new entity classes and new classes of relations can be added as needed. Each entity class represents an ontologically distinct category of concepts (or in the social network language, nodes). Each relation class is a type of link between concepts within entity class 1 and 2. For the sake of illustration, we use a simple form of the ontology in which we identify four entity classes — People, Resources (or Knowledge/Skills), Tasks or Events, and Groups or Organizations (see Table 2 headers). We choose these entity classes as they are sufficient for illustration and they are critical for understanding the structure of teams, groups and organizations. The reader should keep in mind that it is possible to use different entity classes and still think in terms of the meta-matrix conceptualization (as we do in this chapter). The key aspect for our purposes is that the meta-matrix defines a set of entity classes and a set of relation classes. This facilitates thinking systematically about organizational structure and provides a limited hierarchy for structuring the network of concepts.

Table 2: Original meta-matrix conceptualization

Meta-Matrix entities	People	Knowledge/ Resources	Events/ Tasks	Groups/ Organizations
People	Social network	Knowledge Network/ Resource Network	Attendance Network/ Assignment Network	Membership network
Knowledge/Resources		Information Network/ Substitution Network	Needs network	Organizational capability
Events/Tasks			Temporal Ordering/ Task Flow/ Precedence	Institutional support or attack
Organizations				Interorganizational network

Based on Carley (2002, 2003)

Between any two entity classes there can be one or more classes of relations. For example, between people and people we can think of a number of relations including, but not limited to, communication relations, friendship relations, or money/exchange relations. To orient the reader, in Table 2, common labels for the network formed by linking the row and column entity classes are identified. The data in a meta-matrix represents the structure of the group or organization at a particular time. It can be analyzed to locate vulnerabilities, strengths, features of the group, to identify key actors, and to assess potential performance. In summary, the meta-matrix approach allows analysts to model and analyze social systems according to a theoretically and empirically founded schema (Carley, 2003). By employing this approach as an ontology, we enable the analyst to extract and analyze social systems as described in texts.

Combining NTA and Meta-Matrix Approaches

In texts, the links between words (concepts) are implicit. Hence, extracting a network of concepts from a text, and classifying this network via the meta-matrix ontology, requires an inference process. The links, or relations, between concepts must be extracted based on the semantic, syntactic, and contextual information given in a text (Carley, 1986; Carley, 1988; Popping, 2003). Making the meta-matrix approach available for NTA can provide analysts with a novel technique for extracting textual networks that reveal the relationships within and between the elements that compose a network and that were classified *a priori* according to the meta-matrix model. The features of the textual data that are relevant to the analyst can then be represented as a network structure of the meta-matrix entity classes and the connections between these classes. Such a network makes the structure of social systems, which is implicitly contained in texts visible and analyzable.

How did we combine and formalize the meta-matrix approach and map analysis technique, which is a specific type of NTA? We utilized the meta-matrix model as an extension of NTA in general and map analysis in specific by instantiating the following five step procedure:

1. **Concept Identification:** identify the concepts in texts that are relevant to the analyst's research question. As part of this process, the analyst may first want to generalize many text-level concepts into higher-level concepts.

2. **Entity Identification:** define an ontology for capturing the overall structure described in the text. We use the basic meta-matrix. Other analysts may wish to adapt this to their research question. Note, step 1 and 2 can also be done in reverse order.

3. **Concept Classification:** classify the identified concepts into the relevant entity classes in the meta-matrix. Given the vagaries of the language it may be that some concepts need to be cross-classified in two or more entity classes.

4. **Perform Map Analysis:** automatically extracting the identified concepts and the relations among them from the specified texts. This results in a map or conceptual network. Since the concepts are classified by entity classes, the resulting concept network is hierarchically embedded in the ontology provided by the meta-matrix. In essence then, there are three networks. First, there is the concept network where the nodes are concepts (many of which are higher-level concepts). Second, there is the entity network where the nodes are the entity classes and the links are the connections among and between the entity classes. Third, there is the network embodied in the meta-matrix thesaurus, connecting concepts in entity classes to concepts in the same or other entity classes.

5. **Graph and Analyze Data:** the final step is to take the extracted data for each text, the network, and graph and analyze it in general and by cells in the meta-matrix. As part of this analysis, the resultant networks from different texts can be combined and compared. Note the analysis can occur at the concept network level (map analysis), the entire meta-matrix level (meta-matrix text analysis), and the sub-cell level (sub-matrix text analysis).

We refer to these five steps as the method of meta-matrix text analysis. With this novel technique we hope to contribute towards the analysis of complex, large-scale data and social systems and providing profound multi-level access to the meaning of textual data. We note that these steps begin to bridge the gap between NTA and a more interpretive analysis of texts. The meaning of concepts is revealed by virtue of other concepts they are connected to. In the meta-matrix approach, the meaning of concepts is revealed both by what other concepts they are connected to and by what type of entity classes into which they fall.

Implementation of Meta-Matrix Text Analysis

We have implemented our formalization of the technique of meta-matrix text analysis in a network text analysis tool called AutoMap (Diesner & Carley, 2004). AutoMap is a software application that helps analysts to extract, analyze, represent, and compare mental models from texts. The tool performs computer-supported content analysis, map analysis, meta-matrix text analysis, and sub-matrix text analysis. The latter two types of analysis we discuss in this section. The more classic content analysis and map analysis were previously described in Carley and Palmquist (1992) and Carley (1997a).

Steps 1 to 3 in meta-matrix text analysis may involve a thesaurus. A thesaurus in general is a two-columned collection that associates text-level concepts with higher-level concepts (Burkart, 1997; Klein 1997). The text-level concepts represent the content of a data set, and the higher-level concepts represent the text-level concepts in a generalized way. Thesauri are created by reading a set of texts, using pre-defined material, and/or deriving pairs of concepts and higher-level concepts from theory (Burkart 1997; Kelle 1997; Klein, 1997; Zuell & Alexa 2001). The terminology of a thesaurus depends on the content and the subject of the data set.

Thesauri play a key role in any AutoMap coding. AutoMap in performing content analysis or map analysis can utilize a generalization thesaurus. In this thesaurus, the analyst can reclassify words in relation to other words on the basis of shared meaning, spelling errors, aliases, etc. Further, phrases that refer to a single ideational kernel — such as "Weapons of Mass Destruction" — can be reclassified as a single concept — WMD. When texts are pre-processed by AutoMap, using a generalization thesaurus, idiosyncratic differences in writing style, multi-word-concepts and wording errors can be eliminated. This generalization process facilitates identifying true conceptual similarities and differences across texts. The creation of the generalization thesauri is step 1, concept identification, in the coding procedure.

When AutoMap is used to perform a meta-matrix text analysis, a second type of thesaurus can also be employed. This second thesaurus, the meta-matrix thesaurus, contains the translation of concepts into the entity classes in the meta-matrix. When texts are processed with a meta-matrix thesaurus, the organizational structures described in the text can be extracted. Since one concept might be indicative of several meta-matrix entity classes, a meta-matrix thesaurus can consist of more than two columns. For example, the concept military falls into two entity classes — Organization and Resource. The specific entity and relation classes used for the meta-matrix approach in this chapter are presented in Table 3.

Note that in applying the meta-matrix conceptualization to terrorist groups, we have extended the original conceptualization (see Table 2) by treating Knowledge and Resource as separate entities (Carley & Reminga, 2004) and by adding Location as a primary entity. Further, we generalized people into Agent to reflect the fact that often names are not known and people are identified by actions such as "victim killed." Since this is an extensible ontology, these changes pose no harm to the underlying theory. We did this extension as knowledge, resources, and location are meaningfully unique entities

Table 3. Meta-matrix model formalization used in AutoMap — entity classes and relation classes

Meta-Matrix Entities	Agent	Knowledge	Resources	Tasks/ Event	Organizations	Location
Agent	Social network	Knowledge network	Capabilities network	Assignment network	Membership network	Agent location network
Knowledge		Information network	Training network	Knowledge requirement network	Organizational knowledge network	Knowledge location network
Resources			Resource network	Resource requirement Network	Organizational Capability network	Resource location network
Tasks/ Events				Precedence network	Organizational assignment network	Task/Event location network
Organizations					Inter-organizational network	Organizational location network
Location						Proximity network

for research in the area of covert networks. By extending the meta-matrix as shown in Table 3, we have done step 2, entity identification, of the coding procedure.

The analyst can use none, one or both types of thesauri, generalization and meta-matrix, to analyze texts with AutoMap. In general, the analyst may find it useful to first create a word list, then a generalization thesaurus, then a meta-matrix thesaurus. Building these thesauri can be done iteratively as new texts are added to the available set, as AutoMap minimizes the cost of coding and recoding texts. The larger the corpus of texts being analyzed, the more time is saved.

When using the meta-matrix thesaurus, AutoMap allows the analyst to associate a text-level concepts or higher-order concepts from the generalization thesauri with one, multiple or no entity classes, and to add user-defined entity classes. This process of associating concepts with entity classes is step 3, concept classification, in the coding procedure.

When AutoMap applies the meta-matrix thesaurus, it searches the text set for the concepts denoted in the meta-matrix thesaurus and translates matches into the corresponding meta-matrix entity classes as specified by the analyst. When performing meta-matrix text analysis, AutoMap links the meta-matrix entity classes in the texts that were pre-processed with a meta-matrix thesaurus into statements, and builds one concept network per text that is cross-coded in terms of the meta-matrix, thus resulting also in a meta-matrix. This automated network creation is step 4, perform map analysis, in the coding procedure.

The resulting networks can be analyzed at varying levels during step 5, graph and analyze data. For example, the analyst might be interested in seeing and analyzing the networks of the text-level concepts that represent all or only some of the meta-matrix categories. We implemented this functionality as sub-matrix text analysis. Each cell in Table 3 denotes a sub-matrix. Sub-matrix analysis distills one or several sub-networks from the meta-matrix and presents text-level concepts in the chosen entity classes. This routine enables a more thorough analysis of particular sections of the meta-matrix, such as Agent-by-Agent networks (social networks), or Organization-by-Resource networks (organizational capability networks). When performing sub-matrix text analysis, AutoMap links the concepts representing the meta-matrix entity classes selected by the analyst into networks.

With the implementation of meta-matrix text analysis and sub-matrix text analysis in AutoMap, we hope to contribute to the investigation of the network structure of social and organizational systems that are represented in texts. With these techniques we aim to provide a reasonable extension of the base technology of computer-supported network text analysis and a practical implementation of the meta-matrix model. In the next section we demonstrate how these novel techniques can help analysts to detect the meaning and underlying social structure inherent in textual data in order to answer related research questions.

Illustrative Example of the Application of Network Text Analysis

To demonstrate the meta-matrix approach to NTA we use a small sample data set of 18 texts. Each text will be coded using the proposed approach and the AutoMap software.

Data

This text sample is a sub-sample drawn from a larger text collection that consists of 191 texts collected at CASOS about six major terrorist groups that operate in the West Bank. These groups are the Al Aksa Martyrs Brigades, Al Fatah, Al Qaeda, Hamas, Hezbollah, and the Islamic Jihad. We gathered the texts from LexisNexis Academia via exact matching Boolean keyword search for each of the groups. The media that we searched with LexisNexis were *The Economist, The Washington Post*, and *The New York Times*. The time frame of our data set ranges from articles published in 2000 to 2003. We sorted the retrieved texts by relevance, screened the top most texts, and selected up to three texts per organization and year for our dataset. The sub-sample from this corpus that we work with in this chapter consists of one text per terror group from each medium from 2003 (Table 4). This sub sample of 18 texts contains 3,035 unique concepts and 13,141 total concepts. The number of unique concepts considers each concept only once, whereas the number of total concepts also counts repetitions of concepts. The reader should keep in mind that the small size of this data set and the fact that the texts were chosen across groups rather than within groups is likely to lead to more overall concepts and fewer relations among them. A discussion of Hamas and Yassin may be unlikely to refer to a discussion about al Qaeda and bin Laden; whereas, it is more likely to refer to Rantissi.

This text set is a suitable illustrative example because the detection of covert networks such as terrorist groups is one application domain for meta-matrix analysis (Carley, Dombrowski, Tsvetovat, Reminga & Kamneva, 2003). Since texts are a widely used source of information about terrorist groups, a technique for pulling networks classified according to the meta-matrix scheme from this type of data is needed. The results of this sample study are neither a valid indication of these terrorist groups nor a formal validation of the method of meta-matrix text analysis, but show what information the analyst can gain from this novel technique.

Data Pre-Processing (Concept Identification)

The quality of the map (or network) extracted from the text can be enhanced by pre-processing the data prior to running the analysis: Text pre-processing condenses the data to the concepts that capture the features of the texts that are relevant to the analyst. This technique is also the first step in the procedure of performing meta-matrix text analysis (see section 4). In a previous publication we have described text pre-processing strategies and results with AutoMap in detail (Diesner & Carley, 2004). As a first pre-processing technique we applied a delete list customized for this dataset[1]. Deletion removes non-content bearing concepts such as conjunctions and articles from texts (Carley, 1993). This reduces the number of concepts the analyst needs to consider when forming thesauri. Then we stemmed the texts with the AutoMap stemmer, which is based on the Porter Stemmer (Porter, 1980). Stemming detects inflections and derivations of concepts in order to convert each concept into the related morpheme (Jurafsky & Martin, 2000). Stemming simplifies the process of constructing a generalization thesaurus and can often eliminate spelling errors and typos. Then we used AutoMap's Named-Entity Recognition functionality. Named-Entity Recognition retrieves concepts such as proper names, numerals, and abbreviations contained in a text set (Magnini, Negri, Prevete & Tanev, 2002). This technique helps to index agents, organizations, places, and events and facilitates building the meta-matrix thesaurus. There were 591 named entities in our dataset. This list of named entities was used to:

1. Translate relevant phrases into a unit that will be recognized as a single concept. This can be realized in the generalization thesaurus in AutoMap by, e.g., replacing the spaces by words that are separated with underscores.

Table 4. Dataset — number of texts that terror group appears in

Source	Aksa	Fatah	Hamas	Hezbollah	Islamic Jihad	al Qaeda
The Washington Post	2	1	2	1	1	2
The New York Times	1	2	3	2	2	1
The Economist	1	2	4	1	2	1
Total	4	5	9	4	5	4

Copyright © 2005, Idea Group Inc. Copying or distributing in print or electronic forms without written permission of Idea Group Inc. is prohibited.

Examples:

> Holi War into Holy_War. The apparent misspelling of Holi results from stemming.
>
> Golan Height into Golan_Heights.

2. Translate people's names, various versions of their names as they appear in the data set, aliases and synonyms that these people use into the organization that this person is associated with.

Examples:

> Dr. Abdel Aziz Rantisi and Dr. Rantisi into Aziz_Al-Rantisi, who is a member of Hamas.
>
> Mahmoud Abba and Abu Mazen into Mahmoud_Abbas, who is a member of the Palestinian Authority.

3. Translate various spellings of a group and synonyms for groups into one unique name of the related group or organization.

Examples:

> Hizbullah into Hezbollah.
>
> Islamic Resistance Movement into Hamas.

Thesaurus Creation

The resulting 170 pairs of associations of text-level concepts with higher-level concepts formed a generalization thesaurus. As noted, a generalization thesaurus translates text-level concepts into higher-level concepts. A single higher-level concept typically has multiple text-level entries associated with it in a thesaurus. For example, Imad Falouji (the higher-level concept), a Hamas member, appeared in the text set as Imad Falouji and Mr. Falouji (two related text-level concepts). The more text-level entries are associated with a higher-level concept, the greater the level of generalization being employed by the analyst.

Since no pre-defined thesaurus was available to us that would have matched terrorism-related concepts to meta-matrix entity classes, we built a second generalization thesaurus. After applying the generalization thesaurus, we built and applied a second generalization thesaurus with 50 entries that translates people's names into organizations or more abstract groups with which these people are associated. We used four basic guidelines:

1. Members of the six terrorist groups that the data set focuses on into the related terrorist organization.

Examples:

> Aziz Al-Rantisi into Hamas.

2. Representatives of the governments of various countries into the country's government.

Examples:

> Omar Sulieman into Egypt_Government.
> Mahmoud Abbas into Palestinian_Authority.

3. People's names into organizations or abstract groups that they belong to.

Examples:

> Hans_Blix, Kofi_Annan, and Michael_Chandler into UN.
> Hanadi Jaradat and Saed Hanani into Suicide_Bomber.
> Haviv_Dodon, Muhammad_Faraj
> Samer_Ufi into Victim_Killed.

In doing this, the basic principle we were applying was to retain specific actors — those who appeared to play primary roles, whereas secondary actors were reclassified by their role, such as victim. Not all names of people that can be associated with a group were translated into the related group. We applied this strategy in order to enable us to retranslate the entity class Agent, to which we assigned these names in the meta-matrix thesaurus that we applied after the second generalization thesaurus, into the names of key players relevant to us in a sub-matrix text analysis that can be run after the meta-matrix text analysis. Names that we decided not to match with an organization are for example Osama bin Laden, Yasser Arafat and Ariel Sharon. This level of maintenance of detail of information always depends on the research question or goal. Our goal was to detect the network structure of terrorist groups.

After finishing the generalization process[2] we built and employed a meta-matrix thesaurus. In order to support the analyst in matching text-level concepts against meta-matrix categories, AutoMap offers the options to: a) load a list of all unique concepts appearing in the text set into the left most column of the meta-matrix thesaurus or b) save a list of a union of all unique concepts on a directory of the analyst's choice. In the next step the analyst has to manually go through this list and to decide whether or not to associate each single concept with meta-matrix categories. Our dataset contained 2,083 unique concepts after applying the generalization thesauri. Of these unique concepts, 303 were assigned to a single entity class in the meta-matrix, and 23 of them to two entity classes (Table 5, sum of column one). A total of 1780 of the 2083 unique concepts we did not assigned to any meta-matrix entity class, but they were kept as non-categorized concepts. The creation of a meta-matrix thesaurus is step 3, concept classification, in the procedure of performing meta-matrix text analysis (see section 4).

Table 5. Creation and application of meta-matrix thesaurus (sorted by frequency)

Category	Cumulated sum of assignment of concepts to entity classes in the meta-matrix thesaurus	Cumulated sum of appearance of entity classes in texts after application of meta-matrix thesaurus	Cumulated sum of linkage of concepts associated with meta-matrix entity classes into statements
Organization	48	569	434
Location	81	404	404
Agent	54	250	217
Resource	75	261	188
Task-Event	27	168	146
Knowledge	41	134	128

In the next step we applied the meta-matrix thesaurus to the data set[3] and ran a meta-matrix text analysis on the pre-processed text set[4]. This technique forms step 4, perform map analysis, in the procedure of performing meta-matrix text analysis (see section 4).

Characteristics of the Textual Networks as Meta-Matrices (Graph and Analyze Results)

In this section, we report the results of the meta-matrix text analysis and sub-matrix text analysis we ran on our data set. This task is step 5 in the procedure of performing meta-matrix text analysis. The intent in this section is to illustrate the type of results and graphs possible using the proposed meta-matrix approach to NTA, not to present a comprehensive analysis of terrorist networks. In doing this example, we will analyze: 1) unique and total frequencies of the concepts and statements, 2) unique and total frequencies of the statements that were formed from concepts associated with meta-matrix entity classes, and 3) the distribution of statements formed from meta-matrix entity classes across the data set.

For our analysis we considered the six meta-matrix entity classes in Table 3. Therefore, we have six unique entity level concepts. Considering only concepts that fall into one or more of these categories, we found an average of 99.2 total concepts per text, ranging from 37 to 163. Based on these concepts, on average of 18.9 unique statements (ranging from 8 to 29) and 45.7 total statements (ranging from 12 to 84) were formed per text. Thus, on average, each unique statement appeared 2.4 times per text. Theoretically, each text could contain up to 36 unique statements. The theoretic maximum would be achieved if there existed at least one concept associated with each entity, and at least one concept of each entity formed a statement with at least one concept in each other entity class. The multiple occurrences of unique statements are expressed in the number of total statements.

Across the 18 meta-matrices extracted from our sample texts, 822 total statements were formed within and between the cells of the meta-matrix (see Table 6 for distribution of total statements across meta-matrix). Notice that the upper and lower triangle of the meta-matrix in Table 6 are not symmetric. For example, in Table 6 from Resource (row) to Organization (column) there are a total of 23 statements, but from Organization (row) to Resource (column) there are a total of 35 statements. Indeed, there is no need for symmetry as the relations between concepts (edges between nodes) found with AutoMap are directed, which is inherently pre-defined by the directed structure of language. The results in Table 6 show that concepts associated with each meta-matrix entity class appears approximately as often in posterior positions of statements (last row in Table 6) as in anterior positions (last column in Table 6). Thus, the in-degree or receptivity of a meta-matrix entity class approximately equals the out-degree or expansiveness of the class. This is due, in part, to the use of proximity in the text to place links among concepts and reflects, if anything, the lack of overly stylized sentential form.

Within the meta-matrix, the entity class that linked most frequently to other entity classes was Organization (179 links), followed by Location (108), Agent (95), Resource (71), Task-Event (66), and Knowledge (53). If we do not look at these absolute values, but at percentages of the linkage of meta-matrix entity classes to the same or other entity classes, our results reveal that concepts in the entity class Task-Event are more likely to be connected to concepts in classes other than Task-Event. In contrast to Task-Event, concepts in the entity class Location are most likely to link to other Location concepts (Table 7).

Furthermore, the results indicate that within the networks that we extracted from the texts, most information refers to membership networks (13.8% of all statements, Figure 1).

Table 6. Number of links (total number of statements) between meta-matrix categories

Meta-Matrix	Agent	Knowledge	Resource	Task-Event	Organization	Location	Sum
Agent	24	8	8	12	55	12	**119**
Knowledge	10	18	9	3	20	11	**71**
Resource	8	9	39	11	23	20	**110**
Task-Event	13	7	9	10	20	17	**76**
Organization	58	23	35	19	90	44	**269**
Location	9	10	17	25	47	69	**177**
Sum	**122**	**75**	**117**	**80**	**255**	**173**	**822**

Table 7. Linkage of meta-matrix entity classes

Meta-Matrix entity class	With same entity class (%)	With other entity classes (%)
Task-Event	13	87
Agent	20	80
Knowledge	25	75
Organization	33	67
Resource	35	65
Location	39	61

Figure 1: Total number of links between meta-matrix categories

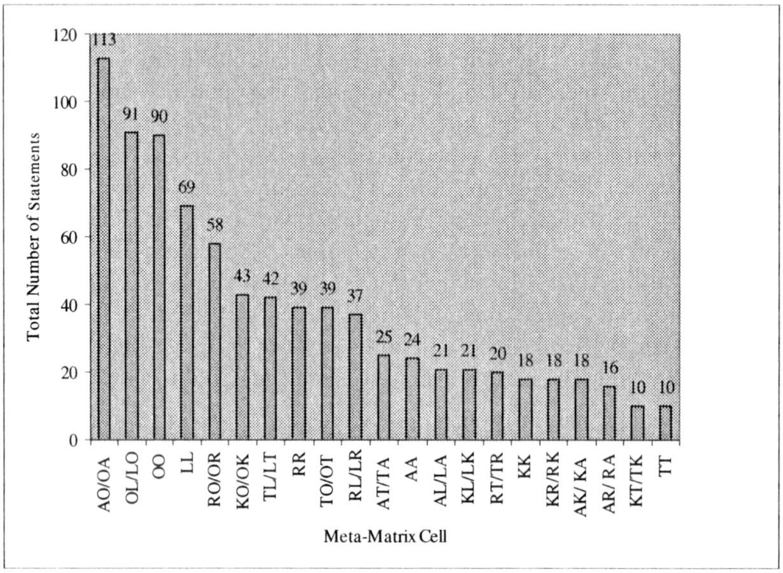

Although there is also substantial information on inter-organizational networks (11.1%) and organizational location networks (10.4%). The least information is provided on precedence networks (1.2%) and knowledge requirement networks (1.2%). This suggests that more is known, or at least presented in the news, about who the terrorists are and where they are than about what they do when and what they need to know in order to engage in such actions or why.

The analysis of the distribution of statements formed from meta-matrix entity classes across the text set reveals that all entities are covered in at least one third of the texts. In addition, Organization, Location, and Agent classes appear in more than half of the texts (Table 8). Again, this suggests that more is reported about who and where than about what, how and why. We note that a human reading of these texts may pick up a little more about what and how, although such information does appear to be less common in general in the texts used for this purely illustrative analysis.

Table 8: Number of texts in that links appears

Meta-Matrix	Agent	Knowledge	Resource	Task-Event	Organization	Location	Sum
Agent	13	5	6	10	17	9	**10.0**
Knowledge	7	9	5	3	9	5	**6.3**
Resource	4	4	9	7	12	11	**7.8**
Task-Event	9	3	7	4	11	10	**7.3**
Organization	17	11	13	11	18	16	**14.3**
Location	7	7	10	11	17	14	**11.0**
Sum	9.5	6.5	8.3	7.7	14.0	10.8	**9.5**

Copyright © 2005, Idea Group Inc. Copying or distributing in print or electronic forms without written permission of Idea Group Inc. is prohibited.

In Figure 1 and Tables 6 and 8, we have been discussing the total links or statements. Looking at the total links provides information about the overall structure of the discussion and the elements of the structure (agents, knowledge, etc.) that are considered critical by the authors or for which they have a wealth of information. It is often useful to ask about unique links, however, if we want to understand the structure itself. In Figure 2, we display the number of links per sub-matrix that are unique. That is, a link or statement is only counted once regardless of how many texts it appears in.

Comparison of Figures 1 and 2 shows that a great deal of information — particularly in the Agent-to-Agent sub-matrix is repeated across texts. This suggests that either many of the texts were discussing the same information (repetition), or they got their information from the same source. Note that if we knew that each source was unique, then the difference between the total (Figure 1) and the unique (Figure 2) would be an indicator of the reliability of the information.

The overall structure for this covert network is very sparse. In some sense, based on these texts, more is known about the affiliations, locations, resources, and knowledge of agents and organizations than is known about the interrelations of knowledge, resources and tasks (Table 9). Further, if we compare the number of unique links (Table 9) to the number

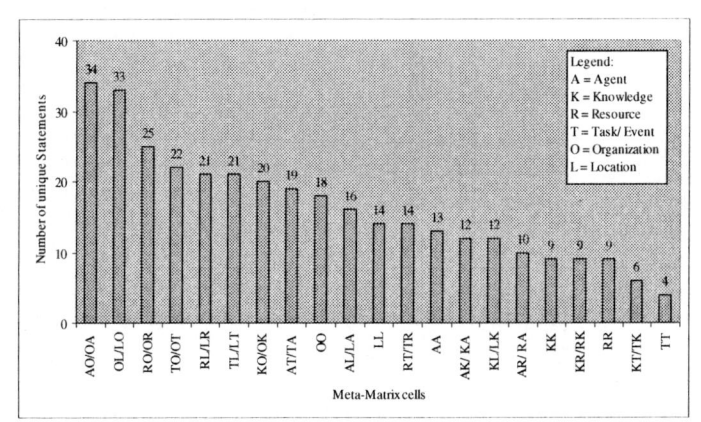

Figure 2. Number of unique links between meta-matrix categories

Table 9. Number of links (unique number) between meta-matrix categories

Meta-Matrix	Agent	Knowledge	Resource	Task-Event	Organization	Location
Agent	13	12	10	19	34	16
Knowledge		9	9	6	20	12
Resource			9	14	25	21
Task-Event				4	22	21
Organization					18	33
Location						14

of texts that contain links (for each sub-matrix) (Table 8) we see that the two tables are similar. In other words, many links appear in only one text. It is interesting to note which sub-matrices have more unique links than texts – e.g., the Agent-by-Knowledge and the Organization-by-Knowledge sub-matrices. This indicates that the texts that discuss the knowledge network tend to do so by discussing multiple linkages (e.g., all of these people know item z). Whereas texts that discuss, e.g., the social network (Agent-by-Agent) are more likely to simply talk about a single pair of actors and the nature of their relationship. Whether this pattern of reporting would hold in other cultures is debatable.

Beyond learning about the network structure of the meta-matrices and the distribution of concepts and connections between them across the sample data, analysts might be interested in investigating in more detail the concepts and links contained in the meta-matrix. In order to gain this knowledge, sub-matrix text analysis[5] can be run. For

Table 10: Who has what means? Organizational capability network (organization by resource)

Statements formed from Higher-Level Concepts (Sub-Matrix Analysis)	
Sample text 1:	Sample text 2:
1 Al-Qaeda – training camp	1 Al-Aksa - assets
1 network- Hawala	1 Al-Aksa - money
1 Hawala – money	1 Hamas - sponsoring
1 finance – network	1 aid - Hamas
1 camp - US-Government	1 aid - Treasury Department
	1 money - Hamas
	1 support - Hamas
	1 Treasury - assistance
	1 US-Government - assistance
	1 assets - Treasury Department

Table 11: Who knows what? Knowledge network (agent by knowledge)

Statements formed from Higher-Level Concepts (Sub-Matrix Analysis)	
Sample text 1:	Sample text 2:
1 chairman – monitoring	1 FBI - Analyst
1 evidence – Saddam Hussein	

Table 12: Who is located where and does what? (Localized assignment network: agent by task-event by location)

Statements formed from Higher-Level Concepts (Sub-Matrix Analysis)	
Sample text 1:	Sample text 2:
1 Saddam Hussein - Iraq	1 arrest - Leader
	1 Leader - Germany

illustrating the results of this procedure, we show a map from the same text in Tables 10 to 12. A map contains one coded statement per line and its frequency.

These various sub-matrix networks enable a better understanding of what attributes of the meta-matrix link to other attributes, and with what strength. All three sub-matrices together enable a broader view of the situation. Figures 3 and 4 illustrate this broader picture. The comparison of figures 3 and 4 illustrates that text 1 presents a more disconnected story than does text 2. Further, even if the two stories were combined, the

Figure 3: Visualization of sub-matrices from sample text 1

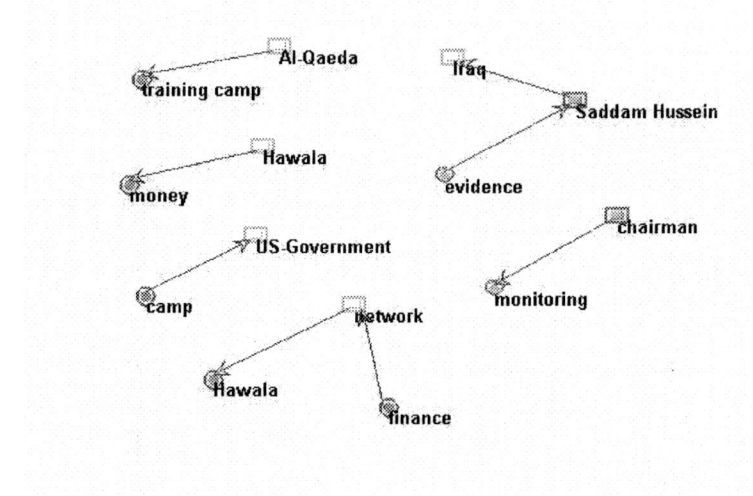

Figure 4: Visualization of sub-matrices from sample text 2

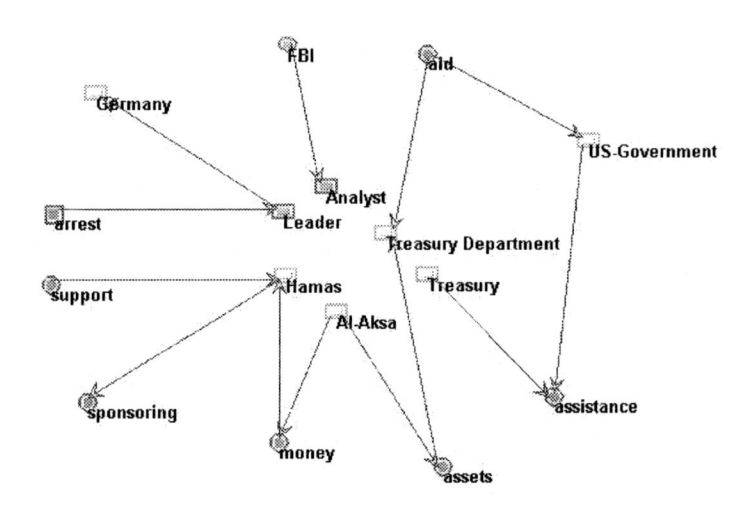

overall map would tell us little about the structure of the two terrorist groups — al-Qaeda and Hamas.

Meta-matrix data and sub-matrix data generated with AutoMap can be saved and then re-analyzed outside of AutoMap using standard social network analysis tools. AutoMap can both code these networks and then output them in two useful exchange formats for use with other network analysis tools — DL for UCINET and DyNetML for ORA (www.casos.cs.cmu.edu/projects/ORA, Carley and Reminga, 2004). For this chapter, we use ORA as it enables the analysis of all the cells in the meta-matrix at once. In either case, the combination of text and network analysis enables the analyst to readily combine rich textual data with organizational data connected through other methods, thus enhancing the analysis process.

Discussion-Features and Limitations

The techniques of meta-matrix text analysis and sub-matrix text analysis described herein can support analysts in investigating the network structure of social and organizational systems that are represented in textual data. Furthermore, these novel and integrative methods enable analysts to classify words in texts into entity classes (node types) associated with networks common to organizational structures according to a theoretically and empirically validated ontology — the meta-matrix.

The validity of the method and the results presented in this chapter are constrained by the little experience we gained so far with these novel techniques, the small number of texts analyzed, and the implementation of the techniques into one software. The tool should also be applied to multiple larger data sets.

Lessons Learned

In general, we find that the entity-name recognizer greatly enhances the ability to locate concepts associated with the meta-matrix ontology. In particular, it facilitates locating Agents, Organizations, and Locations. For entity classes that are less associated with proper nouns, the name recognizer is of less value.

Coding texts using AutoMap is not a completely automated process. However, AutoMap does provide a high degree of automation that assists the user and increases the efficiency and effectiveness of meta-matrix text analysis in comparison to manual coding. As with most text analysis techniques that seek to extract meaning, significant manual effort needs to be expended on constructing the delete list and thesauri, even though the method is computer-supported. For example, the delete list used in this study took 30 minutes to construct. However, the thesauri (and there are three) took four days to construct. Thesauri enable the minimization of miscoding, as in missed relations, due to aliases and misspellings, and differences due to the underlying languages. Analysts have to decide on an optimal trade-off between speed of the computer-supported research process and enhancement of the quality of automated coding caused by the manual creation and refinement of pre-processing tools according to their goals and resources.

It is worth noting that significant improvement over straight manual coding can be achieved by building thesauri and delete lists based on only a fraction of texts. As more texts in this domain are coded, we will have to expend relatively little additional effort to expand the delete and thesauri list. For example, we suspect that hundreds of additional texts will be codable with maybe only a day more attention to the thesauri. The reason is that, when in the same domain, construction of thesauri is like building a sample via the snowball method (i.e., with each iteration fewer and fewer novel concepts are found). How large that fraction should be is a point for future work. However, preliminary studies suggest 10% is probably sufficient. Future work should explore whether intelligent data mining and machine learning techniques can be combined with social network analysis and text analysis to provide a more automated approach to constructing thesauri on the fly.

We also find that the higher the level of generalization used in the generalization thesaurus, the greater the ability to compare two diverse texts. Not counting typographical errors, often the translation of two to ten text-level concepts per high-level concept seems sufficient to generate a "language" for the domain being studied.

We note that when forming thesauri, it is often critical to keep track of why certain types of concepts are generalized into others. At the moment there is no way to keep that rationalization within AutoMap. In general, the user should keep a lab notebook or read-me file for keeping such rationalizations.

Finally, we note that for extracting social or organizational structure from texts a large corpus is needed. The point here is comprehensiveness, not necessarily a specific number of texts. Thus, one might use the entire content of a book that describes and discusses an organization or a large set of newspaper articles. In building this corpus, not all texts have to be of the same type. Thus, the analyst can combine newspaper reports, books, board-of-directors reports, Web pages, etc. Once the networks are extracted via AutoMap they can be combined into a comprehensive description of the organization being examined. Further, the analyst needs to pre-define what the basic criteria are for including a text in the corpus — e.g., it might be publication venue, time frame, geographic area, specific people, organizations, or locations mentioned.

Considerations for Future Work

We also note that the higher the level of generalization, the more ideas are being inferred from, rather than extracted from, the texts. Research needs to be done on the appropriate levels of generalization. Note that the level of generalization can be measured as the average number of text-level concepts associated with each higher level concept.

One of the strengths of NTA is that the networks extracted from the texts can be combined in a set theoretic fashion. So we can talk about the network formed by the union or intersection of the set of networks drawn from the set of texts. When combining these networks we can, for each statement, track the number of texts that contained that statement. Since a statement is a relation connecting two concepts, this approach effectively provides a weight for that relation. Alternatively, the analyst can compute whether any text contained that statement. In this case, there are no weights and the links in the network are simply present or not (binary). If these texts represent diverse sources of information, then the weights are indicative of the certainty or verifiability of a relation. Future work might also explore utilizing Bayesian learning techniques for estimating the overall confidence in a relation rather than just summing up the number of texts in which the statement was present.

We also note that when people read texts there is a process of automatic inference. For example, when people read about a child talking to a parent they infer based on social experience that the child is younger. Similarly, it appears that such inferences are common between the entity classes. For example, if Agent X has Resource Y and Knowledge K is needed to use Resource Y, then in general Agent X will have Knowledge K. Future work needs to investigate whether a simple inference engine at the entity class level would facilitate coding. We note that previous work found that using expert systems to assist coding in terms of adding general social knowledge was quite effective (Carley, 1988). Thus, we expect this to be a promising avenue for future research.

Finally, we note that the use of an ontology adds a hierarchical level to the coding. This is invaluable from an interpretative perspective. There is no reason, conceptually, why multiple hierarchical levels could not be added, denoting finer and finer levels of detail. We suspect however, based on the use of hierarchical coding schemes in various scientific fields (e.g., biology and organization theory) that: a) such hierarchies are likely to not be infinitely deep, b) a certain level of theoretical maturity and consensus in a field is needed for such a hierarchy to be generally useful, and c) eventually we will need to move beyond such a "flat" scheme for extracting meaning. As to this last point, by flat what we are referring to is the fact that a hierarchy can be completely represented in two dimensions. We found, even when doing this limited coding that some text-level concepts and higher-level concepts needed to be cross-classified into two or more entity classes. As more levels are added in an ontological hierarchy, such cross classification is likely to occur at each level, resulting in a network of inference, not a simple hierarchy and so a non-flat structure. Future work should examine how to code, represent, and reason about such networks.

Conclusion

One of the key advantages of classic content analysis was that macro social change could be tracked by changes in content, and over- or under-representation of various words. For example, movements toward war might be signaled by an increasing usage of words describing hostile acts, foreign powers, and weapons. One of the key advantages of Network Text Analysis (NTA) over standard text analysis is that it enables the extraction of meaning and enables interpretation by signaling not just what words are used but how they are used. This enables differences and similarities in viewpoints to be examined, and it enables the tracking of micro social change as evidenced by changes in meaning. By adding an ontology to NTA, differences and similarities in viewpoints about a meta-structure described or discussed in the text can be examined.

In this chapter, we used the meta-matrix ontology as we were interested in the underlying social/organizational structure described in the texts. Several points are critical to note. First, the mere fact that we used an ontology to define a set of meta-concepts enables the extraction of a hierarchy of meaning thus affording the analyst with greater interpretive ability. Second, any ontology could be used, and the analyst needs to consider the appropriate ontology for their work. In creating this ontology the analyst wants to think in terms of the set of entity classes and the relations among them that define the second level network of interest. For us, these entity classes and relations were those relevant to defining the organizational structure of a group.

The proposed meta-matrix approach to text analysis makes it possible to track more micro social change in terms of changes, not just in meaning, but in the social and organizational structures. Using techniques such as this facilitates a more systematic analysis of groups, broadens the types of questions that can be effectively answered using texts, and brings the richness of textual information to bear in defining and understanding the structure of the organizations and society in which we live.

Acknowledgments

We want to thank Maksim Tsvetovat and Jeffrey Reminga from CASOS, CMU for helping with generating the visualizations.

References

Alexa, M. (1997). *Computer-assisted text analysis methodology in the social sciences.* Arbeitsbericht: ZUMA.

Bakker, R.R. (1987). *Knowledge graphs: Representation and structuring of scientific knowledge.* Dissertation. University Twente.

Batagelj, V., Mrvary, A., & Zaveršnik, M. (2002). *Network analysis of texts.* In T. Erjavec & J. Gros (Eds.), *Proceedings of the 5th International Multi-Conference Information Society - Language Technologies* (pp. 143-148). Ljubljana, October. Jezikovne tehnologije / Language Technologies, Ljubljana.

Burkart, M. (1997). Thesaurus. In M. Buder, W. Rehfeld, T. Seeger, & D. Strauch (Eds.), *Grundlagen der Praktischen Information und Dokumentation: Ein Handbuch zur Einführung in die Fachliche Informationsarbeit* (pp. 160-179) (4th edition). München: Saur.

Carley, K.M., & Reminga, J. (2004). *ORA: Organization risk analyzer.* Carnegie Mellon University. School of Computer Science, Institute for Software Research International, Technical Report CMU-ISRI-04-101.

Carley, K.M. (2003). Dynamic network analysis. In R. Breiger, K.M. Carley, & P. Pattison (Eds.), *Summary of the NRC workshop on social network modeling and analysis* (pp. 133-145). Committee on Human Factors, National Research Council.

Carley, K.M. (2002). Smart agents and organizations of the future. In L. Lievrouw & S. Livingstone (Eds.), *The handbook of new media* (pp. 206-220). Thousand Oaks, CA: Sage.

Carley, K.M. (1997a). Extracting team mental models through textual analysis. *Journal of Organizational Behavior*, 18, 533-558.

Carley, K.M. (1997b). Network text analysis: The network position of concepts. In C.W. Roberts (Ed.), *Text analysis for the social sciences* (pp. 79-102). Mahwah, NJ: Lawrence Erlbaum.

Carley, K.M. (1993). Coding choices for textual analysis: A comparison of content analysis and map analysis. In P. Marsden (Ed.), *Sociological Methodology*, 23, 75-126. Oxford: Blackwell.

Carley, K.M. (1988). Formalizing the social expert's knowledge. *Sociological Methods and Research*, 17(2), 165-232.

Carley, K.M. (1986). An approach for relating social structure to cognitive structure. *Journal of Mathematical Sociology*, 12, 137-189.

Carley, K.M., Dombrowski, M., Tsvetovat, M., Reminga, J., & Kamneva, N. (2003). Destabilizing dynamic covert networks. *Proceedings of the 8th International Command and Control Research and Technology Symposium.* Washington, DC. Evidence Based Research, Vienna, V.A.

Carley, K. M., & Hill, V. (2001). Structural change and learning within organizations. In A. Lomi & E.R. Larsen (Eds.), *Dynamics of organizations: Computational modeling and organizational theories* (pp. 63-92). Live Oak, CA: MIT Press/AAAI Press.

Carley, K.M., & Krackhardt, D. (1999). A typology for C2 measures. In *Proceedings of the 1999 International Symposium on Command and Control Research and Technology.* Newport, RI, June.

Carley, K.M., & Palmquist, M. (1992). Extracting, representing, and analyzing mental models. *Social Forces*, 70(3), 601-636.

Carley, K.M., & Reminga, J. (2004). *ORA: Organizational risk analyzer.* Carnegie Mellon University, School of Computer Science, Institute for Software Research International, Technical Report CMU-ISRI-04-106.

Carley, K.M, Ren, Y., & Krackhardt, D. (2000). Measuring and modeling change in c3i architectures. In *Proceedings of the 2000 Command and Control Research and Technology Symposium.* Naval Postgraduate School, Monterrey, CA, June, 2000.

Copyright © 2005, Idea Group Inc. Copying or distributing in print or electronic forms without written permission of Idea Group Inc. is prohibited.

Corman, S.R., Kuhn, T., Mcphee, R.D., & Dooley, K.J. (2002). Studying complex discursive systems: Centering resonance analysis of communication. *Human Communication*, 28(20), 157-206.

Danowski, J. (1993). Network analysis of message content. In W.D. Richards & G.A. Barnett (Eds.), *Progress in communication science, XII* (pp. 197-222). Norwood, NJ: Ablex.

Diesner, J., & Carley, K.M. (2004). *AutoMap1.2 - Extract, analyze, represent, and compare mental models from texts*. Carnegie Mellon University, School of Computer Science, Institute for Software Research International, Technical Report CMU-ISRI-04-100.

Galbraith, J. (1977). *Organizational design*. Reading, MA: Addison-Wesley.

Hill, V., & Carley, K.M. (1999). An approach to identifying consensus in a subfield: The case of organizational culture. *Poetics*, 27, 1-30.

James, P. (1992). Knowledge graphs. In R.P. van der Riet & R.A. Meersman (Eds.), *Linguistic instruments in knowledge engineering* (pp. 97-117). Amsterdam: Elsevier.

Jurafsky, D., & Marton, J.H. (2000). *Speech and language processing*. Upper Saddle River, NJ: Prentice Hall.

Kelle, U. (1997). Theory building in qualitative research and computer programs for the management of textual data. *Sociological Research Online*, 2(2). Retrieved from the WWW at: *http://www.socresonline.org.uk/2/2/1.html*

Klein, H. (1997). Classification of text analysis software. In R. Klar & O. Opitz (Eds.), *Classification and knowledge organization: Proceedings of the 20th annual conference of the Gesellschaft für Klassifikation e.V.* (pp. 255-261). University of Freiburg, Berlin. New York: Springer.

Kleinnijenhuis, J., de Ridder, J.A., & Rietberg, E.M. (1996). Reasoning in economic discourse: An application of the network approach in economic discourse. In C.W. Roberts (Ed.), *Text analysis for the social sciences* (pp. 79-102). Mahwah, NJ: Lawrence Erlbaum.

Krackhardt, D., & Carley, K.M. (1998). A PCANS model of structure in organization. In *Proceedings of the 1998 International Symposium on Command and Control Research and Technology Evidence Based Research* (pp. 113-119). Vienna, VA.

Magnini, B., Negri, M., Prevete, R., & Tanev, H. (2002). A WordNet-based approach to named entities recognition. In *Proceedings of SemaNet'02: Building and Using Semantic Networks* (pp. 38-44). Taipei, Taiwan.

March, J.G., & Simon, H.A. (1958). *Organizations*. New York: Wiley.

Monge, P.R., & Contractor, N.S. (2003). *Theories of communication networks*. Oxford University Press.

Monge, P.R., & Contractor, N.S. (2001). Emergence of communication networks. In F.M. Jablin, & L.L. Putnam (Eds.), *The new handbook of organizational communication: Advances in theory, research and methods* (pp. 440-502). Thousand Oaks, CA: Sage.

Popping, R. (2003). Knowledge graphs and network text analysis. *Social Science Information,* 42(1), 91-106.

Popping, R. (2000). *Computer-assisted text analysis.* London, Thousand Oaks: Sage.

Popping, R., & Roberts, C.W. (1997). Network approaches in text analysis. In R. Klar & O. Opitz (Eds.), *Classification and Knowledge Organization: Proceedings of the 20th annual conference of the Gesellschaft für Klassifikation e.V.* (pp. 381-389), University of Freiburg, Berlin. New York: Springer.

Porter, M.F. (1980). *An algorithm for suffix stripping. I,* 14(3), 130-137.

Reimer, U. (1997). Neue Formen der Wissensrepräsentation. In M. Buder, W. Rehfeld, T. Seeger & D. Strauch (Eds.), *Grundlagen der praktischen Information und Dokumentation: Ein Handbuch zur Einführung in die fachliche Informationsarbeit* (pp. 180-207) (4th edition). München: Saur.

Ryan, G.W., & Bernard, H.R. (2000). Data management and analysis methods. In N. Denzin & Y. Lincoln (Eds.), *Handbook of qualitative research* (pp. 769-802) (2nd edition). Thousand Oaks, CA: Sage.

Scott, J.P. (2000). *Social network analysis: A handbook* (2nd edition). London: Sage.

Simon, H.A. (1973). Applying information technology to organizational design. *Public Administration Review,* 33, 268-78.

Sowa, J.F. (1984). *Conceptual structures: Information processing in mind and machine.* Reading, MA: Addison-Wesley.

Wasserman, S., & Faust, K. (1994). *Social network analysis. Methods and applications.* Cambridge: Cambridge University Press.

Zuell, C., & Alexa, M. (2001). Automatisches Codieren von Textdaten. Ein Ueberblick ueber neue Entwicklungen. In W. Wirth & E. Lauf (Eds.), *Inhaltsanalyse – Perspektiven, Probleme, Potenziale* (pp. 303-317). Koeln: Herbert von Halem.

Endnotes

[1] The delete list was applied with the rhetorical adjacency option. Rhetorical adjacency means that text-level concepts matching entries in the delete list are replaced by imaginary placeholders. Those place holders ensure that only concepts, which occurred within a window before pre-processing, can form statements (Diesner & Carley, 2004).

[2] We did not choose the thesaurus content only option. Thus, adjacency does not apply.

[3] We used the thesaurus content only option in combination with the rhetorical adjacency. Thus, the meta-matrix categories are the unique concepts.

[4] We used the following statement formation settings: Directionality: uni-directional, Window Size: 4, Text Unit: Text (for detailed information about analysis settings in AutoMap see Diesner & Carley, 2004).

⁵   Sub-Matrix selection was performed with the rhetorical adjacency option.

ⁱ   This work was supported in part by the National Science Foundation under grants ITR/IM IIS-0081219, IGERT 9972762 in CASOS, and CASOS – the Center for Computational Analysis of Social and Organizational Systems at Carnegie Mellon University (*http://www.casos.cs.cmu.edu*). The views and conclusions contained in this document are those of the authors and should not be interpreted as representing the official policies, either expressed or implied, of the National Science Foundation or the U.S. government.

Appendix

Software: AutoMap: Diesner, J. & Carley, K.M. (2004). *AutoMap1.2: Software for Network Text Analysis.*

AutoMap is a network text analysis tool that extracts, analyzes, represents, and compares mental models from texts. The software package performs map analysis, meta-matrix text analysis, and sub-matrix text analysis. As an input, AutoMap takes raw, free flowing, and unmarked texts with ASCII characters. When performing analysis, AutoMap encodes the links between concepts in a text and builds a network of the linked concepts. As an output, AutoMap generates representations of the extracted mental models as a map file and a stat file per text, various term distribution lists and matrices in comma separated value (csv) format, and outputs in DL format for UCINET and DyNetML format. The scope of functionalities and outputs supported by AutoMap enables one way of analyzing complex, large-scale systems and provide multi-level access to the meaning of textual data.

Limitations: Coding in AutoMap is computer-assisted. Computer-assisted coding means that the machine applies a set of coding rules that were defined by a human (Ryan and Bernard, 2000, p.786; Kelle, 1997, p. 6; Klein, 1997, p. 256). Coding rules in AutoMap imply text pre-processing. Text pre-processing condenses the data to the concepts that capture the features of the texts that are relevant to the user. Pre-processing techniques provided in AutoMap are Named-Entity Recognition, Stemming, Deletion, and Thesaurus application. The creation of delete lists and thesauri requires some manual effort (see Discussion section for details).

Hardware and software requirements: AutoMap1.2 has been implemented in Java 1.4. The system has been validated for Windows. The installer for AutoMap1.2 for Windows and a help file that includes examples of all AutoMap1.2 functionalities are available online under http://www.casos.cs.cmu.edu/projects/automap/software.html at no charge. More information about AutoMap, such as publications, sponsors, and contact information is provided under http://www.casos.cs.cmu.edu/projects/automap/index.html.

AutoMap has been written such that the only limit on the number of texts that can be analyzed, the number of concepts that can be extracted, etc., are determined by the processing power and storage space of the user's machine.

Chapter V

Belief Function Approach to Evidential Reasoning in Causal Maps

Rajendra P. Srivastava
University of Kansas, USA

Mari W. Buche
Michigan Technological University, USA

Tom L. Roberts
University of Kansas, USA

Abstract

The purpose of this chapter is to demonstrate the use of the evidential reasoning approach under the Dempster-Shafer (D-S) theory of belief functions to analyze revealed causal maps (RCM). The participants from information technology (IT) organizations provided the concepts to describe the target phenomenon of Job Satisfaction. They also identified the associations between the concepts. This chapter discusses the steps necessary to transform a causal map into an evidential diagram. The evidential diagram can then be analyzed using belief functions technique with survey data, thereby extending the research from a discovery and explanation stage to testing

Copyright © 2005, Idea Group Inc. Copying or distributing in print or electronic forms without written permission of Idea Group Inc. is prohibited.

and prediction. An example is provided to demonstrate these steps. This chapter also provides the basics of Dempster-Shafer theory of belief functions and a step-by-step description of the propagation process of beliefs in tree-like evidential diagrams.

Introduction

The main purpose of this chapter is to demonstrate the use of evidential reasoning approach under Dempster-Shafer (D-S) theory of belief functions (Shafer, 1976; see also, Srivastava & Datta, 2002; and Srivastava & Mock, 2000, 2002) to analyze revealed causal maps. The Revealed Causal Mapping (RCM) technique is used to represent the model of a mental map and to determine the constructs or variables of the model and their interrelationships from the data. RCM focuses on the cause/effect linkages disclosed by individuals intimately familiar with a phenomenon under investigation. The researcher deliberately avoids determining the variables and their associations *a priori*, allowing both to emerge during the discourse or from the textual analysis (Narayanan & Fahey, 1990). In contrast, other forms of causal mapping begin with a framework of variables based on theory, and the associations are provided by the participants in the study (cf. Bougon, et al., 1977).

While RCM helps determine the significant variables in the model and their associations, it does not provide a way to integrate uncertainties involved in the variables or to use the model to predict future behavior. The evidential reasoning approach provides a technique where one can take the RCM model, convert it into an evidential diagram, and then use it to predict how a variable of interest would behave under various scenarios. An evidential diagram is a model showing interrelationships among various variables in a decision problem along with relevant items of evidence pertaining to those variables that can be used to evaluate the impact on a given variable of all other variables in the diagram. In other words, RCM is a good technique to identify the significant constructs (i.e., variables) and their interrelationships relevant to a model, whereas evidential approach is good for making if-then analyses once the model is established.

There are two steps required in order to achieve our objective. One is to convert the RCM model to an evidential diagram with the variables taken from the RCM model and items of evidence identified for the variables from the problem domain. The second step is to deal with uncertainties associated with evidence. In general, uncertainties are inherent in RCM model variables. For example, in our case of IT professionals' job satisfaction, the variable "Feedback from Supervisors/Co-Workers" partly determines whether an individual will have a "high" or "low" level of satisfaction. However, the level of job satisfaction will depend on the level of confidence we have in our measure of the variable. The Feedback from Supervisors/Co-Workers may be evaluated through several relevant items of evidence such as interviews or surveys. In general, such items of evidence provide less than 100% assurance in support of, or negation of, the pertinent variable. The uncertainties associated with these variables are better modeled under Dempster-Shafer theory of belief functions than probabilities as empirically shown by Harrison, Srivastava and Plumlee (2002) in auditing and by Curley and Golden (1994) in psychology.

We use belief functions to represent uncertainties associated with the model variables and use evidential reasoning approach to determine the impact of a given variable on another in the model. This combination of techniques adds the strength of prediction to the usefulness of descriptive modeling when studying behavioral phenomena. Evidential reasoning under Dempster-Shafer theory of belief functions thereby extends the impact of revealed causal mapping.

The chapter is divided into eight sections. Section II provides a brief description of the Revealed Causal Mapping (RCM) technique. Section III discusses the basic concepts of belief functions, and provides an illustration of Dempster's rule of combination of independent items of evidence. Section IV describes the evidential reasoning approach under belief functions. Section V describes a causal map developed through interviews and surveys of IT employees on their job satisfaction. Section VI shows the process of converting a RCM map to an evidential diagram under belief functions. Section VII presents the results of the analysis, and Section VIII provides conclusions and directions for future research.

Revealed Causal Mapping Technique

Revealed causal mapping is a form of content analysis that attempts to discern the mental models of individuals based on their verbal or text-based communications (Carley, 1997; Darais et al., 2003; Narayanan & Fahey, 1990; Nelson et al., 2000). The general structure of the causal map can reveal a wealth of information about cognitive associations, explaining idiosyncratic behaviors and reasoning.

The actual steps used to develop the IT Job Satisfaction revealed causal map in the present paper are outlined in Table 1. The research constructs were not determined *a priori*, but were derived from the assertions in the data. The sequence of steps directly develops the structure of the model from the data sample.

First, a key consideration in using RCM is the determination of source data (Narayanan & Fahey, 1990). Since this study assessed the job satisfaction of IT professionals, it was logical to gather data from IT workers in a variety of industries. Interviews were conducted with employees of IT departments, and responses were analyzed to produce the model presented later in the chapter.

Second, the researchers identified causal statements from the original transcripts or documents. The third step in the procedure is to combine concepts based on coding rules

Table 1. Steps for revealed causal mapping technique

Step	Description
1	Identify source data
2	Identify causal statements
3	Create concept dictionary
4	Aggregate maps
5	Produce RCM and analyze maps

(Axelrod, 1976; Wrightson, 1976), producing a concept dictionary (see Appendix A). Synonyms are grouped to enable interpretation and comparison of the resultant causal maps. Care must be taken to ensure that synonyms are true to the original conveyance of the participant. For example, two interviewees might use different words that hold identical or very similar meanings such as "computer application" and "computer program." In mapping these terms, the links are not identical until the concepts are coded by the researcher. It is preferable for investigators to err on the side of too many concepts, rather than inadvertently combine terms inappropriately for the sake of parsimony.

Next, the maps of the individual participants were aggregated by combining the linkages between the relevant concepts. The result of this step is a representative causal map for the sample of participants (Markoczy & Goldberg, 1995).

RCM produces dependent maps, meaning that the links between nodes indicate the presence of an association explicitly revealed in the data (Nadkarni & Shenoy, 2001). The absence of a line does not imply independence between the nodes, however. It simply means that a particular link was not stated by the participants. This characteristic of RCM demonstrates the close relationship of the graphical result (map) to the data set. Therefore, it is vital that the sample be representative of the population of interest. The following section introduces belief functions and the importance of evidential reasoning in managerial decision making.

Dempster-Shafer Theory of Belief Functions

Dempster-Shafer (D-S) theory of belief functions, which is also known as the belief-function framework, is a broader framework than probability theory (Shafer and Srivastava, 1990). Actually, Bayesian framework is a special case of belief-function framework. The basic difference between the belief-function framework and probability theory or Bayesian framework is in the assignment of uncertainties to a mutually exclusive and collectively exhaustive set of elements, say Θ, with elements $\{a_1, a_2, a_3, ... a_n\}$. This set of elements, $\Theta = \{a_1, a_2, a_3, ... a_n\}$, is known as a *frame of discernment* in belief-function framework. In probability theory, probabilities are assigned to individual elements, i.e., to the singletons, and they all add to one. For example, for the frame, $\Theta = \{a_1, a_2, a_3, ... a_n\}$, with n mutually exclusive and collectively exhaustive set of elements, a_i's, with i = 1, 2, 3, ... n, one assigns a probability measure to each element, $1.0 \geq P(a_i) \geq 0$, such that

$$\sum_{i=1}^{n} P(a_i) = 1.$$

Under belief functions, however, the probablity mass is distributed over the super set of the elements Θ instead of just the singletons. Shafer (1976) calls this probability mass distribution the *basic probability assignment* function, whereas Smets calls it *belief masses* (Smets 1998, 1990a, 1990b). We will use Shafer's terminology of probability mass distribution over the superset of Θ.

Basic Probability Assignment Function (m-Values)

In the present context, the *basic probability assignment function* represents the strength of evidence. For example, suppose that we have received feedback from a survey of the IT employees of a company about whether their work is challenging or not. On average, the employees believe that their work is challenging but they do not say this with certainty; they put a high level of comfort, say 0.85 (on a scale 0 – 1.0), that their work is challenging. But, they do not say that their work is not challenging. This response can be represented through the *basic probability assignment* function, m-values[1], on the frame, {'yes$_{CW}$', 'no$_{CW}$'}, of the variable 'Challenging Work (CW)' as: m(yes$_{CW}$) = 0.85, m(no$_{CW}$) = 0, and m({yes$_{CW}$, no$_{CW}$}) = 0.15. These values imply that the evidence suggests that the work is challenging to a degree 0.85, it is not challenging to a degree zero (there is no evidence in support of the negation), and it is undecided to a degree 0.15.

Mathematically, the *basic probability assignment* function represents the distribution of probability masses over the superset of the frame, Θ. In other words, probability masses are assigned to all the singletons, all subsets of two elements, three elements, and so on, to the entire frame. Traditionally, these probability masses are represented in terms of m-values and the sum of all these m-values equals one, i.e., $\sum_{B \subseteq \Theta} m(B) = 1$, where B represents a subset of elements of frame Θ. The m-value for the empty set is zero, i.e., $m(\emptyset) = 0$.

In addition to the *basic probability assignment* function, i.e., m-values, we have one other function, Belief function, represented by Bel(.), that is of interest in the present discussion. As defined below, Bel(A), determines the degree to which we believe, based on the evidence, that A is true. This function is discussed further below.

Belief Functions

The function, Bel(B), defines the belief in B, a subset of elements of frame Θ, that is true, and is equal to m(B) plus the sum of all the m-values for the set of elements contained in B, i.e., $= Bel(B) = \sum_{C \subseteq B} m(C)$. Let us consider the example described earlier to illustrate the definition. Based on the Survey Results, we have 0.85 level of belief that the employees have challenging work, zero belief that the employees do not have challenging work. This evidence can be mapped in the following belief functions by using the above definition:

$$Bel(yes_{CW}) = m(yes_{CW}) = 0.85,$$
$$Bel(no_{CW}) = m(no_{CW}) = 0.0,$$
$$Bel(\{yes_{CW}, no_{CW}\}) = m(yes_{CW}) + m(no_{CW}) + m(\{yes_{CW}, no_{CW}\})$$
$$= 0.85 + 0.0 + 0.15 = 1.0.$$

The belief values discussed previously imply that we have direct evidence from surveying the employees that the work is challenging to a degree 0.85, no belief that the work is not challenging, and the belief that the work is either challenging or not challenging is 1.0. Note that in our example there is no state or element contained in 'yes$_{CW}$' or 'no$_{CW}$'. Thus, m-values and Bel(.) for these elements are the same.

Dempster's Rule of Combination

Dempster's rule of combination is similar to Bayes' rule in probability theory. It is used to combine various independent items of evidence pertaining to a variable or a frame of discernment. As mentioned earlier, the strength of evidence is expressed in terms of m-values. Thus, if we have two independent items of evidence pertaining to a given variable, i.e., we have two sets of m-values for the same variable then the combined m-values are obtained by using Dempster's rule. For a simple case[2] of two items of evidence pertaining to a frame Θ. Dempter's rule of combination is expressed as:

$$m(B) = K^{-1} \cdot \sum_{\substack{i,j \\ B_i \cap B_j = B}} m_1(B_i) m_2(B_j),$$

where m(B) represents the strength of the combined evidence and m_1 and m_2 are the two sets of m-values associated with the two independent items of evidence. K is the renormalization constant given by:

$$K = 1 - \sum_{\substack{i,j \\ B_i \cap B_j = \emptyset}} m_1(B_i) m_2(B_j).$$

The second term in K represents the conflict between the two items of evidence. When K=0, i.e., when the two items of evidence totally conflict with each other, these two items of evidence are not combinable.

A simple interpretation of Dempster's rule is that the combined m-value for a set of elements B is equal to the sum of the product of the two sets of m-values (from each item of evidence), $m_1(B_1)$ and $m_2(B_2)$, such that the intersection of B_1 and B_2 is equal to B and renormalize the m-values to add to one by eliminating the conflicts.

Let us consider an example to illustrate Dempster's rule. Consider that we have the following sets of m-values from two independent items of evidence pertaining to a variable, say A, with two values, 'a', and '$\sim a$', representing respectively, that A is true and is not true:

$m_1(a) = 0.4, m_1(\sim a) = 0.1, m_1(\{a, \sim a\}) = 0.5,$
$m_2(a) = 0.6, m_2(\sim a) = 0.2, m_2(\{a, \sim a\}) = 0.2.$

As mentioned earlier, the general formula of Dempster's rule yields the combines m-value for an element or a set of elements of the frame of discernment by multiplying the two sets of m-values such that the intersection of their respective arguments is equal to the element or set of elements desired in the combined m-value, and by eliminating the conflicts and renormalizing the resulting m-values such that the resulting m-values add to one. This reasoning yields the following expressions as a result of Dempster's rule for binary variables:

$m(a) = K^{-1}[m_1(a)m_2(a) + m_1(a)m_2(\{a,\sim a\}) + m_1(\{a,\sim a\})m_2(a)],$
$m(\sim a) = K^{-1}[m_1(\sim a)m_2(\sim a) + m_1(\sim a)m_2(\{a,\sim a\}) + m_1(\{a,\sim a\})m_2(\sim a)],$
$m(\{a,\sim a\}) = K^{-1}m_1(\{a,\sim a\})m_2(\{a,\sim a\}),$
and
$K = 1 - [m_1(a)m_2(\sim a) + m_1(\sim a)m_2(a)].$

As we can see above, m(a) is the result of the multiplication of the two sets of m-values such that the intersection of their arguments is equal to '*a*' and the renormalization constant, K, is equal to one minus the conflict terms. Similarly m(~*a*) and m({*a*,~*a*}) are the results of multiplying two sets of m-values such that the intersection of their arguments is equal to '~*a*' and ({*a*,~*a*}), respectively.

Substituting the values for the two m-values, we obtain:

$K = 1 - [0.4 \times 0.2 + 0.1 \times 0.6] = 0.86,$
$m(a) = [0.4 \times 0.6 + 0.4 \times 0.2 + 0.5 \times 0.6]/0.86 = 0.72093,$
$m(\sim a) = [0.1 \times 0.2 + 0.1 \times 0.2 + 0.5 \times 0.2]/0.86 = 0.16279,$
$m(\{a,\sim a\}) = 0.5 \times 0.2/0.86 = 0.11628.$

Thus, the total beliefs after combining both items of evidence are given by:

$Bel(a) = m(a) = 0.72093, Bel(\sim a) = m(\sim a) = 0.16279,$
and
$Bel(\{a,\sim a\}) = m(a) + m(\sim a) + m(\{a,\sim a\}) = 0.72093 + 0.16279 + 0.11628 = 1.0.$

The above values of beliefs in '*a*' and '~*a*' represent the combined beliefs from two items of evidence. Belief that '*a*' is true from the first item of evidence is 0.4; from the second item of evidence it is 0.6, whereas the combined belief that '*a*' is true based on the two items of evidence is 0.72093; a stronger belief as a result of the combination. The combined belief would have been much stronger if we did not have the conflict.

Evidential Reasoning Approach

Strat (1984) and Pearl (1990) have used the term "evidential reasoning" for decision making under uncertainty. Under this approach one needs to develop an evidential diagram (as shown in Figure 4 in the next section; see also Srivastava & Mock (2000) for other examples) containing all the variables involved in the decision problem with their interrelationships and the items of evidence pertaining to those variables. Once the evidential diagram is completed, the decision maker can determine the impact of a given variable on all other variables in the diagram by combining the knowledge about the variables. In other words, under the evidential reasoning approach, if we have knowledge about one or more variables in the evidential diagram, then we can *make predictions about the other variables* in the diagram given that we know how these variables are interrelated. Usually, the knowledge about the states of these variables is only partial, i.e., there is uncertainty associated with what we know about these variables. As mentioned earlier, we use Dempster-Shafer theory of belief functions to model these uncertainties.

In the present case, variables in the evidential diagram represent the "constructs" of the model obtained through the Revealed Causal Mapping (RCM) process, and the interrelationships represent how one variable or a multiple of variables influence a given variable. Such relationships among the variables can be defined either in terms of categorical relationships such as, 'AND', and 'OR', or in terms of uncertain relationships, such as a combination of 'AND' and 'OR', or some other relationships as discussed in the next section.

In order to illustrate the evidential reasoning approach, let us first construct an evidential diagram using a simple hypothetical decision problem involving three variables, X, Y, and Z (see Figure 1). Let us assume for simplicity that these variables are binary, i.e., each

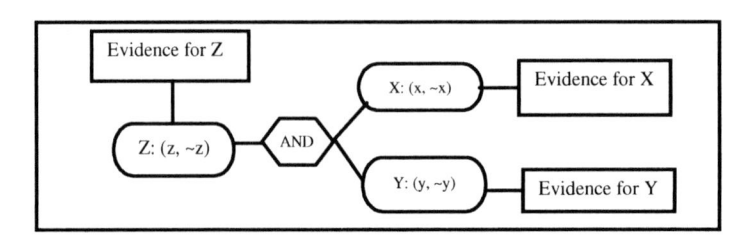

Figure 1: Example of an evidential nework*

*Rounded boxes represent variables (constructs), hexagonal box represents a relationship, and rectangular boxes represent items of evidence pertinent to the variables they are connected

variable has two values: either the variable is true (x, y, and z) or false (~x, ~y, and ~z). Also, let us assume that variable Z is related to X and Y through the 'AND' relationship. This relationship implies that Z is true (z) if and only if X is true (x) and Y is true (y), but it is false (~z) when either X is true (x) and Y is false (~y), or X is false (~x) and Y is true (y), or both X and Y are false (~x, ~y). Now we draw a diagram consisting of the three variables, X, Y, and Z, represented by rounded boxes and connect them with a relational node represented by the hexagonal box. Further, connect each variable with the corresponding items of evidence represented by rectangular boxes. Figure 1 depicts the evidential diagram for the above case.

As mentioned earlier, an evidential reasoning approach helps us infer about one variable given what we know about the other variables in the evidential diagram. For example, in Figure 1, we can predict about the state of Z given what we know about the states of X and Y, and the relationship among them. Under the belief-function framework, this knowledge is expressed in terms of m-values. For example, knowledge about X and Y, based on the corresponding evidence, can be expressed in terms of m-values[3], m_X at X, and m_Y at Y, as: $m_X(x) = 0.6$, $m_X(\sim x) = 0.2$, $m_X(\{x,\sim x\}) = 0.2$, and $m_Y(y) = 0.7$, $m_Y(\sim y) = 0$, $m_Y(\{y,\sim y\}) = 0.3$. The first set of m-values suggests that the evidence relevant to X provides 0.6 level of support that X is true, i.e., $m_X(x) = 0.6$, 0.2 level of support that X is not true, i.e., $m_X(\sim x) = 0.2$, and 0.2 level of support undecided, i.e., $m_X(\{x,\sim x\}) = 0.2$. One can provide a similar interpretation of the m-values for Y. The 'AND' relationship between X and Y, and Z can be expressed in terms of the following m-values: m({xyz, x~y~z, ~xy~z, ~x~y~z}) = 1.0. This relationship implies that z is true if and only if x is true and y is true, and it is false when either x is true and ~y is true, ~x is true and y is true, or ~x and ~y are true.

Based on the knowledge about X and Y above and the relationship of Z with X and Y, we can now make inferences about Z. This process consists of three steps which are described in Appendix C in detail. Basically, Step 1 involves propagating[4] beliefs or m-values from X and Y variables to the relational node 'AND' through vacuous[5] extension. This process yields two sets of m-values at 'AND', one from X and the other from Y:

Table 2: List of symbols related to m-values used in the propagation process in Figure 1

Symbol	Description
x, y, and z	These symbols, respectively, represent that the variables X, Y, and Z, are true.
~x, ~y, and ~z	These symbols, respectively, represent that the variables X, Y, and Z, are not true.
$\Theta_X = \{x,\sim x\}$	The frame of X which represents all the possible values of X.
$\Theta_Y = \{y,\sim y\}$	The frame of Y which represents all the possible values of Y.
$\Theta_{AND} = \{xyz, x\sim y\sim z, \sim xy\sim z, \sim x\sim y\sim z\}$	The frame of 'AND' relationship. The elements in the frame are the only possible values under the logical 'AND' relationship between Z, and X and Y.
$m_X(\{.\})$	m-value for the element or the set of elements {x,~x} in the argument for variable X.
$m_Y(\{.\})$	m-value for the element or the set of elements {y,~y} in the argument for variable Y.
$m_{AND}(\{.\})$	m-value for the elements in the argument for the 'AND' relationship.
$m_{AND \leftarrow X}(\{.\})$	m-value for the element or elements in the argument propagated to 'AND' relationship from variable X.
$m_{AND \leftarrow Y}(\{.\})$	m-value for the element or elements in the argument propagated to 'AND' relationship from variable Y.
$m_{Z \leftarrow AND}(\{.\})$	m-values propagated from 'AND' to variable Z in Figure 1.

$m_{AND \leftarrow x}$ and $m_{AND \leftarrow y}$ (See Table 2 for definitions of symbols). Also, we already have one set of m-values, m_{AND}, at the relational node 'AND'. Step 2 involves combining the three sets of m-values at the 'AND' node using Dempster's rule. Step 3 involves propagating the resulting m-values from the 'AND' node to variable Z by marginalization[6]. This process yields $m_{Z \leftarrow AND}$. These m-values are then combined with the m-values at Z, m_Z, obtained from the evidence pertaining to Z. The resultant m-values will provide the belief values whether Z is true or not true. As mentioned earlier, the details of the propagation process[7] are discussed in Appendix C through a numerical example.

Modeling Uncertain Relationships among Variables

Srivastava and Lu (2002) have discussed a general approach to modeling various relationships under belief functions. We will use their approach to model the assumed relationships among various variables in Figure 4. As given earlier, the 'AND' relationship among X, Y and Z, under belief functions can be expressed in terms of the following m-value:

$$m_{AND}(\{xyz, x\sim y\sim z, \sim xy\sim z, \sim x\sim y\sim z\}) = 1.0.$$

The argument of m-value above determines the possible states of the joint space defining the 'AND' relationship. Similarly, the 'OR' relationship can be expressed as:

$$m_{OR}(\{xyz, x\sim yz, \sim xyz, \sim x\sim y\sim z\}) = 1.0.$$

A relationship representing 60% of 'AND' and 40% of 'OR' can be expressed as:

$$m_R(\{xyz, x\sim y\sim z, \sim xy\sim z, \sim x\sim y\sim z\}) = 0.6, \text{ and } m_R(\{xyz, x\sim yz, \sim xyz, \sim x\sim y\sim z\}) = 0.4,$$

where the subscript R stands for the relationship.

Propagation of Beliefs in a Network of Variables

The evidential diagram becomes a network if one item of evidence pertains to two or more variables in the diagram. Such a diagram is depicted in Figure 2 for a simple case of three variables. Even though the evidential diagram of IT Job Satisfaction model obtained through the RCM approach in the current study is not a network (see Figure 4), we describe the approach of propagating beliefs or m-values through a network of variables for completeness. The propagation of m-values through a network is much more complex and thus we will not go into the details of the propagation process in this chapter. Instead, we will briefly describe the process and advise interested readers to refer to Shenoy and Shafer (1990) for the details. Also, Srivastava (1995) provides a step-by-step description of the process by discussing an auditing example.

Basically, the propagation of m-values (i.e., beliefs) through a network of variables involves the following steps. First, the decision maker draws the evidential diagram with all the pertinent variables and their interrelationships in the problem along with the related items of evidence. This step is similar to creating an evidential diagram for the case of a tree-type diagram. Second, the decision maker identifies the clusters of variables over which m-values are either obtained from the items of evidence in the evidential diagram or defined from the assumed relationships among the variables. For example, in Figure 2, the four items of evidence yield the following clusters of variables: {X}, {Y}, {Z}, {X,Y}, and the 'AND' relationship defines m-value for the cluster {X,Y,Z}. Thus, in Figure 2, we have the following clusters of variables over which m-values are defined: {X}, {Y}, {Z}, {X,Y}, and {X,Y,Z}.

The third step in the propagation process in a network is to draw a Markov[8] tree based on the identified clusters of variables as above. This step is not needed for a tree-type evidential diagram. One can propagate m-values through a tree-type evidential diagram without converting the diagram to a Markov tree. The fourth step is to propagate m-values through the Markov tree by vacuously extending and marginalizing the m-values from all the nodes in the Markov tree to the node of interest. The basic approach to vacuous extension and marginalization remains the same as described earlier through endnotes 5 and 6.

Since the process of propagating m-values in a network becomes computationally quite complex, several software packages have been developed to facilitate this process (see, e.g., Shafer et al., 1988; Zarley & Shafer, 1988; and Saffiotti & Umkehrer, 1991). The software developed by Zarley and Shafer (1988) and Saffiotti & Umkehrer (1991) require programming the evidential diagram in LISP. Also, these software programs do not provide friendly user interfaces. On the other hand the software, "Auditor Assistant," developed by Shafer et al. (1988) has a friendly user interface and does not require any programming language to draw the evidential diagram. In fact, one can draw the evidential diagram using the graphic capabilities of the software. The evidential diagram drawn by using "Auditor Assistant" looks very similar to the one drawn by hand. The internal engine of the program converts this diagram into a Markov tree and propagates m-values once they are entered in the program. The program can be instructed to evaluate the

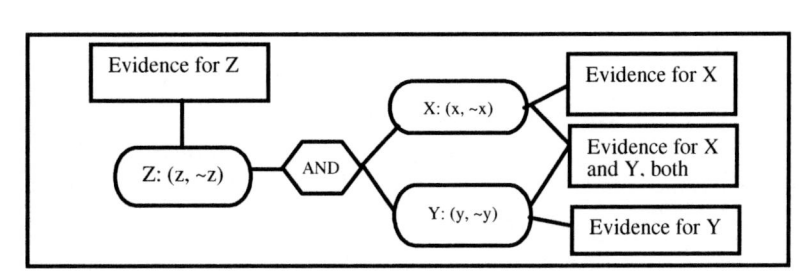

Figure 2: Evidential diagram as a network

network which then provides the aggregated m-values at each cluster of variables in the network. One can then analyze how one variable impacts another variable by making changes in the input m-values in the network.

Since the evidential diagram in our case is a simple tree, it is pretty straight forward to propagate m-values through such a tree as described Appendix C. In order to analyze the model in Figure 4, we develop a spreadsheet program that combines different m-values at each variable and then propagates them through the tree to the desired variable. This process is elaborated in Section VI.

Illustration of Evidential Reasoning: Causal Map of IT Job Satisfaction

Job satisfaction of information technology (IT) workers has been the focus of several information systems studies (e.g., Igbaria & Guimaraes, 1993; Gupta et al., 1992; Thatcher et al., 2003). Organizations want to retain their best IT workers as long as they possess the skills necessary to accomplish the job. However, there is growing concern that many long term IT employees no longer fit the needs of their employers.

The general consensus from the research is that job satisfaction is negatively related to turnover intention (e.g., Thatcher et al., 2003). In other words, workers who are highly satisfied with their jobs are less likely to contemplate seeking other employment and many unsatisfied workers enter the job market. In the current environment of radical role changes (Darais et al., 2003) and selectivity in hiring, IT workers within firms are experiencing anxiety and frustration, wondering what skills they will need to remain marketable in the future. The current trend with offshoring many IT jobs has exacerbated this problem for many workers. IT workers with traditionally secure positions are not immune to the pressures of this dynamic job environment.

In the present study, the IT Professional Job Satisfaction Model was developed based on 83 discovery interviews with IT workers in various job positions including systems analysts, programmers, technical specialists, and systems project managers. Table 3 shows the demographics for the interview sample.

These workers were from eight different corporations in a variety of industries (e.g., banking and insurance, manufacturing, education, state and local government). They voluntarily discussed their opinions on a number of job-related issues, generally focusing on their feelings of uncertainty regarding their personal contributions and job security (see the Interview Protocol in Appendix B). Interviews were generally 30 – 45 minutes in length and tape recorded, with the consent of the participant. Then, the interviews were transcribed and the causal statements were highlighted and analyzed according to the RCM technique described in Section II of this chapter. The causal map (Figure 3) was created based on the concepts represented in the transcripts.

In analyzing the data, one clear finding is that most of the IT personnel interviewed had difficulty describing how they fit within the corporate structure. They acknowledged that

Table 3. Interview sample demographics

Demographic	Mean (n=83)	SD or Percent
Number of years experience with current project	5.80	6.10
Tenure (# of years with the organization)	10.77	8.61
Age (years)	41.25	9.16
Gender		
Female	35	42%
Male	48	58%
Education:		
High School	13	15.7%
Associates Degree	14	16.9%
BA/BS	40	48.2%
MA/MS/MBA	14	16.8%
Post-Graduate Degree	2	2.4%

their contributions were important, but they felt they were personally expendable. Several persons similarly stated, "I'm just a cog in the wheel." As many researchers and practitioners have noted (e.g., Darais et al., 2003), in order to survive in the IT field, workers must continue to retrain and learn new skills. Therefore, acknowledgement of the need to change is depicted as the first node in the IT Professional Job Satisfaction Model (see Figure 3, Item 1). The interviewees indicated that skills stagnation often threatened job security. This realistic fear of job loss (Figure 3, Item 2) is a powerful motivator in pursuing necessary training.

IT workers in the interviews discussed the importance of seeking out training opportunities (Figure 3, Item 3), whether offered by the corporation as in-house training, enrollment in formal college courses, or on-line, computer-aided learning. These courses might entail attaining certification credentials, college credit, or practical experience. According to a majority of interviewees, if training is available at the place of work, and offered during work hours, employees are more likely to take advantage of the instruction. In contrast, off-hours training, to be completed outside of work on one's personal time, was less attractive to these employees. However, there is no guarantee that participation in training courses produces adequate knowledge for accomplishing new tasks.

Beyond merely gaining new knowledge and skills (Figure 3, Item 4), interviewees stressed that they must also be able to practice and apply the new skills in a meaningful way (Figure 3, Item 5). In other words, they believe that their training must be utilized on work projects in order for the new skills to become part of workers' permanent skill sets. Unfortunately, technical skills are often lost if they are not used soon after the course is completed (Radding, 1997).

Some of the relevant elements of job satisfaction (Figure 3, Item 9) that emerged from this study were perceived feedback from supervisors and co-workers (Figure 3, Item 6), participation in challenging projects (Figure 3, Item 7), and autonomy within the work setting (Figure 3, Item 8). Many IT projects involve teams working together to accomplish defined objectives. Direct feedback obtained from supervisors and co-workers (Figure 3, Item 6) increases job satisfaction because there is less ambiguity about perceived performance. For instance, the interviewees stated that they like to receive continuous feedback in order to determine whether they have adequately satisfied the user requirements and specifications during systems development.

Next, challenging projects (Figure 3, Item 7) provide intrinsic motivation for IT workers. Interviewees remarked that they were anxious to tackle difficult problems for the basic joy of simply discovering new solutions. But, beyond the initial pleasure of design development is the pride of successful implementation and user adoption of their creative solutions. These accomplishments instill job satisfaction at a deep level for IT problem-solvers.

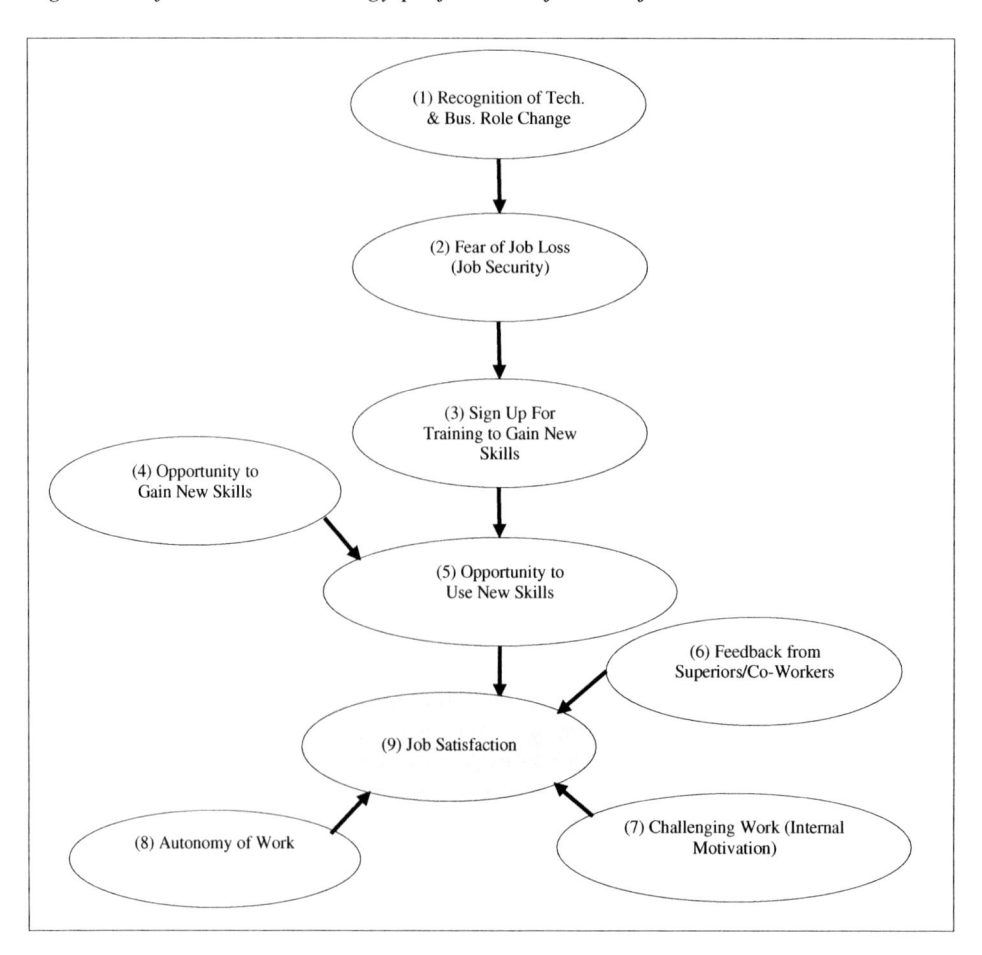

Figure 3. Information technology professional job satisfaction model

Finally, the level of autonomy (Figure 3, Item 8) positively affects job satisfaction because most IT employees prefer freedom and independence in determining relevant job-related decisions (Ang & Slaughter, 2001; Hackman & Oldham, 1976). According to the interviewees, they derive positive affect from exercising autonomy in project completion, resulting in increased job satisfaction.

Table 4 shows evidence used to support the construct measures. For this study, evidence was obtained from survey data. The survey was developed as an extension of a study in which the RCM technique was used to develop a model of work identity for IT professionals (Buche, 2003). Other possible examples of evidence would be additional interviews, observation, evaluation of documentation, and reviewing physical artifacts. Some of the elements could be gathered from supervisors and secondary sources, triangulating the evidence to analyze the model and to predict job satisfaction of IT professionals.

Table 4. Variables, symbols and respective sources of evidence

Variable (from RCM)	Symbol	Possible Values	Evidence	Source (Survey Data)
Recognition of Role Change	RR	$\{yes_{RR}, no_{RR}\}$	E1	• In my role I am most valued for my technical abilities. • My business knowledge is my most important contribution to the organization. • In my organization, I am perceived to be a technical expert. • I could not be successful this job without broad knowledge of the business domain.
Fear of Job Loss (Job Security)	JT	$\{yes_{JT}, no_{JT}\}$	E2.1 E2.2	• Actual layoffs reported in the firm, industry, media • Job security.
Sign Up For Training	ST	$\{yes_{ST}, no_{ST}\}$	E3	• Availability of training to learn new skills.
Opportunity to Gain New Skills	GS	$\{yes_{GS}, no_{GS}\}$	E4	• Opportunities to learn new things from my work.
Opportunity to Use New Skills	US	$\{yes_{US}, no_{US}\}$	E5	• Opportunities to apply new skills in my work.
Feedback from Superiors/Co-workers	FS	$\{yes_{FS}, no_{FS}\}$	E6	• My managers or co-workers often let me know how well I'm doing on my job. • I'm frustrated by the fact that my supervisor and co-workers almost never give me any feedback about how well I am doing my work. • My supervisor gives me specific inputs on how well I am performing my responsibilities.
Challenging Work	CW	$\{yes_{CW}, no_{CW}\}$	E7	• Stimulating and challenging work.
Autonomy of Work	AW	$\{yes_{AW}, no_{AW}\}$	E8	• I have a lot of autonomy in my job. That, is, I decide how to go about doing my projects. • The job denies me any chance to use my personal initiative or judgment in carrying out the work. • My job gives me considerable opportunity for independence and freedom in how I do my work.

Conversion of Revealed Causal Map into Evidential Diagram and Belief Propagation

In this section we first discuss how a revealed causal map can be converted to a belief function evidential diagram and then discuss how beliefs can be propagated through this evidential diagram. Our example is displayed in Figure 3.

Conversion of Revealed Causal Map into Evidential Diagram

The conversion process of revealed causal map into evidential diagram can be described in the following five steps:

1. Identify the main variables (i.e., constructs) in the revealed causal map.
2. Determine the possible values of these variables (such as, 'true/false', or 'high/medium/low').
3. Determine the relationships among the variables (see the details below).
4. Connect the variables through the corresponding relationships.
5. Identify potential items of evidence pertaining to the variables in the diagram and connect these items of evidence to the relevant variables.

The above approach yields the desired evidential diagram for belief-function analysis. In Steps 1 and 2, we have identified nine variables (i.e., constructs; see Figure 3) and their corresponding categorical values (Table 4).

Step 3 (determining the relationships among various variables) is a somewhat difficult process. Expert judgments about these relationships must be rendered. For example, the relationship R1 defining the relationship between 'Role Recognition (RR)' and 'Job Security (JT)' was extremely difficult to model. In this case, the survey data provided only information on whether the subjects recognize their changing role on the job and did not specify any details on how this knowledge might influence 'Job Security'. For IT personnel, 'Role Recognition' might mean that 'yes' there is 'Job Security', but it also may mean that there is no 'Job Security'. Thus, lacking any other information, we assume, for the present discussion, that when 'Role Recognition' is yes, 'Job Security' is 50% 'yes', and 50% 'no'. However, when there is no knowledge about 'Role Recognition', there is no knowledge about 'Job Security'. Such a relationship can be expressed in terms of m-values as given below.

m-values for R1:

$$m_{R1}(\{(yes_{RR}, yes_{JT}), (no_{RR}, yes_{JT}), (no_{RR}, no_{JT})\}) = 0.5,$$
$$m_{R1}(\{(yes_{RR}, no_{JT}), (no_{RR}, yes_{JT}), (no_{RR}, no_{JT})\}) = 0.5.$$

The above relationship propagates[9] 50% of $m_{E1}(yes_{RR})$, the belief on 'Role Recognition' being 'yes' from evidence E1 (Figure 4), to 'yes$_{JT}$,' 50% of $m_{E1}(yes_{RR})$ to 'no$_{JT}$', and 100% of $m_{E1}(no_{RR})$ and $m_{E1}(\{yes_{RR}, no_{RR}\})$ to $(\{yes_{JT}, no_{JT}\})$, as described in the assumed relationship. In other words, the m-values propagated from variable 'Role Recognition (RR)' to variable 'Job security (JT)' are given as:

$$m_{JT \leftarrow RR}(yes_{JT}) = 0.5 m_{E1}(yes_{RR}), m_{JT \leftarrow RR}(no_{JT}) = 0.5 m_{E1}(yes_{RR}), \text{ and}$$
$$m_{JT \leftarrow RR}(\{yes_{JT}, no_{JT}\}) = m_{E1}(no_{RR}) + m_{E1}(\{yes_{RR}, yes_{RR}\})$$

For the relationship R2 we assume the following. On average, a person with the knowledge that there is no job security will sign up for job training with 90% belief and a person with the knowledge that there is no problem with the job security will not sign up for job training with 90% belief. This relationship can be modeled in the following way:

m-values for R2:

$$m_{R2}(\{(yes_{JT}, no_{ST}), (no_{JT}, yes_{ST})\}) = 0.9, \text{ and}$$
$$m_{R2}(\{(yes_{JT}, yes_{ST}), (yes_{JT}, no_{ST}), (no_{JT}, yes_{ST}), (no_{JT}, no_{ST})\}) = 0.1.$$

Similar to endnote 9, one can easily show the following m-values to be the result of m-values propagated from variable 'Job Security (JT)' to variable 'Sign up for Job Training (ST)' through the relationship R2:

$$m_{ST \leftarrow JT}(yes_{ST}) = 0.9 m_{JT}(no_{JT}), m_{ST \leftarrow JT}(no_{ST}) = 0.9 m_{JT}(yes_{JT}), \text{ and}$$
$$m_{ST \leftarrow JT}(\{yes_{ST}, no_{ST}\}) = 0.1 + 0.9 m_{JT}(\{yes_{RR}, yes_{RR}\}).$$

We assumed the following m-values for R3 (see Table 4 for the definitions of the symbols):

m-values for R3:

$$m_{R3}(\{(yes_{ST}, yes_{US}), (no_{ST}, no_{US})\}) = 0.75, \text{ and}$$
$$m_{R3}(\{(yes_{ST}, yes_{US}), (yes_{ST}, no_{US}), (no_{ST}, yes_{US}), (no_{ST}, no_{US})\}) = 0.25.$$

The relationship previously discussed implies that if variable 'ST' is 'yes', i.e., a person sings up for training, then variable 'US' will be 'yes', i.e., the person will have the opportunity to use the new skill with 0.75 belief, and the remaining 0.25 belief is assigned to ignorance. Similarly, the relationship implies that if 'ST' is 'no' then 'US' is 'no' with belief 0.75, i.e., if one does not sign up for job training then he/she will not have the use of new skill with belief 0.75. The remaining 0.25 belief represents ignorance.

For the relationship R4, we assume the following m-values:

m-values for R4:

$$m_{R4}(\{(yes_{GS}, yes_{US}), (no_{GS}, no_{US})\}) = 1.0.$$

This relationship implies that if 'GS' is 'yes' then 'US' is 'yes' with 1.0 belief. Also, if 'GS' is 'no' then 'US' is 'no' with 1.0 belief. In other words, if one has the opportunity to gain new skills on the job then there is 1.0 belief that there is opportunity to use the new skills. Similarly, if there is no opportunity to gain new skills on the job then there is no opportunity to use the new skills.

The relationship R5 relates variables 'US', 'FS', 'AW', and 'CW' to the variable 'Job Satisfaction (JS)'. We have assumed the following relative weights, 0.125, 0.125, 0.25, and 0.5, respectively, for 'US', 'FS', 'AW', and 'CW' when propagating information (m-values) to the variable 'JS'.

Step 4 simply represents a diagram with all the variables interconnected through the assumed relationships (see Figure 4). In Step 5, we identify various items of evidence pertaining to different variables and connect them to the corresponding variables. Table 4 provides a list of evidence pertaining to the nine variables in Figure 4. Once these items of evidence are connected to the corresponding variables, we develop the evidential diagram shown in Figure 4 for the analysis.

Propagation of Beliefs through Evidential Diagram

In order to propagate information in terms of m-values from all the variables to the variable of interest, say, 'Job Satisfaction (JS)' in Figure 4, we need to follow the following steps. First, gather all the information (m-values) at 'Role Recognition (RR)', propagate that information (m-values) to variable 'Job Security (JT)' through the relationship R1 by first vacuously extending to the space of R1, combining it with the m-values at R1 using Dempster's rule, and then marginalizing the resulting m-values to the space of 'JT'. Combine this information (m-values) with the m-values at 'JT' obtained from evidence E2.1 and E2.2, again using Dempster's rule. Next step is to propagate the resulting m-values at 'JT' through R2 to the variable 'Sign up for Training to Gain New Skills (ST)'. This is achieved again by vacuously extending the total m-values at 'JT' to the space of R2, combining them with the m-values at R2 using Dempster's rule, and then marginalizing them to the space of variable 'ST'. Combine this information (m-values) with the m-values obtained from evidence E3 for 'ST'. The resulting m-values are then propagated to the variable 'Opportunity to use New Skills (US)'. Combine these m-values with the m-values obtained from the variable 'Opportunity to Gain New Skills on the Job (GS)' and the m-values from evidence E5 for 'US'.

In the final step, we need to propagate all the m-values from the four variables, 'US', 'FS', 'AW', and 'CW' through the relationship R5 to the variable 'Job Satisfaction (JS)' by vacuously extending the respective m-values to the space of R5, combine these m-values with the m-values defining R5 and then marginalize them to the space of 'Job Satisfaction'. The marginalized m-values on 'Job Satisfaction (JS)' can be written as:

$$m_{JS}(yes_{JS}) = 0.125 m_{US}(yes_{US}) + 0.125 m_{FS}(yes_{FS}) + 0.25 m_{AW}(yes_{AW}) + 0.5 m_{CW}(yes_{CW}).$$
$$m_{JS}(no_{JS}) = 0.125 m_{US}(no_{US}) + 0.125 m_{FS}(no_{FS}) + 0.25 m_{AW}(no_{AW}) + 0.5 m_{CW}(no_{CW}).$$
$$m_{JS}(\{yes_{JS}, no_{JS}\}) = 1 - m_{JS}(yes_{JS}) - m_{JS}(no_{JS}).$$

These m-values provide the impact of all the variables in the evidential diagram in Figure 4.

Given that the evidential diagram in Figure 4 is a tree, the propagation of m-values from various variables to the variable of interest, 'Job Satisfaction' is much easier than propagation in a network of variables. We programmed the logic of vacuous extension, marginalization, and Dempster's rule of combination in a spreadsheet program in MS Excel, which then was used to perform various analyses as discussed in the next section.

Decision Analysis of Causal Map Using Belief Functions

In this section, we discuss how one can analyze the impact of one variable on the other variables in the network given in Figure 4. Such an analysis allows the decision maker to isolate an independent variable while holding the rest of the variables in the model constant. In this example, the overall belief in job satisfaction is 0.803 given the inputs from the Survey Results and industry data. The above value implies that based on the subjects responses, on average, employees are satisfied with their jobs in the environment surveyed with 0.803 level of belief. In order to investigate the impact of a number of variables on the level of job satisfaction, we use a range of possible responses (0 to 1.0) for the variables while keeping the inputs from other items of evidence fixed at values obtained from the survey as given in the respective figures.

First, we investigate the impact of 'Job Security' on 'Job Satisfaction'. We vary the input belief from evidence E2.2 for the negation of 'Job Security' from 0 to 1.0, keeping the rest of inputs fixed. As seen in Figure 5, the impact of 'No Job Security' is pretty severe. As the belief in no job security increases the belief in job satisfaction decreases with increasing rate. In other words, if an employee sees strong evidence in support of 'no job security' then he/she will have very low job satisfaction.

The second sensitivity analysis is conducted on the impact of having an opportunity to use new skills on the job. This analysis reveals that the opportunity to use new skills has

Figure 4. Evidential diagram* of the causal map in Figure 3

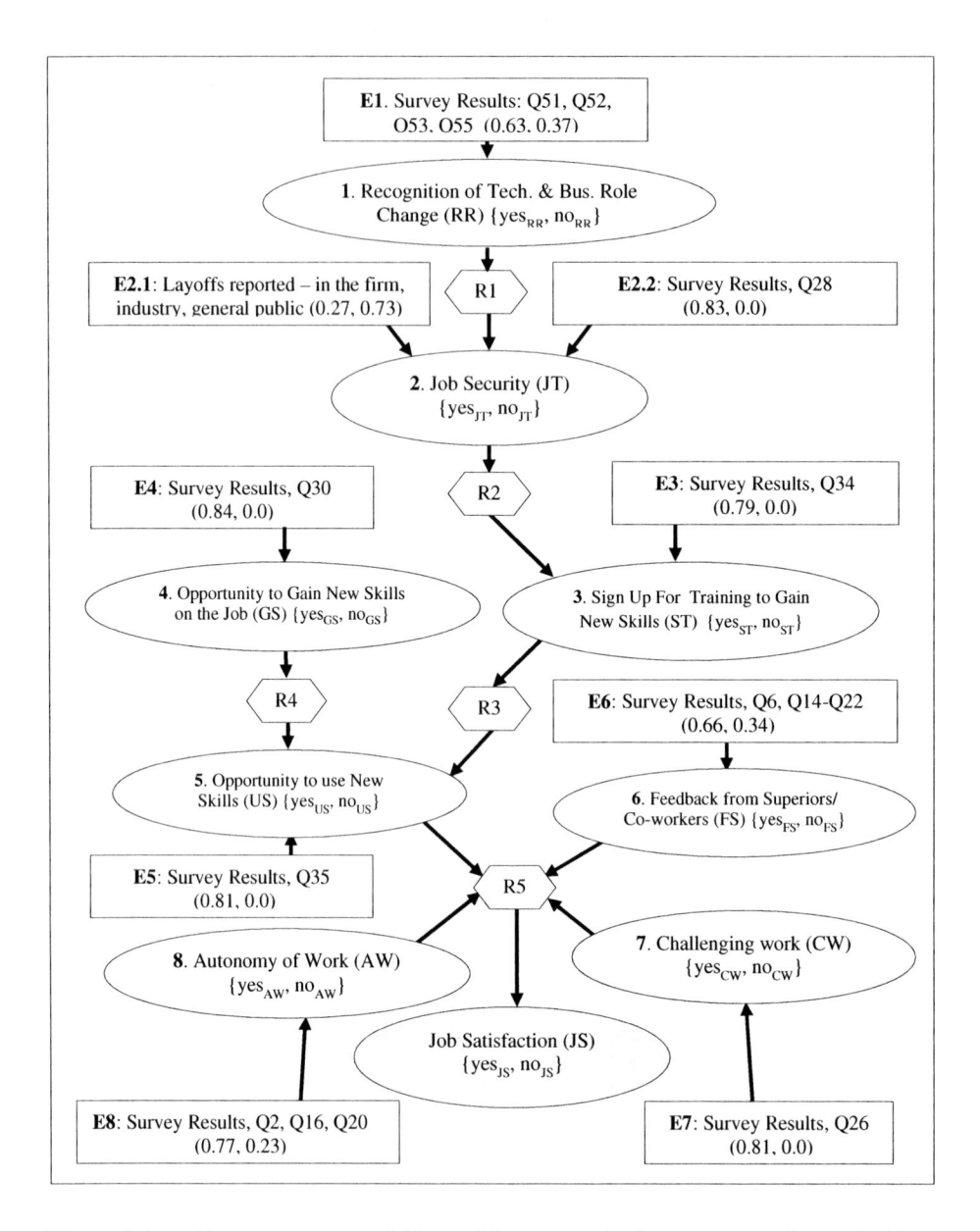

*The oval shaped boxes represent variables and the rectangular boxes represent items of evidence. The numbers in a rectangular box represent the level of support for and against the variable it is connected to. These numbers were determined from the Survey Results except for E2.1 which was determined from the industry data.

Figure 5. Belief in job satisfaction versus belief in no job security*

[Graph: Impact of Belief in 'No' Job Security on Belief in Job Satisfaction. X-axis: Belief in 'No' Job Security (0 to 1). Y-axis: Belief in Job Satisfaction (0.65 to 0.75).]

*The following input m-values in Figure 4 were used for the graph: $m_{E1}(yes_{RR})=0$, $m_{E1}(no_{RR})=0$, $m_{E2.1}(yes_{JT})=0.27$, $m_{E2.1}(no_{JT})=0.73$, $m_{E2.2}(yes_{JT})=0$, $m_{E2.2}(no_{JT})=0$, $m_{E3}(yes_{ST})=0$, $m_{E3}(no_{ST})=0$, $m_{E4}(yes_{GS})=0$, $m_{E4}(no_{GS})=0$, $m_{E5}(yes_{US})$ varied from 0 - 1, $m_{E5}(no_{US})=0$, $m_{E6}(yes_{FS})=0.66$, $m_{E6}(no_{FS})=0.34$, $m_{E7}(yes_{CW})=0.81$, $m_{E7}(no_{CW})=0$, $m_{E8}(yes_{AW})=0.77$, $m_{E8}(no_{AW})=0.23$.

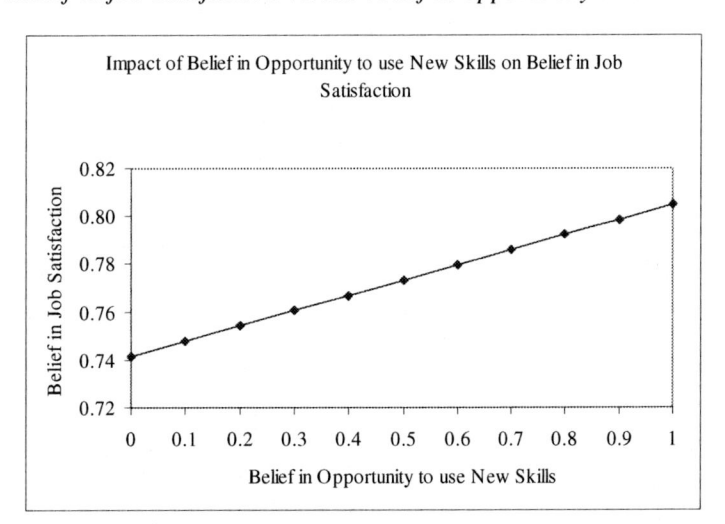

Figure 6. Belief in job satisfaction versus belief in opportunity to use new skills*

[Graph: Impact of Belief in Opportunity to use New Skills on Belief in Job Satisfaction. X-axis: Belief in Opportunity to use New Skills (0 to 1). Y-axis: Belief in Job Satisfaction (0.72 to 0.82).]

*The following input m-values in Figure 4 were used for the graph: $m_{E1}(yes_{RR})=0$, $m_{E1}(no_{RR})=0$, $m_{E2.1}(yes_{JT})=0.27$, $m_{E2.1}(no_{JT})=0.73$, $m_{E2.2}(yes_{JT})=0$, $m_{E2.2}(no_{JT})=0$, $m_{E3}(yes_{ST})=0$, $m_{E3}(no_{ST})=0$, $m_{E4}(yes_{GS})=0$, $m_{E4}(no_{GS})=0$, $m_{E5}(yes_{US})$ varied from 0 - 1, $m_{E5}(no_{US})=0$, $m_{E6}(yes_{FS})=0.66$, $m_{E6}(no_{FS})=0.34$, $m_{E7}(yes_{CW})=0.81$, $m_{E7}(no_{CW})=0$, $m_{E8}(yes_{AW})=0.77$, $m_{E8}(no_{AW})=0.23$.

a significant positive impact on 'Job Satisfaction' as seen from Figure 6. As the belief in opportunity to use new skills increases, the belief in job satisfaction increases. We find an 8.5% increase in job satisfaction over the range from 0 – 1.0 for belief in opportunity to use new skills. This impact is linear, unlike the previous case.

The third variable analyzed is 'Feedback from Supervisors/Co-workers'. As shown in Figure 7, the results demonstrate a substantial positive impact of feedback on the job satisfaction. In particular, job satisfaction increases about 19% as we progress from the lower to higher levels of perceived feedback. It is obvious that feedback is a powerful variable in predicting job satisfaction.

Next, we conduct a sensitivity analysis with the independent variable, 'Challenging Work'. 'Job Satisfaction' was extremely sensitive to increases in the perceived level of challenging work. From no belief that the job is challenging to the higher range of belief, 1.0, the model indicates that the belief in job satisfaction moves from 0.388 to 0.838; a 129% increase as seen in Figure 8. These results indicate that challenging work is the most powerful variable in the model in the prediction of job satisfaction.

Finally, a sensitivity analysis was conducted on 'Autonomy of Work'. The results indicate that 'Autonomy of Work' has a significant impact on the dependent variable, 'Job Satisfaction'. Job satisfaction was found to be very sensitive to autonomy. As the perceived autonomy increases from 0 to 1.0, job satisfaction improves from 60% to 85%, an increase of 41.6%. These results are presented in Figure 9.

These sensitivity analyses have shown the impact on job satisfaction from a broad range of variables and their corresponding beliefs. However, we do want to point out that the

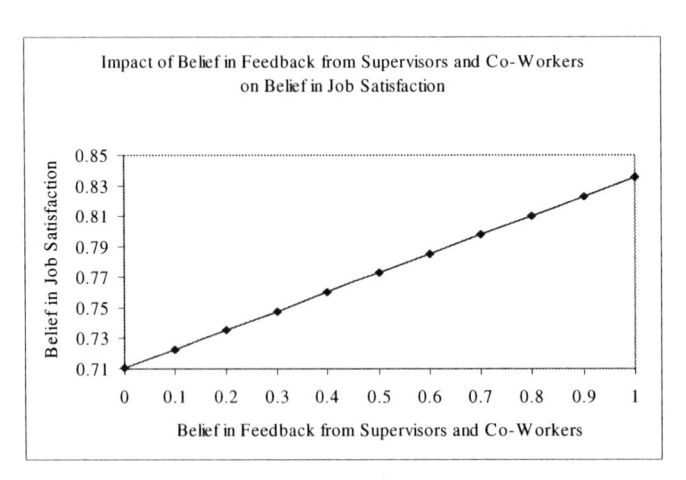

Figure 7. Belief in job satisfaction versus belief in feedback from supervisors and co-workers*

*The following input m-values in Figure 4 were used for the graph: $m_{E1}(yes_{RR})=0$, $m_{E1}(no_{RR})=0$, $m_{E2.1}(yes_{JT})=0.27$, $m_{E2.1}(no_{JT})=0.73$, $m_{E2.2}(yes_{JT})=0$, $m_{E2.2}(no_{JT})=0$, $m_{E3}(yes_{ST})=0$, $m_{E3}(no_{ST})=0$, $m_{E4}(yes_{GS})=0$, $m_{E4}(no_{GS})=0$, $m_{E5}(yes_{US})=0.81$, $m_{E5}(no_{US})=0$, $m_{E6}(yes_{FS})$ varied from 0 - 1, $m_{E6}(no_{FS})=0$, $m_{E7}(yes_{CW})=0.81$, $m_{E7}(no_{CW})=0$, $m_{E8}(yes_{AW})=0.77$, $m_{E8}(no_{AW})=0.23$.

Figure 8. Belief in job satisfaction versus belief in challenging work*

[Graph: Impact of Belief in Challenging Work on Belief in Job Satisfaction. X-axis: Belief in Challenging Work (0 to 1). Y-axis: Belief in Job Satisfaction (0.30 to 0.90).]

*The following input m-values in Figure 4 were used for the graph: $m_{E1}(yes_{RR})=0$, $m_{E1}(no_{RR})=0$, $m_{E2.1}(yes_{JT})=0.27$, $m_{E2.1}(no_{JT})=0.73$, $m_{E2.2}(yes_{JT})=0$, $m_{E2.2}(no_{JT})=0$, $m_{E3}(yes_{ST})=0$, $m_{E3}(no_{ST})=0$, $m_{E4}(yes_{GS})=0$, $m_{E4}(no_{GS})=0$, $m_{E5}(yes_{US})=0.81$, $m_{E5}(no_{US})=0$, $m_{E6}(yes_{FS})=0.66$, $m_{E6}(no_{FS})=0.34$, $m_{E7}(yes_{CW})$ *varied from 0 - 1,* $m_{E7}(no_{CW})=0$, $m_{E8}(yes_{AW})=0.77$, $m_{E8}(no_{AW})=0.23$.

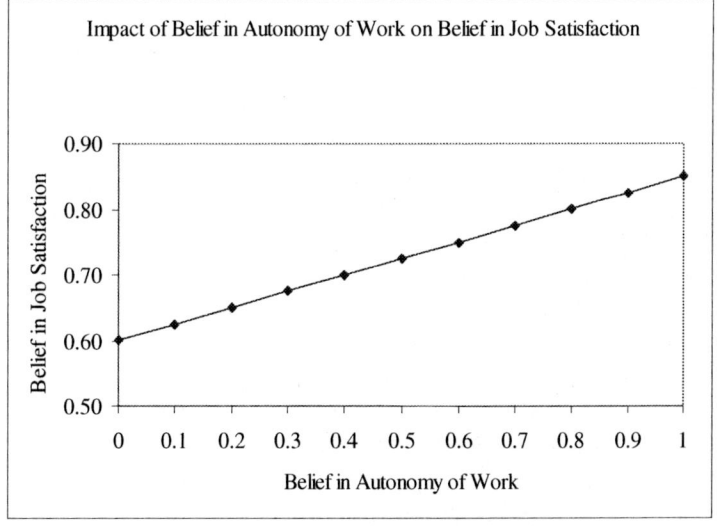

Figure 9. Belief in job satisfaction versus belief in autonomy of work*

[Graph: Impact of Belief in Autonomy of Work on Belief in Job Satisfaction. X-axis: Belief in Autonomy of Work (0 to 1). Y-axis: Belief in Job Satisfaction (0.50 to 0.90).]

*The following input m-values in Figure 4 were used for the graph: $m_{E1}(yes_{RR})=0$, $m_{E1}(no_{RR})=0$, $m_{E2.1}(yes_{JT})=0.27$, $m_{E2.1}(no_{JT})=0.73$, $m_{E2.2}(yes_{JT})=0$, $m_{E2.2}(no_{JT})=0$, $m_{E3}(yes_{ST})=0$, $m_{E3}(no_{ST})=0$, $m_{E4}(yes_{GS})=0$, $m_{E4}(no_{GS})=0$, $m_{E5}(yes_{US})=0.81$, $m_{E5}(no_{US})=0$, $m_{E6}(yes_{FS})=0.66$, $m_{E6}(no_{FS})=0.34$, $m_{E7}(yes_{CW})=0.81$, $m_{E7}(no_{CW})=0$, $m_{E8}(yes_{AW})$ *varied from 0 - 1,* $m_{E8}(no_{AW})=0$.

interrelationships among the intermediate variables and the relative weights assigned to 'Opportunity to use New Skills', 'Feedback from Supervisors and Co-Workers, 'Challenging Work', and 'Autonomy of Work', have direct impact on the results for the dependent variable, 'Job Satisfaction'.

In summary, the above analysis provides an example of how an evidential reasoning approach under Dempster-Shafer theory of belief functions can be used to determine the impact on a given construct or constructs of other constructs in a revealed causal map. It should be noted that a revealed causal map of a decision problem is only a static model while an evidential diagram of a revealed causal map provides a dynamic model for analyzing the behaviors of various constructs under different conditions.

Conclusions and Future Directions for Research

In this chapter we have demonstrated the use of evidential reasoning approach under Dempster-Shafer (D-S) theory of belief functions to analyze revealed causal maps. As an example, we used a simplified causal map obtained through a Revealed Causal Mapping (RCM) technique where the participants were from information technology (IT) organizations who provided the concepts to describe the target phenomenon of 'Job Satisfaction'. They also identified the associations between the concepts. After creating the causal map of the problem being investigated, we developed an evidential diagram. This diagram consists of the variables or constructs of the causal map, interconnected to the other variables with some relationships. These relationships were defined by the decision maker based on experience. Various items of evidence were identified that pertained to different variables. Estimates of the beliefs in terms of m-values in support of, or negation of, the variables were made for each item of evidence using survey questions (Buche, 2003, particularly Appendix C). These m-values were then propagated through the evidential network to obtain the overall belief of 'Job Satisfaction'.

To illustrate the usefulness of the evidential reasoning approach under Dempster-Shafer theory of belief functions, we performed various sensitivity analyses to determine the impact of different variables on 'Job Satisfaction'. This technique enables researchers to predict the level of job satisfaction when given evidence for the other variables in the model. As further validation for our findings, our results are directly in line with previous literature on job satisfaction for workers in general. IT personnel are very similar to other professions and vocations. An evidential diagram similar to the one discussed here would be useful in predicting whether a specific work environment would be more or less satisfactory to an employee before joining the job.

In this chapter we have explained the steps necessary to convert revealed causal maps into evidential diagrams. The analysis of the transformed diagram is useful in forming predictions about human behavior. This technique incorporates the existence of uncertainty in the level of belief associated with the evidence. Therefore, the researcher is able to include in the diagram personal intuition and confidence based on direct experience. Another advantage of the evidential reasoning approach over a revealed causal map is that the former provides a dynamic model of a decision problem while the later provides only a static model. As a limitation, the evidential reasoning approach may become quite complex especially when variables or constructs in the diagram are highly integrated. For ease of instruction, the example discussed herein was fairly simplistic, with primarily linear associations.

References

Ang, S., & Slaughter, S.A. (2001). Work outcomes and job design for contract versus permanent information systems professionals on software development teams. *MIS Quarterly, 25,* 321-350.

Axelrod, R. (1976). *Structure of decisions: The cognitive maps of political elites.* Princeton, NJ: Princeton University Press.

Bougon, M.G., Weick, K., & Binkhorst, D. (1977). Cognition in organizations: An analysis of the Utrecht Jazz Orchestra. *Administrative Science Quarterly,* 22, 606-639.

Bovee, M, Srivastava, R. P., & Mak, B. (2003, January). A conceptual framework and belief-function approach to assessing overall information quality. *International Journal of Intelligent Systems,* 18(1), 51-74.

Buche, M.W. (2003). *IT professional work identity: Constructs and outcomes.* Unpublished dissertation, University of Kansas, Lawrence, KS.

Carley, K. (1997). Extracting team mental models through textural analysis. *Journal of Organizational Behavior,* 18, 533-558.

Curley, S. P., & Golden, J.I. (1994). Using belief functions to represent degrees of belief. *Organization Behavior and Human Decision Processes,* 271-303.

Darais, K.M., Nelson, K.M., Rice, S.C., & Buche, M.W. (2003). Identifying the enablers and barriers of IT personnel transition. In C. Shayo & M. Igbaria (Eds.), *Strategies for managing IS/IT personnel* (pp. 92-112). Hershey, PA: Idea Group.

Gupta, Y.P., Guimaraes, T., & Raghunathan, T.S. (1992). Attitudes and intentions of information center personnel. *Information & Management, 22,* 151-160.

Hackman, J.R., & Oldham, G. (1976). Motivation through the design of work: Test of a theory. *Organizational Behavior and Human Performance, 16,* 250-279.

Harrison, K., Srivastava, R.P., & Plumlee, R.D. (2002). Auditors' Evaluations of Uncertain Audit Evidence: Belief Functions versus Probabilities. In R. P. Srivastava & T. Mock (Eds.), *Belief functions in business decisions,* (pp. 161-183). Heidelberg: Springer-Verlag.

Huff, A.S. (1990). *Mapping strategic thought.* Chichester, UK: Wiley.

Igbaria, M., & Guimaraes, R. (1993). Antecedents and consequences of job satisfaction among information center employees. *Journal of Management Information Systems, 9,* 145-174.

Markoczy, L., & Goldberg, J. (1995). A method for eliciting and comparing causal maps. *Journal of Management, 21,* 305-333.

Nadkarni, S., & Shenoy, P.P. (2001). A Bayesian Network approach to making inferences in causal maps. *European Journal of Operational Research, 128,* 479-498.

Narayanan, V.K., & Fahey, L. (1990). Evolution of revealed causal maps during decline: A case study of Admiral. In A. Huff (Ed.). *Mapping strategic thought* (pp. 109-133). London: John Wiley & Sons.

Nelson, K.M. (2000). *IT personnel transition and organization transition strategy.* National Science Foundation Grant.

Nelson, K.M., Nadkarni, S., Narayanan, V.K., & Ghods, M. (2000). Understanding software operations support expertise: A causal mapping approach. *MIS Quarterly, 24,* 475-507.

Pearl, J. (1990). Bayesian and belief-functions formalism for evidential reasoning: a conceptual analysis. In *Readings in uncertain reasoning* (pp. 540-574). San Mateo, CA: Morgan Kaufmann.

Radding, A. (1997). Rock-solid incentives. *Network World, 14,* 31-34.

Saffiotti, A., & Umkehrer, E. (1991). Pulcinella: A general tool for propagating uncertainty in valuation networks. *Proceedings of the Seventh National Conference on Artificial Intelligence* (pp. 323-331), University of California, Los Angeles.

Shafer, G. (1976). *A mathematical theory of evidence.* Princeton University Press.

Shafer, G., Shenoy, P.P., & Srivastava, R.P. (1988, May). Auditor's Assistant: A knowledge engineering tool for audit decisions. *Proceedings of the 1988 Touche Ross/University of Kansas Symposium on Auditing Problems* (pp. 61-79).

Shafer, G., & Srivastava, R.P. (1990). The Bayesian and belief-function formalisms: A general perspective for auditing. *Auditing: A Journal of Practice and Theory,* (Supplement), 110-148.

Shenoy, P.P. (1991). Valuation-based system for discrete optimization. In P.P. Bonissone, M. Henrion, L. N. Kanal, and J. Lemmer (Eds.), *Uncertainty in artificial intelligence,* (Vol. 6, pp. 385-400). Amsterdam: North-Holland.,

Shenoy, P.P., & Shafer, G. (1990). Axioms for probability and belief-function propagation. In *Uncertainty in artificial intelligence.* Elsevier Science Publishers.

Smets, P. (1998). The transferable belief model for quantified belief representation. In P. Smets (Ed.), *Quantified representation for uncertainty and imprecision,* (Vol. 1). Kluwer Academic Publishers.

Smets, P. (1990a, May). The combination of evidence in the transferable belief model. *IEEE Transactions on Pattern Analysis and Machine Intelligence, 12,* 5.

Smets, P. (1990b). Constructing the pignistic probability function in a context of uncertainty. In M. Henrion, R.D. Shachter, L.N. Kanal & J F. Lemmer (Eds.), *Uncertainty in artificial intelligence 5*. North-Holland: Elsevier Science Publishers B.V.

Srivastava, R.P. (1995, March). The belief-function approach to aggregating audit evidence. *International Journal of Intelligent Systems,* 10(3), 329-356.

Srivastava, R.P. (1993, Fall). Belief functions and audit decisions. *Auditors Report,* 17(1), 8-12.

Srivastava, R.P., & Datta, D. (2002). Belief-function approach to evidential reasoning for acquisition and merger decisions. In R. P. Srivastava & T. Mock (Eds.), *Belief functions in business decisions* (pp. 220-248). Heidelberg: Springer-Verlag.

Srivastava, R.P., & Liu, L. (2003). Applications of belief functions in business decisions: A review. *Information Systems Frontiers* (forthcoming).

Srivastava, R.P., & Lu, H. (2002, October). Structural analysis of audit evidence using belief functions. *Fuzzy Sets and Systems,* 131(1), 107-120.

Srivastava, R.P., & Mock, T.J. (2002). *Belief functions in business decisions*. Heidelberg: Springer-Verlag.

Srivastava, R.P., & Mock, T.J. (2000, Winter). Evidential reasoning for Webtrust assurance services. *Journal of Management Information Systems,* 10(3), 11-32.

Strat, T.M. (1984). Continuous Belief functions for evidential reasoning. *Proceedings of the National Conference on Artificial Intelligence*, Austin, Texas (pp. 308-313).

Thatcher, J.B., Stepina, L.P., & Boyle, R.J. (2002-2003). Turnover of information technology workers: Examining empirically the influence of attitudes, job characteristics, and external markets. *Journal of Management Information Systems,* 19, 231-261.

Wrightson, M.T. (1976). Coding rules. In R. Axelrod (Ed.), *Structure of decisions: The cognitive maps of political elites* (pp. 291-332). Princeton, NJ: Princeton University Press.

Zarley, D. Y. T., & Shafer, G. (1988). Evidential Reasoning using DELIEF. *Proceedings of the National Conference of Artificial Intelligence.*

Endnotes

[1] See the following references for more discussion on belief functions and their applications: Bovee et al. (2003), Srivastava (1993), Srivastava and Datta (2002), Srivastava and Liu (2003), and Srivastava and Mock (2000).

[2] For three independent items of evidence, Dempster's rules can be written as:

$$m(B) = K^{-1} \cdot \sum_{\substack{i,j,k \\ B_i \cap B_j \cap B_k = B}} m_1(B_i) m_2(B_j) m_3(B_k), \text{ where } K = 1 - \sum_{\substack{i,j,k \\ B_i \cap B_j \cap B_k = \varnothing}} m_1(B_i) m_2(B_j) m_3(B_k).$$

One can easily generalize the above formula for n independent items of evidence (see Shafer, 1976, for details).

[3] The argument of m-function represents the state for which the value is assigned and the subscript describes the evidence from which the value is derived. For example, $m_X(x) = 0.6$ represents 0.6 level of support for 'x' from an item of evidence pertaining to the variable X.

[4] Propagation is the process by which m-values on a variable or a set of variables are moved (mapped) to another variable or a set of variables. For example, m-values from variable X in Figure 1 can be propagated to the relational variable 'AND' that consist of three variables, X, Y, and Z.

[5] Vacuous extension is the process through which m-values on a smaller frame are extended to a larger frame. For example, m(x) when vacuously extended to the joint space of X and Y, i.e., the frame {xy, x~y, ~xy, ~x~y}, yields m(x) = m({xy, x~y}).

[6] Marginalization of m-values is opposite to the vacuous extension. This process is similar to marginalization in probability theory; it involves eliminating all the unwanted variables by summing the m-values over the unwanted variables. For example, assume that we have the following m-values on the joint space of X and Y, $\Theta_{X,Y}$ = {xy, x~y, ~xy, ~x~y}: m({xy}) = 0.1, m({xy, x~y}) = 0.6, and m({xy, x~y, ~xy, ~x~y}) = 0.3. The marginalized m-values onto the space of X variable are: m({x}) = 0.1 + 0.6 = 0.7, and m({x, ~x}) = 0.3. Similarly, the marginalized m-values onto the Y space are: m({y}) = 0.1, m({y, ~y}) = 0.9.

[7] Through this example we are illustrating the details of the propagation process of beliefs or m-values through a tree of variables as this is what is needed in our model of IT job satisfaction obtained through the RCM process. A discussion on the details of the propagation of beliefs through a network of variables is beyond the scope of this chapter. Interested readers should see Srivastava (1995) and Shenoy and Shafer (1990) for this kind of propagation.

[8] A Markov tree is characterized by a set of nodes N and a set of edges E where each edge is a two-element subset of N such that (Srivastava, 1995; see also, Shenoy, 1991):

- (N,E) is a tree.

- If N and N' are two distinct nodes in N, and {N, N'} is an edge, i.e., $\{N,N'\} \in E$, then N∩N' ≠ ∅.

- If N and N' are distinct nodes of N, and X is a variable in both N and N', then X is in every node on the path from N to N'.

9   As described in Section IV, in order to propagate m-values from 'RR' to 'JT' through the relationship R1, one needs to vacuously extend the m-values from the space of 'RR', $\{yes_{RR}, no_{RR}\}$, to the space of R1, which is the joint space of 'RR' and 'JT', i.e., $\{(yes_{RR}, yes_{JT}), (yes_{RR}, no_{JT}), (no_{RR}, yes_{JT}), (no_{RR}, no_{JT})\}$, combine the m-values at R1, and then marginalize to the space of 'JT', $\{yes_{JT}, no_{JT}\}$.

10   This semi-structured interview guide was also part of NSF grant proposal and Transition Study research project (Nelson, 2000; Buche, 2003).

Appendix A: Concept Dictionary with Examples

Construct	Description	Example
Role not valued	Company no longer needs certain skill sets to support certain roles.	Generalists such as myself…don't see that role being valued much.
Role change	Expectations of workers experience transition.	I got into the analyst role, being the leader and doing the coordination.
Fear of job loss	Lack of job security.	Anyone would be worried about their career.
Sign up for training	Training is provided by a company for workers to develop new skills.	We just look at the classes, sign up for them.
Opportunity to gain new skills	Workers are taught new skills in classroom or self-paced training.	Once you learn programming, and you have that skill.
Opportunity to use new skills	The job environment provides the opportunities for workers to practice the skills learned during training.	Using new skills to make the company more competitive.
Feedback form superiors and co-workers	Direct reaction obtained from supervisors and co-workers that reduces ambiguity about perceived performance.	The users let me know if the system meets their needs.
Challenging projects	Work assignments provide an intrinsic motivation because the problem-solving aspect takes effort.	Technical challenges of the job.
Autonomy of Work	Workers have freedom and independence in determining relevant job-related decisions.	Nobody really tells me what to do or how to do it.
Job satisfaction	Affective response to the current job environment.	Pleasant work environment.

Appendix B: Interview Protocol[10]

1. What motivates you to come to work here every day?
2. What is the best thing about your current work environment?
3. What is the worst thing about your current work environment?
4. What is the most important thing you contribute to this organization?
5. What could you contribute to your organization that you currently are unable to contribute?
6. What barriers keep you from making this contribution?
7. Where do you realistically see yourself professionally in five years?
8. Where would you ideally like to see yourself professionally in five years?
9. What barriers might keep you from your ideal situation?
10. How much do you like change?
11. How much do you think the IT field, in general, is changing?
12. How much do you think the IT field at your company is changing?
13. How do you feel about this level of change?
14. How is your organization supporting you in personally making these changes?
15. What barriers do you see in making these changes?
16. What is your primary, one year professional goal?
17. How can your organization help you achieve you goals?
18. In summary, how do you see yourself fitting into the organization's "big picture"?
19. Would you like to add any further comments or observations?

Appendix C: Propagation Illustration in Figure 1

In this appendix we describe in detail the three steps involved in the propagation of m-values from variables X and Y in Figure 1 to variable Z.

Step 1: Propagation of m-values from X and Y to 'AND' node:

In order to propagate m-values from variable X, a smaller node with one variable and the frame $\Theta_X = \{x, \sim x\}$, to the 'AND' node, a larger node consisting of three variable X, Y, and

Z with the frame $\Theta_{AND} = \{xyz, x\sim y\sim z, \sim xy\sim z, \sim x\sim y\sim z\}$, we vacuously extend the m-values at X to the space $\{xyz, x\sim y\sim z, \sim xy\sim z, \sim x\sim y\sim z\}$ defined by the 'AND' node. This process yields the following non-zero m-values from X to the 'AND' node:

$$m_{AND \leftarrow X}(\{xyz, x\sim y\sim z\}) = m_X(x) = 0.6,$$
$$m_{AND \leftarrow X}(\{\sim xy\sim z, \sim x\sim y\sim z\}) = m_X(\sim x) = 0.2,$$
$$m_{AND \leftarrow X}(\{xyz, x\sim y\sim z, \sim xy\sim z, \sim x\sim y\sim z\}) = m_X(\{x, \sim x\}) = 0.2.$$

Similarly, we obtain the following non-zero m-values at the 'AND' node when the m-values from Y are propagated to the 'AND' node:

$$m_{AND \leftarrow Y}(\{xyz, \sim xy\sim z\}) = m_Y(y) = 0.7$$
$$m_{AND \leftarrow Y}(\{xyz, x\sim y\sim z, \sim xy\sim z, \sim x\sim y\sim z\}) = m_Y(\{y, \sim y\}) = 0.3$$

Step 2: Combine m-values from X and Y with the m-values at 'AND'

We have the following set of m-values at the 'AND' node; one from X, one from Y, and one at the 'AND' node defining the relationship.

m-values from X:

$$m_{AND \leftarrow X}(\{xyz, x\sim y\sim z\}) = 0.6, m_{AND \leftarrow X}(\{\sim xy\sim z, \sim x\sim y\sim z\}) = 0.2, \text{ and}$$
$$m_{AND \leftarrow X}(\{xyz, x\sim y\sim z, \sim xy\sim z, \sim x\sim y\sim z\}) = 0.2.$$

m-values from Y:

$$m_{AND \leftarrow Y}(\{xyz, \sim xy\sim z\}) = 0.7,$$
$$m_{AND \leftarrow Y}(\{xyz, x\sim y\sim z, \sim xy\sim z, \sim x\sim y\sim z\}) = 0.3.$$

m-values at the 'AND' node:

$$m_{AND}(\{xyz, x\sim y\sim z, \sim xy\sim z, \sim x\sim y\sim z\}) = 1.0.$$

After we combine the above m-values using Dempster's rule, we obtain the following m-values:

$$m(\{xyz\}) = m_{AND \leftarrow X}(\{xyz, x\sim y\sim z\}).m_{AND \leftarrow Y}(\{xyz, \sim xy\sim z\}).$$
$$m_{AND}(\{xyz, x\sim y\sim z, \sim xy\sim z, \sim x\sim y\sim z\}) = 0.6 \times 0.7 \times 1.0 = 0.42,$$
$$m(\{xyz, x\sim y\sim z\}) = m_{AND \leftarrow X}(\{xyz, x\sim y\sim z\}).$$
$$m_{AND \leftarrow Y}(\{xyz, x\sim y\sim z, \sim xy\sim z, \sim x\sim y\sim z\}).m_{AND}(\{xyz, x\sim y\sim z, \sim xy\sim z, \sim x\sim y\sim z\})$$
$$= 0.6 \times 0.3 \times 1.0 = 0.18,$$
$$m(\{\sim xy\sim z\}) = m_{AND \leftarrow X}(\{\sim xy\sim z, \sim x\sim y\sim z\}).m_{AND \leftarrow Y}(\{xyz, \sim xy\sim z\}).$$
$$m_{AND}(\{xyz, x\sim y\sim z, \sim xy\sim z, \sim x\sim y\sim z\})$$
$$0.2 \times 0.7 \times 1.0 = 0.14,$$
$$m(\{\sim xy\sim z, \sim x\sim y\sim z\}) = m_{AND \leftarrow X}(\{\sim xy\sim z, \sim x\sim y\sim z\}).$$
$$m_{AND \leftarrow Y}(\{xyz, x\sim y\sim z, \sim xy\sim z, \sim x\sim y\sim z\}).$$
$$m_{AND}(\{xyz, x\sim y\sim z, \sim xy\sim z, \sim x\sim y\sim z\}) = 0.2 \times 0.3 \times 1.0 = 0.06,$$
$$m(\{xyz, \sim xy\sim z\}) = m_{AND \leftarrow X}(\{xyz, x\sim y\sim z, \sim xy\sim z, \sim x\sim y\sim z\}).$$
$$m_{AND \leftarrow Y}(\{xyz, \sim xy\sim z\}).m_{AND}(\{xyz, x\sim y\sim z, \sim xy\sim z, \sim x\sim y\sim z\}) = 0.2 \times 0.7 \times 1.0 = 0.14,$$
$$m(\{xyz, x\sim y\sim z, \sim xy\sim z, \sim x\sim y\sim z\})$$
$$= m_{AND \leftarrow X}(\{xyz, x\sim y\sim z, \sim xy\sim z, \sim x\sim y\sim z\}).$$
$$m_{AND \leftarrow Y}(\{xyz, x\sim y\sim z, \sim xy\sim z, \sim x\sim y\sim z\}).$$
$$m_{AND}(\{xyz, x\sim y\sim z, \sim xy\sim z, \sim x\sim y\sim z\}) = 0.2 \times 0.3 \times 1.0 = 0.06.$$

The above m-values are propagated to variable Z by marginalizing them to Z as described next.

Step 3: Propagate m-values from 'AND' node to Z

The third step deals with propagating beliefs or m-values from 'AND' node to variable Z. Since the "AND' is a bigger node consisting of three variables, X, Y, and Z, the m-values have to be marginalized to variable Z. As discussed in endnote 6, marginalization of belief functions or m-values is similar to marginalization of probabilities. The unwanted variables are eliminated by summing the m-values over the variables. We obtain the following m-values on variable Z as a result of propagation of m-values from X and Y through the relationship 'AND' by marginalization of m-values at the 'AND' node:

$$m_{Z \leftarrow AND}(\{z\}) = m(\{xyz\}) = 0.42,$$
$$m_{Z \leftarrow AND}(\{\sim z\}) = m(\{\sim xy\sim z\}) + m(\{\sim xy\sim z, \sim x\sim y\sim z\}) = 0.14 + 0.06 = 0.20,$$
$$m_{Z \leftarrow AND}(\{z, \sim z\}) = m(\{xyz, x\sim y\sim z\}) + m(\{xyz, \sim xy\sim z\}) + m(\{xyz, x\sim y\sim z, \sim xy\sim z, \sim x\sim y\sim z\})$$
$$= 0.18 + 0.14 + 0.06 = 0.38.$$

This completes the process. We now know that belief that Z is true is 0.42 (i.e., Bel(z) = 0.42), given that we know that X is true with belief 0.6 and Y is true with belief 0.7. Similarly, we know that Z is not true with belief 0.20, i.e., Bel(~z) = 0.20, given the knowledge about X and Y expressed in terms of the following m-values: $m_X(x) = 0.6$, $m_X(\sim x) = 0.2$, $m_X(\{x, \sim x\}) = 0.2$, and $m_Y(y) = 0.7$, $m_Y(\sim y) = 0$, $m_Y(\{y, \sim y\}) = 0.3$.

Chapter VI

An Empirical Comparison of Collective Causal Mapping Approaches

Huy V. Vo
Ho Chi Minh City University of Technology, Vietnam

Marshall Scott Poole
Texas A&M University, USA

James F. Courtney
University of Central Florida, USA

Abstract

Recently, capturing and evaluating group causal maps has come to attention of IS researchers (Tegarden and Sheetz, 2003; Lee, Courtney & O'Keefe, 1992; Vennix, 1996; Kwahk and Kim, 1999). This chapter summarizes two studies that formally compare three approaches to building collective maps: aggregate mapping, congregate mapping, and workshop mapping. We first provide a conceptual comparison of the three methods. Then we empirically compare models derived with the three methods using both objective and subjective measures. The results suggest that the aggregate method performs best at the group level, whereas the congregate method performs best at the organizational level. The results also indicate that the workshop method was best

Copyright © 2005, Idea Group Inc. Copying or distributing in print or electronic forms without written permission of Idea Group Inc. is prohibited.

at promoting knowledge sharing. These studies suggest that the workshop method can be used in combination with aggregate mapping or congregate mapping methods to improve the collective mapping process.

Introduction

Research on causal mapping has been an active area in information systems (IS) research. Causal mapping has been applied in information systems requirements analysis (Montazemi and Conrath, 1986) and for planning network services (Dutta, 2001). Boland, Tenkasi & Teeni (1994) argue that causal mapping can be used to capture subjects' perspectives for use in decision making, system design, and other activities. Several information systems have been designed to support causal mapping (Eden, 1989; Zhang, Wang & King, 1994; Boland, Tenkasi & Teeni, 1994; Kwahk and Kim, 1999; Hong and Han, 2002). Sheetz, Tegarden, Kozar & Zigurs (1994) proposed a group support system as an aid in uncovering causal maps of users.

Developing and evaluating group or collective causal maps has been the subject of several recent IS studies (Tegarden and Sheetz, 2003; Lee, Courtney & O'Keefe, 1992; Vennix, 1996; Kwahk and Kim, 1999). Ackerman, Eden & Williams (1997), Massey and Wallace (1996) and Vennix (1996) have maintained that collective maps can be used to broaden problem solvers' perspectives by taking alternative views into account in the definition of a messy problem situation. In their view collective maps can be viewed as a means to access multiple perspectives for problems with no definitive formulation. This is a particularly important application, because several researchers (Checkland, 1981; Courtney, 2001; Linstone, 1984; Mitroff and Linstone, 1993; Senge, 1990) have proposed that systems-based multiple perspective approaches are required to deal with problems in organizations and society today. Different perspectives are assumed to hold different models, and it is through the juxtaposition and combination of models that perspectives can be mediated. To gain the precision necessary to compare, contrast, and combine multiple perspectives, it is necessary to build models of the situation. However, it is by no means straightforward to develop group or collective maps. Tegarden and Sheetz (2003) found that merging causal maps of individuals into a collective causal map has been problematic and argued that the creation of collective causal maps is impractical for many organizational situations.

The research reported in this chapter focuses on the use of modeling to mediate multiple perspectives on problems through the development of group causal maps. We focus on the comparison of existing modeling approaches that are capable of representing multiple perspectives through collective maps. Our research questions are: What approaches are available to formulate collective causal maps based on multiple perspectives? Are some approaches superior to others?

This chapter has three objectives. First, it discusses and compares at a conceptual level three methods of constructing collective causal maps. These three approaches represent fundamental distinctions in methods of collective causal mapping and each has some track record of success. Second, it reports the results of two studies conducted to compare the three methods in terms of various criteria. The criteria include objective measures such as map complexity, density, and map distance ratio and subjective measures such as user perceptions of the adequacy of problem representation, solution implications, stakeholder implications, and degree to which the collective maps capture different perspectives. These studies test two hypotheses regarding map complexity and the perceived utility of collective maps for the aggregate, congregate, and workshop mapping procedures. The results of these studies should help illuminate the relative strengths and weaknesses of the different approaches to building collective causal maps and suggest guidelines for selecting the best procedure to fit the modeler's situation.

This chapter starts with a conceptual comparison of three methods for constructing collective maps. We then detail a research design for two studies that compare the three methods. In Study 1 we built collective causal maps to facilitate problem formulation for a sales problem in a Vietnamese company and in Study 2 we built collective maps to support the development of a research model of the impacts of infrastructure and infrastructure projects on a large urban area. In each study we empirically compare models derived with the three methods on both objective and subjective measures.

Methods for Constructing a Collective Map/Model

A map is an aggregation of "interrelated information" (O'Keefe and Nadel, 1978). Maps help represent people's perceptions about their environments (Weick and Bougon, 1986). A causal map consists of nodes and links (or arrows) that one may use to understand a situation (Axelrod, 1976). Nodes stand for factors, labels, concepts, or variables. Links represent relationships or associations. If causal relationships are used, the maps are called causal maps. Most researchers (Eden, Jones & Sims, 1981; Hart, 1977) do not differentiate causal maps from cognitive maps. However, Weick and Bougon (1986) believe that the concept of a cognitive map is broader than a causal map as the former may have other relationships than causal—such as "contiguity, proximity, resemblance, and implication." For consistency, we use the term causal map throughout the chapter.

Causal maps were originally devised to elicit mental models for individuals (Axelrod, 1976; Eden, 1989). A number of researchers (Landfield-Smith, 1992; Bougon, 1992; Weick and Bougon, 1986; Schneider and Andgelmar, 1993; Nicolini, 1999; Laukkanen, 1994; Lant and Shapira, 2001) have extended the application of the concept to a group, collective or organization. Three common methods found in the literature for constructing collective mental models are aggregate mapping, congregate mapping, and workshop mapping. A conceptual comparison of these approaches is provided in Table 1.

In the *aggregate mapping approach*, the focus is on representing all individual maps as fully as possible in the collective map. All labels and links from each individual causal map are included in the collective map. As a result, the aggregate map may become quite complex. The aggregate approach does not emphasize the causal loops in the collective map. For this reason, it may not provide a full representation of social systems, because typically social systems consist of many actors with significantly diverse viewpoints. *Aggregating* is also referred to as "merging" or "overlaying" (Eden, 1989; Eden, et al., 1983), or the "structural/relational join" operation (Lee et al., 1992), or "combination" (Kwahk and Kim, 1999).

The *congregate mapping approach* centers on the identification of key causal loops that drive system dynamics (Bougon, 1992). The study of causal loops or cycles in causal mapping and causal modeling has been emphasized by systems dynamics researchers (Bougon et al., 1990; Forrester, 1961; Senge, 1990). To these researchers, if a causal map or model is used to represent a social system, causal loops are essential elements that are responsible for the system's identity and change (Bougon, 1992) and for the system's complex behaviors (Forrester, 1961). In the congregate approach, only labels and links that contribute to forming loops are entered into the collective map. As a result, the congregate map may be simpler than the sum of individual maps.

In the *workshop mapping approach*, the focus is on consensual model building at the group level. Group members exchange their perceptions of a problem situation to foster consensus (Vennix, 1996). Workshops are group meetings where the group as a whole builds a model aided by a facilitator. The purpose of the workshop is to reach agreement on what elements should be entered into the collective map. As a result of group discussion and interaction in the workshop, the workshop collective model is expected to be shared among group members. In some cases, individual maps are not used in the workshop method, but the facilitator leads the group in building a collective map from scratch.

Hypotheses

With respect to comparing the three methods for developing collective maps we propose two hypotheses regarding map complexity and the perceived utility of collective maps. Researchers in organizational cognition tend to use some simple analyses to measure causal map complexity. The simplest form of map analysis is based on the number of nodes. This approach suggests that the more nodes (or constructs) in a map, the more complex is the map. Eden and Ackermann (1992) note that the number of nodes should be treated with great care as a measure of complexity, because the number of concepts surfaced depends on the interviewing skills of the map builders and the length of interviews. The major weakness of this measure is that it does not include the total number of links in a map, which is associated with the density of the map. Eden and Ackermann (1992) suggest that links-to-nodes ratio (L/N) better represents a map's density. A higher links-to-nodes ratio "indicates a densely connected map and supposedly a higher level of cognitive complexity."

Hart (1977) proposed an alternative measure of map complexity—*map density*— as a measure of degree of interconnection. It is measured by dividing the total number of links by the maximum possible number of links (L/N(N-1)). Klein and Cooper (1982) use map density to measure the cognitive complexity of decision makers. In a set of maps they constructed, they found that maps with largest densities were also the three smallest

Table 1. A comparison of different approaches to building a collective map

	Aggregation	Congregation	Workshop
Work that has used the approach	Lee et al. (1992), Kwahk and Kim (1999), Eden, et al. (1981), and Eden (1989)	Bougon (1992) Hall (1984), Diffenbach (1982)	Langfield-Smith (1992), Massey and Wallace (1996), Vennix (1996)
Core processes	Joining, merging individual maps through common concepts.	Looking for congregating labels, forming loops.	Workshop mapping, group meeting/discussion, consensus building, group facilitation.
Procedure	Unique concepts are merged directly to the composite map while common concepts are merged taking care not to introduce conflicts. Merge two maps at a time until the group maps are exhausted. Use common concepts as coupling device to combine two maps.	Individual maps are connected to form loops through "cryptic" labels, which are repeatedly used by the subjects. Individual maps remain separate, intact in the congregate map.	Group members add concepts (or labels) and relationships (or connections) between concepts, discuss and decide whether they should be included in the group map under the guidance of a group facilitator.
Applications	Organizational memory (Lee et al., 1992), Business Process Reengineering (BPR) (Kwahk and Kim, 1999). Distributed decision making (Zhang et al., 1994).	Strategic planning, organizational identity analysis (Bougon, 1992) Understanding the dynamics of organizations (Hall, 1984).	Group decision support systems (GDSS) (Eden, 1989), solving messy problems (Vennix, 1996).
Advantages	Merging is simple and straight forward; It can be automated with an algorithm; Conflict detection.	Loops help understand the dynamics of the system; Better at capturing multiple perspectives on the problem situation.	May have more beliefs than individuals' maps; Individual biases can be overcome with group interaction.
Disadvantages	A simple merging of all maps may not be a "shared" map; There is no chance to mitigate biases in individual maps.	Difficult to identify the congregating labels; Complex and difficult to automate; Hard to apply as it requires perspectives of all stakeholders.	Premature consensus (groupthink) due to dominant perspectives; Unresolvable conflicts prevent convergence on single map.

maps. In smaller maps the concepts tend to be of central importance to the situation, thus the decision makers acknowledge many relationships between them, making the maps dense.

Building a map by aggregation involves combining individual maps so that all concepts and links in the individual maps are included. When the number of group members increases, complexity of aggregate maps will increase enormously. Thus, the aggregate mapping method is expected to produce collective maps with the highest degree of complexity. In contrast, congregate mapping samples a set of links and nodes from individual maps by identifying key loops or cycles in one or more individual maps, which should result in a simpler representation than the aggregate map yields. When the number of group members increases, the complexity of congregate maps will increase slowly. Thus, the congregate mapping method is expected to produce collective maps with the lowest degree of complexity. Workshop mapping relies on the efforts of a group to identify nodes and links. In view of the limited information processing capacity of group discussion, a workshop map should also be simpler than an aggregate map. The workshop mapping method is expected to produce maps with intermediate degrees of complexity, which depends on the nature and skill of the facilitator. Therefore, we propose the first hypothesis:

Hypothesis 1: Aggregate maps will be more complex than either congregate or workshop maps.

Subjective measures have been used in the literature to evaluate and compare maps. For example, Nicolini (1999) used the subjects' feedback/knowledge to compare maps. Massey and Wallace (1996) used the knowledge of a panel of experts to judge the maps using a Multi-Attribute Value (MAV) model (Massey and O'Keefe, 1993; Massey and Wallace, 1996; Sakman, 1985). The MAV model consists of five attributes (or criteria): structure, stakeholders, solution implication, level of focus, and clarity. The aggregate measure was the weighted sum of the scores on these attributes. In this chapter, we use three attributes: representation of the problem situation, solution implication or direction, and representation of stakeholders or multiple perspectives to evaluate the effectiveness of derived group maps.

Workshop mapping relies on a high level of member involvement. By contrast, aggregate and congregate maps can be built through analysis of individual maps, and thus require much lower levels of participant involvement. Even in cases when subjects play a role in developing the aggregate and congregate maps, they must follow a well-codified set of rules and procedures for developing the map and this will restrict their degree of involvement in the process compared to workshop mapping. The second hypothesis is based on the expectation that the degree to which members participate in building a map is positively related to their evaluation of it:

Hypothesis 2: Subjects will evaluate a map developed using the workshop approach more favorably than with those developed using the congregate or aggregate approaches.

We conducted two studies to compare the three mapping methods and to test the two hypotheses.

Research Design

Two studies were conducted to carry out the comparison of the three approaches. Research designs for the two cases were similar in general respects, but they differed in some details. Some of the differences between the two cases are highlighted in Table 2.

As the detailed designs were different for the two cases, we did not expect that the two cases would produce exactly similar results, but we expected that the patterns fund in the two cases would be comparable. We believe that to the extent similar patterns emerge from different studies we can have more confidence in our conclusions. Conversely, if we find different patterns for the two studies, this highlights areas that require more nuanced judgment and further research. Study 1 commenced before Study 2. Some of the lessons learned (such as the procedure, questionnaire design, etc.) from Study 1 were incorporated into Study 2. It happened that Study 2 was completed before Study 1. Thus some insights gained from Study 2 were also fed back to the conducting of Study 1.

Study 1

The objective in Study 1 was to develop an understanding of the causes of a problem in HALONG, a Vietnamese retail organization, through building a collective causal map. Established as a private company in 1986, HALONG has about 120 employees and manufactures and distributes construction products in Vietnam. It has three plants, near Ho Chi Minh City, in DaNang and in Can Tho and its annual revenue is 10 million USD. According to the President of HALONG, the company grew steadily for the period from 1990 to 1996, but sales had been declining from 1996 to 2001. The objective of the mapping

Table 2. Comparison of the two studies

	HALONG (Study 1)	HOUSTON (Study 2)
Problem/issue	A particular problem was identified based on discussion with the management team. The problem we arrived at was: "Sales situation and factors that affect sales at the organization."	The problem was developing a model of the relationship of infrastructure growth to quality of life of Houstonians based on the expertise of the research team, which was composed of scholars of different disciplines.
Groups involved in the study	Six groups were formed. Two groups were assigned to each of three treatments. Each treatment was one of the methods of building collective causal maps. Four subjects were in each group.	There was one group, which was the research team, but it was composed of scholars with different perspectives on the problem.
Limitations of factors and relationships	The number of factors in individual maps was limited to 15 and the number of relationships was limited to 35. We wanted subjects to focus on important factors and their relationships.	There was no attempt to limit the number of factors and relationships in individual maps and group maps. We wanted a rich picture of the issue.
Data sources for the models	Only subjects' reports of their cognitive constructs were used to build the models.	A variety of data sources were used to build the models, including relevant literature, interview transcripts with infrastructure decision makers, and the subjects' interdisciplinary knowledge.
Treatments	The aggregate and congregate methods were designed to include group model construction. For all three methods, group members worked together to construct their collective map.	The aggregate and congregate methods were designed not to include group model construction. The aggregation and congregation of individual maps were carried out by the researcher. The subjects only participated in the workshop method.

process was to develop a collective understanding of the causes underlying the decline in sales. Different members of HALONG were expected to have different degrees of familiarity with the issue and to have different perspectives on the problem. After some discussion with managers in HALONG, the issue was framed in terms of creating a causal map depicting the "sales situation and factors that affect sales at HALONG." The relevance of this problem to the livelihoods of the subjects ensured their involvement in the study.

All three methods were employed to construct the collective maps. The mapping process consisted of two stages: individual causal mapping and group mapping. Individual maps were obtained for three reasons. First, they provided the basis for comparison with the collective maps. Second, the individual stage provided the subjects with an opportunity to learn and become accustomed to the mapping method and the researchers. Finally, the individual maps improved the quality of the group mapping process by encouraging members to advance their own individual ideas.

The specific process was incorporated into a five-step experimental procedure: (1) Subjects were asked to identify lists of factors important to understanding the problem; (2) Based on these lists, subjects created their own causal maps; (3) The groups built maps using the particular method assigned to them; (4) Subjects were then asked to update their own causal maps if they wished; and (5) Subjects completed the questionnaire and were debriefed. These steps will now be described in more detail.

(1) *List of factors.* Subjects were first asked to identify variables that may be used to describe the problem. In the HALONG case, the problem variables most commonly identified were sales, profit, and customer satisfaction. Subjects were asked next to identify causal factors that have impacts on the problem variables and to identify consequent factors that the problem may have impacts on. This was facilitated with an open questionnaire that had blanks for the subjects to list factors in.

(2) *Individual causal maps.* Individual causal mapping sessions were held with all subjects in the conference room at their workplace. We followed the procedure described in Markoczy and Goldberg (1995) to capture individual causal maps[1]. This procedure is well documented and easy to follow for the subjects. Subjects were asked first to identify possible sensible influences among factors and specify the type, the sign, and the strength of influences. After that they were asked to review their maps and revise them wherever applicable. Specific guidelines for map revision (also included in the questionnaire) were provided. Finally, subjects were asked to identify important feedback loops in their maps. During the individual mapping process, the researcher and two colleagues were available for questions and guidance. The result of this step was a collection of individual causal maps about the problem.

(3) *Group maps.* The subjects met for about 60 - 90 minutes to build group maps. Each group member was given a detailed instruction sheet that they were expected to follow. The researcher and two of his colleagues were present to answer questions and to make sure subjects followed the instructions. Summaries of the group process for each method are as follows:

The Aggregate method. The subjects took turns: i) introducing a factor with a brief description if needed (determined by other members); ii) a member in charge wrote down this factor on a sheet and asked other members whether they agreed to include this factor in the group map; iii) the group then decided whether the factor should be included (if all members agreed, the factor was entered into the group map; if a majority did not favor it the factor was left out; if there were mixed opinions, the factor was marked on the group map with a different color for a second round of discussion); and iv) the process was repeated until all new factors were exhausted. During the factor entry process, relationships were entered into the group map in a similar manner. At the end, the groups were asked to revise their maps by discussing the marked elements. These elements remained in the group maps if group members agreed (including if they agreed that these elements were relevant from other perspectives that they had no knowledge about). Otherwise, the marked elements were left out. Groups were encouraged to add new information into the group map as a result of group discussion and interaction.

The Congregate method. The subjects took turns: i) introducing a causal loop with a brief description if needed (determined by other members); ii) a member in charge recorded this loop on a blackboard and asked other members whether they agreed this loop should be included in the group map; iii) the group then decided whether the loop should be included (if all members agreed, the loop was entered into the group map; if a majority did not favor it the loop was omitted; if there were mixed opinions, the loop was marked on the group map with a different color for a second round of discussion) and; iv) the process was repeated until no more loops were identified. During the loop entry process both factors and relationships were entered into the group map at the same time. At the end, the groups were asked to revise their map by discussing the marked loops or elements. These loops remained in the group maps if group members agreed (including if they agreed that these elements were relevant from other perspectives that they had no knowledge about). Otherwise these loops were omitted. Groups were encouraged to form new loops in the group map as a result of group discussion and interaction.

The Workshop method. The subjects took turns describing the problem situation by identifying problem variables, consequence factors, and causal factors that affect the problem variables, and causal relationships between them. The facilitators recorded these factors/variables and their relationships on blackboards and asked other members whether they agreed to include these elements in the group map and agreed with the story being told. If members all agreed, these elements were put on the group map. If a majority did not advocate inclusion, they were left out. If there were mixed opinions, they were marked with a different color for a second round of discussion. The process was repeated until element entries were exhausted. At the end, the groups were asked to revise their map by discussing the marked elements and considering reducing the number of zero in-degree and out-degree nodes. The agreed-upon elements remained in the group maps and elements on which there was disagreement were left out.

(4) *Individual map update.* After their group meeting, the subjects were asked to revise/update their individual maps (either on the questionnaire or on the diagram/

map) to include any insights they had from the group meeting and from viewing the group map.

(5) *Post experiment.* The subjects were asked to give feedback on the experiment via a questionnaire. This questionnaire gathered information that was used to calculate the subjective measures to evaluate the collective causal maps, described below.

The treatments for this experiment were the three methods of deriving collective maps: aggregate mapping, congregate mapping, and workshop mapping. Subjects were selected from employees of HALONG who work in the sales, production, and accounting departments. They were randomly assigned to groups A, B, C and D. Groups A and B were assigned to the aggregate method, and groups C and D to the congregate method. Due to time restriction, sales reps were randomly assigned to groups E and F (the workshop method).

Measures

The collective maps were compared in terms of both objective measures and subjective measures. Objective measures consist of map complexity and distance ratios between collective models and individual models. These were calculated by the researchers based on comparison of the maps. Subjective measures were based on participants' ratings. These included the degree to which the maps gave a full and accurate representation of the problem representation, the degree to which the maps suggested effective solutions to the problem, and the degree to which the map fairly represented different stakeholders' views. These subjective attributes are based on a Multi-Attribute-Value (MAV) model developed for evaluating causal maps (Massey and O'Keefe, 1993; Massey and Wallace, 1996; Sakman, 1985). These responses were elicited from subjects with the questionnaire that was filled out in the final step of the study. Indices calculated from these responses were used as criteria to measure the effectiveness or utilities of the derived collective maps. Because the two studies used quite different samples and addressed different problems, the questionnaires and procedures for administering them differed, and details of this are given in the description of Study 2.

To analyze the results of Study 1, we used ANOVA, nesting subjects within groups to evaluate the impact of grouping and the impact of the method used on the effectiveness of the composite map in understanding the problem at the individual level. At the group level we were not able to employ statistical tests, but looked for patterns in results.

Table 3. Grouping and treatments

Treatments	Aggregate method	Congregate method	Workshop method
Grouping	Group A (5 subjects)	Group C (5 subjects)	Group E (5 subjects)
	Group B (5 subjects)	Group D (5 subjects)	Group F (5 subjects)

Copyright © 2005, Idea Group Inc. Copying or distributing in print or electronic forms without written permission of Idea Group Inc. is prohibited.

Study 2

In Study 2, the objective was to construct a systems model of infrastructure for the city of Houston that represented the perspectives of a multidisciplinary research team. The research team, composed of engineers, environmental scientists, and social scientists, had been trying to build a decision support system for infrastructure decision making as part of a larger project. The team desired to build a systems model of infrastructure that reflected commonalities among their perspectives, a "best science" model of factors that influenced infrastructure growth and the positive and negative impacts that infrastructure growth had on the urban area. The basic approach taken was similar to Study 1: first build individual causal maps for the researchers, derive collective causal maps using different methods, and compare the methods in terms of which the researchers felt yielded best fit. The first step was to define a problem/issue. After consultation with members of the group, we framed the issue as: "The impact of infrastructure growth on quality of life of Houstonians." The second step was to select participants. We had seven members, who were involved in developing a conceptual framework[2] for the city's infrastructure decision making system, participate in the experiment. The experiment consisted of two stages: individual causal mapping and building group maps.

We followed the same procedure as in Study 1 to capture individual causal maps. Individual maps provided the basis for building collective maps and also provided a standard of comparison for the final group maps. Participating in the individual stage provided the subjects with an opportunity to learn and become accustomed to the mapping method. Based on the interview transcripts[3] and related literature (Forrester, 1969; Lee, 1995), we developed a list of 16 factors or constructs. The subjects were asked to select factors that are relevant to the problem of study and assess possible causal relationships between pair-wise selected factors. The purpose was to gather information that would enable us to draw a causal diagram that shows how the subjects believed infrastructure resource allocation affects the city. The process was assisted using a questionnaire (available from the authors).

After the individual maps were constructed, we applied the aggregate and congregate methods to build the aggregate and congregate maps based on the individual maps. Unlike Study 1, the subjects did not build the aggregate or congregate maps in groups. The experimenters constructed the maps. The subjects were then gathered in a workshop under the researcher's facilitation to build the workshop map using a procedure similar to that described in Study 1. Following the completion of the workshop maps, subjects filled out a questionnaire similar to that utilized in Study 1.

Results of Study 1

In the actual implementation of the experiment, only 24 out of 30 planned subjects were able to participate in the experiment throughout the entire period of the study. (One participant was absent. Two persons left after the individual cognitive mapping because

Table 4. Grouping and treatments

Treatments	Aggregate method (M1)	Congregate method (M2)	Workshop method (M3)
Grouping	Group A (4 subjects)	Group C (4 subjects)	Group E (4 subjects)
	Group B (4 subjects)	Group D (4 subjects)	Group F (4 subjects)

they developed "headaches." Three other people left due to urgent duties). The outcomes of this experiment were six derived group maps (A, B, C, D, E, and F), which are provided in the Appendix. Each method of developing group maps was utilized for two groups. Information about treatments for these groups is provided in Table 4.

Objective Measures

A straightforward measure of map complexity is the number of links and nodes in the maps. Table 5 compares the total nodes (links) of group maps to the average number of nodes (links) in individual maps. An average individual map has ten nodes with a standard deviation of 2.6 nodes. The minimum number of nodes is four and the maximum number 15. Generally, the group maps have more nodes than the average individual maps, as indicated by the group/individual node ratio shown in Table 5. This observation is consistent across all groups. The use of the congregate method (groups C and D) tends to produce group maps that have relatively more nodes than average individual maps.

On average the individual maps have 15 links (minimum 8, maximum 22). The group maps have more links than the average individual maps, with the exception of group C, as indicated by the group/individual link ratios in Table 5. The use of the aggregate method

Table 5. Total number of nodes in individual and group maps

		Groups					
		A	B	C	D	E	F
Nodes	Group	11	11	11	11	15	11
	Individual Average	9.25	9.25	9.00	8.25	12.75	10.75
	Individual Std. Dev.	4.03	1.50	1.63	3.50	2.36	0.50
	Group/Individual Ratio	1.19	1.19	1.22	1.33	1.18	1.02
Links	Group	22	22	17	16	19	21
	Individual Average	11.5	12.75	17.75	11	18.5	16.25
	Individual Std. Dev.	2.08	2.22	5.32	4.08	4.73	2.50
	Group/Individual Ratio	1.91	1.73	0.96	1.45	1.03	1.29

Note: A and B use the aggregate method; C and D use the congregate method; E and F use the workshop method.

Table 6. Links/nodes ratios

L/N ratios	A	B	Avg (A & B)	C	D	Avg (C & D)	E	F	Avg (E & F)
Group	2.00	2.00	2.00	1.70	1.45	1.58	1.27	1.91	1.59
Individuals	1.38	1.39	1.38	1.95	1.50	1.72	1.47	1.52	1.49
STD (ind.)	0.28	0.10	0.20	0.43	0.44	0.47	0.27	0.25	0.24

Note: A and B use the aggregate method; C and D use the congregate method; E and F use the workshop method

(groups A and B) tends to produce the group maps with more links than the average individual maps.

From the link and node data another measure of map complexity, the links to nodes ratio (L/N) was calculated. The links to nodes ratio indicates how dense the maps are in terms of linkages among the concepts (nodes) in the maps. These ratios are shown in Table 6. The individual maps in our experiment have an average links to nodes (L/N) ratio of 1.54 with a standard deviation of 0.3 (maximum L/N ratio for individuals was 2.4; minimum L/N ratio for individuals was 1.0). Generally, the group maps have an average ratio of 1.7 with a standard deviation of 0.3 (maximum 2.0, minimum 1.27).

As shown in Table 6, only for the aggregate method did the collective maps consistently have higher L/N ratios than the individual maps. For both congregate and workshop methods, the collective maps have about the same ratios as the individual maps with large variances. The aggregate models consistently have higher ratios than either the congregate or the workshop models, even though the individual maps for the aggregate method had lower L/N ratios on the average than did the other groups' individual maps. One other interesting result was for congregate group C: this group had by far the highest individual L/N ratio, yet the resulting collective map was simpler than both aggregate maps and one of the workshop maps. This suggests that congregate mapping may simplify the collective map more than aggregate mapping.

Although Eden and Ackermann (1992) report typical ratios of 1.15–1.20 for maps elicited from interviews, several studies reported higher ratios. For example, Hart's (1977) maps have ratios ranging from 1 to 1.4. The causal maps of subjects in Klein and Cooper (1982) have ratios ranging from 1.2 to 1.7. The causal maps in Laukkanen (1994) have ratios of 1.96 and 1.67. Thus our average individual ratio of 1.5 is consistent with other studies.

Table 7. Map density as a measure of map complexity

Map density	A	B	C	D	E	F
Group map	0.20	0.20	0.19	0.15	0.09	0.19
Average individual maps	0.21	0.18	0.25	0.30	0.13	0.16
STD (individuals)	0.10	0.06	0.05	0.25	0.03	0.03

Note: A and B use the aggregate method; C and D use the congregate method; E and F use the workshop method.

The reason for smaller ratios reported by Eden and Ackermann is that their maps contain a large number of nodes and their method of eliciting maps results in less links than the cross-impact method that was used in this research. In the cross-impact method, the map builder considers many possible impacts of every factor on all other factors, while in the interviewing method the map builder only considers direct impacts.

As shown in Table 7, the individual maps have an average density of 0.20 (with a standard deviation of 0.12). In terms of map density as an indicator of map complexity, there were no statistically significant differences between the group maps and average individual maps. This result is not consistent with the results obtained using the L/N ratios, in which the aggregate models have higher ratios than average individual maps. However, inspection of Table 6 indicates that for both the congregate and workshop methods, one of the two groups had lower density than the two groups employing the aggregate method. There seemed to be more variation in density for the congregate and workshop methods than for the aggregate method.

Our maps are denser than those reported in previous studies. For example, maps in Hart (1977) have an average density of 0.03 (ranging from 0.024 to 0.042). The causal maps of subjects in Klein and Cooper (1982) have density ratios ranging from 0.06 to 0.21. The causal maps of subjects in Laukkanen (1994) have ratios of 0.09 and 0.10. The maps in this study are denser than those reported in the literature because these maps have smaller numbers of nodes[4] and the method we used to elicit maps was "cross-impact" rather than "interviewing" or coding from documents or transcripts. Our result is consistent with the observation that Klein and Cooper (1982) drew from their studies: the smaller the maps, the larger density. They explain that in smaller maps the concepts tend to be of central importance to the situation, and thus the decision makers identify many relationships between them, making the maps dense.

Finally, we used the distance ratio (DR) proposed by Markoczy and Goldberg (1995) and the program provided by the authors to calculate DRs between the group maps and the individual maps. A summary of distance ratios between collective maps and individual maps is given in Table 8. On average, the DR between group maps and individual maps is 0.13 with a standard deviation of 0.03. The maximum DR is 0.19 and the minimum 0.08. The results shown in Table 8 suggest that the method used to construct group maps has an impact on the average DR from the collective map to the individual maps. To test this

Table 8. Distance ratios between collective maps and individual maps

Groups	A	B	C	D	E	F
Group- individual distance ratios	0.19	0.15	0.19	0.13	0.1	0.15
	0.17	0.14	0.19	0.11	0.08	0.1
	0.15	0.14	0.16	0.13	0.09	0.11
	0.12	0.17	0.12	0.12	0.08	0.12
Average	0.16	0.15	0.17	0.12	0.09	0.12

Note: A and B use the aggregate method; C and D use the congregate method; E and F use the workshop method.

observation, we conducted a one-way ANOVA with method as the factor and distance ratios between the collective maps and the respective individual maps as the dependent variable. For each method, we had eight cases. We found that the workshop mapping method had the lowest DR as compared to the congregate method ($p < .006$) and the aggregate method ($p < .001$). However, there was no difference between the aggregate and the congregate methods.

In summary, the results obtained for the links-to-nodes ratio and the distance ratio measures are supportive of the expectation that the aggregate method would produce more complex collective maps than the congregate method and the workshop method. And while the map density results were not significantly different, the pattern was also consistent with this expectation.

Subjective Measures

Subjective evaluation of the experimental outcomes was conducted three months after the comparative experiment under the guidance of an assistant. The rating process was supported by an evaluative questionnaire (available from the authors). The questionnaire consisted of eight maps or figures (six maps from the outcome of the comparative experiment, one map of the management team, and one synthesized map). Subjects were not told which maps were which. The questionnaire was designed based on a multi-attribute value (MAV) model (Massey and O'Keefe, 1993; Massey and Wallace, 1996; Sakman, 1985) with three attributes or criteria: problem representation (C1), solution implication (C2), and stakeholder implication (C3). Subjects were asked to evaluate the figures in two steps. In step one, they identified the information in each map that was critical. In step two, they rated the map on the three criteria. The first step provided the basis for the second step. For example, for problem representation, the raters were asked to mark elements (factors and relations between factors) with þ (or 0) symbols if the raters agreed (disagreed) that these elements represented the problem situation. For solution implication, they were asked to mark relationships that had important implications for solving the problem. For stakeholder implication, subjects were asked to indicate how well various groups of stakeholders and their needs, interests, and power[5] were incorporated in the map. They rank ordered these groups in terms of which were represented the best, second best, and so forth.

All HALONG subjects were contacted and asked to evaluate the maps. Half of them completed the questionnaire. To obtain a more robust evaluation of whether the maps represented the situation at HALONG, three senior management personnel who had not participated in building the maps were also recruited to evaluate them. In addition to HALONG personnel, 30 M.B.A. students who had been in management positions and ten lecturers in a Vietnamese school of management were recruited to rate the maps. Twenty-eight usable questionnaires (21 from M.B.A. students, seven from lecturers) were obtained from this sample.

The measures in this study were three attributes of the group map that were defined above: problem representation (C1), solution implication (C2), and stakeholder implication (C3). The attributes were measured on a 0-10 scale, in which 0 indicates "strongly disagree" and 10 indicates "strongly agree."

Table 9. A plan for comparison of results of mapping across the groups

Treatments	M1 (Aggregate)		M2 (Congregate)		M3 (Workshop)	
Group	A	B	C	D	E	F
Raters	G1 (HL) / G2 (non-HL)		G1 (HL)/ G2 (non-HL)		G1 (HL)/ G2 (non-HL)	

As illustrated in Table 9, the comparison of the results is organized in the following manner. For each method (M1, M2, M3), we compared the two groups of raters (HALONG raters, indicated by G1, versus non-HALONG raters, indicated by G2) in terms of the three criteria (C1, C2, C3) to determine whether independent evaluations (non-HALONG raters) were significantly different from participant evaluations (HALONG raters). Originally we had planned to contrast HALONG participants' perceptions with the perceptions of the three non-participating HALONG managers, but there were no significant differences between these two sets of ratings, so they were combined for this analysis. We also compared the pairs of group maps derived with the same method on the three criteria to determine whether they received significantly different evaluations. Finally, we compared the three methods over the three criteria for all raters combined to determine the relative performance of the methods.

Comparison of means for the two aggregate collective maps constructed by groups A and B indicated that the two maps differed (see Figure 1). Although the maps for groups A and B were derived using the same method, B received significantly higher ratings than A for problem representation (t = -2.24, df = 84, p = .02, 2 tailed). The differences are near significant in terms of solution implication (t = -1.85, df = 83, p = .068) and stakeholder

Figure 1. Evaluation of the aggregate method over three criteria

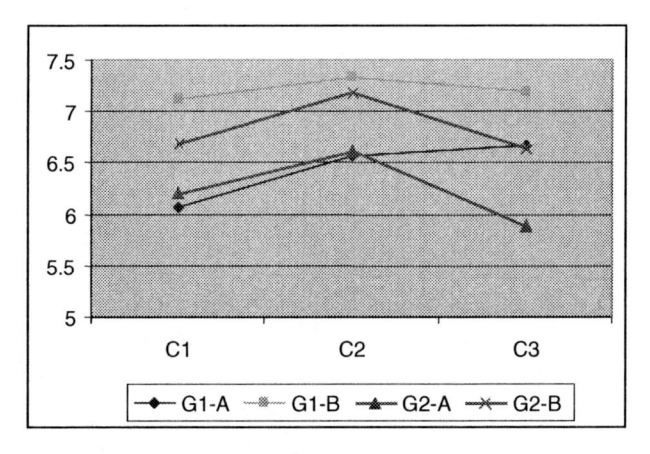

Notes: G1 stands for the HALONG rater group; G2 for the non-HALONG rater group. A and B are the two group maps constructed in the experiment using the aggregate method. C1 is the average ratings of the groups for problem representation criterion, C2 for solution implication criterion, and C3 for stakeholder implication criterion. So, G1-A represents the ratings given by HALONG raters (G1) to the first aggregate group map (A). G1-B represents the ratings of the second aggregate group map (B) by the HALONG raters (G1). G2-A represents the ratings of the first aggregate group map (A) by the non-HALONG raters (G2). G2-B represents the ratings of the second aggregate group map (B) by the non-HALONG raters (G2).

Figure 2. Evaluation of the congregate method over three criteria

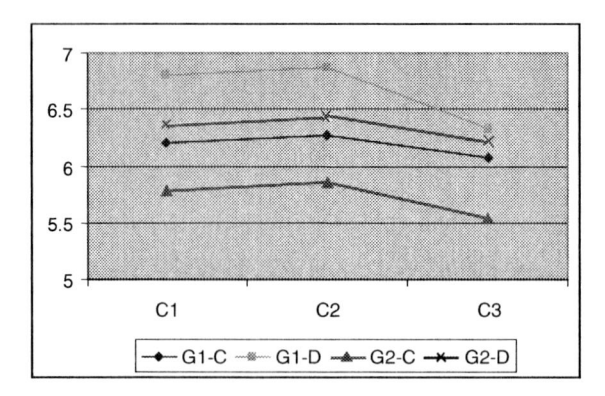

Notes: G1 stands for HALONG raters; G2 for non-HALONG raters; C and D are the two group maps constructed in the experiment using the congregate method. C1 stands for problem representation criterion, C2 for solution implication criterion, and C3 for stakeholder implication criterion. See Figure 1 note for further explanation.

implication (t = -1.891, df = 83, p = .062). No significant difference was found in the evaluations between the HALONG and non-HALONG raters for C1 and C2 (p>.1). HALONG raters gave slightly higher ratings to C3 than independent raters with a 10% level of significance (t = 1.777, df = 83, p = .07).

Figure 3. Evaluation of the workshop mapping method over three criteria

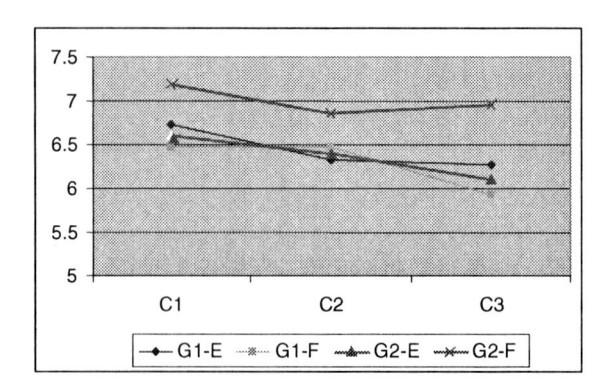

Notes: G1 stands for HALONG raters; G2 for non-HALONG raters; E and F are the two group maps constructed in the experiment using the workshop method. C1 stands for problem representation criterion, C2 for solution implication criterion, and C3 for stakeholder implication criterion. See Figure 1 note for further explanation.

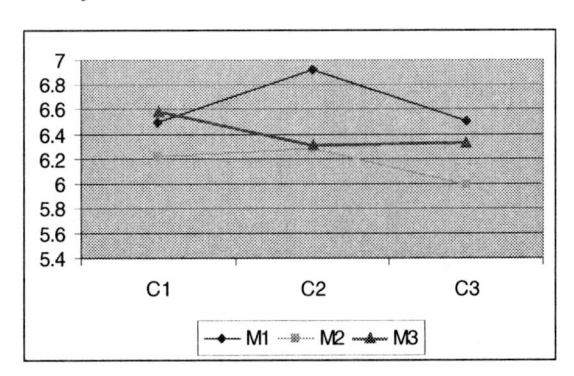

Figure 4. Comparison of the three methods over three criteria

[Chart showing M1, M2, M3 across C1, C2, C3]

Notes: M1 stands for the ratings averaged across all raters for both maps constructed with the aggregate method, M2 the ratings averaged across all raters for both maps constructed with the congregate method, and M3 the ratings averaged across all raters for both maps constructed with the workshop method. C1 stands for problem representation criterion, C2 for solution implication criterion, and C3 for stakeholder implication criterion

Comparison of means for groups C and D for the congregate mapping method (see Figure 2) indicated no significant differences between groups. The difference was near significance for problem representation (t = -1.956, df = 84, p = .054, 2 tailed), but it was not significant for either solution implication (t = -1.754, df = 84, p = .083) or stakeholder implication (t = -1.612, df = 84, p = .111). Although the figure suggests a tendency for HALONG subjects to rate outcomes higher than non-HALONG subjects, the difference was not statistically significant (p > .10).

The result of the means comparison between the maps of groups E and F, which utilized the workshop mapping method, indicated significant differences between the two maps (see Figure 3) for the non-HALONG raters. While the HALONG group rated the maps for groups E and F as approximately equal on the three criteria, the non-HALONG subjects rated group F's map as better than group E's on all three criteria (t = 2.44, df = 84, p = .017 for problem representation; t = 2.02, df = 84, p = .046 for solution implication; and t = 2.30, df = 84, p = .024 for stakeholder implication).

The effectiveness ratings for the three methods of constructing maps for all raters combined are shown in Figure 4. To test for differences in effectiveness between the three methods we conducted one way ANOVAs with methods as the factor for each of the three dependent variables (C1, C2, and C3). The ANOVAs revealed a significant main effect for the method factor for solution implication (C2: F = 4.123, df = 2/254, p = .017). A marginally significant main effect was also found for stakeholder implication (C3: F = 2.263, df = 2/254, p = .106). No significant effect was found for problem representation (C1). Post-hoc tests revealed that the aggregate mapping method was rated as superior to the other two methods on solution implication (p < .015) and to the congregate method in terms of stakeholder implication (p < .03)

Discussion

The results of Study 1 suggest that aggregate maps are more complex than congregate and workshop maps. They also suggest that aggregate maps are perceived to be more effective in suggesting solutions than both congregate and workshop maps and more effective in representing stakeholders' views than congregate maps. However, the results also showed that groups using the congregate and workshop methods could vary widely in the objective properties of the maps they created. Moreover, ratings of maps varied between groups using the same method for all three mapping approaches.

Differences between groups using the aggregate and congregate methods may be due to the skill of members involved. In the aggregate and congregate methods, facilitators were not directly involved in the process of building group maps. Groups followed the instructions for each method in their own way. It may be the case that the skill of members in carrying out the mapping process had an impact on the outcome. If facilitators had been more involved, there may have been more consistent results. It is well documented in the literature that facilitation plays an important role in group process outcomes (Hackman, 1990; Phillips and Phillips, 1993; Vennix, 1996).

Differences between the two groups using the workshop mapping method, which was aided by a facilitator, may be due to the nature of the facilitation. One of the facilitators in the study had a good deal more experience than the other. Eden and Ackermann (1992) observed that: "[I]nexperienced mappers [facilitators] tend to generate a map with a smaller number of constructs than those identified by an experienced mapper and in addition they generate more links." As indicated in Table 5, the less experienced facilitator for group F created a map with 11 factors and 21 links, whereas the more experienced facilitator for group E created a map with 15 factors and 19 links. Thus, group facilitation may account for the variance in the links/nodes ratios for the collective mapping method.

The congregate method fared worst in terms of subjective ratings and also yielded models with quite different objective properties for the two groups. This may be because subjects were not familiar with thinking in terms of feedback loops (Hall, 1984; Weick and Bougon, 1994; Richardson, 1991; Steinbruner, 1974; Levi and Tetlock, 1980). Without special training it is difficult to identify important feedback loops, which in some cases may require time to think through. Some feedback loops may be associated with long delays that may take a long time to be effective. For many people, it is much easier to think about a problem in terms of a "shopping list" in which only one-way impacts are identified.

The HALONG raters consistently rated the two maps derived from the workshop method as equally good, but the non-HALONG raters tended to rate one map of each pair as significantly better than the other. This difference between the two groups of raters is not difficult to explain. The HALONG raters are likely to have relied more on content when making their judgments (e.g., whether the maps reflected the problem situation), while the non-HALONG raters are likely to have relied more on the structural characteristics[6] of the map (e.g., the amount of information in the maps).

Table 10. Correlations between objective and subjective measures

Correlations	C1	C2	C3
L/N ratio	-0.60	-0.13	-0.39
Density ratio	-0.82	-0.36	-0.67
Links	0.66	0.50	0.68

Note: C1 stands for problem representation criterion, C2 for solution implication criterion, and C3 for stakeholder implication criterion.

In an attempt to illuminate the relationships between the subjective and objective measures, we ran correlations between some objective measures (number of nodes, number of links, L/N ratios, map density ratios, out-degree and in-degree of problem variable – sales) and the subjective measures (problem representation, solution implication, stakeholder implication). Some of the interesting correlations are reported in Table 10.

Problem representation (C1) and stakeholder implication (C3) are negatively correlated with map complexity and L/N ratio, yet positively correlated with number of links. Correlations are weaker for stakeholder implication (C3) than for problem representation, and weaker still for solution implication (C2). Subjective measures have higher correlations to map complexity than to the L/N indicator. No significant correlations were found between subjective measures and the number of nodes, out-degree and in-degree of the problem variable (sales).

The relationships between objective and subjective measures are interesting and may suggest some implications for the conditions when the methods may be best applied. The negative correlations between the subjective measures and complexity suggest that maps with higher levels of complexity are not perceived to be as useful or as representative as simpler maps. One implication of this, for example, is that the aggregate method may not work well in larger and heterogeneous groups, as it tends to increase group map complexity as the number of group members or the distinct perspectives increases. On the contrary, the congregate method may be more suited to larger and heterogeneous groups as it is able to handle heterogeneous perspectives via causal loops. An increase in the number of causal loops does not necessarily increase group map complexity. The positive correlation between the number of links in group maps and the effectiveness of group maps is reasonable. Relationships in a map indicate the content or information in a map, and thus a greater number of relationships may imply more information-content in the map. However, too many relationships may increase map complexity, and this may reduce the effectiveness of the group map for observers.

Results of Study 2

Seven individual maps were elicited from members of the research team following procedures described above. These were used to build collective maps with the

Table 11. Descriptive statistics on individual causal maps

	Individual Researchers							
	P1	P2	P3	P4	P5	P6	P7
Number of Factors (Nodes)	20	23	10	27	17	18	16
Number of Relationships (Links)	45	44	25	47	49	43	46
L/N ratio	2.25	1.91	2.50	1.74	2.88	2.39	2.88
Density ratio	0.12	0.09	0.28	0.07	0.18	0.14	0.19

aggregate and congregate methods. Summary information about individual maps is presented in Table 11. On average, an individual map had 19 factors (with a standard deviation of 5.4), 43 links or relationships (with a standard deviation of 8), an L/N ratio of 2.36 (with a standard deviation of .44), and a density ratio of 0.15 (with a standard deviation of .07).

The aggregate model was built by the researcher without the assistance of the group. In the aggregate method, all the factors and links from each individual map were included in the collective map. The result was that the aggregate map had 39 factors and 193 unique links. Its L/N ratio was 4.95 and density ratio was 0.13. Because the aggregate map was quite complicated, we split it into two parts: a unique map and a common map. The unique map (referred to as the aggregate map henceforth) contained unique relationships extracted from individual maps. Relationships that appear in at least two individual maps were entered into the common map (referred to as the common aggregate map henceforth).

The congregate model was built by the researcher, who identified the common causal loops in the individual causal maps of Houston's infrastructure and folded them into a common model. The process of building the congregate model consisted of four steps: (1) identification of key actors and their goals and behaviors in the infrastructure system, (2) formulation of reference knowledge based on the interview transcripts, (3) identification of causal loops in individual maps matching reference knowledge and formulation of hypothetical causal loops to match the unexplained reference knowledge, and (4) construction of a map incorporating a theory of the problem based on a model that congregates causal loops identified in (3) with a consideration of temporal dynamics. The

Table 12. Descriptive statistics on common causal maps

	Nodes	Links	L/N	Density
Aggregate	39	193	4.95	0.13
Common Aggregate(*)	21	51	2.43	0.12
Congregate	16	32	2.00	0.13
Workshop	38	57	1.50	0.04
Average of Individual Map Statistics	29	83	2.72	0.11

Note: (*) The common aggregate map contains those beliefs (or relationships) that appear in at least two individual maps.

resulting congregate model had 16 factors and 32 links. Its L/N ratio was 2.00 and density ratio was 0.13.

The workshop model was built by five out of the seven researchers in a mapping workshop. The workshop was initiated by a problem description that was based on the interview transcripts of interviews previously conducted by the researchers. Each participant received a ten-step instruction sheet to guide discussion. The subjects took turns in describing the problem situation by identifying problem variables, consequent factors, causal factors that affected the problem variables, and causal relationships between them. The facilitator (the first author) recorded these factors/variables and their relationships on a whiteboard and asked other members whether they agreed to include these elements and agreed with the story being told in the group map. The process was repeated until element entries were exhausted. The workshop took about an hour. The resulting workshop model had 38 factors and 57 links. Its L/N ratio was 1.50 and its density ration was 0.04.

In terms of map density ratio, shown in Table 12, we found that the aggregate method produced the most complex collective map of the three methods, followed by the congregate and workshop methods. The common aggregate map is simpler than the whole aggregate map but it is still more complex than the workshop and the congregate maps (in terms of L/N ratio). Although the workshop map has a great number of factors, it is the simplest map in terms of L/N and map density ratio.

When compared to the individual maps within each group, only the congregate map has fewer factors, while the workshop and aggregate maps have more factors than the average individual map. In terms of the number of links, both congregate and workshop maps have fewer links, while the aggregate map has more links than the individual maps. In terms of L/N ratio, both congregate and workshop maps are less complex but the aggregate map is more complex than the individual maps. In terms of map density ratio, the workshop map is less dense while both congregate and aggregate maps are denser than the individual maps.

Distance ratios (DRs) between the collective maps and the individual maps are shown in Table 13. On average, the DR between group maps and individual maps is 0.07 with a standard deviation of 0.02. The maximum DR is 0.12 and the minimum 0.05.

We observe from Table 13 that the method used to construct group maps might have some impact on the average DR from the collective map to the individual maps. To test this observation, we used one-way ANOVA with one factor (method) and one dependent variable (DR). For each method, we had seven cases. The results of the ANOVA revealed

Table 13. Distance ratios between collective maps and individual maps

	P1	P2	P3	P4	P5	P6	P7
Aggregate	0.08	0.12	0.08	0.07	0.08	0.09	0.12
Common Aggregate	0.07	0.11	0.06	0.05	0.08	0.06	0.09
Congregate	0.07	0.10	0.05	0.06	0.06	0.07	0.09
Workshop	0.05	0.06	0.06	0.06	0.07	0.06	0.07

Figure 5. Comparison of group maps in terms of Problem Representation

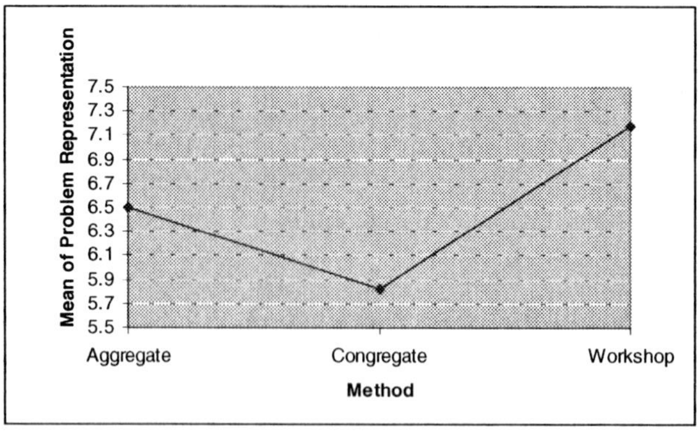

a significant main effect for the method factor that had an impact on DR ($F = 3.941$, $df = 3/27$, $p = .02$). Post-hoc tests (LSD) revealed that the aggregate map had higher DRs than both the workshop ($p < .002$), and the congregate methods ($p < .05$).

Subjects were asked to evaluate the maps in terms of problem representation, solution implication and stakeholder implication, as described in Study 1. Figure 5 shows the means on problem representation for the three methods: the congregate method had the lowest rating, followed by the aggregate method, with the workshop method receiving the highest rating. There was no consensus on what model was best in terms of problem representation among the raters. Three raters believed that the model based on the workshop method was best, while two raters chose the model based on the aggregate as the best and one rater preferred the model based on the congregate method.

A preparatory step in the rating for solution implication asked the rater to identify critical paths that indicated where the problem was and what he/she agreed could be useful in developing some resolution directions for the problem. Based on this activity, the rater was asked to rate the degree to which the model could help in developing policies to resolve the problem on a scale from 0 (strongly disagree) to 10 (strongly agree). The workshop model received higher ratings than did the congregate model, which received higher ratings than the aggregate model. However, none of these differences was statistically significant.

Stakeholder implications were rated with reference to six groups of stakeholders: elected officials, the city public works department, citizens, businesses, contractors, and media.

Table 14. Comparison of the three methods on stakeholder implications

Stakeholders	Workshop	Congregate	Aggregate
Elected Officials	7	4.8	4.7
City Departments	6.2	5	4.2
Citizens	6.5	5.5	5
Businesses	6.8	6.2	5.8
Contractors	5.5	5	4.3
Media	5	4.5	3.5

Copyright © 2005, Idea Group Inc. Copying or distributing in print or electronic forms without written permission of Idea Group Inc. is prohibited.

Table 15. Comparison of the three methods on multiple perspectives implication

Perspectives	Workshop	Congregate	Aggregate
Economic	8	7.2	7
Political	7.8 (a)	5 (a)	4.2 (a)
Technical	7.3 (b)	4.5 (b)	4.3 (b)
Environment	6.2	4.7	6
Social	6.2	5	4.8
Ethical	2.3	1.8	1.8

Note: Means in the same row labeled with (a) are significantly different at $p < .05$; means in the same row labeled with (b) are significantly different at $p < .10$.

Raters were also allowed to identify additional stakeholder groups that were not listed in the questionnaire. As a result, two stakeholder groups were added to the set: environmentalists and engineers. For each group of stakeholders, the rater was asked to circle a number on a scale from 0 (strongly disagree) to 10 (strongly agree) indicating how well the needs and interests of that stakeholder group were incorporated into the model. Results are displayed in Table 14. On average, the workshop method received the highest ratings for all stakeholders while the aggregate model received the lowest ratings. The congregate model received intermediate values. However, these differences were not statistically significant.

The three methods were compared on one additional criterion, multiple perspectives implication, the degree to which the collective causal map is able to capture various perspectives on the problem situation. In this study, multiple perspectives implication indicated how adequately a group map represents six perspectives on infrastructure: economic, political, technical, environmental, social, and ethical. Although raters were asked to identify additional perspectives that were not listed in the questionnaire, they did not suggest any. For each perspective, the rater was asked to circle a number on a scale from 0 (strongly disagree) to 10 (strongly agree) to indicate how well the perspective was represented in the model. Results are reported in Table 15. On average, the model derived from the workshop method received the highest ratings for all perspectives, while the aggregate model received the lowest ratings with the exception of the environmental perspective. The congregate model was intermediate. ANOVA tests revealed that the workshop model was able to better capture the political and technical perspectives of the problems. Other differences were not statistically significant. Of interest is the fact that none of the methods was judged able to capture the ethical perspective on the situation as perceived by the raters.

Discussion

In this study, we also found that the aggregate method produced the most complex collective map. In terms of distance ratios between collective maps and individual maps, we found that workshop maps had the lowest DRs, aggregate next lowest, and congregate the highest DRs. An implication of this pattern is that the workshop method may enhance the effects of knowledge sharing among group members, while the congregate mapping method may have difficulties in gaining acceptance from group members. In terms of problem implication and solution implication, workshop maps were perceived to be superior to aggregate or congregate maps, with congregate maps faring worse than aggregate maps. The workshop model was also rated better in terms of stakeholder implications and multiple perspective implications, with congregate maps next and aggregate maps receiving the lowest ratings. Many of these results were not, however, statistically significant due to the low power of the tests.

It is interesting to note the differences between subjective judgments of complexity and the objective measures of complexity. Our observation during this study was that human subjects tend to make judgments that are similar to the simplest objective measure (the number of nodes) while placing less emphasis on objective measures based on both nodes and links (L/N ratio or density). Most raters believed that the congregate map was the simplest. One rater commented that "we don't like it [the congregate map] because it is too simple" compared to the other maps. However as indicated in Table 11, the congregate map is actually more complex than the workshop map in terms of L/N ratio and map density.

Summary and Conclusion

The results of both studies lend support for the hypothesis that the aggregate method would produce the most complex collective maps, whereas the congregate method would produce collective maps lower in complexity. The workshop method tended to produce collective maps with an intermediate degree of complexity. This result is particularly evident for the L/N ratio, but is also reflected in several map density comparisons. In terms of distance ratios between individual maps and the collective maps, the congregate and workshop methods were less distant than the aggregate method in both cases.

In terms of subjective ratings of the methods, Study 1 suggested that the aggregate method was rated better than the congregate method for all criteria. Moreover, the aggregate and the workshop mapping methods were equally good in terms of problem representation and stakeholder implication. However, the aggregate method outperformed the workshop mapping method in terms of solution implication. In Study 2 a different pattern of results emerged. Workshop mapping was generally superior to aggregate and congregate approaches across all four criteria. Further, congregate maps generally received somewhat better ratings than aggregate maps. Together the two studies lend mixed support to Hypothesis 2.

It is useful to consider the relationships between the objective and subjective results. The objective results were for the most part consistent across the two studies, but there were differences in the subjective results. Aggregate mapping fared better in Study 1 than in Study 2, whereas congregate mapping fared better in Study 2 than in Study 1. Workshop mapping was rated well for the most part in both studies. In Study 1 its ratings were equivalent to those of aggregate mapping (except for solution implication), whereas in Study 2 it was rated much higher than aggregate or congregate mapping. This suggests that map complexity and the degree to which the map corresponds to individual representations had different meanings for the two samples. In Study 1 map complexity did not seem to correlate with lower ratings, whereas in Study 2 it did. In Study 1, degree of difference between collective and individual maps did not correlate with ratings, whereas in Study 2 it was positively correlated.

At least three explanations for this difference can be advanced. First, and most plausible to us, the average number of links and nodes was much higher in the individual maps in Study 2 than in Study 1 (an average of 10 nodes and 15 links in the individual maps in Study 1 versus an average of 29 nodes and 83 links in the individual maps in Study 2). Hence, the aggregate maps in Study 2 were likely to be much more complicated and difficult to interpret than those in Study 1. This may have resulted in lower ratings by the subjects. In addition subjects in Study 1 may have been able to see their own concepts and ideas in the aggregate maps more easily than subjects in Study 2, and thus they might be disposed to rate it higher than in Study 2. Both groups rated the workshop method high, which suggests that higher levels of participation increase perceived value of the collective map.

A second explanation is that the use of groups to build maps in all three conditions in Study 1, but only for the workshop method in study 2, influenced ratings. Participation in Study 1 may have mediated subject ratings of the maps, particularly those of the subjects who built the maps. In Study 2, however, subjects only participated in finalizing the maps for the workshop map and may have seen the aggregate and congregate maps as "alien." If this explanation is accurate, then one implication is that the aggregate method used in a workshop is superior to the other methods although it performs less well when the facilitator builds the maps. A third possible explanation for the results is that they stem from cultural differences between the subjects in the two studies. However, it is not apparent what cultural differences could account for the differences in results.

Lessons Learned

We can advance several lessons learned about the three methods. The advantage of the aggregate method is that it is simple and easy to implement. It is also very good at pooling information from group members' individual maps. As the comparative study suggested, the aggregate method works best when individual maps are not very complex and/or when the group is relatively homogeneous (as in Study 1). The disadvantage of the aggregate method is that group maps derived from this method tend to be complex and dense. In larger and more heterogeneous groups, the aggregate method may not be effective as it is in small and homogeneous groups (as in the setting of this experiment).

It seems likely that the congregate method would be more effective in larger and heterogeneous groups. The advantages of the congregate method are two-fold. First, it is less complex (than the aggregate method). An increase in the number of causal loops does not necessarily increase group map complexity. Second, it is better in representing the interactions of multiple perspectives via causal loops. In organizational problem

Table 16. Dependency of method effectiveness on group size

Effectiveness Rank	Group size		
	< 5	5 to 7	> 7 (hypothesized)
Best	Aggregate method	Workshop method	Congregate method
Intermediate	Workshop method	Aggregate method = Congregate method	Workshop method
Worst	Congregate		Aggregate method

formulation, the congregate method is proposed to apply at the organizational level, where the number of groups is many and groups have more distinct perspectives. At the organizational level, the congregate method will help identify different perspectives to be included in the organizational model.

The workshop method fared best in terms of least complexity and highest subjective ratings across the two studies. This is likely due, in part, to the higher level of involvement subjects have in the map-building process. The workshop method can be used alone or in combination with other methods to improve the shared effect of collective maps. Other researchers (Ackermann et al., 1997; Diffenbach, 1982; Eden, 1989) have suggested that such combinations improve the group mapping outcome. The workshop method can replace the aggregate method at the group level when individual maps cannot be obtained for some reason. This substitution may not seriously affect the effectiveness of group maps. In combination with the workshop approach, the congregate method has potential in handling multiple perspectives in complex systems.

One final point to bear in mind is that Study 1 showed that, in terms of objective measures, the congregate and workshop methods had more variation in results than the aggregate method. This is probably due to the fact that these require more judgment on the part of the modeler and group than the aggregate method, which is for the most part based on clear-cut rules. Subjective judgment may well be perceived as bias by some participants, which may create a sense that both the congregate and workshop methods are not representative of some user perspectives.

Based on the results of the two studies, we can also advance some suggestions concerning the relationship between group size and effectiveness of mapping methods. We propose that when group size increases, the effectiveness of the aggregate method will decrease significantly, while the effectiveness of the workshop method may increase slightly, and that of the congregate method will increase.

Table 16 summarizes our hypothesized relationship. This relationship may suggest the best fit method for a given group size. Further study is, however, needed to fully test this relationship because we are going beyond the four-person groups used in the first study and the seven-person group in the second.

References

Ackermann, F., Eden, C., & Williams, T. (1997). Modelling for litigation: Mixing qualitative and quantitative approaches. *Interfaces, 27,* 48-65.

Axelrod, R. (Ed.) (1976). *Structure of decision: The causal maps of political elites.* Princeton, NJ: Princeton University Press.

Boland, R. J., Tenkasi, R. V., & Teeni, D. (1994). Designing information technology to support distributed cognition. *Organization Science, 5,* 456-475.

Bougon, M. G. (1992). Congregate causal maps: A unified dynamic theory of organization strategy. *The Journal of Management Studies, 29,* 369-389.

Checkland, P. (1981). *Systems thinking, systems practice.* New York: John Wiley & Sons.

Courtney, J. F. (2001). Decision making and knowledge management in inquiring organizations: A new decision-making paradigm for DSS. *Decision Support Systems, 31,* 17-38.

Diffenbach, J. (1982). Influence diagrams for complex strategic issues. *Strategic Management Journal, 3,* 133-146.

Dutta, A. (2001). Business planning for network services: A systems thinking approach. *Information Systems Research, 12,* 260-283.

Eden, C. (1989). Using causal mapping for strategic options development and analysis (SODA). In J. Rosenhead (Ed.), *Rational analysis for a problematic world: Problem structuring methods for complexity, uncertainty, and conflict* (pp. 21-24). Chichester, UK: Wiley.

Eden, C., & Ackermann, F. (1992). The analysis of cause maps. *The Journal of Management Studies, 29,* 309-323.

Eden, C., Jones, S., & Sims, D. (1983). *Messing about in problems: An informal structured approach to their identification and management..* New York: Pergamon.

Forrester, J. W. (1969). *Urban dynamics.* Cambridge, MA: Productivity Press.

Forrester, J. W. (1961). *Industrial dynamics.* Cambridge, MA: Productivity Press.

Hall, R. I. (1976). A system pathology of an organization: The rise and fall of the old Saturday Evening Post. *Administrative Science Quarterly, 21,* 185-211.

Hart, J. A. (1977). Causal maps of three Latin American policy makers. *World Politics, 30,* 115-140.

Hong, T., & Han, I. (2002). Knowledge-based data mining of news information on the internet using causal maps and neural networks. *Expert Systems with Applications, 23,* 1-8.

Klein, J. H., & Cooper, D. F. (1982). Causal maps of decision makers in a complex game. *Journal of the Operational Research Society, 33,* 63-71.

Kwahk, K. Y., & Kim, Y. G. (1999). Supporting business process redesign using causal maps. *Decision Support Systems, 25,* 155-178.

Langfield-Smith, K. (1992). Exploring the need for a shared causal map. *The Journal of Management Studies, 29,* 349-368.

Langfield-Smith, K., & Wirth, A. (1992). Measuring differences between causal maps. *The Journal of the Operational Research Society, 43,* 1135-1150.

Lant, T. K., & Shapira, Z. (2001). *Organizational cognition: Computation and interpretation.* Mahwah, NJ: Lawrence Erlbaum.

Laukkanen, M. (1994). Comparative cause mapping of organizational cognitions. *Organization Science, 5,* 322-343.

Lee, S., Courtney, J. F., & O'Keefe, R. M. (1992). A system for organizational learning using causal maps. *Omega, 20,* 23-36.

Lee, S. Y. (1995). *An integrated model of land use/transportation system performance: System dynamics modeling approach.* Ph.D. Dissertation, University of Maryland, College Park.

Levi, A., & Telock, P. E. (1980). A cognitive analysis of Japan's 1941 decision for war. *Journal of Conflict Resolution, 24,* 195-211.

Linstone, H. A. (1984). *Multiple perspectives for decision making: Bridging the gap between analysis and action.* New York: North-Holland, Elsevier Science.

Markoczy, L., & Goldberg, J. (1995). A method for eliciting and comparing causal maps. *Journal of Management, 21,* 305-333.

Massey, A. P., & O'Keefe, R. (1993). Insights from attempts to validate a multi-attribute model of problem definition quality. *Decision Sciences, 24,* 106-125.

Massey, A. P., & Wallace, W. A. (1996). Understanding and facilitating group problem structuring and formulation: Mental representations, interaction, and representation aids. *Decision Support Systems, 17,* 253-274.

Mitroff, I. I., & Linstone, H. A. (1993). *The unbounded mind: Breaking the chains of traditional business thinking.* New York: Oxford University Press.

Montazemi, A. R., & Conrath, D. W. (1986). The use of causal mapping for information requirements analysis. *MIS Quarterly, 10,* 44-55.

Nicolini, D. (1999). Comparing methods for mapping organizational cognition. *Organization Studies, 20,* 833-861.

O'Keefe, J., & Nadel, L. (1978). *The hippocampus as a causal map.* Oxford, UK: Clarendon.

Richardson, G. P. (1991). *Feedback thought in social science and systems theory.* Philadelphia: University of Pennsylvania Press.

Sakman, M. (1985). *An empirical study of three methods of problem definition in ill-structured situations.* Ph.D. dissertation, University of Wisconsin, Madison.

Schneider, S., & Angelmar, R. (1993). Cognition in organizational analysis: Who's minding the store? *Organization Studies 14,* 352-374.

Senge, P. M. (1990). *The fifth discipline: The art and practice of the learning organization.* New York: Doubleday/Currency.

Sheetz, S. D., Tegarden, D. P., Kozar, K. A., & Zigurs, I. (1994). A group support systems approach to causal mapping. *Journal of Management Information Systems, 11,* 31-57.

Steinbruner, J. D. (1974). *The cybernetic theory of decision: New dimensions of political analysis.* Princeton, NJ: Princeton University Press.

Tegarden, D. P., & Sheetz, S. D. (2003). Group causal mapping: A methodology and system for capturing and evaluating managerial and organizational cognition. *Omega, 31,* 113-125.

Vennix, J. A. M. (1996). *Group model building: Facilitating team learning using system dynamic*. Chichester, UK: Wiley.

Weick, K. E., & Bougon, M. G. (1986). Organizations as causal maps: Charting ways to success and failure. In H. Sims & D. Gioia (Eds.), *The Thinking Organization* (pp. 102-135). San Francisco: Jossey-Bass.

Zhang, W. R., Wang, W., & King, R. S. (1994). A-pool: An agent-oriented open system shell for distributed decision process modelling. *Journal of Organizational Computing, 4,* 127-154.

Endnotes

[1] In the analysis, we use their distance ratio (DR) formula to measure the distance between collective maps and individual maps.

[2] This framework and a prototype of sustainable decision support systems were developed to improve policy planning and decision making regarding urban infrastructure investments such as investments in roads and bridges, fresh water supply systems, waste water treatment, drainage and so forth.

[3] These interviews were conducted by the participants and other researchers with people who are involved with the city's infrastructure management.

[4] It was our intention to limit the number of nodes to 15 (maximum).

[5] The power-related implications of a map can be surfaced if it can be used to show how one group of stakeholders is advantaged in the current situation and how this contributes to the problems or how one group can manipulate the organization to serve their interests.

[6] The map, which had more links, thus, higher degree of map density ratio, received a higher rating.

Appendix

Cognitive Maps from Houston Case

Collective map created with aggregate method

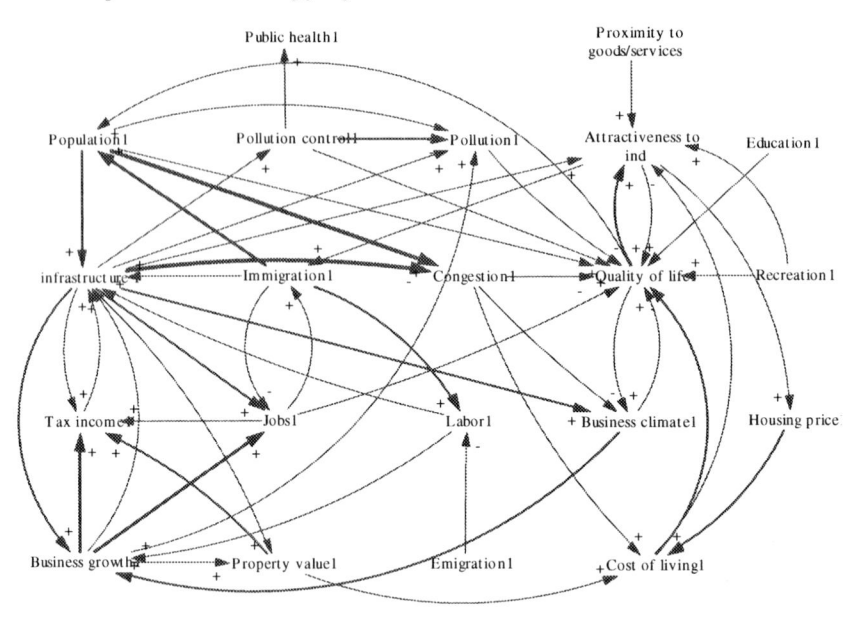

Collective map created with congregate method

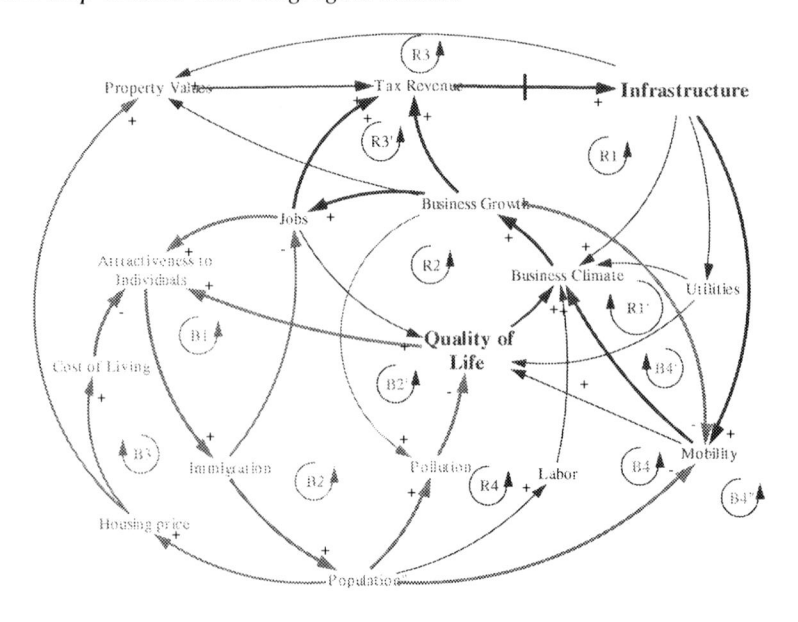

Collective Causal Mapping Approaches 173

Collective map created with workshop mapping method

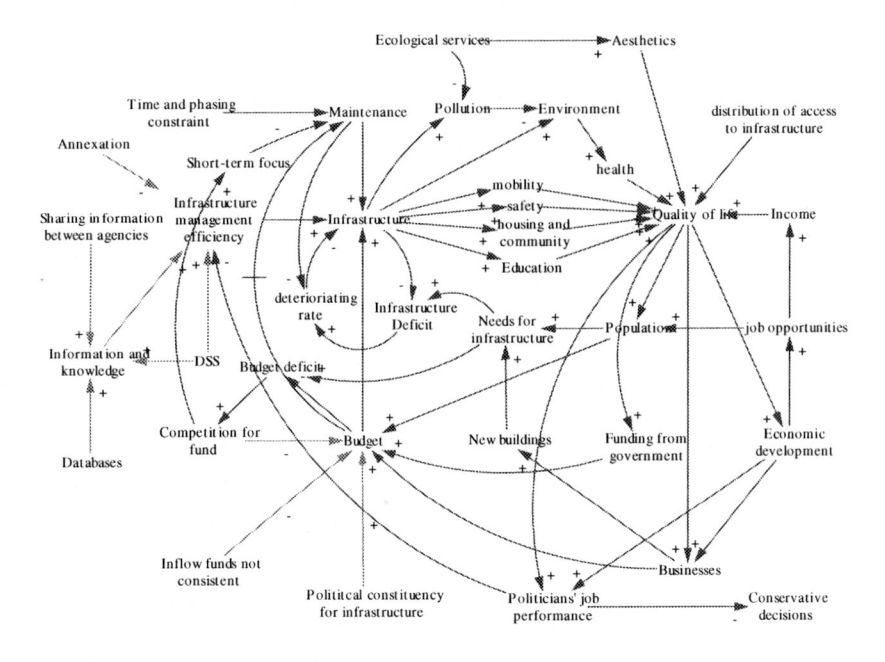

Chapter VII

Expanding Horizons:
Juxtaposing Causal Mapping and Survey Techniques[1]

Deborah J. Armstrong
University of Arkansas, USA

V.K. Narayanan
Drexel University, USA

Abstract

In this chapter, we compare the findings from causal maps derived from semi-structured interviews with that obtained from survey respondents, using a data set originally constructed to characterize object-oriented (OO) software development expertise. To compare the results, we invoke three different theories to capture evoked concepts in the interviews, but discover one theory provided more robust theoretical constructs in embracing the evoked concepts. The survey responses were factor analyzed to explore if the factor structure matched the structure derived from revealed causal maps. Although there was significant similarity between the results, the survey yielded more factors than predicted by the theory. The lessons learned from this process are discussed.

Copyright © 2005, Idea Group Inc. Copying or distributing in print or electronic forms without written permission of Idea Group Inc. is prohibited.

Introduction

The original work of Axelrod (1976) on causal mapping has remained a standard adopted by others extending the technique to discovery (e.g., Fiol & Huff, 1992), evocative (e.g., Nelson, Nadkarni, Narayanan & Ghods, 2000) and intervention (Hodgkinson & Wright, 2002) settings to name a few. While some methodological properties of causal mapping have recently come under scrutiny (Mohammed, Klimoski & Rentsch, 2001; Nadkarni & Narayanan, in press), one fundamental question remains unanswered: How do the data yielded by causal mapping techniques compare with the data obtained by other methods? Without works comparing alternate methodologies, we cannot be fully confident of the meaning of the data yielded by causal mapping, much less the appropriateness of the technique to different research settings.

In this chapter we advance the causal mapping method using a comparative study that links causal mapping data with data obtained from surveys. We take a cue from Nelson et al. (2000), who argued that causal maps are a starting point for capturing concepts in an exploratory context, but the concepts then become the basis of constructing large sample surveys for validation and hypothesis testing. The domain used for this study is object-oriented (OO) software development, which is a developing domain, and as such robust theories that capture this domain are absent. This necessitates exploratory works and we employ causal mapping to characterize the domain. We validate the causal maps by administering a relatively large sample survey that in turn provides a basis of comparison for the causal maps.

Thus the central objective of this chapter is to demonstrate an approach to couple revealed causal maps (RCMs) developed in "evocative" domains (Nelson et al., 2000) and large scale surveys designed for statistically based hypothesis testing. Put another way, we propose a strategy for systematically linking discovery and hypothesis testing contexts. An ancillary objective is to demonstrate how the approach triangulates the causal mapping technique with survey methods, thus exploring the validity of the causal mapping technique

To meet these objectives we organize the paper as follows: First, we establish the context of the study, OO software development; second, we summarize the conceptual underpinnings of the study and the strategy for triangulation; third, we provide a detailed description of the methodology used; we then report the results of the study and finally discuss the lessons learned.

The Context: Object-Oriented (OO) Software Development

"OO software development" refers to a set of principles guiding software development that emphasizes organization based on both information and processing, and that manipulates the information according to the real-world objects that the information describes (Brown, 1997). Unlike other approaches such as procedural software development, OO has come into vogue more recently and theories about OO are still evolving. As software development is knowledge work, its most important resource is expertise (Faraj & Sproull, 2000). Yet, a systematic identification of the major constructs for object-oriented software development expertise has yet to receive significant attention. While there has been an exploratory study linking cognition and OO concepts (Sheetz & Tegarden, 2001), to date no research has empirically tested the evoked theories of OO software development. This provides the perfect context to evoke and empirically test theories of expertise. As noted by Nelson et al. (2000, p.482), "in evocative studies, domain experts are available, but work is needed to evoke their knowledge and cast it into available theoretical frameworks to construct domain specific theories."

We conducted an extensive review of theoretical literature to identify the frameworks available to investigate OO software development. Theoretical sources we reviewed included textbooks on traditional software development (e.g., Dennis & Wixom, 1999; Hoffer, Valacich & George, 2001), OO software development (e.g., Brown, 1997; Martin & Odell, 1995; Norman, 1996), "classic" books on OO software development (e.g., Booch, 1994; Coad & Yourdon, 1991a, 1991b; Henderson-Sellers, 1992; Rumbaugh, Blaha, Premerlani, Eddi & Lorensen, 1991) and seminal articles in OO software development (e.g., Detienne, 1995; Fichman & Kemerer, 1992; Rosson & Alpert, 1990; Villeneuve & Fedorowicz, 1997). Table 1 lists a sample of the potential OO theories that could be used as a starting point for this research.

The abundance of theoretical frameworks is one indicator that OO theory development is in the early stages. To reduce the number of theories to a manageable set, we employed two criteria: comprehensiveness and diversity. Since this was an exploratory study, we wanted to use frameworks that represented the widest range of conceptualizations possible. *Comprehensiveness* was defined as the number of concepts identified in the

Table 1. Sample of potential OO theories used in classification scheme

Author	Theoretical Framework	Comments
Armstrong	Four OO Characteristics: Behavior, Structure, OO Modeling/Analysis and OO Development	Included second largest percentage of overlap with concepts elicited in this study (42%)
Bansiya and Davis	OO Design concepts: messaging, composition, inheritance, polymorphism, class hierarchies	Did not include a significant percentage of the concepts elicited in this study (16%)
Coad and Yourdon	Five OO Characteristics: encapsulation, inheritance, message-passing, objects, polymorphism	Did not include a significant percentage of the concepts elicited in this study (26%)
Henderson-Sellers	OO Triangle consists of encapsulation, abstraction, and polymorphism	Framework included third largest percentage of overlap with concepts elicited in this study (37%)
Rosson and Alpert	Four OO characteristics: communicating objects, abstraction, problem oriented design, and shared behavior	Framework included largest percentage of overlap with concepts elicited in this study (53%)
Sutcliffe	Four features of OO models: abstraction, classification, inheritance and encapsulation	Did not include a significant percentage of the concepts elicited in this study (21%)
Wegner	OO concepts: complex objects, object identity, methods, encapsulation, typing and inheritance	Did not include a significant percentage of the concepts elicited in this study (21%)

framework: The more concepts the framework had, the more comprehensive the framework. Several of the frameworks were too restricted in the number and variety concepts they included and thus were not appropriate for this study. *Diversity* was assessed by comparing the frameworks to each other. For example, the Booch (1994) framework was almost identical to the Coad and Yourdon (1991) framework and was thus eliminated as a candidate early in the selection process. As a result, we narrowed the theoretical frameworks to three, the major constructs of each are presented in Table 2.

- *Theoretical Framework I* was developed by grouping concepts based on the categorization scheme presented by Rosson and Alpert (1990) and utilized by Sheetz and Tegarden (2001) in their study linking cognitive activities to object-oriented design complexity. The categories Rosson and Alpert suggested were: Communicating Objects, Abstraction, Problem-Oriented Design, and Shared Behavior. The Communicating Objects category contains concepts such as message passing; the Abstraction category contains concepts such as abstraction and encapsulation; the Problem-Oriented Design category contains concepts such as modeling objects; and the Shared Behavior category contains concepts such as inheritance and class.

- *Theoretical Framework II* was adapted from Henderson-Sellers (1992). His book compiles several research articles into the idea of an object-oriented triangle (see Henderson-Sellers (1992) for a summarization of supporting literature). The first corner includes the concepts of encapsulation and information hiding. The second corner includes the concepts of abstraction, classes and objects. The third corner includes the concepts of inheritance and polymorphism.

- *Theoretical Framework III* was developed from Armstrong (in press). The categories suggested were based on the object-oriented model and consist of Behavior, Structure, OO Modeling/Analysis and OO Development. The Behavior construct contains concepts such as message passing and collaboration and is focused on the object actions within the system. The Structure construct contains concepts such as attribute, class and object and is focused on the relationships between classes and objects and the mechanisms that support the class/object structure. The OO Modeling/Analysis construct contains concepts such as identifying objects and is focused on the analysis phase and identifying the "things" or objects in the problem under study. The OO Development construct contains concepts such as framework and layer and is focused on the overall development of OO.

Table 2. Chosen theoretical framework constructs

Framework 1 Rosson and Alpert	Framework 2 Henderson-Sellers	Framework 3 Armstrong
Shared Behavior	Information Hiding, Encapsulation	Structure
Problem Oriented Design	Abstraction, Class, Object	Behavior
Communication	Inheritance, Polymorphism	OO Modeling /Analysis
Abstraction		OO Development Concepts

The underlying strategy for triangulation of RCMs and surveys employed in this study is anchored in key epistemological underpinnings, which we summarize before we detail the method.

Conceptual Underpinnings of the Methodological Strategy

Analysis of the truth claims of data by any method should rest on its conceptual underpinnings. As persuasively argued by Rescher (1992), knowledge development is itself a practice, the study of which is the domain of epistemology. Rescherian epistemology further isolates two interconnected cycles of practice underlying knowledge development, thus allowing us to categorize different approaches. The first one is a *theoretical* cycle which seeks to maintain internal consistency among theoretical ideas, or "theoretical self-substantiation." The second, an *applicative* cycle, seeks "pragmatic validation" external to theory. Rescher underscores the tension between the two cycles, and maintains that in any vibrant domain of inquiry, the overall legitimization of a methodology for the substantiation of our factual beliefs must unite the two distinct cycles, one toward a systematic coherence at the theoretical level, and the other toward pragmatic validity at the empirical level. See Figure 1(a) for a graphical representation of the cycles.

Figure 1. Rescherian epistemology applied to validation

(a) Two-fold cycle of the legitimization of systemizing methodology (Adapted from Rescher, 1992)

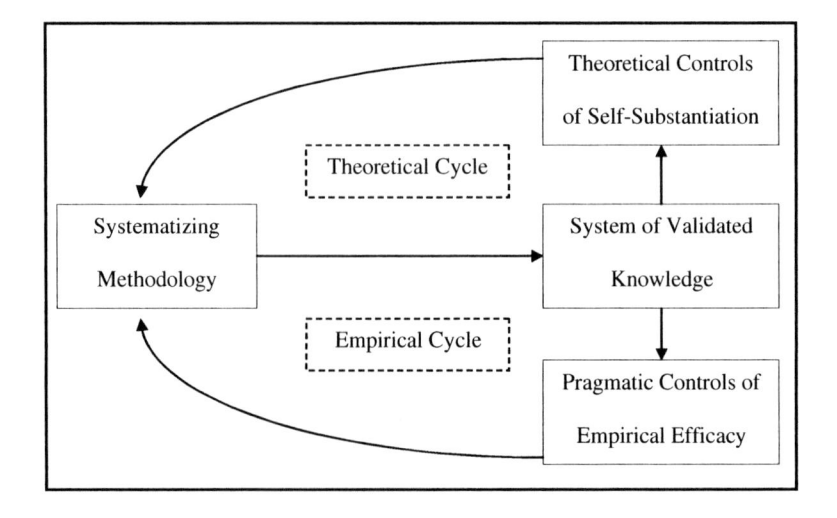

Figure 1. Rescherian epistemology applied to validation
(b) Four stage validation process for RCM

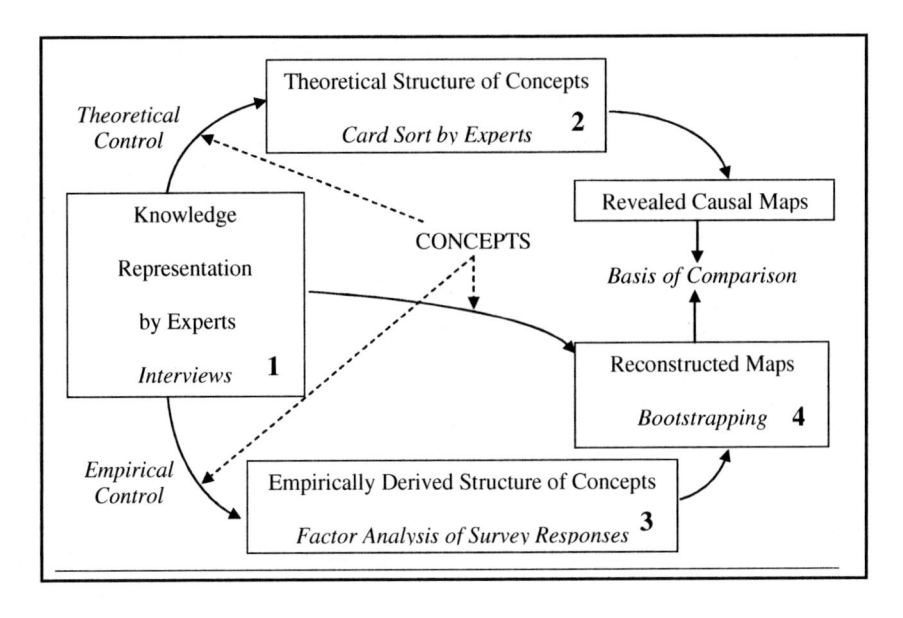

[Figure 1(b): Diagram showing the four-stage validation process. Knowledge Representation by Experts (Interviews) 1 connects via Theoretical Control to Theoretical Structure of Concepts (Card Sort by Experts) 2, which leads to Revealed Causal Maps. These form the Basis of Comparison with Reconstructed Maps (Bootstrapping) 4, which derive from Empirically Derived Structure of Concepts (Factor Analysis of Survey Responses) 3, connected back via Empirical Control. CONCEPTS is shown centrally.]

In this study we engage the two-fold cycle to develop a system of validated knowledge regarding OO software development expertise. In the theoretical cycle we develop theories of OO software development from revealed causal maps (RCMs) of OO experts. In the applicative cycle we compare the findings from the causal maps with those obtained from survey respondents.

Proposed Strategy

Our approach to the analysis of methodological validity of the RCMs is anchored in Rescherian epistemology. Specifically, we adopt a four-stage process as shown in Figure 1(b).

1. First, we engage the applicative cycle, by creating a text of what constitutes OO expertise to isolate concepts in the language of the practitioner. Semi-structured interviews were conducted with OO software development experts to gather their knowledge regarding the concepts that constitute OO development.

2. Second, through a conscious process of choice, we choose a theoretical framework to interpret the concepts, thus engaging the theoretical cycle. As stated above, three theoretical frameworks were initially chosen as candidates. Additional OO experts were asked to assess the congruence of the emergent concepts with each

theoretical framework. Each developer performed a card sort for *each* of the three theoretical frameworks. Based on the results of the card sort, we chose theoretical *Framework III*.

3. Third, we employ the interpretive framework to engage an alternate methodology (survey) for empirical validation. We developed and validated an instrument from the concepts that emerged from the interviews. The validated instrument was then given to a large sample of software developers. Factor analysis identified five factors that explain the pattern of correlations within the data.

4. Finally, we attempt a rapprochement of the tensions between theoretical and applicative cycles through a system of *bootstrapping*: We use the empirical evidence to recast the interpretive framework to contrast the outputs of theoretical and applicative cycles. The factor structure is used as another framework (*Framework IV*) to interpret the interview data. Each causal statement is re-coded using *Framework IV*, and an additional causal map is produced. The two maps, one using *Framework III* and the other using *Framework IV* are then contrasted.

Method

Using the four-stage process detailed above, we conducted two interlinked studies (Armstrong 2001): Study I, incorporating stages 1 and 2 of the validation process (see Figure (1b)), used interview data gathered from expert developers to elicit Revealed Casual Maps (RCMs). Study II gathered survey data from a large sample of software developers to unearth the empirical structure of the raw concepts from interviews and to reconstruct the RCMs through bootstrapping, stages 3 and 4 of the validation process (see Figure 1(b)).

Study I: Revealed Causal Mapping

To represent the knowledge structures of OO software development experts, we followed the causal mapping procedure detailed in Chapter II.

- *Data source.* For this study, the data source was domain experts and the narratives were gathered through semi-structured, open-ended interviews. To accomplish this task, expert OO software developers were identified using a snowball technique (Shanteau, 1987, 1992) and convenience sample (Stone, 1978).

- *Sample.* The participants in the study were expert OO software developers, as acknowledged by their peers. Organizations were selected based on their identification of available "expert software developers" and their willingness to participate. Over 15 organizations of various sizes (15-10,000 employees) and industries (e.g., telecommunications, manufacturing, consulting, and services) provided access to their software developers. In Table 3, we summarize the key characteristics of the respondents.

Table 3 — Study I. OO interview demographic, N=24

Demographic	Mean	SD
Age	39.29	7.35
Gender (% male)	96.3%	-
Years in IT	15.42	6.61
Years with current organization	3.35	2.91
Years of procedural experience	10.40	5.27
Number of procedural projects participated in	20.5	16.73
Years of object-oriented experience	4.73	1.54
Number of object-oriented projects participated in	6.79	9.46

Table 3 — Study II. Survey demographic, N= 142

Demographic	Mean	SD
Age (1 < 21, 2 = 21-30, 3=31-40, 4=41-50, 5=51-60, 6 > 60)	3.77	.870
Gender (% male)	85.9%	-
Years in IT	19.98	8.90
Years with current organization	10.89	8.63
Years of procedural experience	16.52	7.76
Number of procedural projects participated in	32.01	34.86
Years of object-oriented experience	3.46	3.07
Number of object-oriented projects participated in	2.91	2.61

- *Interviews.* The interview process consisted of open-ended interviews with probes (Rossi, Wright & Anderson, 1983). An interview guide was adapted from Nelson, Armstrong and Ghods (2002) to facilitate the interview process (see the Appendix for the Interview Guide). During the interviews respondents were asked questions regarding how they *think* about software development. Based on the respondent's answer to the question, follow-up probes were asked to elicit further details regarding their software development thought process. Each interview lasted from 30 to 90 minutes. The range of interview lengths occurred because the interviewer did not constrain the responses to the questions. The interviews were tape recorded and later transcribed into a document format ranging from four to 14 pages.

Prior to commencement, we estimated the number of interviews necessary to reach redundancy or saturation of concepts at 25. The point of redundancy was reached at 15 participants eliciting a total of 19 concepts. The point of redundancy suggested that the achieved sample of 24 respondents was more than sufficient to capture all of the relevant concepts in the sample.

Deriving Revealed Causal Maps

The causal mapping process used for this study is consistent with the steps provided in Chapter II. We have expanded on those issues not previously addressed or unique to this study.

- *Step 1: Identify Causal Statements.* Due to the cognitive nature of this study it was determined that in addition to explicit causal statements, implicit causal statements should also be recorded. To establish the reliability of the identification procedure, interview texts were coded by the researchers and one of two additional raters. The raters were deemed appropriate to identify the causal statements because of their familiarity with the technique, the domain under study, and they were not participants in any portion of the study. There were two rounds of coding that covered six OO interview texts chosen at random from the interviews. The reliability between the researchers was calculated by measuring the level of agreement on terms and linkages. The level of agreement between the researchers averaged 0.80, suggesting an acceptable level of reliability.

- *Step 2: Construct Raw Causal Maps.* In the second step, the causal statements identified in the first step were separated into "causes" and "effects" to construct the "raw causal maps."

- *Step 3: Develop Coding Scheme.* The relevant concepts were identified from the statements. A software development expert reviewed the statements and independently placed them into conceptual categories. The level of agreement between the researcher(s) and rater averaged 0.87 and a total of 19 OO concepts were identified. Once the conceptual level scheme was developed, the statements were placed into the appropriate concepts.

Tying emergent concepts to established literature has been recommended to develop categories that are distinct and uniform in breadth and level of abstraction (Carley & Palmquist, 1992; Fahey & Narayanan, 1989; Priem, 1994). To do this, we assessed the degree of congruence of the three theoretical frameworks identified in the literature review to the evoked concepts.

Three object-oriented software development experts were asked to assess the congruence of the emergent concepts with each theoretical framework. The developers were provided the constructs from each theoretical framework (see Table 2) and a set of index cards containing each of the 19 concepts, with a definition of the concept provided on the back of the card for their reference. Each developer performed a card sort according to *each* of the three theoretical frameworks. The card sort was conducted using a different framework order for each developer. The average level of agreement among the developers was 0.52 for *Framework I*, 0.33 for *Framework II*, and 0.70 for *Framework III*. Based on the results of the card sort, we chose theoretical *Framework III* as the appropriate construct level classification scheme. The correspondence between the 19 evoked concepts and constructs is presented in Table 4.

- *Step 4: Recast the "raw" maps into Revealed Causal Maps.* Once the classification scheme was completed, the causal statements for each respondent were placed into the appropriate concept and construct level categories. The result is a concept and construct level RCM for each respondent. The individual maps are then aggregated (Axelrod, 1976; Bougon, Weick & Binkhorst, 1977; Nadkarni & Nah, 2003) into one overall map.

Table 4. Construct and concept detail for theoretical Framework III

Construct	Concept
Structure	Abstraction
	Attribute
	Class
	Encapsulation
	Information Hiding
	Inheritance
	Instantiation
	Object
Behavior	Collaboration
	Message Passing
	Method
	Polymorphism
	Relationship
OO Modeling/Analysis	Identifying Objects
	Noun-Verb Analysis
	Object Model
OO Development Concepts	Patterns
	Layer
	OO Development

- *Step 5: Create Measures for the Maps.* The analysis of the maps in this study was based on past research in causal mapping (Bougon et al., 1977; Ford & Hegarty, 1984: Huff, 1990; Narayanan & Fahey, 1990; Nelson et al., 2000). The measures used are borrowed from the social network analysis field (Knoke & Kuklinski, 1982) and include the adjacency and reachability matrices, centrality and density measures (see Chapter II for a detailed discussion of the measures).

Study II: Survey

- *Data source.* We developed an instrument to capture the concepts emerging from the interviews. As a starting point, five statements per concept were selected for inclusion in the instrument based on content and clarity. Internal validity and construct validity were addressed through a pretest sort (Anderson & Gerbing, 1991). Based on the results of the pretest sort statements were re-worded or deleted. The pilot instrument was developed from the remaining list of statements. The pilot instrument was given to 31 software developers. We assessed scale internal consistency reliability using Cronbach's alpha (Huck, 2000). Correlations between variables were analyzed, and questions were deleted or re-worded for clarity. The final instrument covered 19 object-oriented concepts[5].

- *Sample.* The validated instrument was then given to a large sample of software developers. The sample was drawn from organizations selected based on their identification of available "software developers" and their willingness to participate. Thirty-three organizations of diverse industries (e.g., telecommunications, manufacturing, aerospace and financial services) provided access to their software developers. Study respondents were chosen based on a key-informant method (Bagozzi, Yi & Phillips, 1991; Seidler, 1974). Participants in this phase of the study were different than the respondents used in the previous phase of the project. A total of 177 responses were originally recorded with 35 being eliminated due to lack of software development experience, duplicate responses, or other problems with the data, leaving a sample of 142 respondents. A profile of the Study II (survey) sample is presented in Table 3.

- *Factor analysis.* We used an exploratory principal components factor analysis with varimax rotation to reduce the variables to a usable set of constructs for the OO software development expertise framework. Past research has provided guidelines for the minimum sample size needed to conduct factor analysis. Some have suggested the ratio of sample size to number of variables as a criterion: the recommendations range from 2:1 to 20:1 (e.g., Bryant & Yarnold, 1995). Others have suggested using a minimum sample size as the criterion. For example, Lawley and

Table 5. Factor analysis for Framework IV

Construct	Alpha	Concept
Nesting	0.806	Inheritance
		OO Development
		Polymorphism
Object Characteristics	0.918	Attributes
		Class
		Encapsulation
		Instantiation
		Method
Behavior II	0.818	Collaboration
		Message Passing
		Relationship
OO Modeling/Analysis II	0.872	Identifying Objects
		Noun-Verb Analysis
		Object
OO Development Concepts II	0.883	Abstraction
		Patterns
		Information Hiding
		Layer
		Object Model

Maxwell (1971) suggest that there should be 51 more cases than the number of variables. In their 1988 study, Guadagnoli and Velicer found that absolute sample size was more important than functions of sample size in determining stable solutions and recommend 100 to 200 observations. Our sample of 142 respondents fell within the acceptable range for the analysis. The number of respondents represents a sufficient sample to perform principal components analysis.

The resulting factor structure is summarized in Table 5, with the associated Cronbach's alpha reliability scores. As shown in the table, the object-oriented concepts loaded on *five* factors that we named Nesting, Object Characteristics, Behavior II[2], OO Modeling/Analysis II, and OO Development Concepts II, using an *eigen* value >1.00 criterion. Cumulatively, the factors accounted for 71% of variance in the sample. The Nesting construct (a = 0.81) dealt with managing the complexity in the object-oriented mindset (e.g., inheritance, polymorphism). Similarly, the Object Characteristics construct (a = 0.92) dealt with the packages that the basic concepts are put into (e.g., class, instantiation), thus focusing on the development and functioning of an object. The Behavior II construct (a = 0.82) consisted of the communication and relationships between sets of objects (e.g., collaboration, message passing). The OO Modeling/Analysis II construct (a = 0.87) consists of concepts that are the fundamental techniques for object-oriented analysis (e.g., object, identifying things as objects). Finally, OO Development Concepts II (a = 0.88) focused on how objects function within the larger system to make up an object-oriented application (e.g., abstraction, layer), i.e., finding, modifying, and assembling the classes and methods needed to support an entire application.

Results and Discussion

We present the results in three steps. First, we present the constructs revealed in the interviews that are central to understanding OO software development expertise, highlighting the characteristics of the revealed linkages between constructs in the aggregate RCMs. Second, we summarize the results of the recasting of RCMs based on classification suggested by the factor analysis of survey responses. Third, we provide an assessment of the congruence between the original and the reconstructed RCMs.

Study I: Revealed Causal Maps

The aggregate level RCMs from the interview data represented OO software development expertise as being constituted by four major constructs: Structure, Behavior, OO Modeling/Analysis, and OO Development Concepts and is shown in Figure 2(a). The overall density of the map is 1.75, indicating a relatively high interconnectedness. As shown in Table 4, eight concepts comprise the Structure construct, which has a centrality of 0.57, suggesting that it occupies a prominent role in OO software development. The Behavior construct contains five concepts and the centrality is 0.57 suggesting a

Figure 2(a). Aggregated construct level revealed causal map, interview data

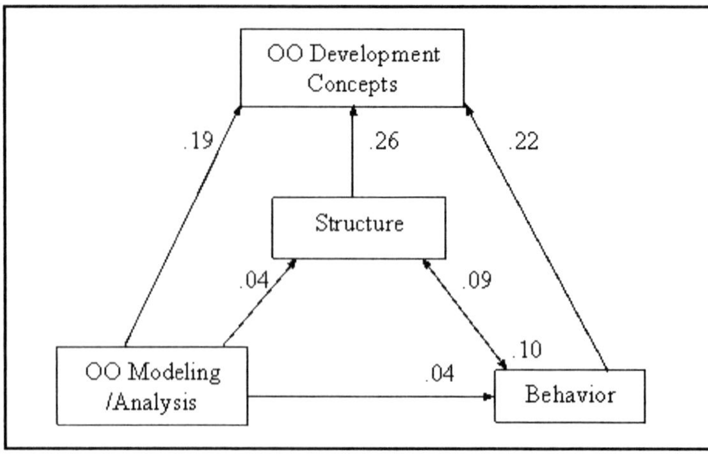

prominent role in OO development. The OO Modeling/Analysis construct evoked in this study contains three concepts and has a centrality of 0.43 suggesting a slightly lesser role in OO software development. The fourth construct, OO Development contains three concepts related to overall OO development. The centrality of the construct is 0.43, suggesting a slightly lesser role in the OO approach. While the results are consistent with those found by Sheetz and Tegarden (2001), this is the first study that has found the importance of these additional concepts as components of OO. The data indicate that the structure and behavior of objects are equally central to OO development, with modeling and overall development slightly less central.

The reachability matrix of the aggregated construct level RCM is presented in Table 6. It reveals that experts see OO Modeling/Analysis as a cause construct (all arrows from the construct) and OO Development as an effect construct (all arrows into the construct). The Structure and Behavior constructs are both cause and effect constructs. The highest reachability occurs for the linkages in which OO Development Concepts is the effect construct.

Study II: Reconstructed RCMs

Recall that the factor analysis of the survey data yielded five factors: Nesting, Object Characteristics, Behavior II, OO Modeling/Analysis II, and OO Development Concepts II. The reconstructed map can be seen in Figure 2(b). The density of the overall map is 1.80. The centrality of the five constructs varied from a low of 0.11 (OO Development Concepts II), 0.33 (Object Characteristics), to 0.44 (Behavior II) to a high of 0.56 (OO Modeling/Analysis II, and Nesting). Table 6 also presents the reachability matrix for the reconstructed (aggregated construct level) RCM based on the survey data. The aggregated RCM of the OO software developers reveals that developers learning OO tech-

Copyright © 2005, Idea Group Inc. Copying or distributing in print or electronic forms without written permission of Idea Group Inc. is prohibited.

Figure 2(b). Data aggregated construct level reveal causal map

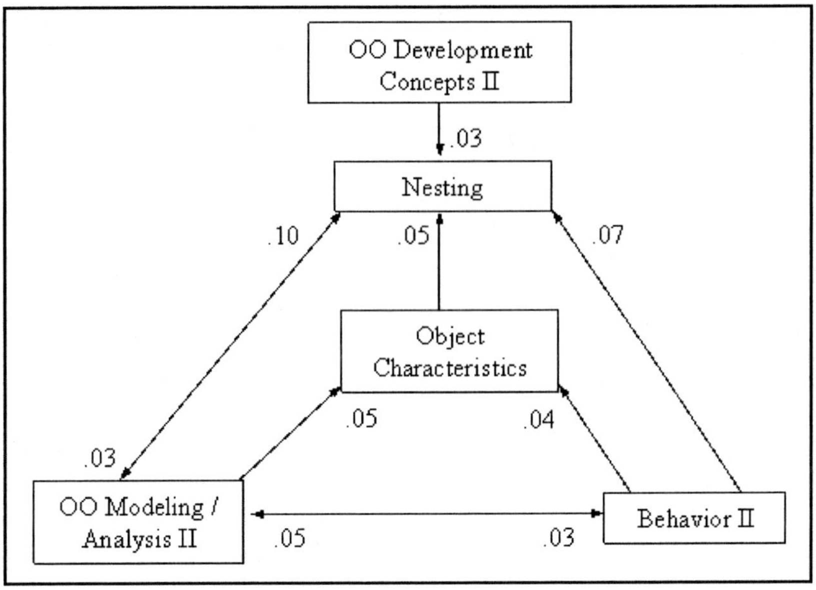

```
                    OO Development
                      Concepts II
                           │
                          .03
                           ▼
                        Nesting
              .10  ↗    .05 ↑    ↖ .07
                           │
                    Object
                    Characteristics
                 .05          .04
         .03 ↙                      ↘
     OO Modeling /  ←───────────→  Behavior II
      Analysis II   .05       .03
```

Table 6³. Reachability matrices for aggregated construct level RCM

Interview	A	B	C	D
A. Structure	■	0.104	-	0.260
B. Behavior	0.094	■	-	0.219
C. OO Modeling/Analysis I	0.042	0.042	■	0.188
D. OO Development Concepts 1	-	-	-	■

Survey	A1	A2	B	C	D
A1. Nesting	■	-	-	0.025	-
A2. Object Characteristics	0.047	■	-	-	-
B. Behavior II	0.074	0.036	■	0.045	-
C. OO Modeling/Analysis II	0.098	0.045	0.031	■	-
D. OO Development Concepts II	0.029	-	-	-	■

niques (with the exception of OO Development Concepts II being a cause construct) do not see clear cause and effect constructs within the OO software development approach. The reachability values between the constructs were fairly consistent (mean .05), with the linkages into the Nesting construct (effect) slightly stronger.

A Comparative Analysis of Revealed and Reconstructed RCMs

There are similarities and differences between the cognitive structures that constitute OO software development expertise yielded by revealed and reconstructed RCMs. See Table 7 for comparison of the concepts and constructs. From the demographics of the two samples we can see that the respondents for the interview data had about one additional year of OO experience, but had completed twice the number of OO projects as the respondents for the survey data. Based on the differences in experience, the difference between the interview (expert) cognitions and the survey cognitions should be quite large. When comparing the OO interview RCMs to the survey RCMs there should be differences because the respondents are at different places in the learning process.

Recall that the factor analysis yielded five constructs, one more than the theoretical framework that best fit the evoked concepts. As shown in Table 7, there was significant overlap between the Behavior, OO Modeling/Analysis, and OO Development Concepts constructs across the two methods. The survey responses separated into two constructs (Object Characteristics and Nesting) what the best fitting theoretical framework combined into one (Structure). This is consistent with general theories of expertise on

Table 7.[4] Comparison of Study I versus Study II concepts and constructs

Study I Construct	Study I Concepts	Study II Constructs	Study II Concepts
Structure	Abstraction	Nesting	Inheritance
	Attribute		OO Development
	Class		Polymorphism
	Encapsulation	Object Characteristics	Attribute
	Information Hiding		Class
	Inheritance		Encapsulation
	Instantiation		Instantiation
	Object		Method
Behavior	Collaboration	Behavior II	Collaboration
	Message Passing		Message Passing
	Method		Relationship
	Polymorphism		
	Relationship		
OO Modeling / Analysis	Identifying Objects	OO Modeling / Analysis II	Identifying Objects
	Noun-Verb Analysis		Noun-Verb Analysis
	Object Model		Object
OO Development Concepts	Patterns	OO Development Concepts II	Abstraction
	Layer		Patterns
	OO Development		Information Hiding
			Layer
			Object Model

software development that asserts that as developers gain expertise they create larger chunks of information with more abstract representations (e.g., Adelson, 1981; McKeithen, Reitman, Rueter & Hirtle, 1981; Murphy & Wright, 1984; Pennington, 1987).

In addition to the basic structure of the maps there are several similarities and differences in the linkages of the maps. As shown in Table 6, the reachabilitiy matrices demonstrate that there is a common linkage from the Behavior construct to the Structure (Nesting and Object Characteristics) constructs. In addition, the OO Modeling/Analysis construct has two linkages in common across the maps, with the Structure (Nesting and Object Characteristics) and Behavior constructs. The centrality measures highlight some differences in the maps. The interview data indicated two layers of centrality, with layer one including the Structure and Behavior constructs, and layer two including the OO Modeling and OO Development constructs. This indicates a relatively flat cognitive structure. In contrast, the survey data indicated three layers, with layer one including the OO Development construct, layer two including the Behavior and Object Characteristics constructs, and layer three including the Nesting and OO Modeling constructs. In addition to more layers, the survey data map had a wider range of centrality scores than the interview data map. This indicates a more hierarchical and complex cognitive structure in which some concepts are more central and others more ancillary to the domain.

The reachability measure provides another mechanism for comparison. In the interview data map the OO Development construct has by far the highest reachability with a large variance among the reachability values. In contrast, in the survey data map the reachability values have a much smaller range with the Nesting construct having the highest reachability. Thus while the content of the maps is quite similar, the main difference in the two maps is in the linkages.

Discussion

Before discussing our results, we should place them in context, noting that OO development techniques have only come into vogue in recent years. This low level of maturity has three correlates: lack of theoretical parsimony, standardization and professionalization. As a field matures, developments are likely to result in parsimonious theory and consequently fewer clearly articulated concepts. This makes possible standardization of approaches, very much akin to the emergence of technical standards. In turn this allows transmission of explicit knowledge thus facilitating professionalization of practitioners. In our search for an adequate theoretical scheme to categorize the evoked concepts in OO, we found a variety of frameworks. Even the best fitting framework could embrace only slightly over half the evoked concepts. The tacit knowledge of the experts seems to be more extensive than represented by the available theoretical frameworks. Clearly, theoretical development in OO software development is far from complete.

Under these conditions, evocative approaches such as RCM appear not merely to be an adornment, but a necessity in research to capture the "true" phenomena under investigation. Against the backdrop of the lack of consensus among theoretical frameworks describing OO, the correspondence between the RCM and survey responses augurs well for the former, newer method, which is alleged to be a more appropriate tool for cognition research (Huff, 1990). This is one of the first studies designed to develop a cognitive representation of expertise in OO software development and then empirically test that representation. Its results, consisting of the concepts, constructs and the linkages among them — in short the cognitive structuring of expertise in OO — provide a starting point for empirically representing knowledge structures.

Lessons Learned

This is arguably one of the first studies designed to juxtapose the RCM method with the survey method, thus we can only draw tentative implications. Nonetheless, we need to point out four potentially significant implications:

1. The four stage validation process — gathering a knowledge representation of experts, choosing a theoretical structure to interpret those concepts, using the evoked concepts to design large sample surveys, and finally using the survey output to re-construct the causal maps — offers a useful approach to juxtapose RCM and survey methods.
2. Although our results point to the empirical validity of the RCM approach in the task of knowledge representation, they highlight the sensitivity of construct-level representations of RCM to the underlying theoretical framework. Great care should be exercised in the choice of theoretical frameworks to group evoked concepts.
3. Perhaps more specifically, our study suggests that the RCM approach can become the basis of other large sample studies in exploratory contexts.
4. In discovery and evocative contexts, i.e., early stages of theory development, where different theories may be competing for accuracy, RCMs derived from experts may provide one method of standardizing the theoretical framework.

Conclusion

One of the significant challenges in theory development in new domains is the task of coupling discovery with verification through normal science methods. To date, there has been no systematic approach to accomplish this, since scholars who engage in discovery are rarely the ones engaged in verification. As we have shown, causal mapping linked to surveys may provide one method by which the linkage between discovery and verification can be systematically juxtaposed. Finally, we would argue that such linkage is consistent with the received wisdom from epistemology.

References

Adelson, B. (1981). Problem solving and the development of abstract categories in programming languages. *Memory and Cognition, 9*, 422-433.

Anderson, J. C., & Gerbing, D. W. (1991). Predicting the performance of measures in a confirmatory factor analysis with a pretest assessment of their substantive validities. *Journal of Applied Psychology, 76*(5), 732-740.

Armstrong, D. (2004). The quarks of object-oriented development. *Communications of the ACM*, in press.

Armstrong, D. (2001). Charting the rocky shoals of an object-oriented mindshift. Unpublished dissertation, University of Kansas, Lawrence, KS.

Axelrod, R. (1976). *Structure of decision: the cognitive maps of political elites.* Princeton, NJ: Princeton University Press.

Bagozzi, R. P., Yi, Y., & Phillips, L. W. (1991). Assessing construct validity in organizational research. *Administrative Science Quarterly, 36*, 421-458.

Bansiya, J., & Davis, C. G. (2002). A hierarchical model for object-oriented design quality assessment. *IEEE Transactions on Software Engineering, 28*(1), 4-17.

Booch G. (1994). *Object-oriented analysis and design with applications,* (2nd edition). San Francisco: Benjamin Cummings Publishing.

Bougon, M., Weick, K., & Binkhorst, D. (1977). Cognition in organizations: An analysis of the Utrecht jazz orchestra. *Administrative Science Quarterly, 22*, 606-639.

Brown, D. (1997). *An introduction to object-oriented analysis: Objects in plain English.* New York: John Wiley & Sons.

Bryant, P.G., & Yarnold, P.R. (1995). Principal components analysis and exploratory and confirmatory factor analysis. In L.G. Grimm & P.R. Yarnold (Eds.), *Reading and understanding multivariate statistics* (pp. 83-97). Washington, DC: American Psychological Association Books.

Carley, K., & Palmquist, M. (1992). Extracting, representing and analyzing mental models. *Social Forces, 70*, 215-225.

Coad P., & Yourdon, E. (1991a). *Object-oriented analysis* (2nd edition). New York: Prentice Hall.

Coad P., & Yourdon, E. (1991b). *Object-oriented design.* New York: Prentice Hall.

Dennis, A., & Wixom, B.H. (1999). *Systems Analysis and Design.* New York: John Wiley & Sons.

Detienne, F. (1995). Design strategies and knowledge in object-oriented programming: Effects of experience. *Human Computer Interaction, 10*, 129-169.

Fahey, L., & Narayanan, V. K. (1989). Linking changes in revealed causal maps and environment: An empirical study. *Journal of Management Studies. 26*(4), 361-378.

Faraj, S., & Sproull, L. (2000). Coordinating expertise in software development teams. *Management Science, 46*(12), 1554-1568.

Fichman, R. G., & Kemerer, C. F. (1992, October). Object-oriented and conventional analysis and design methodologies: Comparison and critique. *IEEE Computer*, 22-39.

Fiol, C. M., & Huff, A. S. (1992). Maps for managers: where are we? Where do we go from here? *Journal of Management Studies*, 29, 267-285.

Ford, J. D., & Hegarty, W. H. (1984). Decision maker's beliefs about the causes and effects of structure: An exploratory study. *Academy of Management Journal*, 27, 271-291.

Guadagnoli, E., & Velicer, W. F. (1988). Relation of sample size to the stability of component patterns. *Psychological Bulletin,* 103, 265-275.

Henderson-Sellers, B. (1992). *A book of object-oriented knowledge.* Englewood Cliffs, NJ: Prentice Hall.

Hodgkinson, G.P., & Wright, G. (2002). Confronting strategic inertia in a top management team: Learning from failure. *Organization Studies,* 23(6), 949-969.

Hoffer, J. A., Valacich, J. S., & George, J. F. (2001). *Modern systems analysis and design* (3rd Edition). New York: Pearson Education.

Huck, S.W. (2000). *Reading statistics and research.* New York: Addison Wesley Longman.

Huff, A. (1990). Mapping the process of problem reformulation: Implications for understanding strategic thought. In A. Huff (Ed.), *Mapping strategic thought.* New York: John Wiley & Sons.

Knoke, D., & Kuklinski, J. H. (1982). *Network analysis.* Newbury Park, CA: Sage.

Lawley, D. N., & Maxwell, A. E. (1971). *Factor analysis as a statistical method.* London: Butterworth.

Martin, J., & Odell, J. J. (1995). *Object-oriented methods: A foundation.* Englewood Cliffs, NJ: Prentice Hall.

McKeithen, K., Reitman, J., Rueter, H., & Hirtle, S. (1981). Knowledge organization and skill differences in computer programmers. *Cognitive Psychology*, 13, 307-325.

Mohammed, S., Klimoski, R., & Rentsch, J. (2001). The measurement of team mental models: We have no shared schema. *Organizational Research Methods,* 3, 123-165.

Murphy, G. L., & Wright, J. C. (1984). Changes in the conceptual structure with expertise: differences between real world experts and novices. *Journal of Experimental Psychology: Learning, Memory and Cognition*, 10, 144-155.

Nadkarni, S., & Nah, F.F.H. (2003). Aggregated causal maps: An approach to elicit and aggregate the knowledge of multiple experts. *Communications of the Association of Information Systems,* 12, 406-436.

Nadkarni, S., & Narayanan, V.K. (2004). Validty of the structural measures of text-based causal maps: An empirical assessment. *Organizational Research Methods*, in press.

Narayanan, V. K., & Fahey, L. (1990). Evolution of revealed causal maps during decline: A case study of Admiral. In A. Huff (Ed.), *Mapping strategic thought* (pp. 109-133). London: John Wiley & Sons.

Nelson, H. J., Armstrong, D., & Ghods, M. (2002). Teaching old dogs new tricks. *Communications of the ACM,* 45(10), 132-137.

Nelson, K. M., Nadkarni, S., Narayanan, V. K., & Ghods, M. (2000). Understanding software operations support expertise: A causal mapping approach. *MIS Quarterly,* 24, 475-507.

Norman, R. J. (1996). *Object-oriented systems analysis and design.* Upper Saddle River, NJ: Prentice Hall.

Pennington, N. (1987). Stimulus structures and mental representations in expert comprehension of computer programs. *Cognitive Psychology,* 19, 295-341.

Priem, R. L. (1994). Executive judgment, organizational congruence, and firm performance. *Organization Science,* 5, 421-437.

Rescher, N. (1992). *A System of Pragmatic Idealism, Volume I: Human Knowledge in Idealistic Perspective.* Princeton, NJ: Princeton University Press.

Rossi, P. H., Wright, J. D., & Anderson, A. B. (1983). *Handbook of Research Methods.* Orlando, FL: Academic Press.

Rosson, M., & Alpert, S. R. (1990). The cognitive consequences of object-oriented design. *Human Computer Interaction,* 5, 345-379.

Rumbaugh, J., Blaha, M., Premerlani, W., Eddi, F., & Lorensen, W. (1991). *Object-oriented modeling and design.* New York: Prentice Hall.

Seidler, J. (1974). On using informants: A technique for collecting quantitative data and controlling for measurement error in organizational analysis. *American Sociological Review,* 39(12), 816-831.

Shanteau, J. (1992). Competence in experts: The role of task characteristics. *Organizational Behavior and Human Decision Processes,* 53, 252-266.

Shanteau, J. (1987). Psychological characteristics of expert decision makers. In J. L. Mumpower, O. Renn, L. D. Phillips, & V. R. Uppuluri (Eds.), *Expert judgment and expert systems* (pp. 289-304). Berlin: Springer-Verlag.

Sheetz, S. D., & Tegarden, D. P. (2001). Illustrating the cognitive consequences of object-oriented systems development. *The Journal of Systems and Software,* 59, 163-179.

Stone, E. (1978). *Research methods in organizational behavior.* Glenview: Scott and Foresman.

Sutcliffe, A. G. (1991). Object-oriented systems analysis: The abstract question. Proc. IFIP WG 8.1 Conference. *The object oriented approach in information systems,* Quebec City, Canada.

Villeneuve, A. O., & Fedorowicz, J. (1997). Understanding expertise in information systems design, or, What's all the fuss about objects? *Decision Support Systems,* 21, 111-131.

Wegner, P. (1987). Dimensions of object-based language design. *ACM Sigplan,* 23(11), 168-182.

Endnotes

[1] An earlier version of this work titled "Juxtaposing Causal Mapping and Survey Techniques to Characterize Expertise" was presented at the Academy of Management Conference, Seattle, WA, August 2003.

[2] The II symbol is used to distinguish the survey driven construct from the interview driven construct.

[3] Gray cells indicate common connections or lack of connections for interview and survey data. Black cells indicate that a construct does not have a causal linkage with itself.

[4] Shaded area indicates common concepts/constructs for interview and survey data.

[5] Instrument available upon request from first author.

Appendix

Interview Guide

1. When a friend asks you "What is object-oriented development?" what do you say?
2. What are the main ideas that define object-oriented development?
3. What is the easiest concept to learn?
4. What is the most difficult concept to master?
5. How is that different from procedural development?
6. Think of a time when you have been given a requirements document (for example, say to develop an accounting system) and asked to produce an object-oriented solution. What was the first thing you did? How did you proceed from there?
7. What problems do you think experienced procedural developers have as they learn object-oriented development?
8. How could the transition from procedural to object-oriented development be made easier?
9. How do you know if an object-oriented developer is an expert?

Chapter VIII

Reflections on the Interview Process in Evocative Settings

Kay M. Nelson
The Ohio State University, USA

Abstract

Revealed causal mapping (RCM) represents one of the best ways to study a phenomenon in a discovery or evocative setting. The RCM method provides rich data that facilitates a deeper understanding of the cognitive facets of a phenomenon not available with other methods. In this chapter I will share insights gained from conducting several interactively elicited causal mapping studies in the discovery and evocative research contexts. I address issues a researcher will encounter during in the interview process, the causal statement identification procedure, and the development of the coding scheme. I conclude with some thoughts on lessons learned in the field.

Introduction

Revealed causal mapping (RCM) is an increasingly powerful tool for several research contexts including discovery, exploratory, hypothesis testing and intervention (see Chapter I for a detailed discussion of the research contexts). This chapter provides insights for conducting research in a discovery or exploratory context. In a discovery (or exploratory) setting the initial data collection process is conducted without any preconceived constructs in mind other than the general issue at hand. When using RCM as a theory *building* or discovery methodology, rather than a theory *confirming* or hypothesis testing methodology, the process must be open to allow constructs to be revealed that had not been initially anticipated by the interviewer. It is important that one decide at the beginning of a RCM study what data collection method is appropriate for the phenomenon under study (see Chapter II). Since I have used the discovery and exploratory research contexts in my work with revealed causal mapping, I will address my comments only to those research contexts and specifically interactively elicited causal maps. To make the process a bit clearer, I will use as a context portions of a much larger study of IT personnel transition[1].

In this chapter I will share what I have learned through the process of conducting revealed causal mapping research. I will begin by discussing the interview process and identifying causal statements from the interview texts. Then I will provide some insights on the development of a coding scheme and will conclude with some thoughts on lessons learned.

Interviews

The goal of the interviews is to guide the respondents to a discussion of the issues without leading them to specific predetermined constructs (Rossi, Wright & Anderson, 1983). To achieve this, the interviews use open-ended questions and do not specifically mention the phenomenon under study. Open-ended questions are augmented with probes (Rossi et al., 1983), where the interviewer is trained to explore a respondent's answer to discover new concepts not originally expected in the interview guide. A sample interview guide is included in the Appendix. Data elicited in the interviews is iteratively validated by going back to the respondents to clarify and confirm their responses. For example, in my study of IT personnel transition, we confirmed the responses by returning to the participants and verifying what was revealed in the interview transcripts and asking for clarification on issues such as time frame, and intended meaning.

Identifying Causal Statements

The interview transcripts are analyzed by identifying causal statements embedded in the answers of the respondents, where a causal statement is defined as a statement that a respondent makes revealing their belief that one thing causes another (Ford & Hegarty, 1984). The analysis of causal statements is an iterative process and does require informed decision making on the part of the research team. By using this inductive approach and allowing constructs to arise out of the interview data, we intentionally refrain from imposing a conceptual or predefined structure on the data (Mitroff & Mason, 1982) in a discovery or evocative setting.

The first stage of data analysis in revealed causal mapping is analyzing the interview transcripts for causal statements, both implicit and explicit. I recommend that the statements be first pulled out of the interview transcripts into a spreadsheet so they can be easily traced back to the original interview document page and paragraph from which they were elicited. The statements need not be put into the spreadsheet verbatim, but rather they can be moved to the spreadsheet either in fragments or paraphrased.

Coding Scheme

Identification of the patterns and frequencies of the construct connections is made with the revealed causal mapping technique, resulting in a theoretical structure that is more purely elicited from the data, not from predetermined biases (Robinson, 1950). This is accomplished through the procedure of developing an initial concept-level coding scheme, identifying the major evoked constructs, and organizing the concepts and constructs.

Each causal statement is analyzed to identify specific concepts, and as new concepts are elicited from the transcripts, a complete list is generated. This first part of the coding process should be done by the members of the interview team when respondents are first interviewed face-to-face. The interviewers are best able to do the initial coding since they were in the room with the respondents and can interpret the interview transcripts with knowledge of the body language, demeanor, and other characteristics of the respondent. If the interviews are performed by telephone, it becomes less critical that the interviewers do the initial coding, although it is still preferred. The number of transcripts chosen to develop the initial coding scheme will vary both by number of respondents and the point of redundancy in the study, which is reached when the number of constructs from interviews converge and no new constructs are found. There is no specific percentage of respondents that drives how many transcripts are used to form the initial coding scheme. Rather, the initial coders will continue to do comparisons for inter-rater reliability until an acceptable level of agreement is reached. The level of agreement between the researchers can be measured using Kendall's coefficient of concordance (Siegel, 1956). The reliability of this process is improved through constant checks of inter-rater concordance.

For the five studies I have done using this methodology in a discovery context, all with fewer than 100 respondents, acceptable concordance was reached by having multiple researchers (in my experience, two to four) each code ten spreadsheets (one spreadsheet per interview transcript) containing the raw causal statements from the transcripts. This should be done individually by each researcher without consultation from the others. No formal coding scheme should be used during this phase of the process. This is done deliberately to let concepts emerge as they are reported by the respondents. Whatever the initial coders believe the cause or effect represents is written down as a code in one to three words. Then the initial coders exchange transcripts and recode each others', checking for inconsistencies. The inconsistencies are worked out by going back to the original transcripts and reading the cause or effect statement in context. This process continues and is refined until all of the transcripts are coded. If ten spreadsheets do not result in an acceptable coefficient of concordance, the process must be continued until concordance. For example, in the IT Personnel Transition Study (Rice & Nelson, 2003) the final coefficient of concordance was 0.75.

Coding Scheme Granularity

From this iterative process a first cut, an initial coding guide is developed that sorts the causal statement codes into three levels of granularity: concepts, categories, and constructs. A concept is the actual idea or information embodied in the statement. A category is a grouping of related concepts that occur at a similar level of granularity (e.g., individual, group, organization). Constructs are the highest level of abstraction and consist of related categories. Once the coding scheme has been determined, the rest of the spreadsheets are coded, again by at least two individuals who cross-check each other's work to maintain reliability. Through trial and error (Nelson, Nadkarni, Narayanan, & Ghods, 2000), we found that having an additional level of granularity — categories — allowed us to group similar concepts that were revealed at different levels of analysis. We call this final guide a construct/concept table, with the acknowledgement that the "category" column of the table sorts out the levels of analysis for each construct.

For example, in the Information Technology Personnel Transition study (Rice & Nelson, 2003) we found that there were some categories that significantly impacted IT personnel in different ways. Within the Environment construct at the individual level, concepts that influenced the individual in the workplace had a different impact on transition than concepts that concern home and family life. Therefore, these concepts were put in different categories. Concepts such as *autonomy, responsibility, flexibility* and *availability of opportunities* were put in the category of Job Environment (organization level). Concepts such as *family, mental health*, and *age* were put in the category that was labeled Individual Environmental factors (individual level). As can be seen, these are both individual-level concepts, but their impact on an individual's ability to transition

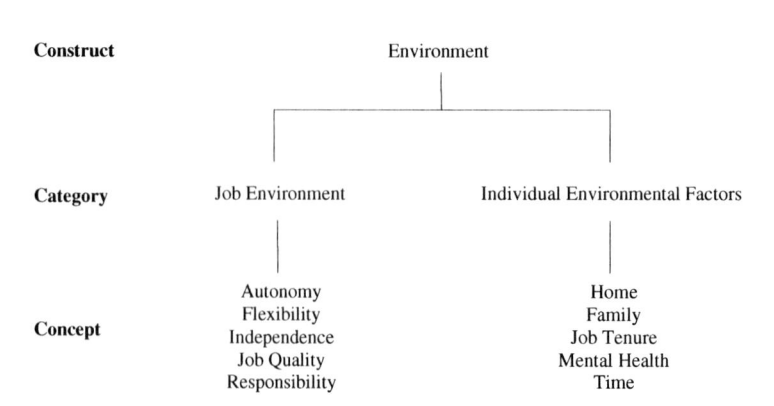

Figure 1. Sample coding scheme hierarchy

Construct	Environment	
Category	Job Environment	Individual Environmental Factors
Concept	Autonomy Flexibility Independence Job Quality Responsibility	Home Family Job Tenure Mental Health Time

is considerably different. These differences require the concepts to be categorized into different groupings even though they are still part of the same construct — in this case, the Environment. See Figure 1 for a representation of these relationships.

Multiple Definitions

When coding for revealed causal mapping, it is critical to examine words that describe cause or effect concepts. Researchers must be very careful because in many cases, the same word may actually describe something reflecting a different concept or the same concept at a different level of granularity. For example, the word "training" emerged from many of the transition interview transcripts. However, when taken in context, "training" was an individual-level concept in the categories of Knowledge Acquisition, Motivation and Personal Outcomes, but "training" was also a concept which was described by the respondents as something that was seen as Corporate Support and Direction which is at the organizational level. Therefore, it is clearly necessary that in the cross-validation procedure, the coding assigned to the cause and effect statements in the spreadsheets must often be traced back to the actual transcript of the interview from which they were taken to reconfirm the proper context. If this is not done very carefully and all the steps followed (Nelson et al., 2000), or coders are not trained properly, it is very likely that concepts will be coded incorrectly.

Lessons Learned

There are several lessons that the researcher interested in this type of study can take away from this chapter. The first is that it is important to develop a well thought out interview guide with open-ended questions. These questions should be focused on guiding the participant to the phenomenon without biasing the participant's response. In addition, the success of the interview often resides in the interviewer's probing skills. Depending on the phenomenon under study, the interviewee may be reluctant to discuss the issue or be unsure as to what "answers" you are looking for. The follow-up probes allow you to fully explore the different facets of the issue, again guiding the participant to the phenomenon.

The second lesson deals with the concept elicitation. As I stated, an open mind is key when eliciting the concepts from the transcripts. With revealed causal mapping (as with other qualitative methods) the researcher should maintain an open mind regarding what concepts and linkages will emerge from the study. Often it is the unexpected that provides the most insight to the phenomenon. The researcher should be attentive to the multiple levels of granularity that a concept may have, as well as the multiple meanings. Care must be taken to accurately capture the words and intent (context) of the participant, so valuable data is not lost.

References

Ford, J. D., & Hegarty, W. H. (1984). Decision maker's beliefs about the causes and effects of structure: An exploratory study. *Academy of Management Journal,* 27(2), 271-291.

Mitroff, I. I., & Mason, R. O. (1982). Business policy and metaphysics: Some philosophical considerations. *Academy of Management Review,* 7(3), 361-372.

Nelson, K. M., Nadkarni, S., Narayanan, V. K., & Ghods, M. (2000). Understanding software maintainer expertise: A causal mapping approach. *Management Information Systems Quarterly,* 24(3), 475-507.

Rice, S., & Nelson, K. M. (2003). Analyzing the revealed relationships of it personnel transition concepts. *Academy of Management Conference 2003,* Seattle, WA.

Robinson, W. S. (1950). Ecological correlations and the behavior of individuals. *American Sociological Review,* 15, 351-157.

Rossi, P., Wright, J., & Anderson, A. (1983). *Handbook of research methods.* Orlando: Academic Press.

Siegel, S. (1956). *Nonparametric statistics for the behavioral sciences.* New York: McGraw-Hill.

Endnote

[1] This research was funded by an NSF Career grant from the Organizations and Innovation Program.

Appendix

Information Technology Personnel Transition Study Interview Instrument

Hi. I'm _____ from the University of XXX. Thank you for agreeing to participate in this interview. I'm going to ask you some unstructured questions and ask for your opinions and feelings on the topics. Are you ready to start?

PROBE PROBE PROBE

1. What motivates you to come to work here at Y every day?
2. How is this motivation _____ tied to your current work environment?
3. What is the best thing about your **current** work environment?
4. What is the worst thing about your current work environment?
5. What is the most important thing you contribute to (your company)?
6. What could you contribute to (your company) that you currently are unable to contribute?
7. What barriers keep you from making this contribution?
8. Where do you see yourself professionally in five years?
9. Where would you **ideally** like to see yourself professionally in five years?
10. What barriers might keep you from your ideal situation?
11. How much do you like change?
12. How much do you think the IT field, in general, is changing?
13. How much do you think the IT field at (your company) is changing?
14. How do you feel about this level of change?
15. How is (your company) supporting you in personally making these changes?
16. What barriers do you see to making these changes?
17. What is your primary, personal, one-year professional goal?

Date: _____
Name: _____
Tape #: _____
E-mail _____

Section III

Causal Mapping in IS/IT:
Research and Applications

Chapter IX

Using Causal Mapping to Uncover Cognitive Diversity within a Top Management Team

David P. Tegarden
Virginia Tech, USA

Linda F. Tegarden
Virginia Tech, USA

Steven D. Sheetz
Virginia Tech, USA

Abstract

The cognitive diversity of top management teams has been shown to affect the performance of a firm. In some cases, cognitive diversity has been shown to improve firm performance, in other cases, it has worsened firm performance. Either way, it is useful to understand the cognitive diversity of a top management team. However, most approaches to measure cognitive diversity never attempt to open the "black box" to understand what makes up the cognitive diversity of the team. This research reports on an approach that identifies diverse belief structures, i.e., cognitive factions, through the use of causal mapping and cluster analysis. The results show that the use of causal mapping provides an efficient and effective way to identify idiosyncratic and shared

Copyright © 2005, Idea Group Inc. Copying or distributing in print or electronic forms without written permission of Idea Group Inc. is prohibited.

knowledge among members of a top management team. This approach allows the cognitive diversity of the top management team to not only to be uncovered, but also to be understood.

Introduction

There continues to be a growing interest in linking cognition to decision making, especially group or team decision making (Schwenk, 1995; Walsh, 1995). One aspect especially important to top management team effectiveness is cognitive diversity (Kilduff, Angelmar & Mehra, 2000; Knight et al., 1999). Cognitive diversity is defined as variation in underlying and invisible cognitive processes such as attitudes, beliefs or values among a top management team (Hambrick & Finkelstein, 1987; Finkelstein & Hambrick, 1990). An important feature of group effectiveness is the dispersion or variation of a group's attributes like tenure, age and differences in beliefs (Hambrick, 1994). Demographic attributes like tenure, age, functional specialties and educational background, are often used as proxies for unmeasured psychological constructs like risk aversion and commitment (Finkelstein & Hambrick, 1990; Hambrick & Mason, 1984). Yet, it is less common for researchers to compile actual psychological profiles of decision-making teams (Jackson, 1992). We focus on the explicit identification of differences among a top management team regarding their perceptions and beliefs about the firm's future direction and strategy, especially regarding their differing perceptions of the situation. While demographic variation implies that there are differences in perception, an actual measurement of these different perceptions can portray the cognitive diversity among a top management team.

A review of the literature suggests that cognitive diversity among a top management team can either enhance or reduce a firm's performance. It is proposed that cognitive diversity in a top management team is important when a firm is operating in complex environments because there is a lack of clarity about the causes of organizational success and failure (Ashby, 1952; Weick, 1979). Multiple beliefs and perspectives, e.g., cognitive diversity, are important in order to capture the wide range of information necessary to interpret complex environments. Kilduff et al. (2000) found that cognitive diversity is positively related to performance during initial decision making stages among simulation teams. As such, an explicit representation of each perspective could be beneficial to the top management team, especially at the initial stage of a strategic planning cycle.

On the other hand, cognitive diversity can also be detrimental to top management team effectiveness. Some researchers have hypothesized that the greater the shared understanding, i.e., the lower the cognitive diversity, that exists between individuals that work together, the greater the team's effectiveness (Cannon-Bowers, Salas & Converse, 1990). Other researchers have found that the degree of consensus about goals and about the means of achieving them influences the effectiveness of the firm (Bourgeois, 1980; Dess, 1987; Dess & Origer, 1987). One approach to increase the shared understanding between individuals is to make the beliefs and perceptions explicit by modeling different interpretations so as to capture and evaluate both the similarities and differences found in the individuals' cognitions (Daft & Weick, 1984; Eden & Akermann, 1998a).

Cognitive diversity is an important dimension for both researchers and decision-makers to explicitly model. It is our contention that by explicitly modeling cognitive diversity (the degree to which beliefs and perceptions differ among a top management team), decision-makers within a top management team can better understand the situation and provide a starting point for deciding on the future direction of the firm. We report on a method that captures both individual and group belief structures. By comparing individual belief structures, it is possible to construct cognitive factions, individuals or subgroups with different beliefs and perspectives. An explicit uncovering of these beliefs can facilitate both researchers interested in investigating the relationship between cognitive diversity and performance and decision-makers interested in investigating and resolving different perspectives within their top management team.

The purpose of this research is to describe a way to uncover cognitive diversity among members of a top management team and to demonstrate, using different analytical techniques, the validity of the identified cognitive factions within the top management team. We identify cognitive factions by grouping individual team members together that have similar belief structures. The number of cognitive factions represents the level of cognitive diversity within the team. As such, the cognitive diversity of the team is represented by the different factions.

As Hambrick (1994) has pointed out, "many top management 'teams' may have little 'teamness' to them . . . By opening the question of how integrated—how team-like—a group of top managers are, we create the opportunity for important advances in research. First, it allows the explicit introduction of top group integration as a construct. . . .[and s]econd, explication of the construct of top group integration will allow its use as a moderator in studies of associations between top group attributes and organizational outcomes." As such, the explicit representation of cognitive diversity, through the identification of cognitive factions, at the beginning of a strategic planning cycle, will benefit the planning process. Explicit representation of multiple perspectives can enhance the team's understanding of the scope of the firm's environment and situation. The views from the factions increase the scope of views and alternatives for the firm to consider. This allows minority views to be explicitly "heard" and discussed that might otherwise be ignored. As such, at the initial stage of a strategic planning cycle, an explicit representation of the different perspectives, belief structures of cognitive factions, prior to the negotiating and bargaining processes can be beneficial to the top management team in developing a better plan.

In the remainder of the paper, we review causal mapping techniques, overview our causal mapping-based approach for capturing individual and deriving collective cause maps, identify the cognitive factions through the use of cluster analysis and describe the factions using various analytical techniques that demonstrate that indeed the factions are different. Next, we discuss the collective causal maps of the cognitive factions and summarize the results. Finally, we discuss implications for managers and researchers.

Table 1. Types of collective cause maps

Type	Data Capture Approach	Data Merging Approach
Congregate Map (Bougon, 1992)	Participant-Driven	Researcher-Driven
Shared Map (Langfield-Smith, 1992)	Researcher- and Participant-Driven	Researcher- and Participant-Driven
Group Map (Eden & Ackermann, 1998a)	Researcher- and Participant-Driven	Researcher-Driven
Oval Map (Eden & Ackermann, 1998a)	Researcher- and Participant-Driven	Researcher- and Participant-Driven
Group Map (Tegarden & Sheetz, 2003)	Participant-Driven	Participant-Driven

Causal Mapping Background

Causal maps have been used to represent managerial cognition at both the individual and group levels (Axelrod, 1976; Eden & Ackermann, 1998a; Huff, 1990; Meindl, Stubbart, & Porac, 1996). From a managerial and organizational cognition perspective, five causal mapping approaches have been used to produce collective causal maps (see Table 1). Most collective causal map approaches capture the data for the collective maps using individual maps. The individual maps tend to be either created using a participant-driven interview, such as the Self Q interview (Bougon, 1983), or a negotiated researcher and participant interview (Eden & Ackermann, 1998a). The advantage of a participant-driven approach is the minimization of the possibility of researcher bias impacting the creation of the individual maps (Nicolini, 1999).

All of the approaches for creating collective maps from individual maps require that the concepts used in individual maps be standardized in order to create collective maps. The use of congregate labels created by the researcher to group similar concepts used across individuals is common to all approaches that merge individual maps into collective maps (Bougon, 1992; Eden & Ackermann, 1998a, 1998b). In the merging processes associated with the first four approaches in Table 1 (congregate, shared, group, and oval maps), this standardization process occurs *after* the individual maps are created. Congregate labels are based on researcher's and possibly participant's identification of similarities of beliefs contained in the individual maps. The congregate labels are then substituted in the individual maps. Once the congregate labels have been placed into the individual maps, the individual maps can then be merged based on the common nodes (congregate labels) contained in the individual maps. As a result, the process of merging individual maps into a collective map is both time consuming and results in a loss of information regarding idiosyncratic differences among individual belief structures. In addition, researcher bias may be present as the research/facilitator usually determines the congregate labels across individual maps (Nicolini, 1999). In contrast, our process (Tegarden & Sheetz, 2003) enables the individuals in a decision-making team to agree upon the congregate labels so that researcher intervention and bias is minimized.

To identify cognitive diversity or what we call cognitive factions in a top management team, we cluster the causal maps created by the members of the top management team based on the similarity of the cause-effect linkages between the nodes (congregating labels). A similar approach was employed by Reger and Huff (1993) to compare cognitive similarities and differences of industry maps across top managers within an industry. In the next section we describe the methodology used to identify the cognitive factions.

Methodology

The company described in this paper is a highly successful information technology company that provides customized solutions for government and commercial clients. They employ 500 professionals in six states. It is a privately held, employee-owned company. The company was founded in 1966 with a focus on operational research of transportation issues. In the mid 1980s, they began developing IT solutions to transportation and distribution business requirements. Since 1989, their revenues have grown by an average of 20% each year. Approximately 80% of that growth can be attributed to repeat business from satisfied customers. They are organized into three divisions: the Information Technology Services Division; the Technical Services Division; and, the Facilities Services Division. Figure 1 describes their organizational structure. The planning team is comprised of these eight executives plus five more from various areas of the organization.

The methodology used in this study consists of three primary steps (Figure 2). First, causal maps were elicited. Second, collective causal maps were derived and analyzed. Third, using the causal maps, cluster analysis, and a set of analytical techniques, cognitive factions were identified and justified. Each of these steps is described.

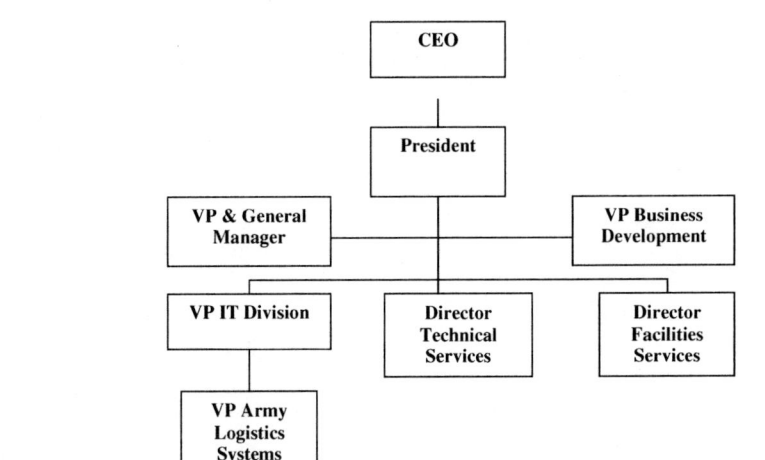

Figure 1. Organizational chart

Figure 2. Cause map elicitation and cognitive faction identification steps

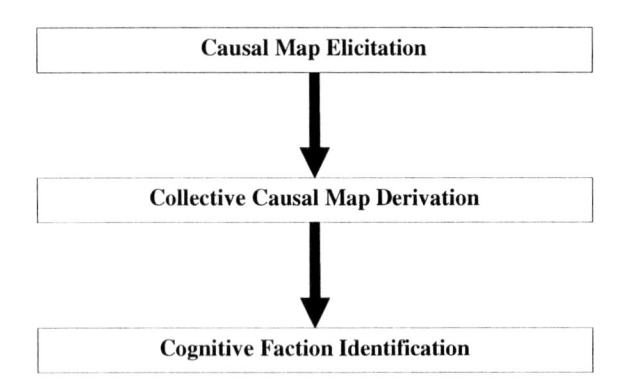

```
┌─────────────────────────────────┐
│     Causal Map Elicitation      │
└─────────────────────────────────┘
                │
                ▼
┌─────────────────────────────────┐
│  Collective Causal Map Derivation │
└─────────────────────────────────┘
                │
                ▼
┌─────────────────────────────────┐
│  Cognitive Faction Identification │
└─────────────────────────────────┘
```

Causal Map Elicitation

As mentioned previously, we use a method where participants identify congregate labels *before* the causal relationships are identified at the individual map level (Tegarden and Sheetz, 2003). This approach minimizes the potential for researcher bias and provides an efficient means for deriving collective maps in a comparatively short period of time. However, once congregate labels are derived, any causal mapping approach can be adapted to construct cognitive factions using the cluster analysis based approach described here. In our approach, both the individual causal maps and collective maps embody the congregate labels. As such, we can analyze differences as well as similarities among the individual causal maps to create an overall collective map and collective maps representing cognitive factions.

The causal mapping methodology used is a modification of the Self-Q Technique (Bougon, 1983; Sheetz, Tegarden, Kozar & Zigurs, 1994). The methodology is supported by a distributed system that runs in a WWW-based environment.[1] The software couples group support systems (GSS) technology with causal mapping to provide a mechanism for the group to identify their own congregating labels. Like most systems that use GSS technology, the software supports anonymity. Anonymity minimizes the effect that the more powerful members of the top management team can have on the other members (Valacich, Dennis & Nunamaker, 1992). Using the software, no one member has any more or less influence on any other member.

The causal mapping elicitation procedures are supported using an agenda of activities implemented in the software. Each activity is supported with an individual tool. Throughout the session, a facilitator provides procedural guidance to the group, e.g., administrative activities such as reading instructions and keeping time. To avoid potential researcher bias, at no time does the facilitator provide feedback on group responses.

Individuals first log on to the system to begin a group causal mapping session. After successfully logging on, individuals identify concepts, define categories from the meanings of the concepts, determine the relative importance of the categories, and

Table 2. Causal mapping elicitation procedures

Activity	Description
1. Elicit Concepts Introduction	Log-in screen and presentation of the framing statement and stall diagram.
Concept Identification	Elicit characteristics, concepts, and/or issues that contribute to strategic situation of the firm in the case. Comments are shared among all participants as they are entered.
2. Identify Categories Category Identification	Elicit categories that group concepts by similarity; agree on category definitions and names. Each participant verbally suggests a category name and definition. Other participants comment on the name and definition. The facilitator lists the names and records the definition using the system.
3. Classify Concepts Concept Categorizations	Each participant classifies the concepts into categories.
4. Rank Categories Category Rating Step	Each participant rates each category on a 9-point scale, from important to extremely important without knowing the responses of other group members.
5. Define Relationships Identify Relationships	Each individual selects from list uses the system to identify causally related categories. Each causal relationship is assigned a direction (positive + or inverse -) and a strength from 1 to 3 for a scale of -3 to +3, from strong negative influence to strong positive influence of one category on another category.

indicate the influence of each category on other categories (Table 2). Each of the steps is described.

Step 1: Concept Identification

The purpose of this step was to allow the participants to identify and exchange their beliefs about the future direction of their firm. A framing statement was presented to the participants to set the context for the brainstorming of concepts. The framing statement used in this case focused on eliciting ideas about the future direction of the firm. Specifically the statement listed four questions:

1. What do we want to accomplish in the next five years?
2. What is it that we do especially well?
3. What other things should we be doing especially well?
4. What present and future constraints do we face in our operations?

During this activity, the participants occasionally experienced a mental block. A stall diagram also was used to alleviate this situation. The stall diagram allowed the participants to cue themselves by presenting ideas associated with the future direction of their firm (Figure 3).

Figure 3. Stall diagram

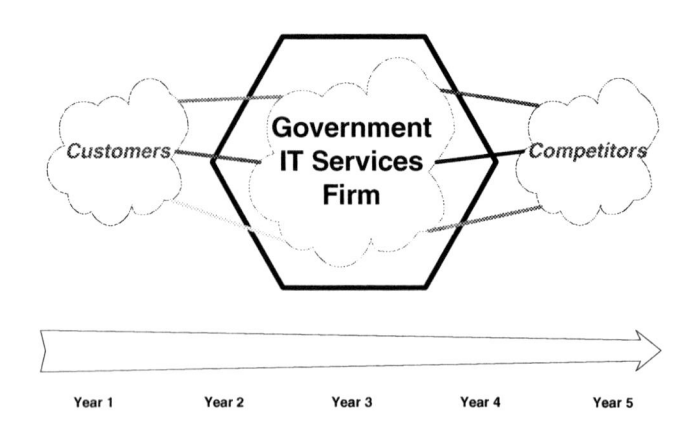

Step 2: Identify and Define Categories

The purpose of this step was to identify and define a set of categories (congregating labels) that group the similar concepts identified in the previous step. Participants looked through the list of concepts to identify those that address a similar issue or idea. The participants then voluntarily proposed a category name and definition to the group. The facilitator recorded the proposed category name on a chalkboard. This continued until the group was satisfied with the group of the proposed categories. At no time did the facilitator provide any guidance as to the completeness or correctness of the group of categories suggested by the strategic planning team. The only types of comments by the facilitator were to ask whether the team wanted to add, delete, and/or merge categories. The facilitator, however, did not provide and suggestions as to what should be added deleted or merged. Since this step was not anonymous, the facilitator took great care to manage the power relationships that existed in this top management team[2]. This process continued until the group was satisfied with the list of categories and their definitions. This step is intended to allow the group to identify the sufficient congregating labels for identifying the causal maps.

Step 3: Classify Concepts

The purpose of this step was to allow the participants to deepen their shared understanding of the categories. In this step, the participants placed each concept into one of the categories defined in the previous step. Concepts that a participant did not feel belonged in one of the categories were placed into an Unknown category. This step was completed when all participants had placed the concepts into categories.

Step 4: Rank Categories

The purpose of this step is two-fold. First, to understand the relative importance of categories to the issues contained in the framing statement. Second, but equally important, this activity is to increase the shared understanding of the meanings of the categories for the participants, i.e., an attempt to ensure that the categories are indeed sufficient congregating labels. In this step, the participants rated the importance of each category to meeting the issues contained in the framing statement.

Step 5: Relationship Identification

Causal relationships are identified between categories. These relationships provide the final component of creating individual causal maps. Relationships are identified without viewing the relationships of other participants. In a causal map, an arrow indicates that a participant perceives that a change in the originating category affects the terminating category. To identify a causal relationship, the participant selects: (1) the origin category, (2) the destination category, and (3) the direction (positive or negative) and amount of influence (strong:3, moderate:2, or slight:1) that the origin category has on the destination category. If the participant decides that they should not have included a relationship that is currently in their map, they may remove it. The participant repeats these steps until the participant is comfortable with the displayed map. At that time, the participant saves the map to the system. This activity is completed when all participants have saved their maps.

Collective Causal Map Derivation and Analysis

In our case, the process of deriving a collective causal map involves determining the number of participants that identified each possible relationship between the categories. This process is possible since the nodes of the derived collective maps have already been agreed upon by the group. As such, the system simply derives a series of collective causal maps from the individual maps by examining each of the possible relationships among the categories. The number of participants that identified the relationship and the average strength of the relationship are computed. The series of collective maps begins with a map containing only the relationships identified by **all** participants (a consensus map) and ends with a map containing relationships identified by any participant (a total map).

There are many techniques in the literature for analyzing causal maps. To begin with, in this study we analyze the complexity of the maps. A simple analysis of complexity is the number of nodes and links in the map and the ratio of links to nodes in the map. Simply put, the higher the ratio of links to nodes, the more complex the map (Eden, Ackermann & Cropper, 1992; Knoke & Kulkinski, 1982; Narayanan & Fahey, 1990). Cognitive centrality has also been used as a measure of the importance of a node in addressing the issues in the framing statement (Eden et al., 1992). As such, we converted the cognitive centrality of each node into a rank ordering of importance for each participant. This is similar to the approach we used in converting the category ratings to rank orders.

Cognitive Faction Identification and Description

To identify the set of cognitive factions within the top management team, we used cluster analysis to group the individual participant maps together. To compute the similarity of one map to another, we computed Jaccard coefficients (Boyce, Meadow & Kraft, 1994) based on the shared causal relationships among the participants, i.e., the structural properties of the maps. The Jaccard coefficient was computed as:

$$\frac{\text{\# shared causal relationships in Map 1 and Map 2}}{\text{\# of causal relationships in Map 1} + \text{\# of causal relationships in Map 2} - \text{\# shared causal relationships in Map 1 and Map 2}}$$

Since the nodes in the individual participant maps are identical, we only have to measure the similarity of the relationships contained in the individual causal maps. In this case, the more shared causal relationships, the greater the similarity is between the maps. For cognitive faction identification purposes, we ignored the strength of the relationships, e.g., if a positive relationship existed between two nodes in two different maps, but they had different strengths, we decided the two maps shared a causal relationship. However, we differentiated the relationships if they had different causal direction (positive vs. negative/inverse). Based on the computed Jaccard coefficients between every pair of individual maps, we clustered the maps together using Ward's method. Ward's method was chosen to attain increased coverage of cases, improved handling of outliers, and to minimize the effects of cluster overlap (Aldenderfer and Blashfield, 1984).

To provide further evidence of the cognitive factions uncovered, we used a set of analytical techniques, beyond that of cluster analysis, to provide independent justification of the identified cognitive factions. The analytical techniques included a productivity measure based on the number of concepts generated by the members of the respective cognitive factions. By looking at the productivity of each cognitive faction, we ensure that we are not simply clustering together the members of the team with similar levels of concept generation, e.g., those with a high-level of commitment to the process and those with a lower-level of commitment. We also used the techniques described previously with the overall group analysis: the complexity analysis, ratings, and cognitive centrality. In this case, we applied the techniques to the cognitive factions and compared the factions among themselves and to the overall group.

We also used Givens-Means-Ends (GME) analysis on the different cognitive faction consensus maps to demonstrate that each faction had different causal insights. GME analysis is an analytical technique that interprets the flow of causality as measured by the ratio of the number of inflows divided by the number outflows for the categories in the causal map (Bougon, Weick & Binkhorst, 1977; Eden et al., 1992; Weick & Bougon, 1986). Givens are identified by having more outflows than inflows of causal influence

Table 3. Sample concepts generated by participants

- Customer satisfaction is our number one strength
- Enhance our ability to attract and retain quality personnel
- Structure the company to support the coming growth
- Growth beyond 200M
- Give the stock actual value
- Develop a Human Resources Planning Process to develop new leaders
- Establish commercial client base
- Obtain capital for growth
- Never lose sight of our values and concern for our service and people
- Proportional growth within all three division/business areas
- Develop training programs to support management growth from within the company
- Provide great service to our customers
- Identify core competencies

(ratio < 1), means as having approximately the same number of inflows and outflows (ratio close to 1), and ends having more inflows than outflows (ratio > 1). Viewing the categories in increasing order of this ratio shows the direction of causality in a causal map (Bougon et al., 1977; Weick & Bougon, 1986). Givens represent the variables in the map that can be manipulated to influence the Ends, which represent the goals of the participants. The Means are moderators of the Given's influence. GME analysis also can be used to identify causal themes contained in a causal map.

Results

This section is organized along the steps of the methodology used: causal map elicitation, collective causal map derivation and analysis, and cognitive faction identification and description. The results from each step are given.

Causal Map Elicitation

The causal map elicitation process elicited 153 concepts or about 12 concepts per participant. A sample of the generated concepts is given in Table 3. The top management team identified 12 categories. The categories and their definitions produced by the team members are given in Table 4.

The explicit importance ratings of the categories given by the top management team members were converted to rank orders and analyzed. The team members reached a moderate level of agreement on the rank ordering of the importance of each category (Kendall's $W = .514$, $X^2 = 73.572$, $p = .000$). Finally, using the categories identified, each member created an individual causal map.

Table 4. Participant identified categories and definitions

Category Name	Definition
Growth	Of the company, customer base, revenues.
Profitability	ROI, stock value, fee, expectations.
Communication	Internal vertically and horizontally.
Personnel Mgmt.	Compensation, recruiting, HR, training, retention.
Organization	Getting better organized, corporate structure, organized to meet goals.
External Image	New logo, stakeholders, reputation, public image, name recognition.
Products	Information technology, services, solutions, expansion.
Customers	Anyone paying us money, internal functions.
Marketing/BusDev	Business development, strategic posturing, how to get customers.
Leadership	Accountability, ethics/corporate values, developing vision.
Quality	How you do the job, meet customer expectations, internal/external, compliance.
Competitors	Anyone who could take our work, internal component, anyone with work we want.

Collective Causal Map Derivation and Analysis

The overall group consensus map for this strategic planning team only contained two categories (nodes) and a single causal relationship from Leadership to Growth giving a link to node ratio of .5 (See Figure 4). Obviously, the complexity of this map is non-existent. On the other hand, the overall group total map contains all 12 categories and 119 causal relationships giving a link to node ratio of 9.9. As expected, the total map is substantially more complex. However, what was not expected is the degree of difference between the two maps. The consensus map only contains 17% of the categories and less than 1% of the actual causal relationships found in the total map. The average cognitive centrality is 1 and 6.7 for the consensus and total maps, respectively.

We also used cognitive centrality as a measure of the perceived importance of a node in addressing the issues in the framing statement. As in the ratings analysis, we converted the cognitive centrality of each node into a rank ordering of importance for each participant. In this case, the participants reached only a low level of agreement on the rank ordering of the importance of each category (Kendall's W = .373, X^2 = 53.406, p = .000). Based on the degree of differences uncovered between the consensus and total maps and the low level of agreement reached on the cognitive centrality based rank orderings, we concluded that further analysis was required to determine whether cognitive factions, i.e., subgroups of belief structures, existed or not.

Figure 4. Overall group consensus map

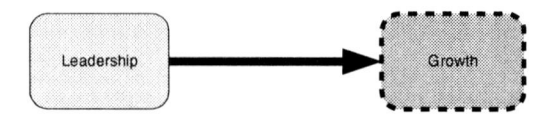

Leadership → Growth

Table 5. Cluster membership

Case	5 Clusters	4 Clusters	3 Clusters
1	1	1	1
2	2	2	2
3	3	3	3
4	4	4	1
5	2	2	2
6	2	2	2
7	3	3	3
8	5	3	3
9	5	3	3
10	3	3	3
11	4	4	1
12	1	1	1
13	3	3	3

Cognitive Faction Identification and Description

As described above, using the shared causal relationships, cluster analysis was used to identify the cognitive factions. In our case, we used the hierarchical cluster analysis in SPSS 12.0. The cluster analysis provided three potential sets of clusters: a three ([1,4,11,12], [2,5,6], [3,7,8,9,10,13]), four ([1,12], [2,5,6], [3,7,8,9,10,13], [4,11]), and five ([1,12], [2,5,6], [3,7,10,13], [4,11], [8,9]) cluster solution (See Table 5). The clusters were

Figure 5: Dendrogram using Ward Method

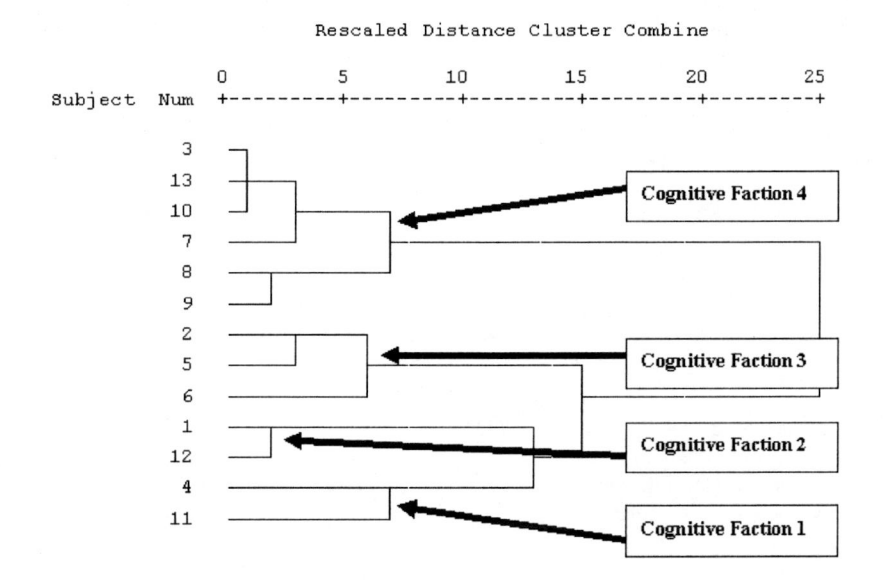

```
                    Rescaled Distance Cluster Combine

              0         5        10        15        20        25
Subject  Num  +---------+---------+---------+---------+---------+
          3
         13
         10
          7
          8
          9
          2
          5
          6
          1
         12
          4
         11
```

Cognitive Faction 4
Cognitive Faction 3
Cognitive Faction 2
Cognitive Faction 1

Table 6. Cognitive faction membership description

Cognitive Faction Number	Company Function — Executive	Support	Business	Total
1	2	0	0	2
2	0	1	1	2
3	0	3	0	3
4	1	1	3	5
Total	3	5	4	12

identified based on the mathematical similarity computed using the Jaccard coefficient (Boyce et al., 1994). The higher the value of the coefficient, the more causal relationships shared among the team members. Using the dendogram in Figure 5, we chose to use four clusters based on the "closeness" or length of the line that merged similar groups together. A shorter line indicates that the Euclidian distance between two groups is smaller, indicating more similarity between the groups. For example, the shortness of the horizontal lines of participant numbers 3, 10, and 13 (at the top of the diagram) demonstrate that they share many causal relationships. Based on a visual inspection of the dendogram, we chose the four cluster solution. This was based on the length of the line that clusters participants 4 and 11 together. We decided that we would not allow any "weaker" clusters to be formed. As such, four cognitive factions were uncovered.

Demographic Analysis

A variety of demographic characteristics (age, experience, education) were compared across the four factions. None were significantly different across the factions. Even though the planning team's ages ranged from 32 to 54 and job tenure at the company ranged from seven to 16 years, the differences were not associated with different belief structures. In addition, there was considerable homogeneity among the managers regarding education, gender and race. All but two of the managers had master's degrees. The other two had bachelor's degrees. All but one manager was male and all were Caucasian.

Table 7. Concept generation within groups

Measures	Overall Group	Cognitive Factions 1	2	3	4
Number of Group Members	13	2	2	3	6
# Concepts Generated	153	22	23	38	70
Avg # Concepts Generated per Category per Member	.98	.92	.96	1.06	.97

The most distinguishing characteristic was type of functional area within the company reported in Table 6. We defined company functions as executive (CEO, President and board member), support functions (Director-HRM, Director-Marketing, Director-Finance, and VP-Business Development), and business areas (VPs and Directors of IT, Logistics and Facilities Management). The president and board member define cognitive Faction 1. This represents two of the three top executives attending the strategic planning session. Cognitive Faction 2 is comprised of the VP of IT and the Director of Finance. IT represents the "newest" business division of the company. Cognitive Faction 3 consists of three support function managers and cognitive Faction 4 consists of logistics and transportation managers (the traditional line of business) as well as a top executive and a supporting general manager.

Description of Factions

When we look at each faction's productivity, as measured by the number of concepts generated by the members of the factions, we find that all members generated about one concept per category (Table 7). This can be viewed as evidence that all faction members were about equally involved in the GCMS process. Next, we perform complexity, ratings, and cognitive centrality analysis for each of the cognitive factions and compare them among themselves and to the overall group. Following that, we present additional evidence that there are four cognitive factions by looking at clusters of categories, shared and idiosyncratic causal relationships, category analysis, and Givens-Means-Ends (GME) analysis for the different cognitive faction consensus maps.

Complexity Analysis

Table 8 presents the complexity measures for the consensus maps for the overall group and the cognitive factions. Visually inspecting Table 8 shows that the cognitive factions had a much higher level of agreement as to the number of nodes and relationships that existed in their consensus maps. Furthermore, there seems to be differences between the cognitive faction groups as to the ratio of links to nodes and average cognitive centrality of the consensus maps. This provides additional evidence that cognitive factions, i.e., subgroups of shared knowledge, existed within the top management team.

Table 8. "Consensus" map complexity

Measures	Overall Group	Cognitive Factions 1	2	3	4
Number of Nodes	2	10	11	7	11
Number of Links	1	11	14	6	13
Ratio of Links to Nodes	0.5	1.1	1.3	.9	1.2
Avg Cognitive Centrality	1	2	2.5	1.7	2.4

Table 9. Average category importance rating (and converted rank) by group

Category	Overall Group	Cognitive Factions 1	2	3	4
Growth	8.31 (1)	8.00 (3)	6.50 (6)	8.67 (1)	8.83 (1)
Leadership	7.69 (2)	7.50 (4)	7.50 (2)	7.00 (4)	8.17 (2)
Personnel Management	7.69 (2)	8.50 (1)	7.00 (4)	7.00 (4)	8.00 (4)
Mkt/Bus Development	7.31 (4)	8.50 (1)	7.50 (3)	6.67 (6)	7.17 (5)
Communication	7.15 (5)	7.00 (5)	8.50 (1)	8.00 (2)	6.33 (7)
Customers	6.54 (6)	5.50 (9)	7.00 (4)	6.33 (7)	6.83 (6)
Quality	6.54 (6)	7.00 (5)	2.00 (10)	6.00 (8)	8.17 (2)
Organization	6.15 (8)	6.00 (8)	5.00 (7)	8.00 (2)	5.67 (9)
Profitability	5.69 (9)	7.00 (5)	5.00 (7)	4.67 (9)	6.00 (8)
Products	4.31 (10)	5.00 (10)	0.50 (11)	4.00 (11)	5.50 (10)
External Image	3.77 (11)	3.00 (11)	4.50 (9)	4.33 (10)	3.50 (11)
Competitors	2.00 (12)	1.00 (12)	0.50 (11)	1.00 (12)	3.33 (12)
Within Group Rank Order Agreement					
Kendall's W	.514	.718	.823	.593	.620
X^2	73.572	15.785	18.099	19.556	40.937
p	.000	.149	.079	.052	.000

Importance Ratings and Cognitive Centrality Analysis

The top part of Table 9 shows the importance ratings for the overall group and the four cognitive factions. It is ordered by the overall group's average importance ratings of categories shown in the second column in the table. The rating values in the table indicate there are differences among the factions and that the factions differ from the overall group. For example, Faction 2 ranks Communication as the most important category, while Faction 3 and 4 see Growth as the most important category. When we analyzed the factions for within group agreement, we found that the level of agreement (Kendall's W) increased among the members of each faction in comparison to the level of agreement reached in the overall group. The increased values range from .593 (Faction 3) to .823 (Faction 2) compared to .514 for the overall group. However, due to the small size of each faction, the statistical significance of the level of agreement decreased. These results provide additional evidence that the beliefs of the individuals in the factions were more similar to each other than they were to the beliefs of the entire team or other combinations of the cognitive factions.

Table 10 displays the average cognitive centrality of each node (category) in the individual maps for the overall group and the cognitive factions. It is ordered by the overall group's average cognitive centrality. A review of the table indicates that the cognitive factions disagree with one another and they all differ from the overall group. Furthermore, the within group agreement is greater for the factions than for the overall group. The level of agreement values ranged from .465 (Faction 4) to .716 (Faction 3) in comparison to .373 for the overall group. However, like the ratings, the statistical significance of the level of agreement decreased due to the small size of each faction. Like the ratings, these results provide additional evidence for the identified cognitive factions.

Table 10: Average cognitive centrality (and converted rank) by group

Category	Overall Group	Cognitive Factions 1	Cognitive Factions 2	Cognitive Factions 3	Cognitive Factions 4
Growth	12.31 (1)	8.50 (1)	10.00 (1)	5.67 (3)	16.00 (1)
Personnel Management	7.46 (2)	7.50 (2)	4.00 (5)	6.67 (1)	9.00 (7)
Quality	7.31 (3)	5.50 (5)	3.00 (10)	3.33 (6)	11.33 (2)
Leadership	7.08 (4)	6.00 (3)	3.50 (9)	4.00 (4)	10.17 (5)
Mkt/Bus Development	6.92 (5)	6.00 (3)	4.00 (5)	2.67 (7)	10.33 (4)
Profitability	6.92 (5)	5.00 (6)	5.00 (3)	2.33 (8)	10.50 (3)
Communication	6.77 (7)	5.00 (6)	4.00 (5)	4.00 (4)	9.67 (6)
Customers	6.15 (8)	4.00 (8)	6.50 (2)	1.67 (10)	9.00 (7)
Organization	5.77 (9)	4.00 (8)	4.50 (4)	6.00 (2)	6.67 (11)
External Image	5.62 (10)	4.00 (8)	4.00 (5)	2.00 (9)	8.50 (10)
Products	5.23 (11)	2.00 11)	2.50 (11)	1.67 (10)	9.00 (7)
Competitors	3.08 (12)	1.50 (12)	2.00 (12)	0.67 12)	5.17 (12)
Within Group Rank Order Agreement					
Kendall's W	.373	.536	.660	.716	.465
X^2	53.406	1.800	14.513	23.627	30.711
p	.000	.379	.206	.014	.001

By reviewing the results reported in Tables 9 and 10, we see that the level of agreement within the factions on both the explicit importance ratings and the cognitive centrality of the categories are greater than what was reached by the overall group. This demonstrates that the members within the cognitive factions agreed with one another more than they agreed with members of the other cognitive factions. By reexamining the average rating and converted rank order of the importance of each category (see Table 9), we see that there is substantial disagreement between the cognitive factions. For example, the Growth category is the most important category for Cognitive Factions 3 and 4, while it is only the sixth ranked category for Cognitive Faction 2. Furthermore when inspecting Table 10, we see that not only does the rank ordering of the categories by cognitive centrality values differ between the cognitive factions, but we also see that the level of connectivity among the categories are different. For example, the causal maps for Cognitive Faction 4 are much more interconnected than the other cognitive factions.

Givens-Means-Ends Analysis

Both the overall group and cognitive faction maps can be evaluated using givens means ends (GME) analysis to determine the flow of causality through the map (Bougon et al., 1977; Eden et al., 1992; Weick & Bougon, 1986). Table 11 presents the Givens, Means, and Ends of the overall group's and cognitive faction's consensus maps. Again, there is little agreement among the cognitive factions. All cognitive factions only agreed to the Growth category as playing the role of an end, or goal. The other six common categories played different roles for different subsets of the cognitive factions. The Communication category was perceived as a given by Cognitive Factions 2, 3, and 4 and as a means by Cognitive Faction 1. The Leadership category was a given for Cognitive Factions 1, 2,

Table 11. Givens-means-ends for consensus maps

Group	Givens	Means	Ends
Overall Group	Leadership		Growth
Cognitive Faction 1	Leadership Mkt/Bus Development Organization	Communication Customers Personnel Mgmt	External Image Growth Quality Profitability
Cognitive Faction 2	Communication Competitors External Image Leadership Products	Customers Organization Personnel Mgmt Profitability	Growth Mkt/Bus Development
Cognitive Faction 3	Communication Leadership Mkt/Bus Development Organization Personnel Mgmt		Growth Profitability
Cognitive Faction 4	Communication Mkt/Bus Development Organization Products	Customers Leadership Quality	External Image Growth Personnel Mgmt Profitability

3 and a means for Cognitive Faction 4. The Organization category was a given for Cognitive Factions 1, 3, and 4 and a means for Cognitive Faction 2. The GME analysis provides additional support for the existence of cognitive factions and the use of causal mapping to uncover them. We refer to the givens, means, and ends of the maps below where we discuss the similarities and differences among the maps.

Discussion

The above results demonstrated that there were higher levels of agreement within the cognitive factions than within the overall group and that there were differences between the cognitive factions. As such, the results provided support for using causal mapping to uncover cognitive diversity within a top management team. In this section, we describe the perceptions and beliefs within each cognitive faction as well as the differences between the cognitive factions.

Figures 4 and 6 through 9 show the actual consensus causal maps for the overall group and the individual cognitive factions. The maps are drawn in a left to right order by Givens-Means-Ends. Givens are shown as a lightly shaded box drawn with a solid outline, Means are shown as an unshaded box drawn with a dashed outline, and Ends are shown as a darker shaded box drawn with a dashed outline. Positive causal relationships are shown with a solid arrow, while negative ones are shown with a dashed arrow. The width of the relationship line portrays the strength (1, 2, or 3) of the relationship.

The overall group consensus map (see Figure 4), only contains a single strong positive causal relationship. As such, there are no Means within this map. Based on the few categories contained within this map, it is obvious that there is a lack of agreement among the members of this strategic planning team.

The consensus map for Cognitive Faction 1 is shown in Figure 6. This faction was comprised of a board member and the president of the organization. As such, not surprisingly, this map shows that this faction believes that Leadership is a very important Given. In fact, the Leadership category causally affects five of the other categories either directly or indirectly: Communication, Customers, Quality, Growth, and Profitability. In fact, the only End that is not affected by Leadership is External Image. Additionally, Growth is a very important End, or goal, for this faction. This faction also believes that issues related to the Organization category, which was defined as "getting better organized, corporate structure, and organized to meet goals" (see Table 4), has a negative, or inverse, causal effect on Personnel Management which has a positive effect on Growth. This faction also believes that the Organization category has a negative or inverse relationship with Growth of the firm. This is due to the indirect relationship that Organization category has on the Growth category via the Personnel Management category. The causal effect from the Organization category to Growth is negative since Organization has negative direct effect on Personnel Management which, in turn has a positive direct effect on Growth. Therefore, if issues related to the Organization category increase, they will cause a decrease in Personnel Management which then will cause a decrease in Growth. This negative causal belief is counter to the other cognitive factions' beliefs in which they feel that Organization has either a direct or an indirect positive relationship to Growth (see Figures 7 through 9).

Figure 7 shows the consensus map for Cognitive Faction 2. This faction consisted of the VP of information technology, a business line in this firm, and the director of finance. This cognitive faction is the only one that included the Competitors category in their

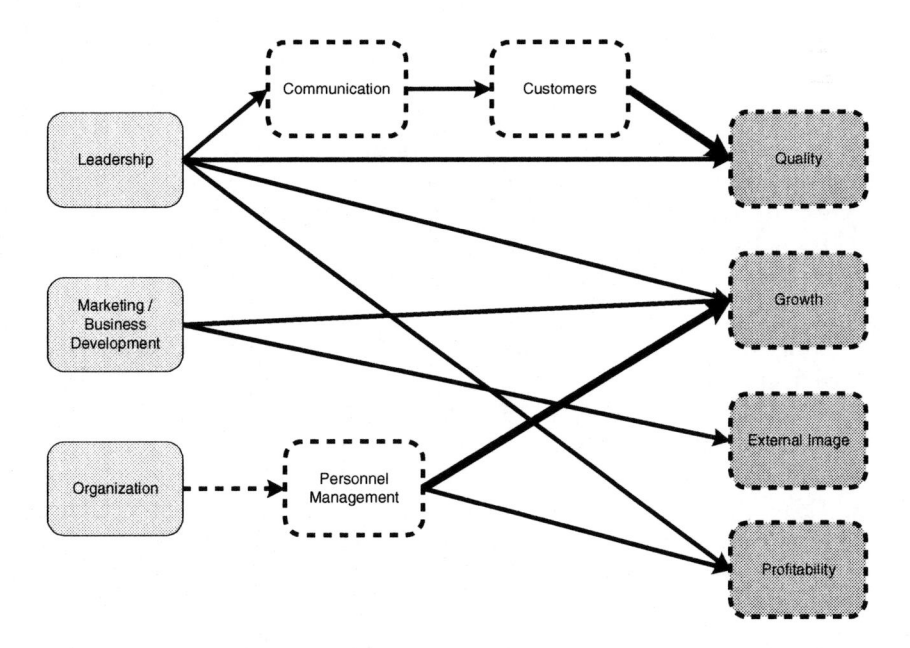

Figure 6. Cognitive Faction 1 consensus map

Figure 7. Cognitive Faction 2 consensus map

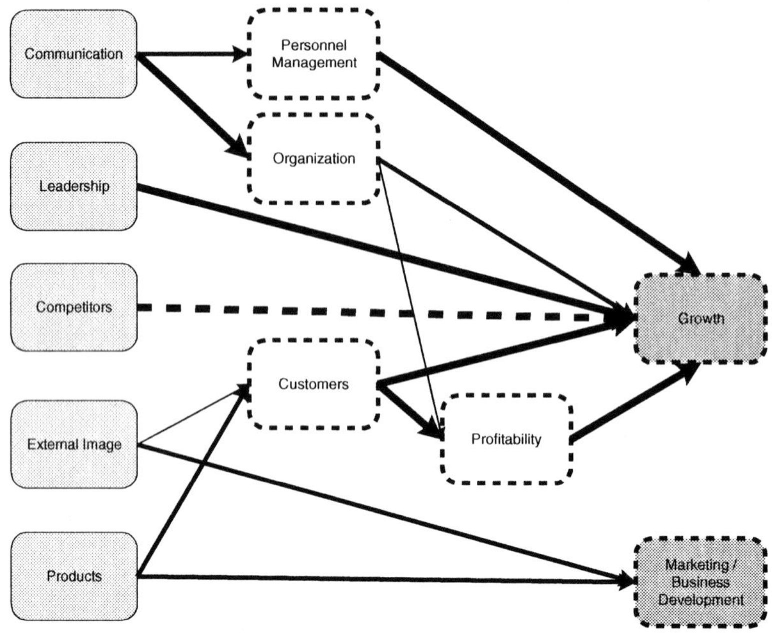

consensus map. They believe that Competitor issues will negatively affect the Growth of the firm. They also have an internal and external causal theme that impacts Growth. The internal theme is driven by the Communication category and mediated by the Personnel Management and Organization categories. Based on this theme and the definition of the Communication category (see Table 4), it is obvious that this faction feels that internal organizational communication plays an important role in the growth of the firm. The external theme is driven by the External Image and Products categories and is mediated by the Customers and Profitability categories. This theme implies that for the firm to grow, the firm must increase their customers which will only occur if the firm's external image is improved and the firm's products are expanded. This external theme is unique to this faction.

The consensus map for Cognitive Faction 3 (see Figure 8) is the simplest of the consensus maps. The members of this faction did not include five of the twelve categories identified by the strategic planning team. Table 8 shows that not only did this faction have the fewest nodes in their consensus map, they also had the fewest number of causal relationships, the smallest ratio of relationships to categories, and the smallest average cognitive centrality. Furthermore, this is the only faction whose map does not have any means. This faction was made up of three support function managers: VP of business development, director of marketing, and a human resource manager. Of the four factions, this one provides the least insight into what the firm needs to address and where the firm

Copyright © 2005, Idea Group Inc. Copying or distributing in print or electronic forms without written permission of Idea Group Inc. is prohibited.

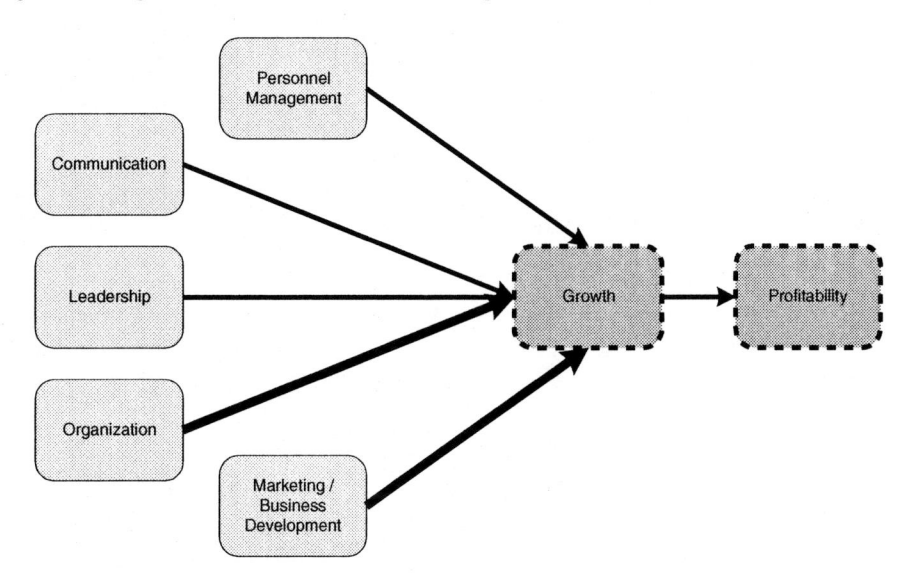

Figure 8. Cognitive Faction 3 consensus map

will go into the future. What we can infer from their consensus map is that they believe that the Givens (Personnel Management, Communication, Leadership, Organization, and Mkt/Bus Development) directly affect the Growth category. And, based on the strength of the relationships, they see issues related to the Organization and Mkt/Bus Development categories contributing the most to that Growth. Based on the membership of this faction, this should not be surprising. Based on the limited information contained in this map, it is very difficult to use it to help set the future direction of the firm. However, it can be used to reinforce ideas that are contained in the maps of the other cognitive factions. For example, the positive causal effect that Organization has on Growth, adds force to the similar belief contained in the consensus maps of Cognitive Factions 2 and 4 (see Figures 7 and 9).

The consensus map for the final cognitive faction, Cognitive Faction 4, is shown in Figure 9. This faction included the CEO, VP and General Manager, VP of Logistics, and directors of logistics, technical services, and facility services—all of which are primary, traditional lines of business of the firm. This faction, like Cognitive Faction 2, has an internal and external set of causal themes. The internal theme shows that Communication issues indirectly affect the Growth of the firm via the Leadership and Quality categories. Interestingly, this is the only faction that did not see Leadership as a Given. Instead, Leadership only mediates the effect of the Communication and Organization issues have on the Growth of the firm. The external theme that this faction has identified is related

Figure 9. Cognitive Faction 4 consensus map

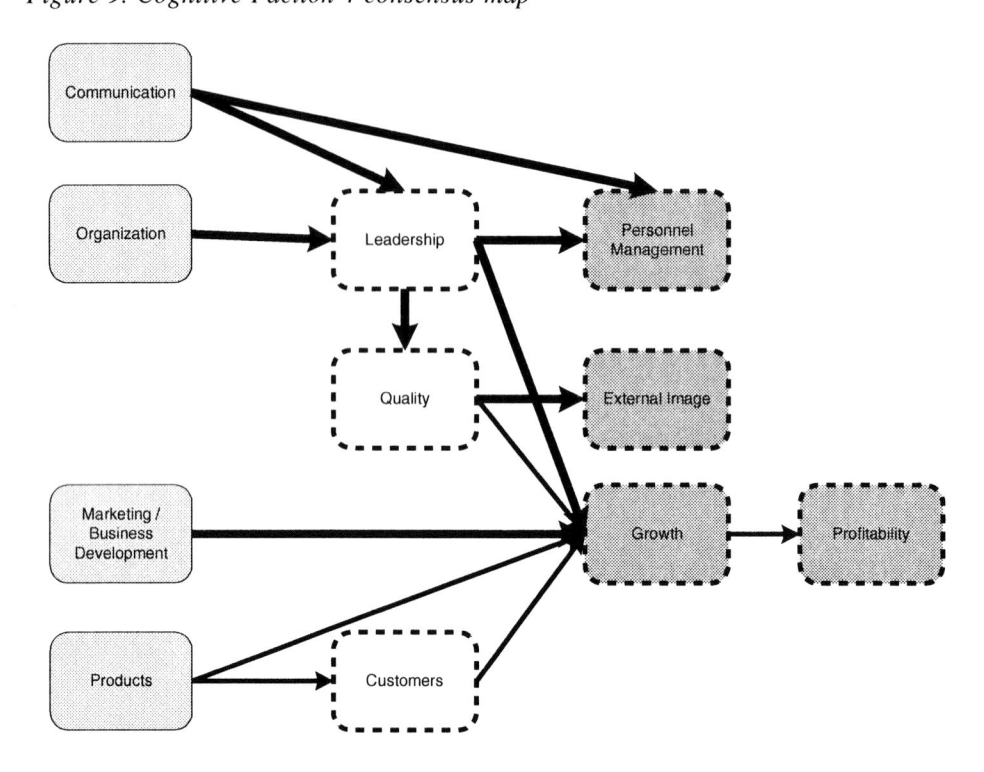

to the one identified by Cognitive Faction 2. In both cases, the Products category affects Growth via the Customers category. This again implies for Growth to occur for the firm, the Customer base must be increased which can be done by increasing the Product offerings. However, the two factions disagree as to the role that the External Image and Mkt/Bus Development categories play, one believes they are Givens, the other Ends.

By careful review of the different causal maps of the cognitive factions, it is clear that the different factions have different underlying belief structures. The identification of the similarities and differences among the cognitive factions allowed the uncovering of potentially important minority views of the form's strategic position and future direction. Without the identification of the cognitive factions within the strategic planning team, these minority views may have been lost. As such, the identification and analysis of cognitive factions is useful as a beginning point in the negotiating and bargaining processes that are part of any strategic planning cycle.

This strategic planning team benefited from the information we uncovered regarding their different beliefs about where and how this company should grow. The issues identified from the factions in this study needed to be addressed by the planning team. It is our contention that the minority views uncovered through the identification and analysis of the cognitive factions would not have been heard if they had not been explicitly identified for the strategic planning team. While the political nature of top management teams results in much bargaining and negotiation, the inclusion of strategic variables may not be the foundation of negotiation. Instead, resource constraints and control by individual managers become bargaining tools to gain a better position within the firm. In this case, the explicit uncovering of different beliefs regarding strategy increased the attention paid to the strategic aspects of the firm.

We also discovered, through discussion of the cognitive faction maps, that the planning team found this approach useful in identifying the key issues associated with their future direction. The friction between the different points of view was apparent throughout the planning retreat by all involved. However, until the cognitive faction maps were presented, it had remained below the surface. As such, the explicit representation through the maps facilitated the strategic planning team in reaching a better understanding of the different perspectives of their strategic situation. Again, the cognitive faction maps ensured that the minority views received (more) attention.

Summary

The use of causal mapping provides an efficient and effective way to identify idiosyncratic and shared knowledge among members of a top management team. By clustering the individual causal maps, based on their shared causal relationships, we were able to uncover a set of cognitive factions within the top management team. The number of cognitive factions represents the level of cognitive diversity within the team. Since our causal mapping approach forces the group to come to a common set of nodes or congregating labels before causal relationships are identified, clustering the maps is very straightforward. Furthermore, by forcing the group to identify the congregating labels, it enabled the creation of group maps to be created without researcher intervention, thus reducing the possibility of researcher bias.

We also provided a set of analyses that can be used to check the validity of the identified factions. We looked at the importance ratings (and their corresponding ranks) of the categories, the level of complexity of the causal maps, and the cognitive centrality (and their corresponding ranks) of the causal maps. We also compared the consensus maps using Givens-Means-Ends analysis. Finally, we compared the consensus maps based on the causal themes contained in them. The identification of the similarities within each cognitive faction and the differences between the cognitive factions is useful for a strategic planning facilitator to have as a beginning point for the typical negotiating and bargaining processes that are part of any strategic planning cycle.

The primary limitation for this approach to uncovering cognitive diversity is the requirement that the individual maps can only be merged once sufficient congregating labels have been identified. Depending on the causal mapping approach used, the identification of the congregating labels can be very labor intensive. By using the methodology incorporated in the GCMS, we were able to avoid this problem. However, once the congregating labels have been identified, and the individual maps have been recast using the congregating labels as the nodes in the causal maps, this approach is straightforward. A second limitation of the reported research is that the results are based on a single top management team. As such, any generalization of the results must be done with care.

Our study did not show a relationship between demographic diversity and cognitive diversity. Even though many aspects of this strategic planning team were homogeneous, their belief structures were not. The assumption that demographic diversity measures cognitive diversity needs further investigation. We did find the cognitive factions to be related to the different functional areas of the organization. This relationship supports the view that divisions operating autonomously will have different experiences and decision contexts.

Further investigation into using causal mapping and cluster analysis to identify cognitive factions in top management teams as a way to uncover cognitive diversity is needed. Moreover, we believe that top management team research can benefit from cognitive diversity measurement that enables the researchers to directly measure relationships between team cognition with other organizational variables like structure, processes, and firm performance. Currently, we are investigating the use of our approach with other teams.

Finally, a more complete comparison of our approach with other approaches to uncover cognitive diversity is necessary. Specifically, how do the other collective cause mapping approaches affect the cognitive diversity of a group? We expect that researcher-driven approaches to either data capture or merging can reduce the diversity uncovered. For a strategic planning session, this may result in consensus too early in the planning process. With complex, diversified firms, the different perspectives of the factions can enhance the analysis of the firm's situation.

Appendix: Description of the Group Cognitive Mapping System[3]

The Group Cognitive Mapping System (GCMS) is a multi-user, client-server system that uses thick-client technology implemented in Java and SQL in conjunction with an Access database. The user interface for the data collection aspect of the system is implemented as a Java applet that runs within a WWW-browser. The data analysis portion of the system is implemented in SQL, C++, VBA, Excel, and SPSS. The researcher can either set up an ODBC connection from Excel or SPSS to the Access data base which allows the researcher to simply execute the appropriate analysis query or they can simply copy the results of a query in Access into an Excel table or SPSS data editor window and run the appropriate analysis tool.

Data Collection Tools

The design of the data collection aspect of the system is based on designs typically associated with group support systems (GSS). As such, the data collection part of the system is organized around the idea of an agenda. Furthermore, all tools guarantee the anonymity of the participant. This helps alleviate any power-type relationships. The facilitator/researcher uses the agenda to control the deployment of the appropriate data collection tools. Currently, there are seven tools that directly support the cause map elicitation step in the methodology used in this study (see Figure 2 and Table 2). Additionally, there is a log-on tool that participants use to get access to the system. Each of the data collection tools is described below.

Concept Identification is supported with a distributed electronic brainstorming tool. In this tool, the subject is presented with a framing statement and is asked to type concepts into the system related to the framing statement. As they type their concepts in, the system distributes them to the screens of all other participants. In the case of a subject suffering from a mental block, the subject can also have the system display a stall diagram (see Figure 3). The stall diagram is essentially a graphical depiction of the framing statement.

Identify and Define Categories is supported using a tool that randomly chooses a participant and asks them to propose a category name and definition that can be used by all participants to categorize the concepts generated in the previous step. This tool provides the "definer" with the list of concepts in the order that they were generated. Once the definer creates a category and definition, the definer shares the proposed category and its definition with the other participants. The tool also includes a "chat room" type of facility that allows all participants to provide feedback on the proposed category and definition. Once the "group" is comfortable with the proposed category and definition, the definer saves them in the system. Next, the system chooses another participant to play the role of definer. This process goes on using a round-robin type of approach until the group is comfortable with the proposed set of categories.[4]

The Classify Concepts step was supported with a categorization tool in which the participants placed each concept into a single category that was defined in the previous step. This tool presents the list of concepts created in the first step, the categories and definitions created in the second step, and the list of concepts that the participant has placed in the current category (at the beginning, these lists are null). To categorize a concept, the participant chooses a concept and category and tells the system to place the concept in the category. It does not matter whether the participant chooses the category or concept first. When the participant chooses a category, both the definition of the category and the concepts currently placed in the category are displayed to the participant. Once the concept has been categorized, it is removed from the list of concepts to be categorized. Occasionally, a participant would like to reclassify a concept. The system supports this action by allowing the participant to remove the concept from a category by placing it back into the list of concepts to be categorized. At that point, the concept can be placed into any category.

Rank Categories is actually supported by two related tools: the Category Rating tool and the Category Rating Discussion tool. These tools support a Delphi-like process that allows the participants to rate the categories, discuss the category ratings, and then re-rate the categories. The Category Rating tool provides the participant with the categories and their definitions along with a slider that allows them to rate each category on a scale of one (1) to nine (9). The tool displays the entire list of categories and their sliders simultaneously. In this manner, the participant can perform both an absolute rating value, and by viewing the pattern of values displayed over the sliders, the participants can ensure that the individual category ratings are reasonable in a relative sense. As such, the tool supports both absolute and relative judgment (Miller, 1956). The Category Rating Discussion tool presents the individual participant ratings on their individual screen. Additionally, the tool displays the average group rating for each category. Again, this allows the participant to see the pattern of group rating values over the entire set of categories, by focusing on the sliders as a set, and to see how each category was rated by them and the group average, thus supporting a relative judgment model. Finally, the Category Rating Discussion tool provides a "chat room" type facility for the group to discuss the current rating values.

Relationship Identification, like Rank Categories, is supported by two related tools: a Relationship Identification tool and a Relationship Discussion tool. Using the Relationship Identification tool, the participants create their individual cause maps using the agreed upon, group-defined categories as nodes in their maps. The tool is set up in a manner that allows the participant to identify the origin category, the destination category, the type of causal relationship (positive or negative), and the strength of the causal relationship (strong:3, moderate:2, or slight:1). Once the participant has made these choices, the tool updates the evolving cause map and redraws it on the screen in a givens-means-end (GME) order. This always allows the participant to see the flow of causality in a left-to-right manner. The discussion tool allows the participants to discuss the current set of causal maps. To do this, the tool provides a chat-room type of facility to allow comments about the maps to be shared in an anonymous manner. The tool also provides a set of display options to allow the participants to see how their map compares to their fellow team members. The display options include:

- Showing individual maps only, collective maps, and/or both.
- Filtering of the maps based on their "strength" levels (3, 2, 1).
- Filtering the collective maps based on the level of agreement reached on the individual causal relationships identified, i.e., the percentage of participants agreed that the relationship existed.

The participants can also use the three options in combination. For example, they can choose to show both the collective and individual maps that portray relationships at least a 50% level of agreement and that the relationships have a strength level of 3.

Data Analysis Tools

The data analysis tools currently supported in the GCMS are divided into three categories: categorization analysis, importance rating and ranking analysis, and causal map analysis. In this section, we describe the tools used in identifying and evaluating cognitive factions. For the interested reader, we refer to Tegarden & Sheetz (2003) for a more complete description of the analysis tools supported.

From a cognitive faction analysis perspective, we have not used any of the categorization analysis tools supported by the GCMS. However, some of the unique tools supported include maps of attention (Huff, 1990), statistical level of agreement on categorization of concepts, parallel coordinate graph based analysis using concept generation order and participant concept categorizations (Inselberg, 1997), and association maps based on the participant's concept categorizations. Most of the tools are implemented using the report generator in Access and SQL. The parallel coordinate graphs are implemented using SQL and Excel.

The GCMS currently supports three independent measures of category importance. In the current study, we described two of them: explicit importance ratings and cognitive centrality. The third that is supported is based on the concept categorizations. The more concepts placed in a category, the more focus on the issues contained in that category. To be able to compare across all three measures, each of the measures are converted to a rank-order scale. SQL queries are used to generate the data necessary to feed SPSS to perform the Kendall's coefficient of concordance (W) computation to determine the level of agreement reached across participants for each measure and at the individual and group level, across the three measures.

Causal Map Analysis

There are many approaches used to analyze causal maps. In the context of cognitive factions, the GCMS supports map complexity computations, givens-means-ends (GME) analysis, the analysis of the level of agreement reached and the strength of relationships contained in the maps, and map similarity. The majority of the techniques are implemented as a set of SQL-based reports.

As described in the paper, there are different ways to compute the complexity of a causal map. The GCMS supports the computation of number of nodes, number of relationships, the ratio of relationships to nodes, and cognitive centrality. Also, using a graph theory program implemented in C++, the GCMS computes many graph theoretic measures (Harary, 1969). The GME, level of agreement, and relationship strength analyses is essentially identical to that described with the Relationship Discussion tool above. In addition to the tool, there are SQL-based reports that are available for the researcher to further analyze the maps.

From a map similarity perspective, the GCMS computes a similarity matrix that can be fed to SPSS for cluster analysis. At this point in time, communication between the GCMS and SPSS is one way. As such, once the clusters have been identified, the collective maps associated with each cluster must be manually identified in the GCMS before further analysis is possible. This is implemented through a set of SQL queries that places the participants into their relevant cluster (faction). Once this has been executed, the map analysis can proceed in the normal manner, i.e., each faction map is simply treated as either a collective map, for within faction analysis, or as an individual map, for between faction analysis.

References

Aldenderfer, M., & Blashfield, R. (1984). *Cluster analysis.* Beverly Hills, CA: Sage.

Ashby, W.R. (1952). *A design for a brain.* New York: Wiley.

Axelrod, R. (Ed.) (1976). The analysis of cognitive maps. In R. Axelrod (Ed.), *Structure of decision: The cognitive maps of political elites* (pp. 55-73). Princeton, NJ: Princeton University Press.

Bougon, M.G. (1992). Congregate cognitive maps: A unified dynamic theory of organization and strategy. *Journal of Management Studies,* 29(3), 369-389.

Bougon, M.G. (1983). Uncovering cognitive maps: The self-q technique. In G. Morgan (Ed.), *Beyond method: Strategies for social research* (pp. 173-188). Beverly Hills, CA: Sage.

Bougon, M.G., Weick, K., & Binkhorst, D. (1977). Cognition in organizations: An analysis of the Utrecht Jazz Orchestra. *Administrative Science Quarterly,* 22, 606-639.

Bourgeois, L.J., III. (1980). Performance and consensus. *Strategic Management Journal,* 1, 227-248.

Boyce, B.R., Meadow, C.T., & Kraft, D.H. (1994). *Measurement in information science.* San Diego, CA: Academic Press.

Cannon-Bowers, J.A., Salas, E., & Converse, S.A. (1990). Cognitive psychology and team training: Shared mental models in complex systems. *Human Factors Bulletin,* 33, 1-4.

Daft, R.L., & Weick, K.E. (1984). Toward a model of organizations as interpretation systems. *Academy of Management Review,* 9, 284-295.

Dess, G.G. (1987). Consensus on strategy formulation and organization performance: Competitors in a fragmented industry. *Strategic Management Journal,* 8, 259-277.

Dess, G.G., & Origer, N.K. (1987). Environment, structure and consensus in strategy formulation: A conceptual integration. *Academy of Management Review,* 12, 313-330.

Eden, C., & Ackermann, F. (1998a). *Making strategy: The journey of strategic management.* London: Sage.

Eden, C., & Ackermann, F. (1998b). Analyzing and comparing idiographic causal maps. In C. Eden & J. C. Spender (Eds.), *Managerial and organizational cognition: Theory, methods, and research* (pp. 192-209). London: Sage.

Eden, C., Ackermann, F., & Cropper, S. (1992, May). The analysis of cause maps. *Journal of Management Studies,* 29(3), 309-324.

Finkelstein, S., & Hambrick, D.C. (1990, September). Top-management-team tenure and organizational outcomes: The moderating role of managerial discretion. *Administrative Science Quarterly,* 35(3), 484-503.

Hambrick, D.C. (1994). Top management groups: A conceptual integration and reconsideration of the "team" label. *Research in Organizational Behavior,* 16, 171-213.

Hambrick, D.C., & Finkelstein, S. (1987). Managerial discretion: A bridge between polar views of organizational outcomes. *Research in Organizational Behavior*, 9, 369-406.

Hambrick, D.C., & Mason, P.A. (1984). Upper echelons: The organization as a reflection of its top managers. *Academy of Management Review*, 9, 195-206.

Harary, F. (1969). *Graph theory.* Reading, MA: Addison-Wesley.

Huff, A.S. (1990). *Mapping strategic thought*, Chichester: John Wiley & Sons.

Inselberg, A. (1997). Multidimensional detective. In J. Dill & N. Gershon (Eds.), *Proceedings Information Visualization 1997* (pp. 100-107). Los Alamitos, CA: IEEE-CS Press.

Jackson, S.E. (1992). Consequences of group composition for the interpersonal dynamics of strategic issue processing. *Advances in Strategic Management*, 8, 345-382.

Kilduff, M., Angelmar, R., & Mehra, A. (2000). Top management-team diversity and firm performance: Examining the role of cognitions. *Organization Science*, 11, 21-34.

Knight et al. (1999). Top management team diversity, group process, and strategic consensus. *Strategic Management Journal*, 20, 445-465.

Knoke, D., & Kuklinski, J.H. (1982). *Network analysis.* Newbury Park, CA: Sage.

Langfield-Smith, K. (1992). Exploring the need for a shared cognitive map. *Journal of Management Studies*, 29(3), 349-368.

Meindl, J.R., Stubbart, C., & Porac, J.F. (Eds.) (1996). *Cognition within and between organizations*. Thousand Oaks, CA: Sage.

Miller, G.A. (1956). The magical number seven, plus or minus two: Some limits on our capacity for processing information. *Psychological Review,* 63, 81-97.

Narayanan, V.K., & Fahey, L. (1990). Evolution of revealed causal maps during decline: A case study of admiral. In A.S. Huff (Ed.), *Mapping strategic thought* (pp. 109-133). Chichester, UK: John Wiley & Sons.

Nicolini, D. (1999). Comparing methods for mapping organizational cognition, *Organization Studies*, 20(5), 833-860.

Reger, R.K., & Huff, A.S. (1993). Strategic groups: A cognitive perspective. *Strategic Management Journal*, 14, 103-124.

Schwenk, C.R. (1995). Strategic decision making. *Journal of Management*, 21, 471-493.

Sheetz, S.D., Tegarden, D.P., Kozar, K.A., & Zigurs, I. (1994). A group support systems approach to cognitive mapping. *Journal of Management Information Systems*, 11(1), 31-57.

Tegarden, D.P., & S.D. Sheetz (2003), Group cognitive mapping: A methodology and system for capturing and evaluating managerial and organizational cognition. *Omega*, 31, 113-125.

Valacich, J.S., Dennis, A.R., & Nunamaker, Jr., J.F. (1992). Group size and anonymity effects on computer-mediated idea generation. *Small Group Research*, 23, 49-73.

Walsh, J.P. (1995). Managerial and organizational cognition: Notes from a trip down memory lane. *Organization Science*, 6, 280-321.

Weick, K.E. (1979). *The social psychology of organizing* (2nd Edition). Reading, MA: Addison-Wesley.

Weick, K.L., & Bougon, M.G. (1986). Organizations as cognitive maps: Charting ways to success and failure. In H. Sims & D. Gioia (Eds.), *The thinking organization: Dynamics of organizational cognition.* (pp. 102-135). San Francisco, CA: Jossey-Bass.

Endnotes

[1] The software is described in the Appendix and in Tegarden and Sheetz (2003).

[2] The GCMS does have the ability to perform this step in an anonymous manner. However, in this particular study, it was decided by the facilitator to use a manual approach instead. This was done for efficiency purposes only.

[3] The material in this appendix is based on Tegarden and Sheetz (2003).

[4] In the current study, to speed up the process, we did not use this tool. Instead, we used the manual process described in the paper.

Chapter X

Causal Mapping for the Investigation of the Adoption of UML in Information Technology Project Development[1]

Tor J. Larsen
Norwegian School of Management, Norway

Fred Niederman
Saint Louis University, USA

Abstract

This research project gathered data about the use of UML and object-oriented analysis and design as the approach to the development of information systems. The data collection method consisted of interviews with information systems application developers with wide ranging differences in background. The authors used causal mapping for analysis of the data gathered. This chapter focuses on the authors' experiences with causal mapping as a method for exploring issues and relationships. Causal mapping was also used to document tips on its use illustrating these with findings regarding UML and object-oriented analysis and design in particular.

Copyright © 2005, Idea Group Inc. Copying or distributing in print or electronic forms without written permission of Idea Group Inc. is prohibited.

Introduction

Productivity in computing hardware for decades has roughly followed Moore's Law in producing doubled power at lower cost every 1.5 years or so. Similarly, the productivity associated with networking technology continues growing exponentially as each new user added creates value for all previously installed users. Only in the arena of software development does productivity seem to be progressing slowly — if at all.

One target area for improving software development productivity has been documentation and requirements structuring. For example data flow diagrams (De Marco, 1978), data modeling (Chen, 1976), and the object-oriented modeling (Brown, 2002) have all been added to the repertoire of systems designers. The underlying concept is that visual representation, accuracy, and a fairly straightforward nomenclature in modeling system characteristics can serve to help bridge understandings among system users, developers, and programmers. Such understandings should allow for reducing the number of systems that are technically valid but don't address business problems and should provide clarity for technical designers and coders to more efficiently translate requirements into artifacts.

Despite the contributions to increased software quality because of the employment of these techniques for representation, problems remain (Sauer, 1999). It is reported that only 12 percent of information system projects are delivered on time and on budget. The most often mentioned reasons for failure are not meeting users' requirements, impaired functionality, and purely technical problems.

Based on these observations, the objective of the present research was formulated as increasing our understanding of how the phenomenon of representation is managed and used in today's business organizations; when does it work; when does it not; what are reasons for its successful or failed employment? We realized that these issues are not only related to projects but also to corporate efforts to define and standardize approaches to software development, education, and outsourcing — just to mention a few dimensions. Techniques for documentation and requirements structuring must be understood in an organizational context.

In this study, we focused on one particular approach to system representation, the Unified Modeling Language (UML) (Booch, Rumbaugh & Jacobson 1999). UML is the most recent among approaches to representation and it is the most complete approach spanning from user-information processes to implementation concerns. It is also widely held to be the future approach to modeling information systems.

The present chapter tells the story of our initial efforts to understand the use of UML in an organizational context. We don't present a traditional report on completed research. Rather, we describe and discuss the issues addressed and the decisions made in our early search for theory, why a data driven approach may be appropriate, why causal mapping was chosen as the method of analysis, emerging results, and lessons learned from this first attempt at creating some kind of order in a highly complex and disjointed research area. The chapter proceeds with theory and research approach. Next follows methodology, followed by material about developing causal maps, leading into challenges in using causal maps and lessons learned. The last section is the conclusion.

Theory and Research Approach

Research and practice reports on UML are diverse and scattered (Cho & Kim, 2001, 2002; Sim & Wright, 2001, 2002; Johnson, 2002). We find documentation of negative as well as positive effects of UML deployment. Also, UML — while studied and described in many computer science papers — has generally not been studied in the evaluative sense: what is its economic contribution to a firm? How does the precision of description it provides trade off against the time it takes to develop and maintain? What is its cost through the lifetime of an application and for use throughout an organizational department? Most profoundly, in our view the established literature typically addresses only a small subset of UML-related issues within a very narrow area of the project effort. Reflecting upon how UML is used in the organizational context, it quickly became apparent that decisions and implementation at multiple levels must be involved. Clearly the organization must permit, if not encourage, its use. Particular projects may subscribe or not subscribe to the UML approach — perhaps for engineering reasons such as a project whose mission is not deemed consistent with this approach or for human resource reasons such as it would take too long to acquire UML development skills to allow the project to be completed on time. We came firmly to believe that use of UML requires the resolution of organizational, project, group, and individual issues. With the exception of textbooks, contributions addressing UML in this larger context could not be found. The challenge of conducting research on UML in an organizational context is further discussed in the subsections of search for a theory, theory-driven versus data-driven research, and use of causal mapping.

Search for a Theory

The lack of an integrative perspective in UML research may not be typical in research addressing similar research objectives. A review of published research within the topic area of management information systems identified diffusion theory as a likely candidate (Fichman, 2000). If we consider UML as a "technology" in the broad sense of a technique and approach to achieving a set of results, the way that it is diffused and adopted among organizations, projects, groups, and individuals would perhaps be a reasonable framework for attempting to address UML usage and the impact it has on project outcomes.

Rogers' (1995) formulation, sometimes called Rogers' theory, has been fairly thoroughly examined using highly precise and rigorous measures — generally gathered through widely distributed survey questionnaires (Brancheau & Wetherbe, 1990; Moore & Benbasat, 1991; Prescott & Conger, 1995; Fichman & Kemerer, 1999). Rogers' theory has also been extensively criticized (Larsen, 2001; Lyytinen & Damsgaard, 2001). For example, organizational IS/IT innovations are more complex than Rogers' theory specifies. The IS/IT innovation processes unfolding in the "adopting" organization are richer and more diverse than sigmoidal. The division of users into the categories of early adopters, early majority, late majority, and laggards is at best unproven but more likely an introduction of social complexity, yet simplicity, that implies semantic meaning contrary to innovation process realities (Van de Ven, Polley, Garud & Venkataraman, 1999). Decisions are not purely individual but distributed among individual actors, groups, project managers, and organizational units. We concluded that using diffusion theory as the platform for studying UML in an organizational context would be inappropriate.

Our concern parallels the debate that has appeared in venues ranging from top journals to informal discussion groups about the "rigor" versus "relevance" and "theory" versus "description" characteristics of research studies (for example, Robey & Markus, 1998; Benbasat & Zmud, 1999; Nurminen & Eriksson, 1999; Goles & Hirscheim, 2001; Weber, 2003). Given how little knowledge links UML to organizational outcomes, the study of UML would suggest "relevance" and "description." At least among the organizations we ended up visiting, the use of UML remains either a new technology that could potentially be adopted or one that is partially in use with the jury still out regarding its precise cost-benefit results. Therefore, adding to the knowledge of UML in the organization would potentially be of benefit to these practitioners. In order to integrate our observations regarding the research characteristics of UML with theories of diffusion, we decided to take a theory building approach.

Theory-Driven vs. Data-Driven Research

We found ourselves in a predicament — staying theoretically pure or reporting on the use of object-oriented analysis and design as it unfolds in organizations today. We came to believe that there is a dialectic struggle between theory and practice (Van de Ven & Poole, 1995). The employment of theory requires a precise definition of constructs, variables, relationships, and units of analysis, or has these elements as the planned outcome of the research effort. Conversely, increasing our understanding of a complex phenomenon, such as the use of object-oriented design and analysis, requires a multilevel research design where the outcome cannot be predicted based on available research reports (Klein & Kozlowski, 2000).

Our research focus on increasing our understanding of UML in its broad organizational setting suggests that many loose ends and disconnected bridges would emerge. The indication is that chaos rules. Although this might be expected, we also believe that some degree of order will exist. In organizational settings, actors allocate time and resources to issues and phenomena that they believe have importance. A high demand for resources in defining and executing action related to the issues and phenomena addressed, as is the case with UML, will increase the likelihood that actors take it seriously. It is reasonable to suggest that actors will concentrate on particular issues and phenomena that they deem as being important. Directing attention to issues and phenomena is a necessary but not sufficient prerequisite for understanding why actors would pay attention. We also believe that actors are concerned about outcome. That is, when time is spent on defining issues and phenomena, attention would also be given to the impact that one of these may have on other issues and phenomena.

Causal Mapping

Our search for an analysis approach that would assist this reality led us to causal mapping. The purpose in selecting causal mapping is not oriented toward defining central tendencies in the data, but rather toward documenting the range of possibilities. In other words, we believe it is too early to test the relative frequency of three theorized causes of UML success when we expect there may be four, five, six, or more potential causes that have not yet been documented. We would consider it too early to even attempt to conclude that in some precise percentage of situations UML increased positive development outcomes by some specific amount. Rather, we use causal mapping to illustrate the range of variables that could influence decisions to implement UML as well as the outcomes should UML be implemented.

The employment of causal mapping in our research setting would differ from most others. For example, Nelson et al. (2000) use the method to define a fairly narrow set of constructs, variables, relationships, and relationship strengths. Although we expected to find constructs, variables and relationships, it is not our goal to demonstrate that our causal map analysis outcome would be reliable across research settings. Rather, we were looking for indications of these as they emerge from the data. Also, we believe that causal mapping would document missing connections (e.g., sometimes it is valuable to know what elements should be absent as well as present in an equation) and bring to light relationships that may not be linear, where a construct at one level may cause negative results, at another level have no impact, and at still another level cause positive results. In conclusion, although we expected to find the same elements as in other research employing causal mapping our objective was not reliability but validity with regard to mirroring the complexity of organizational approach to UML.

Our use of causal mapping has similarity with Fahey and Narayanan (1989). We seek to explore a complex phenomenon (UML) in the wider organizational setting. Our use of causal mapping can be understood in the context of the basic research method challenge of the personal pronouns of we, I, and you (Bohman, 2000). "We" represents the objective approach to research — as in a deductive approach. "I" represents the individualized approach to research — as in an inductive approach. "You" represents the real world subjects and their views, attitudes or behaviors. Obviously, researchers using the voice of "we" or "I" attempt to express salient aspects of "you." Additionally, researchers employ a method within which aspects of "you" are studied and analyzed.

The particular concern in this research was that causal mapping strongly emphasizes a clear definition of the two elements of construct/variable and causal relationship between constructs. Used in a straightforward and narrow manner causal mapping represents the voice of "we" — a deductive and objective approach to research, as in Nelson et al. (2000). The present researchers argue that subjects — the "you" in research — may possess clear views of constructs/variables and causal relationships. However, the presumption, in Nelson et al.'s (2000) research is that these will be parsimonious on the individual level and across individual roles. We believe, however, that our domain of interest, UML within the organizational context, does not have the pre-existing background of prior investigation to allow for identification of those constructs/

variables and causal relationships before examining data, but rather using the data as the source for discovery of these.

Therefore, our data collection method was not intended to define a set of constructs/variables and causal relationships, as in Fahey & Narayanan (1989). Doing so would have the danger in leading respondents to fill in the suggested topics without considering whether the set of topics is complete. That is, since very many constructs/variables and relationships exist in the real world, directing subjects to talk about a pre-selected subset of these phenomena may lead to definitions that reflect the pre-selection rather than represent the real world. In this scenario, the outcome might appear clean, but actually hide the fact of missing elements. Therefore, given the lack of prior research guidance, in this research subjects were encouraged to talk freely while guided toward the present research focus. Our approach should and must be closer to the spirit of having "you" talk as "you" find appropriate. Data collected in this manner would, hopefully, be a good source for defining constructs/variables and causal relationships with a high degree of validity.

Methodology

The first subsection addresses sample definition issues. The thinking behind data collection and lessons learned from it are presented in the subsections of interview guide development, interview execution, and lessons learned from conducting the interviews. The last subsection addresses issues related to coding procedures.

Sample Definition

Organizations likely to meet the qualifications below were asked to participate by inviting volunteers to participate in structured interviews. To qualify as a research participant, the systems development project participants must have had at least three years of work experience and they must have worked on information systems development projects of at least a minimum threshold of size. It was our judgment that very small projects would not require formal documentation. Without knowing an exact threshold where such documentation is needed (in fact one sub-goal of the study is to consider this issue) we projected a minimum of having participated in at least one project involving three full-time project members lasting at least six months. Otherwise the probability of need for formal methods such as UML was viewed as being below an acceptable threshold.

The strategy for selecting participants involved seeking a broad range of systems analysts working on IT development projects in a wide variety of roles. The selection of individuals playing a wide range of roles is based on the primary goal of developing a range of possible states or values for various aspects of UML's role in the development process. Participation was solicited in two ways. First, individuals of personal acquaintance to the researchers meeting the qualifications discussed next were invited to participant. Second, we requested referrals to eligible individuals from organizations likely to have these individuals in their employ. Direct contact with eligible individuals as then initiated.

Although we had a clear description of desired interviewees, we found the need to adjust as opportunities presented themselves. We sought systems developers but ended up with individuals playing a wide array of roles pertaining to system development including corporate strategic information systems planners, project managers, user security officers, information systems consultants, and about 40% systems developers (see Appendix A for a full exposition of the characteristics of the interviewees). This resulted from our collaborators in participating organizations' interpreting our research agenda and the qualifications of likely subjects differently from us. In retrospect, this turned out to enrich the range of perspectives represented in our sample.

Interview Guide Development

As we decided to collect our data using interviews, it was important to develop an interview guide in order to structure the information gathering process. Given that our goal was the solicitation of maximum ideas and insights, we did not expect that each participant follow the identical sequence of questions. However, we did not want to inadvertently miss areas of inquiry with any of the participants.

Questions in the interview guide were mainly derived from our own experience. Our first step involved the development of a "rich picture" (Checkland & Scholes, 1990). It included major relationships among organizational units that may determine strategic issues related to representation, formal educational units, systems development projects (their managers, systems analysts, and programmers), external to the organization units (consultants and vendors), and representation documentation. Literature was also used, for example Booch, Jacobson and Rumbaug (1999) for UML-related issues, Rogers (1995) on diffusion issues, Van de Ven, Polley, Garud and Venkataramann (1999) on innovation issues, but also published research articles on UML. Questions were not copied directly from these or any other source. Rather, these sources were used as a means for checking type and breadth of questions to be included in the interview guide.

In the end, the interview protocol went through nine iterations in its development as we reviewed, combined, separated, and added new questions while tweaking wording of those we intended to use. As part of the development process we read the questions aloud to each other and simulated the sort of responses we expected — looking for alternative interpretations and elements that needed further clarification or terms that needed further definition. We also considered whether the simulated answers would lead to the kind of information that we would want to analyze in later stages in the research project.

In the final version of the interview protocol we had seven sections: background and initiation (Appendix B); description of the most recent IT development project they had worked on; methods and tools used in the most recent project; outcomes they observed from the most recent project; observations about projects within the organization in general; the IT environment in their firm; and the firm's IT strategy. The logic for this sequencing of questions was based on movement from the smallest to largest unit of analysis. We believed that the respondents would be most familiar with their personal experience and concrete observations. As the interview continued, more generalization and global assessments would follow.

Interview Execution

The main approach taken was to conduct interviews at the interviewee's site. The main arguments for this approach was that by doing so interviewees would feel more comfortable with being interviewed and would not have to waste time on travel in a busy work schedule. Nevertheless, four of the interviewees preferred to have the interviews conducted on campus and another at a local coffee shop.

Due to the length of the overall interview, only the first five sections in the interview guide (see Appendix B) were fully covered in all interviews. Within the topical segments, we found the most effective approach was to begin by posing a broad general question intended to gain the participant's uninfluenced view of an area. We then followed up with more specific questions. For example, we would ask a broad general question such as, "What models or approaches did you use for documenting our last IT development project?" We would then continue by asking if the participant used use cases models, then asking if they used sequence diagrams, following the list of UML models. We also asked if they used data flow diagrams, data modeling diagrams, and any other models. This procedure allowed us to receive an uninfluenced view from the interviewee, suggesting ideas most salient from their point of view, while still investigating each of the specific tools comprising UML and, thereby, gaining more detailed insight into the adoption and "customization" of their use of UML toward providing a richer picture of the nature and not just quantity of usage.

Lessons Learned from Conducting the Interviews

We found the interview protocol to be invaluable in two respects. First, during the sessions, it provided a stable background to move through various items of interest with respondents. On occasions when the discussion would go into detail in an area, it gave us a point of reference to return to from which we could continue in another area. Second, in examining our data after completing the interviews and transcriptions, it provided a framework of issues that were addressed in one way or another by each of the interviewees allowing for more systematic comparison of answers in light of differing roles within projects and other differentiating demographic elements of the participants.

One decision that presented difficulties pertained to referencing a particular project. We asked participants to think of a particular project in order to make the questions concretely related to actual experience, rather than derived from how they think "it should be". However, in spite of this, we found that respondents often strayed into more general discussions regarding how they used various approaches across a range of projects. Methodological purity might have suggested forcing the participants back to discussion of the one identified project, however, some of the more interesting points were raised in consideration of the comparison among projects. Our observation is that even as the conversation drifted away from a particular project, it remained based on their experiences, though more generalized across a set of projects. We also found that they might pull details from a variety of project experiences — for example, they might report on their experience with sequence diagrams on one project where they did not use class diagrams, but report on another project using class diagrams but not sequence diagrams. In retrospect, beginning with a single project was probably a good approach because it tended to keep participants from responding only with generalities. But it was also good to allow the respondents to drift away from that particular project in order to report on the broader array of their experiences. In conclusion, we found that the steps taken to strengthen the voice of "you" (Bohman, 2000) was the correct interview approach.

Table 1. Example of the analysis table

C-#	R	P-#	Statement	Cause	Effect
31	2	4	We're still trying to get people to understand the IS model and our roles because people look at us when we say we need to be part of their planning units and their teams and so for, they look at us "We're not ready for IT yet." We say, "No, no, you don't understand. We're a part of your team. We need to understand prior to when you think you need technology so that we can best help you. It also helps us in our planning." So we've got varying degrees of people understanding our role but it is starting to grasp on. People are starting to understand that role and I can't seem to have enough people to fulfill those roles.	Early involvement	User understanding
32	2	4	Also, recently, in the business integration team, we had taken on process mapping, which makes sense because if you don't understand the process, it's difficult to start mapping out a project and mapping out technology. So we are also facilitating and training process mapping so that's also new.	Process mapping	Project organization
33	2	6	We had a team, a fairly large team, that pretty much encompassed a good portion of our IS department internally as well as we brought in external consultants because we didn't feel we had the expertise and knowledge in doing everything that we were going to be embarking upon.	Addition of consultants	Enhance knowledge base for project work
34	2	7	We had some knowledge but it wasn't practical. It was textbook knowledge and we wanted some practical experience so we hired, actually, multiple consultants. We didn't have one firm. We brought in multiple people. We project managed it but we had a project manager from the consulting firm work with us hand-in-hand.	Addition of consultants	Enhance knowledge base for project work
35	2	7	I thought I could because my background seems like I could do that but I very quickly learned that if I got caught too much in the technical details, I couldn't manage the overall scope of the project.	Focus on overview	Project management success
36	2	9	And we went out and personally trained all 100 distributors when we rolled out phase one. They liked that. They thought that was great.	Personalization of training	User satisfaction

Note: The abbreviations in column headings denote: C-# (comment number), R (respondent number), P-# (page number in interview transcript).

Coding Procedures

In general, from this stage on, work was performed by one author and verified by the second author. (It is noted that the reverse was the case for other analyses of the same data). Rather than coding separately then comparing outcomes quantitatively as one does with most communication research coding, we discussed differences to consensus. This method resulted in many observations of differences based more on linguistics than on substantially different understandings. However, we chose this approach because we did not want to start with predefined coding schemes, but rather to generate the language for describing elements based on the content of the interviews themselves.

Coding occurred in two stages. First, we went through each transcript and identified causal statements (or inferred causal statements). These statements were copied and pasted into a table (see Table 1).

The table structure was designed to serve as a tool for organizing further coding efforts. The instantiated tables also provided all relevant information about each statement in a handy and easy-to-use manner. In the end, the transcripts were transformed into a set of tables — one for each transcript.

Second, for each statement we identified "cause" and "effect" labels. Because we examined these at a semantic level — searching for the meaning of the statements rather than keying of specific words or syntactic level structures — we did not develop specific rules, but rather treated each statement as a unique case and applied judgment and discussion to consensus where meanings might have had multiple interpretations. These labels were subject to change in the mapping phase for either of two reasons. First, in the context of the entire interview, the meaning of the particular statement sometimes showed slightly different orientation and second, slight differences in phrasing might be collapsed into a single descriptive term. This occurred often in wording of "effect" variables such as "project success." Slightly different ideas such as project thoroughness, project efficiency, and project learning might all be collapsed into project success. In the end, this process resulted in a total of 270 comments identified from the 11 transcripts (24.4 comments per interview). In addition, some 36 additional cause-effect combinations were observed (where one comment yielded more than one relationship) and another 47 comments contained valuable insights into definition of terms or other matters, but did not yield causal links. In sum, we observed 259 casual links (23.6 links per interview). The complete list of cause concepts and effect concepts are presented in appendices C and D.

Developing Causal Maps

We hasten to say that even though we have accounted for all comments in our current set of causal maps, we continue to find ways of recombining them for the purpose of conducting additional analysis. Following from the verbal description of the content of the statements, visual aids are prepared to help with developing understanding and

Figure 1. Example of a causal segment

Note: The number in the bubble refers to the statement in the table. These numbers make it much easier to return at a later time to the actual text during the writing stage of the project. Also note that the arrow heads show directionality which is derived from the causal or inferred causal statement. On occasion, arrowheads may go in both directions — for example, developers' skills could influence use of UML, but prolonged use could also change the composition of developers' skills. The arrowheads, therefore, represent the observations of the respondents rather than all relational possibilities.

observation of deeper relationships. This also occurred in several stages. First, we transformed each page of the tables into a set of causal segments — each statement generated a pair (occasionally multiple causal relations) of causal relations which were mapped onto PowerPoint slides. This mapping was done one page of table to one PowerPoint slide. Even at this stage, references to a single entity in multiple states would be represented as multiple arrows to or from that entity. In other words if training influenced user skills and user skills influenced use of UML, the segment would be presented as shown in Figure 1.

Each causal segment represents our smallest unit of result documentation. Each interview would yield a number of causal segments. Some of these might be related and some

Figure 2. Consolidated causal map — Interview #8, documentation success

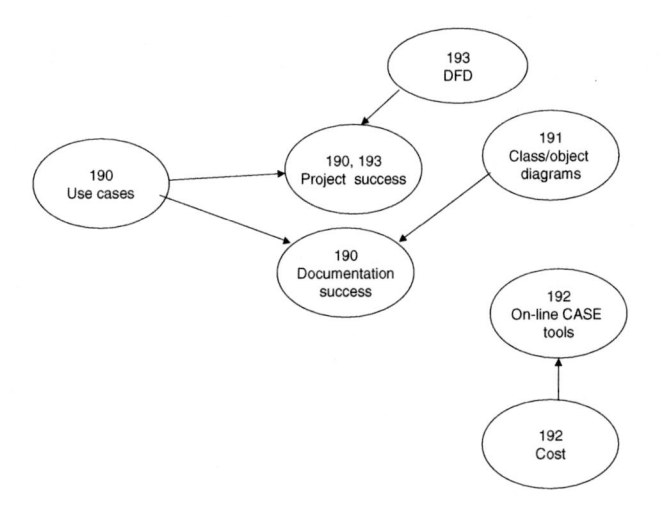

might not — the latter representing stand-alone findings. The mechanism chosen for combining segments derived from one interview was to look for variables that appear in more than one causal segment. A variable that appears across causal segments can take on the role of being either independent or dependent and sometimes both. Based on these principles causal segments from an interview can be combined into a holistic view of the relationships uncovered in that interview (see Figure 2 for an example).

At this point, we had a choice. We could consider each interview a separate case and treat the discussion of findings in terms of a set of 11 case studies following Yin (1994). However, we opted for the second approach given our focus on theory development and understanding the range rather than central tendencies of the data, which was to further consolidate findings across interview participants. Again, we did this by focusing on "target" labels and searching for the entities that influenced them. This work is in process and will, hopefully, yield insights that are publishable in their own right.

Challenges in Using Causal Mapping

Even if convinced that the method has the potential to yield a quality outcome, ending up with insufficient "revelation" of new or interesting information is possible. Ultimately, one may come away with a study that just doesn't show any consistent findings or even suggest different findings consistently among different contingencies. In principle, this would be an excellent scientific "disconfirmation" of prevailing thought, but practically speaking it is often not a favorite observation in the eyes of reviewers.

However, this problem is often tractable where the researchers have become too close to the project and are either not recognizing what is "interesting" about it or not presenting what is "interesting" in a format highlighting what editors and reviewers will also find interesting. This leads to the question: What constitutes an interesting finding? We reflect on this question by discussing the abandoning of Rogers' diffusion theory, surprising elements, and complex relationships emerging from our causal maps.

Abandoning Rogers' Diffusion Theory

The findings support our view that Rogers diffusion theory is invalid as a lens for studying UML in an organizational context (see Table 2).

Our findings confirm that Rogers' theory does not apply. Our conclusion is restricted to the employment of this theory as the overarching platform for our study. However, our analysis covers major prerequisites within Rogers' theory. Still, other aspects of this theory may be relevant, for example, the constructs of trialability and observability. The proposition is that the higher the degree of trialability and observability, the more likely that adoption occurs. However, UML is in its very nature a highly complex phenomenon — in fact so complex that Rogers definition of these terms quite likely does not have meaning.

Table 2. Rogers' diffusion theory and present findings

Aspect of Rogers' diffusion theory	Findings in the present study
The innovation is clearly defined and does not change during the diffusion process	UML is highly complex in its own right and exists in parallel with other methods for representation. UML consists of multiple elements. UML is differently understood among actors. UML is molded according to need during the systems development process. When standard application packages are employed, UML may be an improbable approach.
Over time, the adoption of the innovation is sigmoidal	Even when a corporate strategic unit promotes the employment of UML, projects in the organization may not use it – rendering a smooth cumulative usage curve quite unlikely. Even the concept of use (of UML) in its most narrow interpretation is a difficult issue. We found that a project manager clearly stated that UML was the standard being used. The systems analysts disconfirmed.
Users can be divided into the categories of early adopters, early majority, late majority, and laggards	Awareness and/or belief in UML occur collectively and individually at differing points in time. Adoption of UML is not necessarily a "good thing." Being a laggard might be highly appropriate.
Individual adopters make the adopt/non-adopt decision	Actors on many levels make decisions about UML. More often than not decisions made are not followed through. The issue of mandatory (because of organizational policy) and voluntary use is highly complex.

We cannot suggest in a straightforward manner what a theory that would describe the phenomenon of UML in an organizational context might be. Therefore, listening to the data, we think, is extremely necessary in our effort to increase our understanding.

Surprising Elements

We look for variables that have not been mentioned in the literature. For example, we find in our causal maps that the implementation of standard application packages is not related to successful use of UML. We found this surprising because many organizations today install an integrated standard application package for critical business functions such as accounting, procurement, inventory control, customer order processing, and distribution. The package must be integrated into the portfolio of other information systems in the organization.

However, the structure and architecture of the standard application package generally is not made available to the buyer organization. The reason for this is that the standard application package vendor looks upon the structure and architecture as a competitive element. The vendor does not want to run the risk of having other vendors learn the inner workings of the standard application package — the risk of which would increase to an unacceptable level if a buyer organization were to learn about these in depth.

Therefore, the buyer organization is left with descriptions of input and output data as the basis for integration with other information systems. It does not matter whether the standard application package is developed fully in UML or not. Because of denied access, the buyer organization cannot (fully) integrate the information systems portfolio according to UML principles. In fact, if installing standard application packages becomes the dominant strategy among organizations, the concept of UML may be rendered obsolete in companies other than those creating the packages. The challenge would move from a consistent development of information systems to the integration among them.

Complex Relationships

This study identified several areas where relationships are complex. For example, our data suggest that the amount of documentation has some causal relationship with the amount of documentation success — however, this is probably not a linear relationship at all values. At some point increasing the documentation by one unit provides less than one unit of additional value but continues to cost one unit of time and money. At some point additional documentation may start to erode documentation success, where success is viewed in cost/benefit terms. It also includes multi-directional relationships. Our data suggests that there is a relationship between the success of individual projects and the success of the management of project development as a portfolio in the organization. However, the direction of this relationship could go either way. The success of the organization's project development might simply be conceived as the accumulation of outcomes from each project — the sum if you will. This might be influenced by overall policies, tools, and approaches, which may differ among three groups of stakeholders, the IT management, IT workforce, and of the larger business influences. On the other hand, these same policies, tools, and approaches at the departmental level may influence the success of each project. Note that policies might be applied with wisdom differentially where appropriate to different projects, or they might be applied uniformly helping some projects and retarding others. Note also that some types of policies, perhaps pertaining to standardization or reuse, would have dramatic impact while others pertaining to documentation style or change management would have less impact given different circumstances and projects.

The nature of these relationships might be difficult to detect from the causal mapping *per se*, but hints can be detected where different interview participants use terminology differently, remark on relationships from different perspectives, point out contingencies, or otherwise describe complexity in their responses to questions. The process of coding statements noting causal elements and effect elements tends to blunt the observation of these "semantic" level observations. However, in the consolidation of maps, these tend to show up as variations among elements described by different individuals. Mining the interesting aspects of these complex relationships requires returning to the original text and also some interpretation, inference, and imagination on the part of the investigator. Imagination isn't a term normally associated with "scientific studies," but in the sense that the investigator recognizes that an interviewee is describing a relationship in a particular context and that the relationships could have different aspects outside of that context by imagining or envisioning alternate scenarios, can help bring out the richness of the phenomena, even if it does extend beyond the literal statements made by the participants.

Lessons Learned

Throughout this chapter, we have tried to note our observations about the process of conducting a causal mapping study. We'd like to highlight lessons we've learned in three major areas in this endeavor; the mechanics of conducting a data driven study; the value of planning; looking for consistency and gaps.

The Mechanics of Conducting a Data-Driven Study

The mechanics of conducting this sort of study are significant — you can't let them become overwhelming. In our case, these mechanics included a major detour of time and effort for satisfying the requirements of the institutional review board (a.k.a., human subject committee). In the end, the effort needed to pass muster with for human subjects research forced us into some early planning efforts that paid off. On the other hand, the overhead of record keeping and drafting warning statements to participants for assuring privacy at times seemed highly disproportional in effort for protecting against the small risk and small probability of any harm coming to a study participant. Other mechanical difficulties included the extraordinary time it took for transcriptions and checking transcription. This included manual coding and mapping (though we don't know how much confidence we would have in any software program that claimed to provide coding or mapping at a semantic or meaningful level), and, in our case, coordinating work by researchers residing each on a different continent.

The Value of Planning

Steps taken early in the process can make life easier (or more difficult) in later phases. In particular, we would note the value of planning for causal mapping while creating the interview protocol. It can be argued that questions should be developed pertaining to the domain of investigation without regard to the particular method of analysis. In essence, this is what we did for this study. However, as a result we probably had to do much more inferring of relationships than if we had designed the questions with causal mapping in mind. Because we are looking for explicit illumination of relationships, it would be very helpful to fill an interview protocol with "why" questions, particularly following from open-ended observations, to elicit these types of answers. It would also be interesting to see where respondents base conclusions on observations or extrapolation themselves without having underlying causal models at play.

Therefore, directly eliciting information about causal relationships, drivers, and outcome may be problematic. People may not necessarily think about their experiences in those terms. Raising the issue may make people overtly cognizant about these issues on the expense of other cognitive patterns — for example, unrelated events, events forming networks with no clear causal relationships, or events perceived as hierarchies. The argument that causal relationships that emerge in talks not having this focus may be more trusted than those expressed because the respondent is queued along this line has merit and warrants explicit consideration.

Looking for Consistency and Gaps

We were looking for consistency in cause and effect within as well as across interview transcripts. We find that the causal mapping clearly documents gaps. We raise two issues. First, people might simply not have a unified view of UML. For example, the lack of an implemented organizational and project UML strategy will quite likely enforce this result. People would be left to make their own decisions. Second, the gaps may indicate lack of or inconsistent data. The number of interviewees in our research is only 11, which may not be sufficient for convergence of findings. Our subjects were spread among projects and organizational units and among organizations. Therefore, gaps in the causal mappings may be used to determine additional need for data collection. What roles should additional subjects have and how many within each role would be needed to increase the validity and reliability of the research findings? Hence, causal mapping may be used as a vehicle for detecting inconsistencies in practice as well as in research.

We believe that our approach to data collection was appropriate. We did not use causal mapping principles as the basis for interview guide design. The objective of data collection was to allow the voice of "you" to speak in a fairly free manner. The interview guide therefore focused on UML issues to allow the respondent to express her or his own views. Causal mapping was employed as a method of analysis of interview transcripts. We conclude that although causal mapping may be looked upon as a tool within the deductive school of research it is also well-suited for qualitative and exploratory purposes.

Conclusion

Our research objective was formulated as understanding representation in systems development in an organizational context. The approach to representation investigated was UML. We did not find a theory that would serve as a lens for defining issues, constructs or relationships. As an example, the often-used diffusion theory (Rogers, 1995) was found to be inappropriate, relative to our research needs. We decided that a data-driven approach, allowing practitioners to a large degree to speak in the voice of "you," should be employed.

Because we think that practitioners will be concerned about UML-related issues and the impact of one issue on another — for example, that successful use of UML in system development would result in projects being completed on time and within budget — we turned to causal mapping as the method for data analysis. Although our research isn't completed, we find that causal mapping served us well in documenting constructs, variables, and relationships that practitioners deem relevant. Moreover, causal maps, as we hoped, resulted in the documentation of surprising elements, as well as gaps.

This chapter has focused on describing the methods utilized in a causal mapping study. The emphasis has been on presenting and discussing the decisions that arose during the process. It is not difficult to explain our thinking regarding the directions we selected at various choice points. It is more difficult to propose that these were "the right" or even good decisions. On the whole many of these decisions represent trade-offs – getting a reasonable job done versus holding out for a theoretical perfection; maintaining a usable audit train versus not getting bogged down in our own detailed documentation; understanding in detail the view of our respondents versus emphasizing more general emergent themes that no individual may have directly expressed.

From our personal point of view, the study has significantly created value in providing us with a much richer understanding of the role of UML in IT development – lessons that are extremely helpful in the classroom and working with recruiters of our students. It is our hope that the ultimate observations that will be presented in a final report will be viewed as combining elements of "confirming" or adding weight to commonly held views that remain basically anecdotal in nature and elements of some surprising and new relationships and possibilities.

Acknowledgments

The authors wish to acknowledge the contribution of Saint Louis University for providing a summer grant to the second author for work on this chapter.

References

Benbasat, I., & Zmud, R.W. (1999). Issues and opinions – Empirical research in information systems: The practice of relevance. *MIS Quarterly*, 23(1), 3-16.

Bohman, J. (2000). The importance of the second person: interpretation, practical knowledge, and normative attitudes. In H.H. Kögler & K.R. Stueber (Eds.), *Empathy & agency: The problem of understanding in the human sciences*. Boulder, CO: Westview.

Booch, G., Rumbaugh, J., & Jacobson, I. (1999). *The unified modeling language user guide*. Boston, MA: Addison-Wesley.

Brancheau, J.C., & Wetherbe, J.C. (1990). The adoption of spreadsheet software: Testing innovation diffusion theory in the context of end-user computing. *Information Systems Research*, 1(2), 115-143.

Brown, D.W. (2002). *An introduction to object-oriented analysis: Objects and UML in plain English*. New York: Wiley.

Checkland, P., & Scholes, J. (1990). *Soft systems methodology in action*. Chichester, UK: Wiley.

Chen, P.P.S. (1976). The entity-relationship model – Toward a unified view of data. *ACM Transactions on Database Systems*, 1(1), 9-36.

Cho, I., & Kim, Y.-G. (2001-2002). Critical factors for assimilation of object-oriented programming languages. *Journal of Management Information Systems*, 18(3), 125-156.

De Marco, T. (1978). *Structured analysis and system specification*. New York: Yourdon.

Fahey, L., & Narayanan, V. K. (1989). Linking changes in revealed causal maps and environment: An empirical study. *Journal of Management Studies*, 26(4), 361-378.

Fichman, R.G. (2000). The diffusion and assimilation of information technology innovations. In R.W. Zmud (Ed.), *Framing the Domains of IT Management: Projecting the Future...Through the Past* (pp. 105-127). Cincinnati, OH: Pinnaflex Educational Resources.

Fichman, R.G., & Kemerer, C.F. (1999) The illusory diffusion of innovation: an examination of assimilation gaps. *Information Systems Research*, 10(3), 255-275.

Goles, T., & Hirscheim, R. (2000). The paradigm is dead ... long live the paradigm: the legacy of Burell and Morgan. *Omega*, 28(3), 249-268.

Johnson, R.A. (2002). Object-oriented analysis and design – What does the research say? *Journal of Computer Information Systems*, 42(3), 11-15.

Klein, K., & Kozlowski, S.W. (Eds.) (2000). *Multilevel theory, research, and methods in organizations: Foundations, extensions, and new directions*. San Francisco, CA: Jossey-Bass.

Larsen, T.J. (2001). The phenomenon of diffusion: Red herrings and future promise. In M.A. Ardis & B.L. Marcolin (Eds.), *Proceedings of the IFIP TC8 WG8.6 Fourth Working Conference on Diffusing Software Products and Process Innovation, April 7-10*, (pp. 35-50). Banff, Canada. Boston, MA: Kluwer Academic Publishers.

Lyytinen, K., & Damsgaard, J. (2001). What's wrong with the diffusion of innovation theory? In M.A. Ardis & B.L. Marcolin (Eds.), *Proceedings of the IFIP TC8 WG8.6 Fourth Working Conference on Diffusing Software Products and Process Innovation, April 7-10*, (pp. 173-190), Banff, Canada. Boston, MA: Kluwer Academic Publishers.

Moore, G.C., & Benbasat, I. (1991). Development of an instrument to measure the perceptions of adopting an information technology innovation. *Information Systems Research*, 2(3), 192-222.

Nelson, K. M., Nadkarni, S., Narayanan, V.K., & Ghods, M. (2000). Understanding software operations support expertise: A revealed causal mapping approach. *MIS Quarterly*, 24(3), 475-507.

Nurminen, M.I., & Eriksson, I.V. (1999). Research notes – Information systems research: The 'Infurgic' perspective. *International Journal of Information Management*, 19, 87-94.

Prescott, M.B., & Conger, S.A. (1995). Information technology innovations: A classification by it locus of impact and research approach. *DATA BASE Advances*, 26(2&3), 20-40.

Robey, D., & Markus, M.L. (1998). Beyond rigor and relevance: producing consumable research about information systems. *Information Resources Management Journal*, 11(1), 7-15.

Rogers, E.M. (1995). *Diffusion of innovations*. New York: The Free Press.

Sim, E.R., & Wright, G. (2001-2002). The difficulties of learning object-oriented analysis and design: an exploratory study. *Journal of Computer Information Systems*, 42(2), 95-100.

Sauer, C. (1999). Deciding the future for is failures: not the choice you might think. In W. Currie & B. Galliers (Eds.), *Rethinking management information systems: An interdisciplinary perspective*. Oxford: Oxford University Press.

Van de Ven, A.H., Polley, D.E., Garud, R., & Venkataraman, S. (1999). *The innovation journey*. New York: Oxford University Press.

Van de Ven, A.H., & Poole, M.S. (1995). Explaining development and change in organizations. *Academy of Management Review*, 20(3), 510-540.

Weber, R. (2003). Editor's comment – Still desperately seeking the IT artifact. *MIS Quarterly*, 27(2), iii-xi.

Yin, R.K. (1994). *Case study research: design and methods*. Thousand Oaks, CA: Sage.

Endnote

[1] Authors are listed alphabetically and contributed equally to this article

Appendix A: Respondent Demographics

Employer	Background	Age	G	Management Responsibility	Title
Large accounting/consulting firm Reports to senior manager or VP Organized by industry sectors	Bachelors in Engineering 1994, MBA 96 With firm since 1998	29	M	In projects 2 ½ yrs focus on success & risk, analyzing requirements	Project manager
Medium-sized custom manufacturing Reports to IT director new role/division -IT not quite understood reporting track -president is engineer -CFO -director of IS	BS Computer science	40	F	Manages two teams of business consultants Supports sales and e-commerce helpdesk since 09/2001	Business Integration Manager
Medium-sized custom manufacturing Reports to IT director -president is engineer -CFO -director of IS	Bachelors in Information systems	40	F	two years' tenure manages 13 developers	Application systems manager
Large accounting/consulting firm	Bachelors in Philosophy Business certificate MBA -employed since 1999 in current role	31	M	responsibility is in the middle of the hierarchy last project, 8 people reporting directly, four more reporting in-directly	Development manager
Medium-sized financial brokerage IT dept. has 20yrs old IT in a-transition process	Bachelor of Science in electrical engineering	47	F	mentor for OO/JAVA (80%) acts as liaison between IT department and business line IT users	Lead developer

Copyright © 2005, Idea Group Inc. Copying or distributing in print or electronic forms without written permission of Idea Group Inc. is prohibited.

Appendix A (Continued)

Employer	Background	Age	G	Management Responsibility	Title
Medium-sized financial brokerage -not critically dependent upon IT, makes money! -outsource accounting (new) -move toward std packages -IT department -CMM level 0 but not formally measured -Data management Group	Bachelors in theology & philosophy masters of divinity -12 yrs with firm	50	M	soft supervision, no hiring, etc. technical rather than management track, more consulting than directing	senior technical data consultant
Medium-sized health care facility heavy into IT development -Clinical team within IT department	Bachelors of Science in nursing 1999 MS nursing, emphasis informatics, 2002	42	F	In charge of project implementation, but no reporting employees	Clinical business analyst
Small biotech firm -IT department	college 1 year 1980, computer science -was employee-rehired as individual consultant	41	M	none	Contract programmer/analyst
Small biotech firm -IT department	BS-comp.science, 1983 Worked in field since that time	41	M	In charge of project and one other employee	Software engineering manager.
Large food product company flattened out budgets -IT department -1200 employees	electrical engineering, 1968	50	M	None Technical consulting	Corporate level software architecture
Large food product company -Management System Group -- Organizational Technical Development	Masters in aerospace engineering	42	M	-15 people recently, down to 10 today (08/2002	-MIS consultant

Appendix B: Interview Guide

Systems Development Representations The Unified Modeling Language: Organizational Prerequisites and Use Value

Preamble

We began with informal explanation of who we are and what we were doing. We also read the formal Institutional Review Board – human subjects – approved disclaimer.

1.0 Background and Initiation

Individual characteristics

(demographics, subjective norms, competencies and preferences, styles)

1.1 Your age? _____
1.2 Your educational background? (degrees earned)
1.3 Do you have management responsibilities? (Are there other employees that report to you/that you supervise?)
1.4 Your place in the organization (IT-department, Line unit)?
1.5 Your present position?
1.6 Your work experience (position, start-end, type of projects)?

2.0 The Last Completed Project Worked on, Being a User Oriented System Lasting More than Three Months and Having at Least Three Project Members

2.1 Please briefly describe the intended objectives and deliverables
2.2 Approximately when was it started and completed?
2.3 How would you describe the size or scope of the project (lines of code, # of screens, # of tables, # of reports, # of servers/clients/networks, etc.)?
2.4 How would you describe the personnel involved in the project (# of IS professionals, # of client team members, amount of change of personnel during the project)?
2.5 How would you describe the level of difficulty of the project (system characteristics, management issues, collaboration tasks)?
2.6 To what extent would you characterize the project as developing completely new application software (in contrast to maintenance and upgrading)? To what extent did you utilize vendor developed software in the project? (If so, which product did you use, who was the vendor, how would you describe the documentation, vendor determined, object-oriented, in compliance with UML, structured design — or any other? Changes in the vendor software were made by yourself, the vendor, both?)

3.0 Methods and Tools in the Last Project

3.1 As you work on the analysis and design of the new IT application, what sort of methods do you use for representing requirements and application structures? As you personally see it, would you say your employed methods belong to types of methods? If so, what would be the dominating type? The least used or important one?

3.2 Have you used any of the following analysis and design modeling techniques for representing requirements and application structures? *(For any used, follow up with how extensively, supported by case tool, used alone or part of project team usage, thoughts about using the tools, where/when in the project were they be employed)*

- Use-case
- Class or object diagrams
- Sequence charts
- Collaboration charts
- Activity diagrams
- State transition diagrams
- Data Flow diagram
- Entity Relationship diagram

3.3 When it comes to modeling the requirements, design, and code structure for new system, what methods do you prefer? *(May be answered in earlier question — particularly if using methods not selected themselves)*

3.4 In the execution of the last project, to what extent did you use computer tools that support your standard — that is, how do you actually carry out your descriptions, manually or automated? *(link to CASE tools)*

3.5 Do all members of the project team use the same set of representations and CASE tools or does each member use whatever tools he or she prefers?

3.6 How are descriptions of requirements communicated among project members? Do you typically use any of the following for communication regarding requirements among project members?

Mail

- E-mail
- Shared project specification database
- Meetings and walkthroughs
- Other?

3.7 How would you characterize the user — user participation — IT expert interaction and integration (or lack thereof)?

Do you employ UML or any of its diagrams in these interactions? (As you see it, what are the benefits and what are the drawbacks? How well do users understand these diagrams? How does a user exert influence on choice of diagram or diagram content? Or should the user not have any influence? Why and why not?)

3.8   Did this project include any mechanism for learning or enhancing your abilities regarding the representations and CASE tools?

In your experience, how are representation and tool competence taken care of? (follow-up) How much do you have to learn on your own? Did you have 'methods' discussion groups? Did you attend methods seminars or courses? Is the focus on representation something resembling a 'one shot' or is it an ongoing activity?

4.0 Outcomes (Use — Amount, Density, Distribution, Economic Value, "Correctness of Solutions")

4.1   Considering these same projects, to what degree do you consider them successful? What sort of criteria do you use to judge them?

- Economic?
- Time?
- Quality?
- Amount of completeness?
- Positive feelings among developers?
- Positive feelings among users/sponsors?
- Meeting stated objectives?

4.2   To what extent and in what way did the use of UML, OO analysis and design, and/or CASE tool affect the level of success achieved?

5.0 About Project Work in General

UML/OOAD/CASE — the innovation and its nature (Rogers' aspects, critical mass, OOP infusion — supporting tech, class libraries, application components)

5.1   Having discussed the use of methods in the last project — thinking about the projects you have worked on during the last five years, are there some projects for which you tend to use modeling tools rather than others? What would differentiate projects where you do use the tools from those where you don't?

5.2 Thinking back over the last 5 years or so, what are the most drastic changes with regard to how you work on projects? (organization, people, ITs development, methods)

5.3 What, if any, changes have you made to the standard UML/OOAD/CASE approach to make it useful in your environment?

5.4 Professionally, what would you say is most fun to do?

6.0 IT-Environment (org factors, size (6.1), diversity (6.2), scale (6.3)) — (Following Fichman)

6.1 About how many projects will be active at any one time?

How many employees are there in the IT department who are likely to be engaged in software development at any one time?

About what size is the annual IT budget?

6.2 (Diversity) About how many different programming languages used by the development staff account for at least 5% of development projects?

About how many runtime platforms account for at least 5% of new development projects?

6.3 (Learning related scale) What percentage of application effort goes into new development, integration of systems, maintenance, non-development related activities?

7.0 IT Strategy

7.1 To what extent is there an IT strategy linked to organizational business strategy?

7.2 To what extent is there an articulated IT strategy?

Do you have a development and maintenance strategy for tools and technical support?

Does this strategy include organization issues

- In-house vs. outsourcing?
- Reward system?
- Productivity guidelines?
- Project principles?
- Hiring guidelines?

7.3   Has the strategy any formulation about learning? Keeping the present staff up-to-speed, project learning requirements as part of project management, planning, and control?

7.4   To what extent does your strategy include standardization of hardware, software, and development approach?

7.5   To what extent does the department use OO analysis, design, programming?

7.6   Does the strategy include changing the amount of OO?

THANK YOU

Do you want to be apprised of results of the study?

Name   _____

Address_____

E-mail
_____

Appendix C: Concept List for Independent Variables (Cause)

Ability to translate to other language/culture	OO definition
Abstract thinking	OO design
Active document management	OO programming language
Activity diagrams	OO tool use
Adding requirements into package code	OO use
Addition of consultants	Org strategy
Additions to package	Organizational computing outcome measures
Adoption of standards	Outcome measure
Analysis	Outcome measure (defects)
Analysis process, descriptive	Outcome measure (usage)
Application of OO throughout project	Outcome measures
Application type	Package customization
Architect correctly	Paper prototyping
Architecture level	Pattern of modeling content
Asset management	Paying for changes to specs
Attention to user	Performance
Bugs	Personalization of training
CASE tool use	Phased development with multiple leaders
CASE tool use (Rational Rose and Visio)	Physical arrangement
Change management	Procedural programming skills
Change management process	Process mapping
Change processes	Process time
Class diagrams	Project domain
Class models	Project management
Class or Object Diagrams	Project manager people skills
Clauses where requirements not fulfilled	Project manager technical skills
Communication	Project objective, measure of success
Communication	Project outcome measures
Conflicting assignments	Project size
Consistent modeling	Project size
Consulting firm	Project staffing
Cost	Project staffing
Cost center	Project success measure
Cost per transaction	Prototypes
Culture	Prototyping
Customer knowledge base	Quality assurance
Data modeling	Quality of architecture
Data services layer	Quality of contact with users
Database tool	Rapid evolution, many changes
Decentralization	Rational Rose use
Defined requirements	Rational Rose/UML
Demands on staff versus actual capabilities	Reduction of technical "holds"
Description of analysis process	Relationship of DFD to ER modeling
Description of anticipated development environment	Requirement specification
Descriptive, communication tool	Requirements
Design processes	Requirements determination staffing
Developer acceptance	Requirements Gathering
Developer coordination	Reusability
Developer preference	Reuse
Developer skills	Roles of implementation and domain models
Development environment	Scalability
Development staff skills	Scope creep
Development tasks	Self-training

Appendix C (Continued)

Documentation consistency	Specifying outcomes
Documentation detail	Staff communication between project phases
Documentation method	Staff knowledge and skill
Documentation process description	Staff preferences
Documentation quality	Staff skills
Documentation utility	Staff turnover
Early involvement	Staffing
Early testing	Staffing turnover
Enterprise-level requirements process details	Standardization
ER (data) model	Standardized platform approach
ER diagrams	Standardized use
Faith and trust	Standards
Focus on overview	Success measures
Formal information requirements	Task accounting
Functional area	Task complexity
Guideline design/process	Team size
Hardware capacity	Technology diversity
Hardware/software capacity	Testing/quality assurance
Hierarchy chart	Time, money
Hiring	Tool investment
Ideal documentation approach	Tool platform selection
Implementation issues with ER versus OO	Tool use
Implementation of modeling	Tools
Individual expertise and contribution	Tools description
Individual performance	Training
Information requirements documents	Training methods
IT staff skill levels	UML
Java provides some CASE tool functionality	UML use
Java, OO approach	UML/CASE tools
Leadership	Uncertain situations
Learning / Improvement	Universal development approach
Level at which business process documentation occurs	Use
Linkage of requirements to technical models	Use case
Management mandate	Use of OO
Manual approach	Use of packages
Master scheduling	Use of UML
Matrix organization	Use/non-use of UML
Measurement	User characteristics
Meeting all requirements	User contract
Mentors	User expectations
Metrics	User involvement
Modeling	User liaison
Modeling formality	User satisfaction
Modeling thoroughness	User signoff
Modular training	User survey
Multinational staffing	User type
Narrowed features/simplification	Value of CASE tools, difficult to measure
Need for developer – user communication	Vendor experience
Non-OO design	Vendor selection
Object /class diagrams	Vendor staff turnover
Object diagrams	Visual representation
Object-ERD	Visualization of screens and outputs
On-line CASE tools	Word document
OO	Work expectations
OO Approach	----------------------

Appendix D: Concept List for Dependent Variables (Effect)

Ability to model system	Project cost
Ability to provide documentation	Project difficulty
Ability to provide modeling	Project management organization
Adoption of UML practices	Project management quality
Amount of risk	Project management success
Application success	Project organization
Change management	Project outcomes
Client satisfaction	Project process success (ease/flow)
Client satisfaction	Project quality
Communication requirements	Project success
Communication with users	Prototyping
Component oriented production environment	Quality assurance
Cost	Quality of documentation
Design quality	Quality of information requirements document/
Detailed user requirements	Quality of packaged processes
Developer satisfaction	Quality of tool use
Developer skills	Quality of use of OO
Developer team communication	Quick view
Developer-user communication	Requirements documents
Development guidelines	Reuse
Development model	Role of analysts
Development outcome	Role specialization
Deviation from standards	Satisfaction measure -- questionnaire
Documentation	Scalability
Documentation outcomes	Scope definition
Documentation quality	Scope problems
Documentation success	Sense of closure
Documentation utility	Skill development
Documenting business issues/decisions	Skills
Ease of data retrieval for user	Staff mentoring
Ease of learning OO	Staff skills
Economic value	Staff skills and knowledge
Effective tool use	Staff training
Effort on documentation	Staffing alternatives
Enhance knowledge base for project work	Standardization
ER use	Standardized platform approach
Extra overhead	Standardized use
Formality of documentation	State chart diagram
Formality of modeling	State transition diagrams
Generating user feedback	Subset of CASE tools
Information requirements success	Success measure – fulfill all contracted requirements
In-house use of CASE tool	Sufficient modeling
Insurance against personnel loss	System consistency
Integrating data and process views	System use
Integration of development environments	Technology diversity
Internal versus external staffing	Technology diversity
IT role	Tendency to use OO/UML
Learning curve	Testing effectiveness
Maintenance	Thorough modeling
Model use	Tool use
Modeling formality	Training
Narrowed features/Simplification	Turnover
Need for analysis and documentation	UML use

Appendix D (Continued)

Need for requirements documentation	UML use (sequence diagrams and use case diagrams)
Need for specific tool	Use case
Obligation satisfied	Use levels of ER
On-line CASE tools	Use of DFD and ER
OO	Use of modeling
OO project management	Use of OO approach
OO skill development	Use of sequence diagrams
OO skills	Use of use case
OO success	Used for development
OO tool use	Used for testing
OO use	Usefulness of models
Package customization	User participation
Package stability	User requirements writing
Pattern of modeling content	User satisfaction
Performance	User understanding
Pressure for IT personnel to perform	Version control
Problem understanding	Visualization of documentation

Chapter XI

Using Causal Mapping to Support Information Systems Development:
Some Considerations

Fran Ackermann
Strathclyde Business School, UK

Colin Eden
Strathclyde Business School, UK

Abstract

Identifying what different stakeholders in a business need from Information Systems development has always been seen as problematic. There are numerous cases of failure as projects run over time, over budget, and, most significantly, do not meet the needs of the user population. Whilst having a structured design process can go some way towards reducing the potential of failure, these methodologies do not attend sufficiently to clarifying and agreeing objectives or to considering the social and cultural elements inherent in the ownership and adoption of any new system. Instigating an effective, and structured, dialogue between users, developers and, when appropriate, sponsors, is therefore a critical consideration. Linking user needs, as they see them, to the language of IS developers and vice versa is crucial. Both parties need ownership. This chapter focuses upon the use of causal mapping, supported where appropriate by special software, that facilitates the development of a shared understanding (of both business needs and IT opportunities) and through this common platform enables a negotiated and agreed outcome. The nature of the outcome invites translation to structured design processes.

Copyright © 2005, Idea Group Inc. Copying or distributing in print or electronic forms without written permission of Idea Group Inc. is prohibited.

Introduction

Although Information Systems (IS) are able to provide considerable benefits to organizations, there have been an extensive number of failures. For example, in 1999 the *Financial Times* noted that 50% of systems projects fail to meet their expected rate of return. A later, more spectacular, example is the system developed by ICL for UK Post Office counters — a system which went massively over budget and was never completed in line with the original specification (*Financial Times*, 22 July 1999). Explanations for these problems abound and range from poor communication with users and customers, not learning from past experiences, over-ambitious rates on returns, unexpected demand levels, amongst others (Boddy, Boonstra & Kennedy, 2002).

The use of structured approaches such as Structured Systems Analysis and Design Method (SSADM) (Downs, Clare & Coe, 1988), Information Engineering (Martin, 1986) and other such methodologies were touted as aiding the development of the systems through providing careful, logical procedures to follow. However, experience showed that they still fell short in terms of supporting the process of IS development, as they lacked understanding of the boundaries and properties of the systems starting well down the development process. More recent approaches such as prototyping, and Rapid Application Development (Martin, 1991), which were developed to answer some of the difficulties, are still unable to provide what is required. For example, no aid is provided by these techniques for managing differing, and possibly conflicting, objectives of users, or addressing the organization's social and cultural norms of behaviour. Defining requirements is often regarded as a simple process, or one that can be determined by the Information Systems (IS) staff. As argued by Jayaratna (1994) and Stowell (1995), what is needed is a deeper understanding of the nature of organizations and how the system interacts with the organization

Orlikowski, Walsham, Jones and DeGross (1995) found that even when systems are developed with consideration of the organization's working practices there are problems as appropriation of systems can often be diverted from original intention as user needs change and are refined over time and use. However, they suggest that this is likely to be particularly the case if and when business practices and their socially construed norms are not well understood. Acknowledging the need to attend to the social and ethical considerations, however, is not new, as noted in Enid Mumford's work (1983) and, as Zuboff comments, IS "ultimately reconfigures the nature of work and the social relationships that organize productive activity," (1988) further reinforcing the need.

Therefore, methods and techniques for facilitating dialogue between users, developers and, when appropriate, sponsors is important. Soft Systems Methodology (SSM) — a problem structuring methodology has seen some success in this area (Checkland & Scholes, 1990). As its name suggests, SSM pays particular attention to the "soft" or social issues. The approach recognises that in most situations there is a lack of clarity regarding the objectives of the system in question and that these issues often comprise many aspects and subtleties which make working with the apparently messy IS design situation problematic. Providing some means of surfacing and structuring existing concerns is achieved through the formalism of what is called a "rich picture"— a cartoon-like picture that depicts the aspirations and situations of stakeholders of the system being considered. The process explicitly allows for the social elements to be revealed along with consideration of possible different interpretations of the system (different conceptual models) and so enables an effective dialogue to take place. The process is expected to result in the agreement of an owned outcome.

Another problem structuring method, which is gaining popularity, is the use of causal mapping. There are an increasing number of papers detailing management research and problem solving practices that have effectively applied mapping. These applications appear in a range of research arenas including IS (see Nelson, Nadkarni, Narayanan & Ghods, 2000; Boland, Tenkasi & Te'eni, 1994; Zmud, Anthony & Stair, 1993). Mapping's ability to surface and structure individual theories of the world with their associated detail not only allows the individuals themselves to understand their thinking better but also provides a rich basis upon which to enable the different stakeholders in the group to negotiate a shared understanding and make agreements.

In this chapter we begin by reviewing the background and features of our particular form of mapping before exploring its use in a real-world example, considering what that experience suggests about the requirements of successful IS design, and then finally making some concluding remarks.

Causal Mapping

As is also evident elsewhere in this book, not only are there a number of different ways that causal mapping can support Information Systems, but there are different forms of Causal Mapping. The particular version considered in this chapter is based upon the work of a cognitive psychologist — George Kelly (1955) — whose propositions about how individuals make sense of their world resulted in a powerful body of theory known as personal construct theory (PCT). From this body of theory Kelly developed an instrument: Repertory Grids (Fransella & Bannister, 1977; Bonarius, Holland & Rosenburg, 1981) which has been used in IS research (Hunter & Beck, 2000; Tan & Hunter, 2002). In addition, and, more pertinently for this chapter, cognitive mapping was developed to reflect more depth and greater appreciation of individuality than that which was offered by repertory grids (Brown, 1992; Eden, 1988). However, as many organizational tasks require the involvement of a number of participants, a range of different forms of group mapping have been developed (Ackermann & Eden, 2001; Eden & Ackermann, 1998) to extend the use of causal mapping that is founded in personal construct theory. These different forms include:

The "Oval Mapping Technique" — a manual, rather than computer-assisted, process. Individuals are provided with oval shaped cards (about 11x19cms, or large rectangular post-its) and identical pens (to help increase anonymity). They are asked to write down any concerns, aspirations, issues or assumptions that come to mind. Each contribution is written on a separate oval card. These ovals are posted up on a flipchart paper-covered wall, enabling others to read and "piggyback" off them. During this process of generating a scatter picture of the important aspects of the situation under consideration, a facilitator works at clustering the material into themes so as to manage the large amount of material.

It is not untypical to have 200+ contributions surfaced from a group of eight by the end of a two-hour session. Once the rate of contributions has slowed down or stopped, the group, with the help of the facilitator, works through each cluster exploring how the content of the different statements causally influence one another, both within and across clusters. This process inevitably surfaces further views as different chains of causality are presented and captured. The result is a structured causal map. The map represents not only the different themes/clusters but also their degree of interaction with one another. The process invariably enables the participants to move from an often very divergent view of the situation to a more convergent one.

The second form of group mapping involves the use of a mapping software package — *Decision Explorer*[1] — to capture and structure the material. Instead of having participants write down their contributions, the facilitator captures the contributions as they are stated in facilitated discussion, thus in real time. The facilitator regularly checks with participants that views have been captured correctly, and explores their relationships with other already captured statements. This enables participants to concentrate on the discussion — using the developing map as an aide mémoire. As a result of working electronically the group can interactively "play" with the captured material exploring, for example, the consequences of different options, examining possible alternatives, and agreeing objectives/goals (end points of the causal chains). In doing so they are always aware of the causal ramifications of their developing agreements. In addition, rapid searches can be carried out for statements focusing on a particular topic, as well as a range of analyses used to enable exploration of the structure of the map. Analysis results, such as the identification of "central" statements that influence and are influenced by many others, of "potent options" that can affect many goals, and of significant outcomes or goals, subsequently can be colour coded and categorised. Finally by having a number of views available (similar to spreadsheet packages where there can be a number of sheets) of different aspects, managing the complexity of the large body of material surfaced becomes easier.

The third and final form has participants provided with laptops connected together through a local area network, and connected through *Decision Explorer* to a public screen — the combined system is run through the software *Group Explorer*[2]. This allows participants to directly enter their contributions (both statements and relationships) into the map developing on the public screen as soon as they think of them. This allows for total anonymity and reduces the pressure on the facilitator to capture the material. In addition, this mode of working provides other useful features such as the ability for each participant to rate the importance of statements on a scale or to prioritise them. For example, through using the "preferencing system" participants are able to demonstrate anonymously which of the options they will support and which they will not, providing a reality check on the proposed way forward. Alternatively, participants can use the rating tool, which allows them to explore which of the various options might provide best support for an objective and whether there is any consensus about this.

Each of these has been applied to a range of different decision making areas (see Ackermann & Eden, 2004) including problem structuring (Eden & Ackermann, 2001), strategy development (Eden & Ackermann, 1998) and the modelling of disruptions and delays occurring on large engineering projects (Ackermann et al., 1997).

Using Causal Mapping to Support Information Systems Development   267

In each of these processes the technique of causal mapping provides the means of developing a graphical representation of an individual's or group's perception of issues by building up chains of argumentation. Therefore, statements/nodes (facts, assertions, options, issues, goals, etc.) are captured along with their relationships — where the arrow (relationship) implies causality. In Figure 1, the individual is discussing the use (or not) of a financial information system. Node 13 and 7 are both assertions resulting in the perceived consequences of 9 and 6. This is a small causal map — frequently individual maps comprise 80+ statements and group maps in excess of 400 statements.

Furthermore, the analysis of the structure of the causal map can reveal patterns. For example, busy points typically suggest key issues, superordinate statements (those at the top of the chains of arguments) imply values or goals, and feedback loops imply potential dynamic behaviour. In Figure 1, node 17 has a considerable amount of material supporting it — some of which is shown in detail, e.g., nodes 15, 18, 20 and some of which is currently hidden (nodes 27, 25, 23), suggesting that it is likely to be a key issue. Node 8 is displayed as a goal — this was something that the individual felt was good in its own right. Finally on the left of the figure is a feedback loop (comprising nodes 17, 19 & 20) — in this case operating as a vicious cycle (a self-sustaining negative situation). In this way the user is able to examine both the whole (in terms of emergent properties of its structure) and the detail to help develop a fuller understanding of the interaction of different considerations, and so make a more informed decision.

The map enables a better understanding to be developed as statements are explored alongside their context. Adhering to the formal coding guidelines (see Appendix A) is necessary for the analysis of emergent properties of the map to be reliable, but it also provides a powerful aid to group thinking. For example, the guideline asking that each

Figure 1. An example map

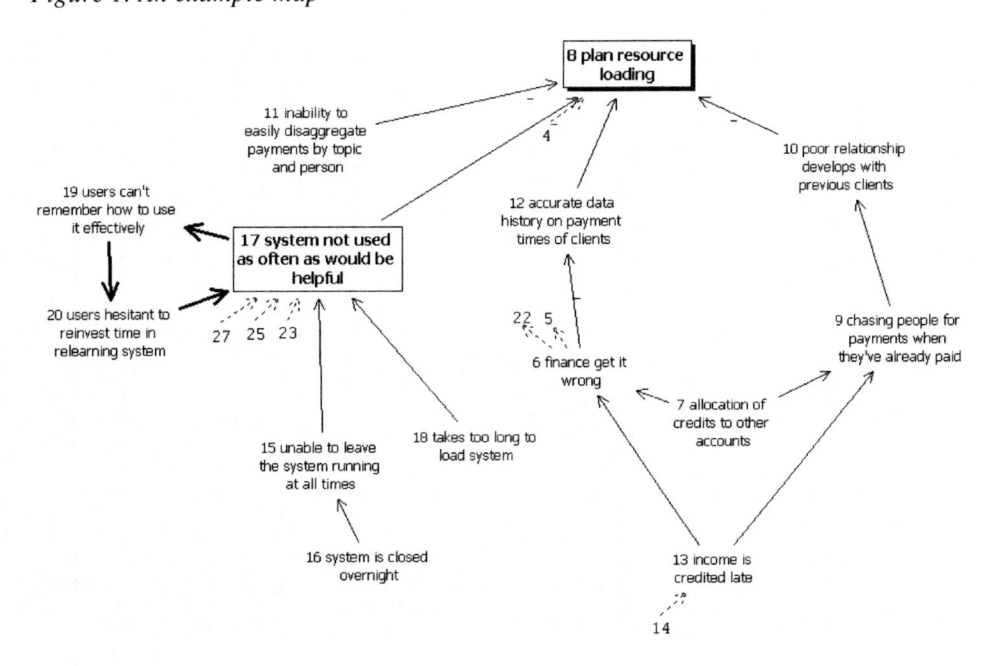

Copyright © 2005, Idea Group Inc. Copying or distributing in print or electronic forms without written permission of Idea Group Inc. is prohibited.

statement be worded in an action-orientated form encourages those developing the maps to be clearer about what might be done and why that would be expressed by an assertion. Attending to the direction of causality between two statements prompts consideration of what is the means and what is the desired end or outcome of two action-oriented statements, often revealing underlying values.

Although mapping can help individuals better understand their world, when considering Information Systems design it is mapping's ability to support group negotiation that is of most interest here. Capturing the views of those participating, along with the full context of their views as chains of argument means individuals are better able to determine what they are concerned about and what they want regarding the system within the context of the opinions of others. Through this extended picture, a greater understanding of meaning is elicited (through the context) and thus an appreciation of the rationale for particular views. Moreover capturing all of the contributions provides participants with a sense that the process is "just" (Kim & Mauborgne, 1991). From this often quite extensive map[3], a shared understanding begins to emerge. One objective is for those involved to begin to understand, in use, what is meant by very general descriptions of the proposed system (Checkland & Holwell, 1998).

Using Mapping to Develop an Information System

As intimated above, developing a clear and shared understanding of the purpose of the system by all who have some stake in its development and use is important for ensuring that the system is used and used within appropriate bounds. Information is always given meaning by its context, and often IS's are designed with a presumption of context. A good understanding can only be derived from a clear knowledge of purpose and the limits to its application.

Understanding who the stakeholders might be, who will give the information meaning and in what way might they be involved (or effect the usage of the system) is critical. Stakeholder analysis and management techniques such as those described in Boddy, Boonstra and Kennedy (2002) or Ackermann and Eden (2003) provide a good starting point.

Ackermann & Eden employ particular forms of mapping to determine not only who the stakeholders are, but also the details regarding their disposition, relationships with others, and the nature of the power and interest they may use to influence the success or otherwise of the information system. By building a grid whose axes are power and interest, participants are able to position stakeholders according to their relative power to influence success (as determined by the purpose of the IS) and interest in usage. The grid usefully shows those who have both the interest and power to ensure success or failure, and so attention to their views regarding the development of the IS will be crucial. A better understanding of these stakeholders can be elicited by exploring in more depth the bases of power and the nature of interest. Those who have power and no interest in the outcome can easily determine failure (intentionally and unintentionally) and so must be carefully managed. Mapping the influence network among these powerful stakeholders provides important clues as to which of them can be used as opinion formers — increasing the chances of success. Analysis of these maps follows the same conventions as those used to analyse causal maps.

By facilitating not only the means of contributing effectively to these deliberations, but also structuring the contributions to enable effective management of the unfolding complexity (rather than reducing it), sufficient and productive time can be spent in the exploration stage. The purpose of the exploration is to consider in depth the emergent properties and develop agreed action packages. This ability through capturing the richness and diversity of views along with managing their structure represents the stages of Intelligence and Design, in what Simon (1959) describes in his four stages of decision making.

By describing a case study that employed mapping as a means of developing an IS, aspects of the process and some of the benefits of mapping will be illustrated and explored. As with most case studies in IS development, the material is sensitive, and so the material presented below is less expansive than preferred.

Developing an Information System for Student Tracking[4]

The organization discussed below is part of a large University. Rather unusually, it is a self-funded unit receiving no public monies. Therefore, it operates in many ways as a business with one of the main objectives being to not make a loss, and make enough surplus to reinvest in its educational products. At least, sufficient revenue is required so that the organization can pay staff, keep the estate in order, and provide its commitment to a high quality total service to students. The major contribution to finances is unsurprisingly student fees, although executive development programmes, amongst other activities, contribute. Currently the unit delivers its key products in many different locations (product offerings not only at home but in four countries in South East Asia, four in the Middle East, and two European countries).

One of the consequences of having such a widely dispersed programme (at any one time the school has around 2,000 students on its books) is that it is paramount that an effective and efficient information system is available to track enquiries, manage admissions, and monitor the progress of students. However as is often the case, an incremental growth in locations and student numbers along with a growing recognition of the power of information technology had resulted in an ad hoc approach to the development of information systems. Consequently, there were six different systems being used, involving a range of different programmes — databases, spreadsheets, and word-processing packages. Getting data from one to another was problematic, frequent errors occurred and thus accurate and timely information was difficult to attain. A new system was required.

In order to ensure that the new system was as effective as possible, it was necessary to take into account views from staff with responsibilities for marketing, operations, academic delivery, and unit management along with those from the computer support group. Moreover in terms of operations, it was important to consider the views not only of those working in the unit but also those operating in the different sites across the globe. Their views needed to be included. Management reviewed the budget and it was agreed that $350,000 would be available for software development with the total budget for staff time and training aiming at a maximum of $750,000 total costs. They were keen to ensure that the new system would be within budget and on time.

As a means of involving the different perspectives and also ensuring a sustainable and achievable product, the unit decided to run a workshop using the causal mapping process and associated software[5]. In this manner, it would be possible to capture all the different views along with their explanations and consequences, thus building up what was hoped to be a full picture of requirements, aspirations, issues, etc. Thus, the workshop was expected to ensure that those attending felt an involvement in the system development and that all users and the computer support staff understood the rationale for the intended system.

The management team spent some time considering specifically who to involve, as they wanted to ensure that two members of staff represented each constituency. They also wanted to employ the services of a neutral party to facilitate, allowing those attending to concentrate purely on contributing. Once the composition of the group was settled, and a facilitator chosen, a date for the workshop meeting was set.

The day commenced with an introduction from the facilitator, who explained the process to be adopted. Each participant had in front of them a networked laptop. Through this medium they would be able to contribute their concerns, aspirations and requirements simultaneously and anonymously. It was believed that this would be helpful, as firstly there was a lot to cover in the day, and secondly there were some concerns that some participants might feel constrained due to the presence of management. The intention was to start with possible reasons for wanting a new system, before eliciting their aspirations for the new system.

The group began by surfacing their concerns about the current situation — the reasons why a new system was needed. They did this by typing in the statement and seeing it appear both on their laptop workstation and on the public screen (which enabled them to see the views of others and so build on them). It soon became clear that many found this a cathartic process — they were obviously very fed up with the present system! After about 10 minutes participants felt that they had covered this topic.

While they had been doing this, the facilitator had been working to position the statements so that they were roughly clustered and hierarchically positioned. This allowed her to then, with help from the group, begin the process of linking them[6] together to develop the causal network where the links represented causal relationships. For example, the group believed that 5 *"rigid structure of the systems rather than flexible structure"* led to 6 *"unable to get decent statistical information"* which in turn meant that 7 *"they experienced difficulties with managing exam board decisions"* (See Figure 2). It was explained that the numbers associated with each statement were for reference only and simply made manipulation easier, and that the three dots (an ellipsis) was a short hand for "rather than" — enabling the capture of contrasting situations.

During the discussion of the triggers for a new system it became clear to the group that they were already surfacing implicitly some of their aspirations for the system (or at least

Using Causal Mapping to Support Information Systems Development 271

the contrast of the goal). Two concerns, namely "drop out rates" and "inefficient management of student progress" were, if managed, important (negatively expressed) goals. To reflect this insight, the facilitator edited the original wording so that these concerns now read in a more aspirational manner (for example, instead of stating "drop out rates too high," the statement now stated: "reduce drop out rates rather than drop out rates too high"). In addition, to reflect the change in status of the statement, a new style (representing through the use of a different font and colour a new category) was created called goals and these two statements given this attribute.

Continuing, the group then spent time considering what might be other goals of the system. Again using their ability to directly type in their contributions along with any links (by now they were familiar with the process) a draft goal system emerged (see Figure 3). Not surprisingly, money featured prominently! However, as the group began to explore the links between the goals, it became apparent that a number of participants felt that they needed to consider the issues more fully — as they were unsure whether they had surfaced all of the goals, or whether they fully understood them. It was time to open up the discussion further.

Using a new view (similar to sheets in Excel) the group then began to consider the new system more deeply. Contributions came rapidly. Within 20 minutes, another 50 or so statements were surfaced. The group began the process of examining this new material (see Figure 4) — suggesting possible links, amending statements to make their meaning more clear, and adding new material. To ensure that there was equal representation, the facilitator created a number of new categories representing the different stakeholder

Figure 2. The first stage: expressing concerns or triggers for a new system (note those statements that are boxed are those that were converted to goals)

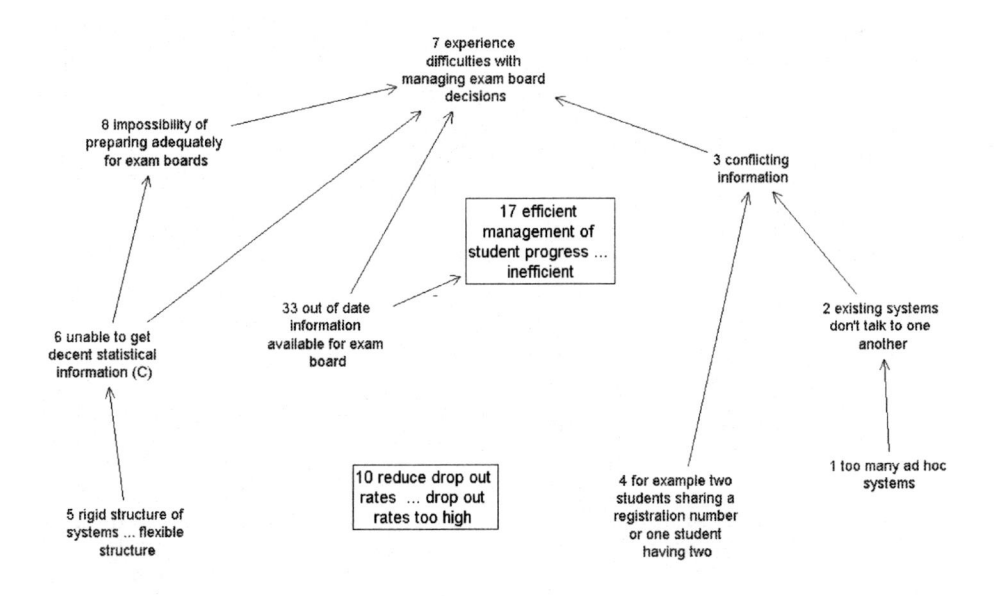

Copyright © 2005, Idea Group Inc. Copying or distributing in print or electronic forms without written permission of Idea Group Inc. is prohibited.

Figure 3. The developing emergent goals system

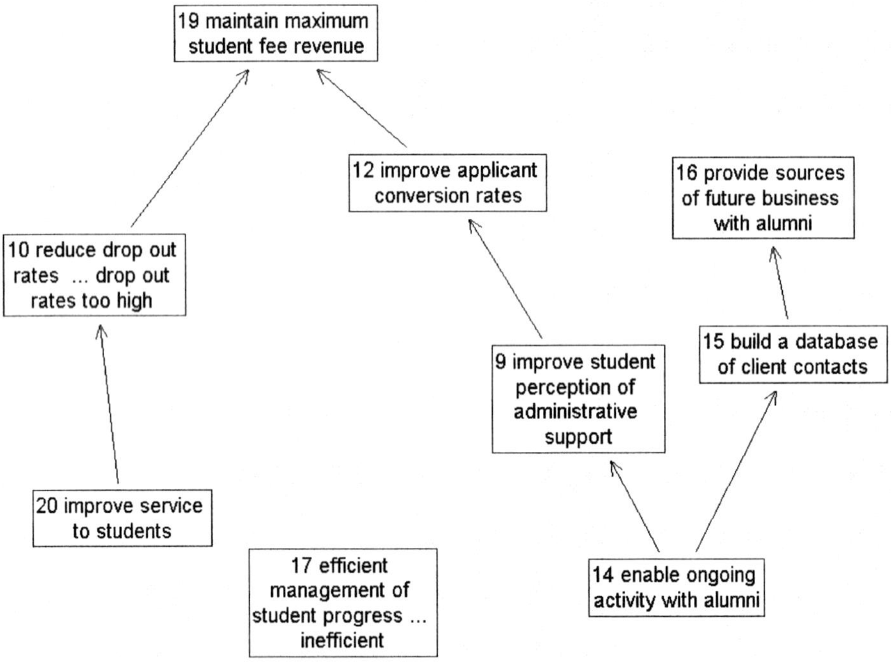

constituencies and with the help of the group applied these to the contributions. Having done this, she was then able to note that both marketing and operations had contributed the most (11 and 20 respectively) with computer services raising 10, academics only raising four statements and management five. Not a surprising result given that both marketing and operations would use the system most, with computer services having to maintain and upgrade it.

This insight prompted further reflection and analysis. By examining the tails (those statements that had no statement linking in/supporting it), it was possible to ensure that all systems implications were addressed by ensuring that each tail was a statement of system requirement, or of system characteristic. Where necessary, this meant adding a statement from computer services staff regarding the particular function or action required. Moreover the group were able to check that each system implication led to a goal, thus ensuring that all system characteristics or requirements did contribute to the stated overall goals. Both these analysis prompted the group to identify further goals — increasing the system of goals from nine goals to 14 goals.

In addition, through using the software's analytical features[7] (discussed above) it was possible to do some logic checks. Firstly, an examination of the "busy" points of the map was undertaken (essentially comprising a count of the number of statements linking in and out). The group were pleased and not surprised that six *"unable to get decent statistical information"* emerged as the most busy (having eight statements linked to it) with 7 *"experience difficulties with managing exam board decisions,"* 17 *"efficient*

Figure 4. Developing the map further

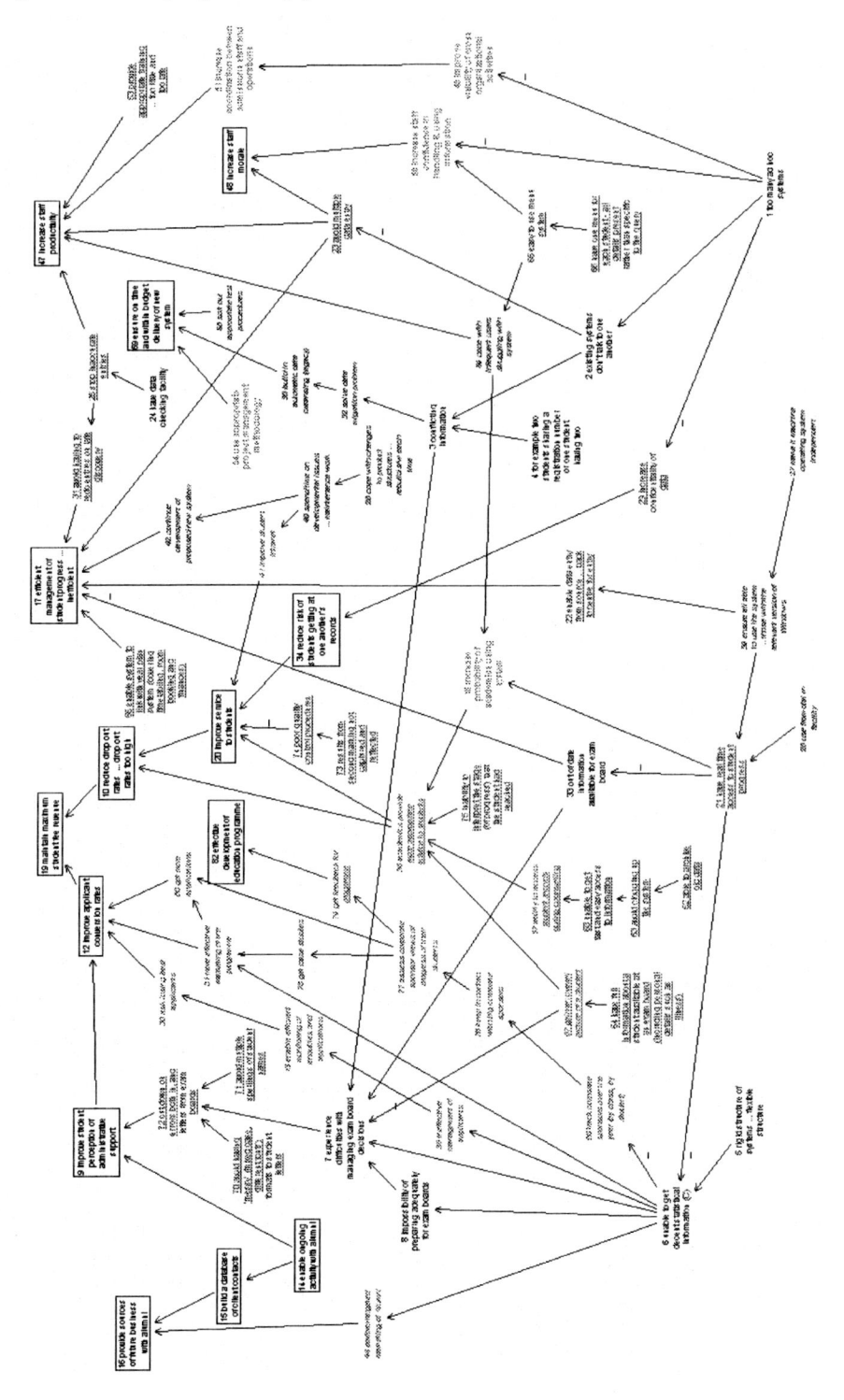

management of student progress rather than inefficient," and 38 *"academics provide more appropriate advice to students"* each having links to seven statements. The group reflected that this seemed correct.

When examining the most potent statements (those statements that supported the greatest number of goals and were therefore important action points) they were also reassured to note that three of the four most potent statements were IT oriented: 28 *"use from dial-in facility,"* 27 *"make it machine operating system independent,"* which was supported by the third 39 *"ensure all are able to use the system rather than those with the relevant version of Windows."* All of these supported the final potent statement, which was 21 *"have real-time access to student progress."*

The workshop ended with a clear agreement of what was wanted from the system, which addressed the needs and concerns of those who would be using it. As a result, it meant that computer services staff were able to put together the document that would be used for the tendering process. In addition the map acted as an organization memory, enabling renegotiation as the development process unfolded and a number of the agreed actions had to be reviewed.

Postscript

The system was seen as very successful. Eighty percent of the users were pleased by the result, the total cost was within budget and the system was delivered on time. The software is the sole record-keeping system in use, substantially reducing errors, and preventing the need for data having to be re-entered. The system, to date, has never failed and application software updates, data migration issues and the occasional bug causing run-time errors on individual desktops are the only causes of system downtime.

However as with all systems, now that the system exists there are additional features desired by users. As with most information systems, these are learned from using the system — with users not aware of them until after the system has been completed — unfortunately mapping can't pick up these (echoing the findings reported by Orlikowski, Walsham, Jones & DeGross, 1995).

This case provides a brief illustration of how the mapping process supports multiple stakeholders in determining an IS development strategy for which all felt a high degree of ownership. It reflected the views of all there: both users and developers — quiet members of staff as well as those who were socially confident. The resultant model helped members to develop a common language and based upon this negotiate an agreed way forward. Most importantly it enabled participants to understand the reasons for requirements and how they causally linked to supporting goals.

How Mapping Can Support the IS Development Process

One of the most difficult aspects in IS development is that of enabling a sensible conversation between IS developers and users, in the manner described above. Managers use a different language from IS developers — one that is driven by the changing needs of the business from day-to-day. With the exception of techno-enthusiasts, managers are unimpressed by the inflexibility of information systems and the requirement to learn new system interfaces beyond those of Microsoft (this was true in the above case where academics who would only infrequently use the system struggled to remember how to access options). Moreover, in addition to managing the different views of managers (who were taking a "sponsor"-like role), a system has to take into account the fact that the users are not universal in their requirements. In the above case, operations staff wanted different capabilities from Marketing, with those staff overseas facing different problems to those based locally. Similarly IS developers use their own particular jargon in a "taken-for-granted" way. Few IS developers have direct business or managerial experience. Consequently causal mapping encourages IS staff to understand the business reasons for their developments, and to justify changes with respect to the mapped goals.

There is little to be achieved by arguing that one group or the other should be different. As with the differences between marketing people and operations people, these differences reflect important specialist expertise particularly so in the case of IS developers, where their expertise can often be more opaque than for other experts in the organization. Organizations function well when multiple perspectives can be fruitfully harnessed. As we have argued above, facilitating mutual understanding and mutual respect depends upon establishing and negotiating linkages between user *roles* and development *possibilities*. The assertion that users do know, or should know, their requirements, is not helpful. Users know something about their role in the organization but can only express requirements when they have an understanding of what can be done, and developers can only express what can be done when they have a better understanding of users requirements (each category having a different set of understandings).

By its very nature, causal mapping is about linkages. Linking statements made by both users and developers in a manner that gradually builds a visual artefact (a map) aids different stakeholders in moving from divergent positions to one of convergence and encourages joint ownership. The meaning of any statement is enhanced through its linkages rather than simply relying on the words in the statement. For example, in Figure 4 the statement regarding *"unable to get decent statistical information"* is given further meaning through the statements explaining it and the six purposes (consequences) realised if it were delivered as "having decent information." Those supporting it are: *"rigid structure of the systems rather than flexible structure"* and *"[NOT][8] have real-time access to student progress."* This means that a statement made by a user that is linked through an explanation or consequence to a statement made by a developer *elaborates the meaning of both statements to both parties*. This is a form of psychological negotiation. Within cognitive psychology this is known as the elaboration of a Personal

Constructs System (Kelly, 1955). The map, as an artefact and a "visual interactive model," is thus a device to aid psychological as well as social negotiation.

The map also serves two other mundane but important outcomes. Whether it is recorded through the use of Oval Mapping on the wall, or through the use of computer-aided representation, it is both a continually *developing and changing set of minutes* (or organisational memory) of the meeting, and a formally constructed *model of means to ends* (record of the consequences of purposeful action).

The formalities of this type of causal mapping require statements to be made in an actionable format, encouraging statements to be made by both users and developers that naturally encourage each to think about "so what?" (consequences) and "how?" (explanations). The hierarchical structure of mapping (with the goals at the top, key issues supporting them, with options and assertions at the bottom) that follows from arrows representing "means to ends," naturally forces thinking about ultimate desired outcomes (goals). The likelihood of multiple consequences and multiple explanations naturally represents goals as being interconnected where each goal supports others and, in turn, is supported by others. Information systems are there to help sensible choices to be made by managers. Therefore information, its timeliness, its setting within the context of other information, and its accessibility are determined by the extent to which it can support goals or help avert negative goals. Inevitably some design requirements for information provision are more potent than others. Because the map shows causal linkages, it becomes easier to make judgments about the relative potency of particular aspects of information system design. Thus, some propositions within the map may have consequences for many goals and also provide for many causal chains to the same goal (and so robustness) and so be more potent. Typically the degree of potency provides important clues for prioritising requirements.

The structure of a map, as nodes (actionable statements) and arrows (causality) invites categorization. Thus, each node can be attributed a particular "style" (usually a particular font and/or colour) indicating, for example, different types of requirements, different resource demands, different a delivery time lines, and different priorities. The categorisation may occur during a workshop, or as the model is used as a part of project management (see Eden & Ackermann, 1998). As categorization emerges the software permits analysis of the categories, for example, which statements occur in specified categories but not in others. This means it is possible to determine which proposals are, for example, both inexpensive and high priorities.

Conclusion

Although there are other problem-structuring approaches that help to develop effective IS requirements — most notably Soft Systems Methodology (SSM) — causal mapping and associated software offers a degree of formal modelling that links easily to more traditional IS development methods. It is also, in practice, a transparent method.

In particular, and as with Soft Systems Methodology, the process of mapping within the context of a workshop enables several stakeholders to see their views within the context of others, develop a richer understanding of possibilities, and avoid miscommunication and possible dysfunctional conflict. Using mapping as a device to help negotiation is also likely to build a more collaborative approach to information systems design. Those developing Information Systems therefore will benefit from using mapping, not only through the added benefit of having a shared agreement for the resultant system but also through being able to involve a wide range of stakeholders.

Mapping provides a natural format for ensuring linkage and integration between IS potential and the business needs of the organisation. Through building up a shared understanding, more effective use of the information systems is likely.

Moreover, as noted by Nelson, Nadkarni, Narayanan and Ghods (2000), mapping can reveal patterns of behaviour, theories in use, which help researchers understand the process of mapping and how it can contribute towards better outcomes. This may help researchers in developing methods for information system design and analysis, that more effectively assist the organization.

Alongside causal mapping, the specially designed Group Support System (*Group Explorer*) software provides the potential for high productivity meetings as well as an online capture that becomes a natural organisational memory and project-planning tool.

References

Ackermann, F., & Eden, C. (2004). Using causal mapping: individual and group; traditional and new. In M. Pidd (Ed.), *Systems modeling: Theory and practice* (pp. 127-145). Chichester: Wiley.

Ackermann, F., & Eden, C. (2003). Powerful and interested stakeholders matter: their identification and management. *Academy of Management Proceedings of the Best Papers*, Seattle, WA.

Ackermann, F., & Eden, C. (2001a). Contrasting single user and networked group decision support systems for strategy making. *Group Decision and Negotiation*, 10, 47-66.

Ackermann, F., & Eden, C. (2001b). SODA - Journey making and mapping in practice. In J. Rosenhead & J. Mingers (Eds.), *Rational analysis in a problematic world revisited* (pp. 43-60). London: Wiley.

Ackermann, F., Eden, C., & Brown, I. (2004). *The practice of making strategy*. London: Sage.

Ackermann, F., Eden, C., & Williams, T. (1997). Modeling for litigation: Mixing qualitative and quantitative approaches. *Interfaces*, 27, 48-65.

Boddy, D., Boonstra, A., & Kennedy, G. (2002). *Managing information systems: An organizational perspective*. Harlow, Essex: Financial Times Prentice Hall.

Boland, R. J., Tenkasi, R. V., & Te'eni, D. (1994). Designing information technology to support distributed cognition. *Organization Science*, 5, 456-475.

Bonarius, H., Holland, R., & Rosenburg, S. (Eds.) (1981). *Personal construct psychology.* London: Macmillan.

Brown, S. (1992). Cognitive mapping and repertory grids for qualitative survey research: some comparative observations. *Journal of Management Studies*, 29, 287-308.

Bryson, J., Ackermann, F., Eden, C., & Finn, C. (2004). *Visible thinking: unlocking causal mapping for practical business results.* Chichester: Wiley.

Bryson, J. M., Ackermann, F., Eden, C., & Finn, C. (1995). Using the 'Oval Mapping Process' to identify strategic issues and formulate effective strategies. In J. Bryson (Ed.), *Strategic Planning for Public and Nonprofit Organisations.* San Francisco: Jossey Bass.

Bryson, J. M., Cunningham, G. L., & Lokkesmoe, K. J. (2001). What to do when stakeholders matter: the case of problem formulation for the African American men project of Hennepin county, Minnesota. *Public Management Review,* 62, 568-584.

Checkland, P., & Holwell, S. (1998). *Information, systems and information systems.* Chichester: Wiley.

Checkland, P., & Scholes, J (1990). *Soft systems methodology in action.* Chichester: Wiley.

Downs, E., Clare, P., & Coe, I. (1988). *Structured systems analysis and design method (SSADM).* London: Prentice Hall.

Eden, C. (1988). Cognitive mapping: A review. *European Journal of Operational Research*, 36, 1-13.

Eden, C., & Ackermann, F. (2001). SODA - The principles. In J. Rosenhead & J. Mingers (Eds.), *Rational analysis in a problematic world revisited* (pp. 21-42). Chichester: Wiley.

Eden, C., & Ackermann, F. (1998). *Making strategy: The journey of strategic management.* London: Sage.

Fransella, F., & Bannister, D. (1977). *A manual for repertory grid technique.* London: Academic Press.

Hunter, M. G., & Beck, G. (2000). Using repertory grids to conduct cross-cultural research. *Information Systems Research,* 11, 93-101.

Jayaratna, N. (1994). *Understanding and evaluating methodologies.* London: McGraw Hill.

Kelly, G. A. (1955). *The psychology of personal constructs.* New York: Norton.

Martin, J. (1991). *Rapid application development.* Englewood Cliffs, NJ: Prentice-Hall.

Martin, J. (1986). *Information engineering.* Carnforth, UK: Savant.

Mumford, E. (1983). *Designing Human Systems: the ETHICS method.* Manchester: Manchester Business School.

Nelson, K., Nadkarni, S., Narayanan, V.K., & Ghods, M. (2000). Understanding software operation support expertise: A revealed causal mapping approach. *MIS Quarterly,* 24, 475-508.

Orlikowski, W. J., Walsham, G., Jones, M. R., & DeGross, J. I. (1995). *Information technology and changes in organizational work*. London: Chapman Hall.

Simon, H. A. (1959, June). Theories of decision making in economics and behavioural science. *American Economics Review*, 263.

Stowell, F. (1995). *Information Systems provision: the contribution of soft systems methodology*. London: McGraw Hill.

Tan, F., & Hunter, G. M. (2002). The repertory grid technique: A method for the study of cognition in information systems. *MIS Quarterly,* 26(1), 39-57.

Zuboff, S. (1988). *In the age of the smart machine*. New York: Doubleday.

Endnotes

[1] *Decision Explorer* is software designed specifically for causal mapping and is available through www.banxia.com.

[2] *Group Explorer* is designed to facilitate the fast and anonymous construction of causal maps for participant groups of 5-15 persons or groups and is available through www.phrontis.com.

[3] It is not untypical to have maps comprising 1000 nodes and 1500 relationships.

[4] This case has been amended for confidentiality reasons and the report considers the very early stages in the process.

[5] See Bryson et al. (2004) *Visible Thinking: Unlocking causal mapping for practical business results,* Wiley, Chichester for more details on the mapping process and additional cases.

[6] For more detail about different modes of working see Ackermann, F. and Eden, C. (2001) 'Contrasting Single User and Networked Group Decision Support Systems," *Group Decision and Negotiation*, Vol 10, 1, pp. 47-66.

[7] The software, *Decision Explorer*, acts as a relational database allowing users to select which parts of the model they wish to examine, view whether there are linkages to other potentially relevant material, categorise statements according to their status, e.g., key issue, and carry out analysis on the structure.

[8] The [NOT] represents the fact that there is a negative link namely "having real time access" leads negatively to "unable to get decent statistical data."

[9] Based upon the Ackoff and Emery typology (Ackoff, R. L. and Emery, F., On Purposeful Systems. London: Tavistock; 1972).

Appendix 1 — The "Formalities" of Mapping

This Support section includes the following:

- Getting the wording of statements right
- Getting the direction of the arrow (causality) right
    - o Being clear about options and outcomes, means and ends, etc.
    - o Dealing with generic statements appropriately
    - o Dealing with assertions and facts
    - o Dealing with feedback loops (see also support 1)
- Goals, negative goals and constraints
- Doing mapping in interviews
- An overview of the mapping hierarchy (encompassing goals, issues, competencies, options/actions) when used for strategic thinking

Wording Statements (nodes)

- Make statements action-oriented by including a verb — without doing violence to what was said where possible
- Aim for six to eight words as this will ensure that each statement is discrete and yet descriptive
- If there is likely to be ambiguity then consider including "who," "what," "where," and "when" in the statement (although this requirement can make the statement too long)
- Exclude words such as "should," "ought," "need," etc. (as this makes it more option-like)
    - o E.g., "we ought to hire more salesmen" becomes "hire more salesmen"
- Avoid using "in order to," "due to," "may lead to," "as a result of," "through," "caused by," etc., as these imply two statements linked together by an arrow
- When a statement includes several considerations, as for example: "postpone writing mapping book, several articles and book chapters, and other books," then it is important to decide whether the statement should become several statements
    - o Ask whether:
- They each have different consequences
- They each have the same importance

- They each might involve different types of actions/explanations in order to create the outcome
    - Thus, in the example:
        - Writing articles may be more important than books or chapters, in which case the statement should be separated into two parts
        - Postponing the mapping book may have different consequences because it involves other colleagues, in which case it should be separated
        - Writing other books may require large chunks of time whereas others can be done using small intervals, in which case it should be a separate statement
    - Therefore, watch the use of "and" as this might suggest two options rather than one
        - e.g., split "increase and improve services" into "increase services" and "improve services" as these might lead to different outcomes and have different explanations

Using Contrasting Poles in a Statement (node)

- The *meaning* of a statement is often best discovered by listening for the contrast
    - For example, the meaning of "warm rather than hot weather" is different from "warm rather than cold weather," "buy two computers rather than six computers" is different from "buy two computers rather than hire more staff," etc.
    - Difficulties arise when each contrast is an option in its own right, and there might be several options. When the contrast illustrates meaning by suggesting a possible alternative outcome, circumstance, etc., (often contrasting past with now, past with future, now with future) then use the contrast as a part of the statement; when the contrast is a clear option then make it a separate statement (sometimes linked without an arrowhead to other options)

Getting the Link Right: Causality

- The direction of arrow should indicate direction of causality and influence: means to ends, options/actions to outcomes.
- One person's means can be another person's ends
    - E.g., A→B might be correct for one person but B→A might be for another
        - For example: "turning things around means we have to win every battle in the next five years" may be coded with "winning every battle" as the

desired outcome from "turning things around," or alternatively "winning every battle" is required in order to "turn things around," depending on the desired ends of the interviewee.

- But, bear in mind some "objective" truths might be subject to debate
    - E.g., "putting more policemen on the beat will reduce crime" may be an objective truth to one person, nevertheless another person might argue the objective truth to be that more crime leads to more policemen on the beat.
- Sometimes A→B can be treated as so consensual that it need not be debated, e.g., "obvious" arithmetical relationships.
    - More sales causes more sales revenue
- Means to ends are most difficult to judge when considering a hierarchy of criteria, values and goals
    - E.g., is "be unhappy and upset much of the time" more disastrous than "crawl into my shell and give up"? That is, does "be unhappy" lead to "into shell" or vice versa? This can only be judged by the person being mapped, or this choice must be open to consideration.
        - It sometimes helps to work with a hierarchy of goals, such as "objectives" lead to "goals" which lead to "ideals or values." So, objectives are shorter term and more easily measurable; whereas goals are expressions of desirable longer term outcomes; whereas ideals or values are unlikely ever to be attained but guide purposeful behaviour[9].
- Avoid mapping time sequences that are not causal relationships (as this will produce flow diagrams or process maps that are not amenable to the same sort of analysis or meaning as cause maps).
- Avoid duplicate and double-headed arrows
    - Ensure that the map does not contain duplication of links
- For example, where the map shows A→B→C→D along with A→C and C→D and A→D — ensure that the latter three links show different causal chains (through additional material)
    - Avoid double-headed arrows as these are implicit feedback loops suggesting either:
        - Muddled thinking that can be resolved by determining means and ends
        - A legitimate feedback loop consisting of additional statements that might provide more intervention options

Dealing with Generic Statements

- It is best to ensure that all members of a category are subordinate to the statement expressing the generic category
    - For example: "buy more saucepans" should in most circumstances lead to "buy more kitchen equipment" — that is, the specific leads to the generic

- When a sub-category has different consequences from those of other members of the category, then it will need its own out-arrow to other consequences (along with the link to the generic).
- Sometimes the generic statement may not be necessary because there are no specific consequences that follow from it, rather they all follow from specific sub-category statements.

Dealing with Assertions and "Facts"

- We presume that when someone makes an assertion then they have a reason to do so, and that it is intended to suggest an implied action is required
    - Thus, if someone states that "Glasgow has a population of over 500,000 people" then we ask why this assertion is being made — what is its meaning in action terms? For example, they might know that it was 600,000 last year and so the statement "obviously" implies that the "Council will be short of taxes next year," which also is stated as a "fact" with implied consequences
- Thus, assertions tend to be at "the bottom" of a map, with consequences following from them.

Goals, Negative-Goals, and Constraints

- Goals are desired outcomes that are "good in their own right" (so much so that they are hardly seen as optional by the interviewee)
- Negative goals are undesired outcomes that are bad in their own right
    - For example, "become bitter"
- Constraints are often stated as if they were goals, but will be subordinate and have consequences that constrain actions, goals, issues, etc.
    - For example: "attaining minimum levels of shareholder return" may act as a constraint on management behaviour, rather than act as a goal (even though shareholders would wish to see it expressed as a goal)

Chapter XII

Strategic Implications of Causal Mapping in Strategy Analysis and Formulation

Douglas L. Micklich
Illinois State University, USA

Abstract

The formulation and implementation of effective strategy at every level within an organization requires that those involved in the process have not only a good overall understanding of the present situation, but also an understanding of the underlying cause and effect relationships which underpin strategy at those levels. This includes understanding the interactions, which occur between the levels of strategy in an organization as well as the benefits of a firm's executive information system. Using various mapping techniques, e.g., concept mapping, cognitive mapping, causal mapping, we investigate the factors that made WorldCom, Inc., a one-time leader in the telecommunications industry, implode and find itself fighting in courts for its very survival.

Introduction

The strategy formulation process for an organization can be described as consisting of the integration of three perspectives of strategy: corporate, business, and functional

(Hax, 1996). The process begins at the uppermost level of an organization, usually with the Board of Directors at the corporate level, and in conjunction with executive management, down through the business level, and finally ending at the functional/operational level. Corporate strategy deals with decisions that by their nature should be addressed with the fullest scope encompassing the overall firm. Business strategy aims at obtaining superior financial performance by seeking a competitive positioning that allows the business to have a sustainable advantage over the firm's competitors. Functional strategies not only consolidate the functional requirements demanded by the corporate and business strategies, but also constitute the repositories of the ultimate capabilities needed to develop the unique competencies of the firm. According to Hax (1996), strategy formulation for the organization is intended to frame all of the key strategic issues of the firm through a sequential involvement of the corporate, business and functional perspectives. The strategy formulation process can also be extended to exist within these perspectives as resources and systems are marshaled to implement that chosen strategy.

When beginning to formulate the overall strategy, concept/cognitive mapping can be used to develop a general understanding of the relationship that exists both between these perspectives/levels of the organization and within these perspectives. Within each level we can use causal mapping to help identify cause and effect relationships that can exist due to various courses of action or of inaction. By looking at these cause and effect relationships that exist among the elements at each level for a given situation, changes in the formulation of strategy (how these elements are used) can be undertaken to correct any unwanted (negative) consequences of a chosen strategy.

In this respect, we use the mapping technique approach to accomplish two objectives. The first is to frame the firm's situations and the elements that surround it. The second is to pinpoint the deficiencies by looking at specific cause and effects and determine a course of action that would correct those deficiencies and allow for the proper allocation of resources throughout the firm.

We begin by first framing the firm's situation and the elements surrounding that situation. We accomplish this by introducing the skills and concepts required in analyzing and formulating a firm's strategy through its various levels. The skills introduced and developed are those of synthesis and analysis. These skills are important both in decomposing strategy into its basic elements and in understanding the relationship that exists between these elements. The concepts introduced are those of Critical Success Factors and Critical Value Activities. These concepts are relative to competitive conditions that exist and issues of the existence of organizational silos as they relate to structure. These skills are important to the development of a general understanding of the circumstances surrounding a given firm's situation and the cause and effect relationships that exist among the levels of strategy from the corporate level through the functional level. Introduced, also, are the concepts of information symmetry and dependence and an explanation how they affect the structural and reporting relationships of the firm and the implementation of strategy through structure.

From here, we go onto our second objective, which is to see where strategy went awry and to be able to diagnose the situation and determine a course of action which would correct any deficiencies and allow for a reallocation of resources. Beginning with an issue in narrative form, and using the concepts and skills, we can identify at the lowest possible level, the point where the problem resides. This is accomplished by using as an example WorldCom, Inc., (see Case in Point at the end of the chapter), where perceptions of these general relationships as well as the specific cause and effect relationships at the various levels will be shown.

Components of Strategy

In this section we are going to introduce two basic concepts in strategy analysis and formulation; Critical Success Factors and Critical Value Activities. These two concepts are highly related in that Critical Success Factors are industry related and can affect the firm's competitive position. Critical Value Activities are those that exist within a firm's value chain that allow them to address the Critical Success Factors in a given industry. These activities can be classified in one of three ways: Business Value-added, Customer Value-added or No Value-added activities. It is the relationship that exists between these activities that will lead a firm in attaining or sustaining its competitive advantage relative to the industry's Critical Success Factors.

Critical Success Factors

In the development of strategy, numerous factors or elements are involved in the process. Two major elements are Key or Critical Success Factors and Critical or Strategy-Critical Activities. These are components of strategy where the organization must excel to outperform its competition in either attaining or maintaining a competitive advantage. This also requires a clear understanding of the core competencies that will be needed to underpin these critical success factors (Johnson, 1999).

Critical Success Factors are those factors, usually three or four in any given industry, that most affect the ability of an organization to prosper in the marketplace. They are prerequisites for industry success (Thompson, 1998). These limited numbers of factors are ones around which managers should have information systems designed and which provide the basis for the organization's success (Jenster, 1986). By its very nature, this would imply a hierarchical structure of constructs. As such, they depict various levels of decomposed relationships describing a complex organizational situation (Jenster, 1986).

Critical Value Activities

Critical value or strategy-critical activities are those activities in the firm's value chain, which are most critical to a firm's achieving its competitive advantage. These are also crucial business processes that have to be performed either exceedingly well or in a closely coordinated fashion for the organization to develop capabilities for strategic success (Thompson, 1998).

These activities are part of the firm's value chain and can be classified in one of three ways: Business value-added activities, which are those that add value to the process from the firm's perspective. An example would be the exploitation of economies of scale in unused process/production capacity. Customer value-added activities are those that add value to the process/product from the customers' perspective. An example would be in the ability to meet the customer's requirements for product quality or timeliness in delivery. No Value-added activities are ones in which neither the firm nor its customers derive any added value and can be considered a candidate for outsourcing. An example here would be the payroll function in many small and medium-sized organizations. Paychex, Inc. is a prime example. By outsourcing this function, client firms are able to redirect resources to those activities that can help their firm increase its competitive ability.

The degree of success that an organization will realize is based on how well they address the industry's Critical Success Factors. Misdiagnosing the industry factors critical to long-term competitive success greatly raises the risk of a misdirected strategy — one that overemphasizes less important competitive targets and under-emphasizes more important competitive capabilities (Thompson, 1998).

As strategy is implemented, the effects of these activities on the success factors may have a tendency to shift over time given a particular situation the firm is facing. The resulting magnitude of these effects will depend on the factors in the situation (reaction by suppliers, competitors, and consumers), and the effect the information system has that links these areas, and on the outcomes in those areas. The information system used is one that will form both the linkages between these activities and the firm's value chain in addressing the industry's critical success factors.

Strategy Analysis and Synthesis

When we begin to formulate strategy, we need to be able to identify the components or elements that comprise a given situation and to understand the relationships between them. To be able to properly understand and map these relationships requires both analysis and synthesis. Analysis has been defined in various ways such as breaking down of a goal or set of intentions into individual or separate steps (Mintzberg, 1994) and the understanding of a company's current position, analyzing what forces drive competition in their industries, and what capabilities can be leveraged to effect a long-term sustainable posture (DeKluyver, 2000). The level of analysis that we use will determine at what level of the organization we will begin strategy formulation.

Synthesis has been defined as an ability to combine parts or elements so as to form a whole, to begin by identifying the components and their relationships to one another, the limitations imposed by the environment and the system's resources (Campbell, 1977) and as an integrated perspective of the enterprise (Mintzberg, 1994). Synthesis is very important for developing an understanding of the relationships that exist not only at each level in which strategy is formulated, but also among levels.

It is through analysis and synthesis that we can progress from cognitive mapping to causal mapping. Using this perspective we can look at those causes and effects of strategy overall, be able to move down and through the various levels, and develop an understanding of the degree of integration within a particular level. It is this movement we will use to drill down in getting to the specifics of a situation. This route is taken for the simple reasoning that you must be able to understand the context of the situation before you can develop it fully and then be able to have an understanding of the cause and effect relationships at any level.

Situational cause and effect outcomes have, in the realm of strategy, two main outcome components. These are long-term outcomes and short-term outcomes. Every level of the organization has some aspects of each of these. For example, at the corporate level a majority are strategic in nature, while at the functional level they tend to be more short-term or operational in nature. The business level would have relatively equal amounts of both. The nature of these components is determined to a great extent by the situational context and time frame horizon given industry and competitive dynamics. In general, we can define long-term as a horizon extending beyond five years and short-term as having a horizon of one year or less (Jones, 2003).

Basic Origins of Causal Mapping

In order to develop a better understanding of the use of causal mapping we need to look first at its origin from concept mapping. The use of concept mapping as a tool in understanding the broad-based (general) relationships and then progressing through cognitive mapping and finally ending with causal mapping is the taxonomy used to understand these relationships and the effects to strategy. To better understand the linkages in this progression, these techniques are defined in Table 1.

The reason for this approach is to gain a better understanding of the need for information in all aspects: quality, quantity, timeliness, relevance, as well as the cause and effect results in deficiencies in these aspects. The need for developing such a framework comes from the fact that "quality information is critical to decision making." (Crockett, 1992)

Table 1. Techniques of mapping

Technique	Definition
Concept Mapping	Diagrams indicating inter-relationships among concepts and representing conceptual frameworks within a specific domain of knowledge (Novak, 1990; Trochim, 1989)
Cognitive Mapping	A general class of physical representations of thoughts or beliefs. These maps can represent individual assertions, or those elicited from a group (Huff, 1990; Montazemi et al., 1986)
Causal Mapping	A sub-class of cognitive maps that focuses on the representation of causal beliefs; A network of causal relations imbedded in an individual's explicit statements, an explicit representation of the deep-rooted cognitive maps of individuals. (Huff 1990; Nelson et al., 2000)

Mapping Relationships

There are two things we must consider when mapping relationships. Primary consideration must be given to the fact that organizations grow and develop, and that existing relationships among and between elements will change over time. Secondary consideration, although of no less importance, are the cause and effect relationships of elements in the firm's internal and external environments and the effect those changes have on strategy formulation and implementation. It is in these areas that the organization evolves in response to competitive conditions, both externally and internally. This evolution is sometimes spearheaded by the type of information system used and the level of its involvement and importance.

When maps are constructed, they are based on a person's perception of a given situation and the factors or areas that will have an impact, positively or negatively, in the situation. As more information surrounding the situation and its factors becomes known and the more we add to or refine a map as it relates to the situation or issue, the greater the sense we will acquire of the whole picture. This is assuming that we have developed an understanding of the relationships that underlie those factors.

While the use of concept/cognitive mapping can give us a general idea of the relationships that exist, and hence the general design of its underlying information system, it is causal mapping that helps us identify the cause and effect relationships of various elements on one another and how they affect the strategic management process. The benefit we gain through defining and illustrating these relationships through mapping, the better the degree of information symmetry and balance that can exist within the organization's structure due to better sharing of information.

Knowing the relative strength of the relationship and the degree of organizational and information dependency can lead to better knowledge management within the firm which in turn, can lead to both improved strategy formulation and implementation. In addition, as we can better understand the structure of the organization, from an IT perspective as well as a competitive perspective, and the cause and effect relationships that exist within that structure, the better will we be able to design information systems to support that structure and those relationships.

Foundations of Symmetry and Dependence

Symmetry

The initial concepts of information symmetry and asymmetry stem from the concept of the universe and its origin as described in Pagel's, "Perfect Symmetry." In his book, he states "the universe begins in a very hot state of utmost simplicity and symmetry and as it expands and cools its perfect symmetry is broken, giving rise to the complexity we see today." We extend this thought into a business context when we consider the various aspects of an organization through the evolution of its strategy and structure. Just as when the universe was first formed, when an organization is created out of nothing, it is in a state of perfect symmetry. Its structure is simple and a degree of balance exists among the elements of the firm, when all things are equal, facilitated by the situational context and information system which is in place. An example of simple structure is shown in Figure 1. In an organizational context, firms that have a high degree of information symmetry (relatively low complexity) are those where the value of information is recognized and easily shared with those areas that require it, and where information is evenly distributed throughout the organization (Frasman, 1990).

A situation of low complexity would exist where there is a high degree of connectivity (i.e., systems "talking" to each other) between systems at a particular level. The importance of information on the decision-making process across lines is easily recognizable to the organization.

As a firm expands through merger and acquisition and contracts through downsizing and consolidation, subsequently changing its structure as it evolves, it goes through various degrees of complexity (Figure 2). As firms move from a simple structure to a more advanced structure, there is a greater chance for departmentalization to exist based on either a functional or a business unit. It is in these instances where we have a greater possibility in moving from degrees of symmetry to asymmetry. This is analogous to the expansion and cooling of the universe.

Operations within the firm can therefore run relatively smoothly and, by the virtue of this balance and distribution of information within the organization, can maintain not only a degree of competitiveness, but also weather the variations that exist in its environment. Where gaps occur or where symmetry is broken, (e.g., in the knowledge base), an effort is made by all areas concerned to gather data and construct information/knowledge to fill those gaps and bring about a degree of symmetry. We can therefore define symmetry as that state of existence where there is a degree of information sharing that exists between elements of the firm to allow the firm to operate competitively with the fewest

Figure 1. Examples of organizational structure

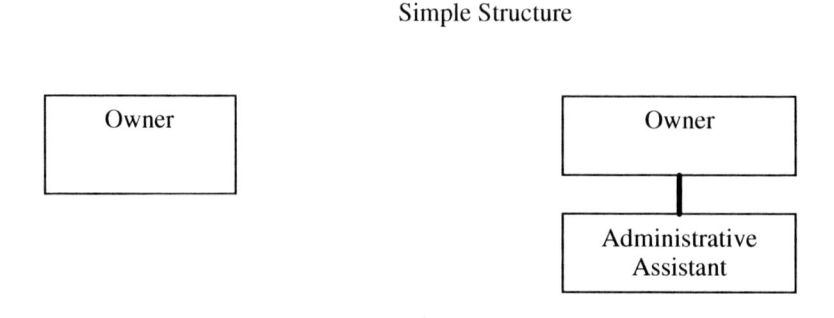

Simple Structure

Owner		Owner
		Administrative Assistant

Simple structure can appear in either one of these two forms. In either case authority is centralized in a single person, flat hierarchy, few rules, and low work specialization (complexity).

Figure 2. Examples of organizational structure

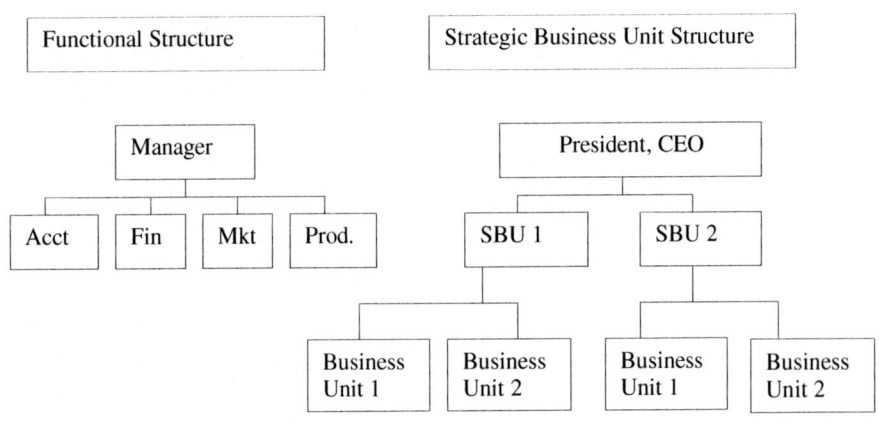

```
Functional Structure                    Strategic Business Unit Structure

        Manager                                  President, CEO
   ┌────┬────┬────┐                             ┌──────┴──────┐
  Acct  Fin  Mkt  Prod.                       SBU 1         SBU 2
                                              ┌──┴──┐       ┌──┴──┐
                                          Business Business Business Business
                                          Unit 1   Unit 2   Unit 1   Unit 2
```

amount of disruptions to strategy. The importance of symmetry in strategy formulation and implementation is found in the cohesiveness and harmony which a firm must use to exist in its environment.

As already stated, as the organization grows and evolves (mergers and acquisitions, new product development, geographic expansion/contraction, downsizing, etc.) it becomes more complex relative to its initial state. The degrees of complexity that arise are caused by the effects, either singularly or in tandem with other elements (states) affecting the firm. These states can be in the form of products, product lines, functional departments, strategic business units (SBU) and the like.

The degree of complexity stems from the relationships that evolve over time as the organization grows and evolves. Complexity can exist in several forms: 1) by virtue of growth in various industries and product lines with information being shared and systems being integrated, 2) growth in industries and product lines with information not being shared and systems not being integrated, and 3) growth in industries and product lines with information being shared but systems not being integrated. These result in emphasizing the effects of asymmetry. Symmetry then moves toward asymmetry by virtue of the changing relationships among and between these elements. These relationships show up as changes in the firm's structure as a result of the implementation of strategy.

Asymmetry does have some benefits to an organization in that it may be required. Because of the degree to which a firm is well-diversified, asymmetry becomes too much of a problem when these resultant changes are not integrated fully into the processes operating within the organization. These changes, again, result in both the structure of the organization and the information systems that underlie it. This can lead to information being asymmetric in the organization. We can define asymmetry as that state of existence where a greater degree of complexity results from information being recognized as having intrinsic value, but not being recognized as having value for the organization as a whole, and therefore not shared. Those areas that require this sharing suffer problems, and as a result, the organization suffers as a whole. Information asymmetry has also been defined as the state of existence where information is unevenly distributed among agents (Fransman, 1998). This uneven distribution can lead to opportunism, which also can present some problems (Williamson, 1990).

Those firms that are highly asymmetric are those where the strategic and operational value of information is not recognized for the firm overall, but just relegated to a particular business unit or area. The asymmetry which results also occurs when the degree of complexity is such that there is a disjointedness or separateness that occurs within the organization. This disjointedness, if not monitored, can result in the formation of "information silos" in the organization, which can affect its functioning and existence.

The concept of information silos is an extension of the line of thought from a functional structure to one associated with a traditional corporate structure. In this way, functional areas are largely autonomous and there is limited communication among functions or areas. Sometimes enterprises are described as being organized into functional "silos" (Martin, 1996). Information silos can be defined as systems that are designed and used to support business units and their functional areas rather than corporate and cross-functional systems.

The outward structure of the organization (e.g., composition of business units, mechanistic vs. organic structure), can appear to be very sound and be in line with corporate growth strategy. However, the existence of information silos, or even when information is dead-ended, can hinder an organization's effectiveness. Information silos exist within structural silos of organizations and can impede not only the strategy formulation process, but also the implementation of strategy.

The greater the degree of asymmetry that exists, the greater the extent to which information silos can exist within the organization. In addition, they further tend to hinder the effectiveness of an organization's decision-making efficiency and the overall competitiveness of the organization. By mapping these areas and functions and understanding their relationships to the organization's strategy and structure, this would lead to an associated reduction of the existence of these unwanted silos. The key is to be able to keep the organization from becoming too asymmetric by recognizing the existing and future relationships and designing systems to facilitate symmetry.

Dependency

Related to issues of symmetry and information silos is the topic of information dependence. In general, the degree of information dependence forms the basis of the relationships which exist among various functional areas or business units of an organization. Dependence forms the basis for interaction through exchange relations, and, as such provides specific structure to the problem of organizational interaction and process coordination (Tillquist, 2002). There are several forms of organizational dependency. Organizational units may operate independently, but may be ultimately dependent upon the pooled efforts of all. They may also be sequentially dependent, where the output of one directly supports another as an input resource. Finally, they may represent a reciprocal dependency where both mutually depend upon the other for needed resources. These differing forms of dependency suggest differing forms of coordination (Thompson, 1967).

Business units and functional departments of a firm which are highly dependent have a large degree of use of common information and information sharing. Hence, there is a greater need for a degree of cooperation and coordination of activities. This is especially important if these relationships exist within a firm's critical value activities that are important for competition and growth. At the functional level, for example, consider the relationship that exists between the marketing, production and human resource departments of an organization. The greater the sales a firm realizes, the greater the need for adjustments to production. This may necessitate an increase in the number of personnel in production or may be caused by an increase in sales by virtue of an increase in the sales force. Likewise an increase in production personnel would signal an increase in production as a precursor to an anticipated increase in sales. An increase in production personnel could signal that a first-strike initiative was being undertaken. In essence, reciprocal dependency occurs when information is not considered as having a one-way path through the organization

Those businesses and departments of the firm that are not as dependent have very little information that is common or needs to be shared. The link to strategy and implementation may also not be strong. For example, at the business level of an organization, the existence of strategic business units is largely independent in a well-diversified firm. The information generated as to each unit's financial posture is largely independent from one to one another, but the information used at the corporate level to assess the overall strategic position of the firm is highly dependent. These areas of a firm would be considered sequentially dependent. This can occur through the data/information aggregation that exists in a firm as it is passed from lower levels to upper levels. Such is the case where the output of a firm's functional units, (accounting) across business units is aggregated as it moves up the hierarchy so as to give not only a picture of the firm's profitability, but also as a control and monitoring mechanism of the implementation of a firm's strategy. Information systems can be designed explicitly for control and coordination of organizational activities by capturing and conveying features of dependency relations (Tillquist, 2002).

Relationships of Symmetry and Dependency

Through using the mapping technique we can determine the type of relationship and nature of that relationship that is perceived to exist among various components/areas of a business with consideration being given to both external and internal relationships. Based on the type and nature of these relationships that exist, we can then develop/design/acquire an information system using appropriate information technology to facilitate that relationship.

As the firm evolves and competitive conditions evolve, initiated by both the external and internal environments, we can show how relationships can change over time, such as changes that occur through activities like mergers and acquisitions. These changes and their effects can be represented simultaneously on map iterations. Additionally, subsequent maps can reveal how we move from various stages of information asymmetry/symmetry and independency/dependency as the firm evolves. Whether we are dealing with external or internal relationships, we must be concerned with the smooth flow of data and/or information.

When the concern is with external relationships (inter-organizational), the question arises as to which relationships/issues were at one time not strategically important that now have become as important. An example is when Sabre Holding Corp., in 2001, sold its IT outsourcing business and internal technology to EDS. This caused American Airlines to bring back in-house some applications development activities because they were now deemed to be strategically important to American's competitiveness (Computerworld, 2001). Other issues are: which businesses/issues contribute to growth and competitiveness, and which have lost or minimized their contribution; for example, the supplier firms to Walmart. Those firms that have good alignment of strategy and IT (compatible systems) with Walmart, who are able to supply what is needed, when and at what level of quality, will have a competitive advantage over those firms that do not. Walmart's recent embracing of Radio Frequency Identification (RFID) technology is such an example (Computerworld, 2003). This represents a change in dependency from independent to dependent and to a greater degree of symmetry.

When the concern is with internal relationships (intra-organizational) such as those that exist between SBUs and functional areas and that are required to support activities/strategies in these areas, we also consider the issue of competitiveness. The systems that connect the various areas of the firm's internal value chain components will impact areas of a firm differently as the type of information required/delivered and the timeliness of such deliveries differs among areas. This is a representation of a change in dependency from independent to reciprocal. The degree of information dependency that exists between areas is determined in part by the significance of each area in relation to its position in the value chain.

Through the "Case in Point: WorldCom, Inc.", at the end of the chapter, we will illustrate how causal mapping can help in determining (showing) how these relationships evolve and the effects they have on a strategy's outcome. They will also help identify, in general, the type of system that needs to be developed.

The ability to map the relationships and issues that exist in firms is not as straightforward as one might be led to believe. As stated earlier, issues of independency/dependency, asymmetry/symmetry, design, construction and implementation of the strategy and systems as well as issues of personal behavior become of increasing importance. Through the mapping technique we can gain a better understanding in determining the type and nature of the relationship that is perceived to exist among various components/areas of a business. These relationships are many times formed from the aggregation of relationships from individuals within the organization. The constructs from which these maps are drawn reflect the frequency that causal linkages appear. Domain-specific constructs are identified and a picture of how these constructs are linked also emerges. Based on this information, we can then be able to develop/design/acquire an information system using appropriate information technology to facilitate that relationship.

The main purpose of using a behavioral simulation is to also take into consideration relationships that develop outside of relationships that tend to form between functional areas and types (i.e., marketing to production), which affect both the formulation and implementation of strategy within the organization. This is done to increase the qualitative aspects of describing an organization's relationships and how those aspects affect the organization, especially in the area of strategy formulation and implementation. The ability to go beyond the predetermined relationships of a computer-based simulation in identifying and understanding how such factors as motivation, hierarchical relationships, identification of information requirements and needs, and the development of systems that facilitate linkages among/between areas is important.

Equally important is the perception of the importance of these relationships as well as any cause and effect impacts these have on a firm's strategy. The more information that can be gathered, aggregated, known and shared about an issue, the better the decisions an organization will hopefully tend to make. This is especially true when you consider the evolution of firms over time as they address issues of both a strategic and operational nature. Through the use of various mapping techniques and their relationships, the better we are able to determine the type and nature of the relationship that is perceived to exist by both individuals and groups among various components/areas of a business. Based on this information, we are then able to develop/design/acquire an information system using appropriate information technology to facilitate that relationship and promote organizational learning at every level.

Behavioral Simulation

Humans have capabilities that are associated with intelligence. They can perceive and comprehend a visual scene, understand language, learn new concepts and tasks, and reason and draw useful conclusions about the world around them (Peterson, 1990). When we combine human capabilities of this nature and business processes with information technology where learning can result, we have created a type of artificial neural network (Marakus, 1999) leading to what can be defined as a type of artificial intelligence in a behavioral setting.

A simulation has been designed to illustrate these concepts and has components of both computer simulations and behavioral components and case analysis in its network. Computer simulation components are found through tools such as scenario analysis using spreadsheets. The behavioral components are found through various human capabilities, such as: judgment, emotion, motivational ability, and behavior, as well as relationships between business units and organizational levels. Case analysis components provide both a historical perspective as well as real-time tracking of the organization.

Using the skills of analysis and synthesis, along with various information technology tools, we are able to draw conclusions about those relationships that exist within and among the levels of strategy. We can then create those causal maps to help us in illustrating and understanding the cause-and-effect relationships that exist.

The subject of this simulation is the capstone management course, Organizational Strategy. Where this type of simulation differs from others is that the class is divided into three levels of strategy: corporate, business, and functional. In this simulation the class assumes a firm's identity, determines a major issue and tracks the firm and its events for a period of 14 weeks, developing a strategic plan that will address that issue. If during the semester the chosen issue is no longer one of priority, then a new issue must be determined. Figures 5–7 illustrate the combined knowledge and understanding of the relationships that exist and the cause and effect of strategy formulation and implementation.

Through these time periods various components of strategy are encountered such as: formulation at the corporate level of the firm's mission and vision statements, diversification strategy for directional growth, competitive strategy and tactics at the business level, and operational strategy at the functional level. This plan goes through a series of formulation and implementation stages from the corporate through the operational level and is illustrated in Figure 3.

Figure 3. Strategic interaction among the levels of srategy

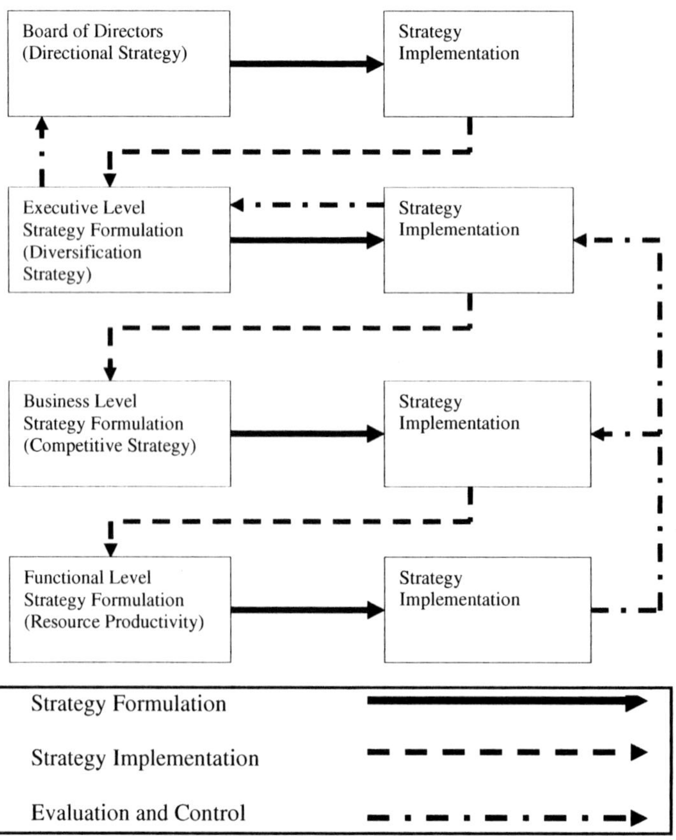

Adapted from Wheelen and Hunger, Strategic Management and Business Policy, 4th Edition, Addison — Wesley Publishing Company Inc., 1992

Copyright © 2005, Idea Group Inc. Copying or distributing in print or electronic forms without written permission of Idea Group Inc. is prohibited.

The corporate level is comprised of a Board of Directors and Executive Management. This level is responsible for defining the mission, scope and issues for the company. The Business level can function in one of two ways: 1) as CEO's of Strategic Business Units, in the case of some type of diversification strategy, or 2) as a Competitive Positioning group when the firm is of a single product focus. The functional level is comprised of Management Information Systems, Accounting, Finance, Marketing, Production/Operations, and Human Resources.

This firm must then track the events in the business world of that company for the course of the semester and develop a strategy that addresses that issue(s). The class is fully aware that issues defined at the beginning of the semester may or may not be the same toward the end of the semester. In addition, internal and external relationships may change as well as the structure of the organization. The mapping technique is used as a tool for helping understand the cause–and–effect relationships imbedded in and as a part of a particular strategy.

Figure 4. Benefits of an executive information system

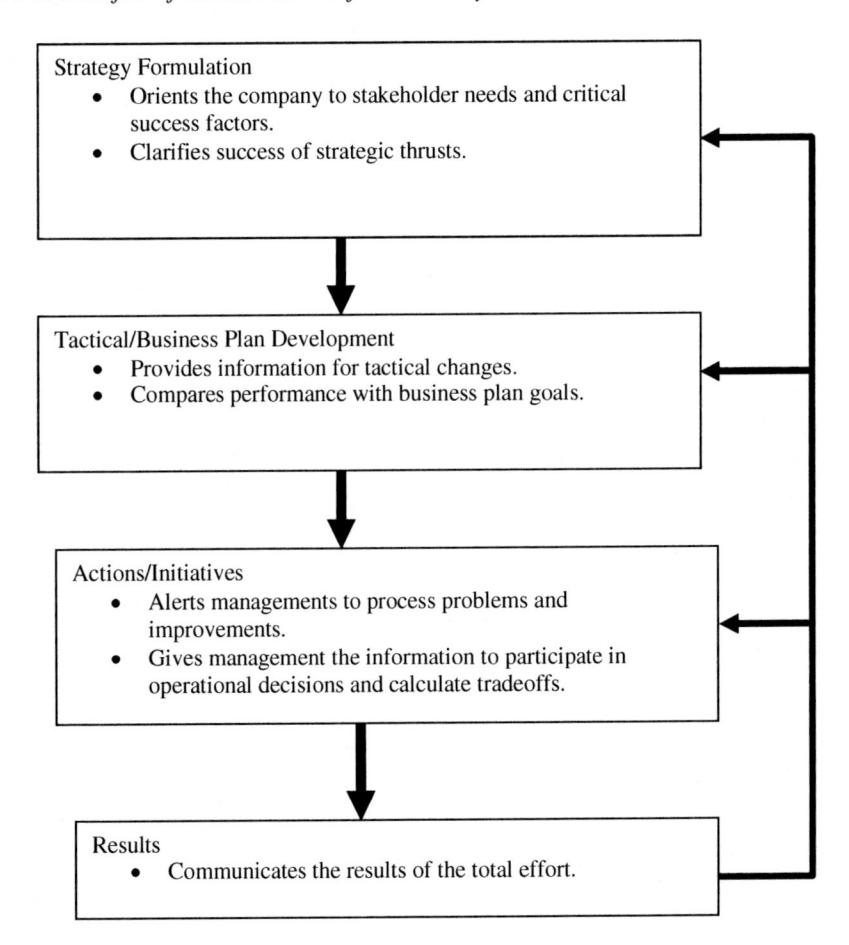

Strategy Formulation
- Orients the company to stakeholder needs and critical success factors.
- Clarifies success of strategic thrusts.

Tactical/Business Plan Development
- Provides information for tactical changes.
- Compares performance with business plan goals.

Actions/Initiatives
- Alerts managements to process problems and improvements.
- Gives management the information to participate in operational decisions and calculate tradeoffs.

Results
- Communicates the results of the total effort.

Let us begin by listing the objectives of the simulation as they relate to strategy:

- Gain an overall understanding of how various areas of the firm relate to each other.
- Gain an understanding of how areas of a firm relate to each other in a given situation.
- Determine, in general, the information requirements that exist between those areas, i.e., the information required for a particular area of operation as well as that required by other areas.
- Determine the cause and effect of information, i.e., the existence or non-existence of it in the execution of strategy.
- Begin to define, in general, what type of systems would need to exist and its functioning at each level of the organization.

The underlying framework for the mapping is one suggested by Crockett (1992). Crockett suggested a framework showing the benefits of an Executive Information System (EIS). In this framework (Figure 4), the performance benefits of such a system result in feedback that influences: 1) strategy formulation, by focusing executives on stakeholders needs and critical success factors, 2) business plan development, by providing information on changes and monitoring progress, and 3) operational activities, by alerting executives to problem areas and improvements. There are three primary problems that retard the flow of quality information into the EIS. These problems are: 1) systems still do not provide (or provide too late) the data that senior managers consider crucial, even after installation, 2) collected data are not linked across functions or strategic areas, and 3) the data that are available help diagnose problems but do not help find solutions (Crockett, 1992).

Implicit within the framework of the EIS are the components of strategy discussed earlier. In general these components can be found in each part of the information system relative to its level in the organization. For example, critical success factors found at the corporate level are used in defining what is necessary for proper organizational growth and value creation. At the business level, the issue is what is required for successful competitive strategies, and at the functional level, what is the maximum resource productivity. Synthesis and analysis would be required in order to make the successful transition from formulation to implementation at each level as well as monitoring the results of those actions and for monitoring the organization as a whole. Failure to give due consideration to these components at any level and the relationships represented, can lead to either ineffective formulation and/or implementation. By using causal mapping, we will be able to address these issues and help provide a path toward gaining a better understanding and assistance in developing a solution to the situation.

Illustrating the Mapping Technique

The information concerning WorldCom, Inc., contained in this case originated from various sources including company press releases, Associated Press articles, USA Today, and CNN's special, "The Rise and Fraud of WorldCom, Inc." The relationships illustrated are those maps representing an aggregation of both student and instructor maps.

When constructing the maps we use various types of arrows to denote the relationships that exist between various areas of the firm. These maps are used to illustrate several facets of any given situation: 1) the factors or players in the situation are illustrated, 2) the strength of the relationship that exists between these factors is shown by arrows (Table 2), with the type of arrow determining the strength of the relationship, and 3) the cause and effect of actions or inactions of strategy are shown. These cause and effect relationships are given by a plus (+) sign designating a positive effect or a minus sign (-), designating a negative effect. The absence of either sign would denote "no effect," but rarely is there "no" effect. These are also shown in the context of information dependency and symmetry and the net effect on other levels of the organization. It should also be noted that the strength of the relationship can range from very strong to very weak regardless of the direction of cause and effect.

Major Case Issues Addressed

The major questions that are addressed using this technique are:

- Why did WorldCom, Inc., a seemingly successful company, fail?
- What were the underlying factors which contributed toward its failure?
- What are the corporate issues, business level issues, and functional level issues?

These questions are used to help define the issue of failure and range from very broad terms to very specific.

Table 2. Relationship indicators for causal mapping

Type of Arrow	Relationship
───────▶	Very Strong
─ ─ ─ ─ ▶	Strong
─ · ─ · ─ ▶	Moderate
·············▶	Weak
·················▶	Very Weak

Issues of Information Dependency

We need to look at this issue from two directions, both independently and simultaneously. When considering issues of organizational structure, we can see various instances of dependency discussed earlier. For example, in the case of the various business units that comprised WorldCom, Inc., as a result of its merger and acquisition activities, there can be shown instances of being independent and reciprocally dependent. Although the business units operated independently, a lack of coordination existed across those business units at both the business and functional/operational levels. This resulted from a lack of reciprocal dependency in not only competitive and pricing strategies, but also in the ability to deliver the service through the same backbone. These units were also sequentially dependent within each business unit as evidenced by the consistency of competitive strategy within the business units.

From the case we find that in the early days of WorldCom, Inc., the strategy of growth was via the merger and acquisition of smaller phone companies to increase their customer base and market coverage. Because of the overriding concern with growth, one of the problems that WorldCom, Inc. ran into was that the individual systems at the functional level, i.e., billing systems, were not integrated. Pricing structures differed among the acquired firms and no attempt was made to integrate these businesses at this level. The dependencies that existed were of being both sequentially dependent and reciprocally dependent.

Figure 5. Functional level symmetry and independence

Causal mapping: Cause and effect of WorldCom's billing system not being integrated in determining corporate profitability

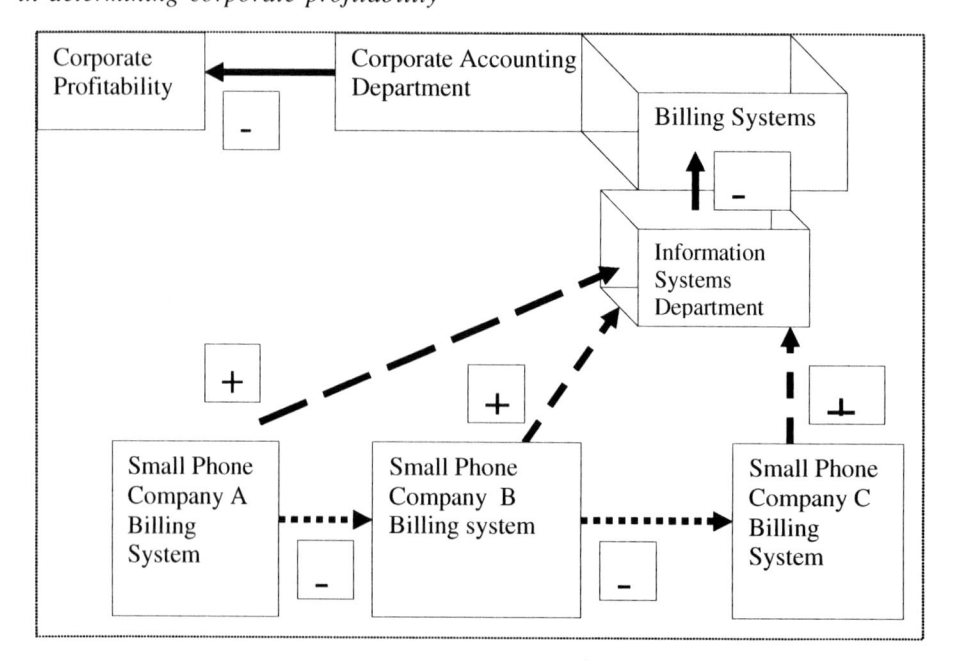

There was a high degree of independence at the business level across business units that necessarily led to a high degree of asymmetry at that level and at the functional and cross-functional levels (Figure 5). This is illustrated by the arrows denoting a very weak relationship between these areas. At these levels reciprocal dependency is needed, as these business units need to share information regarding types of services offered and their associated pricing structure. A lack of information sharing resulted in silos being developed which brought about problems at the business level. The corporate accounting department therefore was lacking the proper quality of information, such as pricing policy, costs, etc., needed to get a true picture of the financial condition of WorldCom, Inc.

Overall, while it can be seen that a high degree of sequential dependence exists toward corporate accounting in the aggregation of information, there is very little linkage (reciprocal) among the systems at that functional level, thereby creating a high degree of information asymmetry. It would appear that a lack of coordination contributed to this issue of dependency. Coordination is the management of dependencies, and organizational change is the adaptation to changing dependencies (Tillquist et al., 2002).

From Figure 5 we can also surmise that the lack of integration (a very weak relationship) between the billing systems at this level had a negative effect on the coordination aspect among the separate business units concerned. There was, however, individually, a strong relationship and a high degree of dependency with the IS department. The relationship between IS and the billing system area of corporate accounting was very strong, as was that of corporate accounting in determining corporate profitability. The positive/negative cause-and-effect relationship shows the actual effect. The lack of systems integration at the functional level had a cumulative negative effect. The billing system at corporate accounting was not able to produce accurate information concerning billed revenue, which in turn gave an inaccurate measure of corporate profitability.

Business Level Dependence and Symmetry

Figure 6 shows the change in dependence resulting from integrating the billing systems at the functional level. You will notice that the cause and effect relationship has changed from negative to positive for many of the existing relationships, beginning at the functional level. This represents a movement from independence to sequential dependence. The relationship of symmetry has moved from asymmetric (very weak) to somewhat more symmetric (moderate). When systems are initially integrated at this level, relationships do not become strong immediately. The degree of change will be slow and is due mainly to the extent to which the systems are integrated. The more complete the integration, the stronger the relationship that exists between those areas and the IS department's ability to deliver quality information. The net effect here is that you are then able to begin to acquire a much truer picture of the condition of the organization and a greater ability to make more effective decisions.

Figure 6. Business level symmetry and dependence
Causal mapping: Cause and effect of WorldCom's billing system being integrated in determining corporate profitability

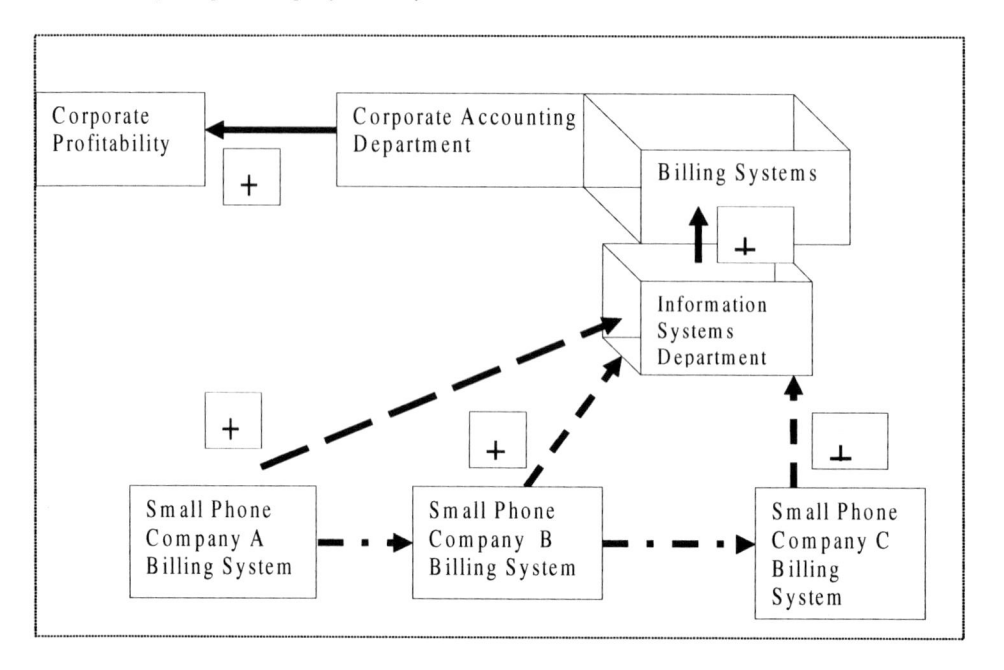

Corporate Level Dependence and Symmetry

One of the pitfalls of a high degree of independence and asymmetry in an organization is that a complete picture of a situation in a given organizational context can rarely or never be obtained. We are not able to and many times cannot coordinate activities of various areas to achieve the mission of the organization. This is evident from the relationships shown in Figures 5 and 6. The mission statement is that vehicle by which all employees can find the general direction in which the firm is headed and be able to periodically determine, via performance measures, progress being made toward that end. Figure 7 shows the relationship of cause and effect due to asymmetry and independence.

From the case, WorldCom's Senior VP of Customer Service, Richard Hudspeth, along with Chris Fouts, Pricing Analyst, posed a major question. This question was, "How in the face of declining revenues, could WorldCom still post large gains," and "How could the numbers given investors on Wall Street remain strong?" This was in light of the fact that revenues in many areas were declining, as a result of a downturn in the economy. As Hudspeth stated, "Because of the lack of integration we were put into a position where the numbers were not going to work, so you had to find a way to make them work." Many in the organization knew that something was not right. Attempts were made to get access to information, to bring pieces of the puzzle together from others who had the required information. This was done in an attempt to gain a clearer picture of what was actually happening, so that courses of action could be formulated and implemented at the

Figure 7. Corporate level symmetry and dependence

WorldCom corporate causal mapping: Cause and effect of information asymmetry on WorldCom's mission statement

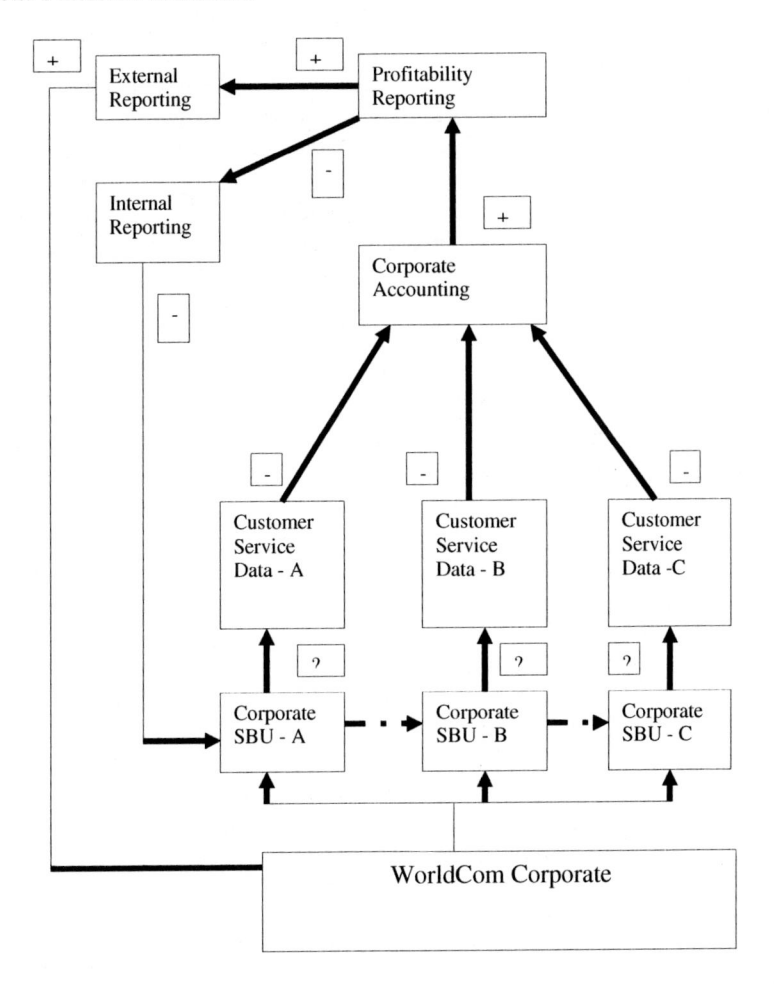

business level. When this had gotten back to people in the corporate office, the returning questions were asked, "Why do you need and why does a certain person need that information?"

By asking questions in this manner, it can be inferred that a high degree or level of independence did exist in the organization and with it a new high degree of asymmetry. A high degree of inferred dependence would have resulted in information being shared with the lower or equal levels. The level of dependence would move from independent to reciprocal dependency and a better sense of symmetry resulting.

From Figure 7, information from the Customer Service areas flow into the corporate accounting office, and in this case was negative in nature although the relationship remained very strong. Information flowing out concerning profitability levels was reported in two ways. The information which was being reported externally was positive while it was known that the current situation from an internal perspective was negative. Asymmetry is also found to originate within the corporate accounting area. Asymmetry arising in this instance is not so much a by-product of the data and information manipulation of the system itself as it is of the people who are a part of that system.

When incomplete information due to independence and asymmetry is present, it is extremely difficult to formulate and implement any course of action. This is represented by the question marks leading from corporate SBU management to the Customer Service Data generated by those strategies from each SBU. The conflict residing in profitability reporting arises from both the negative signs leading into the corporate SBU and the positive signs coming from WorldCom's Corporate Offices. It can also be seen that the relationship that exists between the SBUs at the business level is moderate, illustrating the lack of coordination among the business units. Looking back to Figure 5, we can see this is true because of the lack of coordination among billing systems at the functional level. As was stated in the case, "We were underwriting our own business; in effect, we were competing against ourselves."

Ineffective decision making as a result of asymmetries can be seen in the comments made by Bernie Ebbers regarding the execution of the strategy for WorldCom's growth. The growth strategy as far as the corporate level was concerned was on track due to the positive external reporting, but considerably off-target when considering internal reports. This stems from the failure to adequately address system integration issues at the lowest level of the organization. Referring to Figure 4, we can see that a breakdown in the linkages of the EIS due to asymmetry and independence can potentially have negative consequences in strategy formulation and implementation at all levels.

Summary

This chapter has focused on using causal mapping as an analysis and synthesis tool to understand the relationships which exist among various areas of a firm. This technique helps us to determine strategy's impact on a particular area of a firm as well as its overall impact. It was found that the effects of a strategy, and in some cases, a non-strategy or even an abandoned one, can be felt throughout the organization.

In helping understand what it takes for an organization to function well, we introduced the concepts of symmetry and dependency as they relate to an organization's growth and development. These two concepts are highly related to a third, that of organizational complexity. Organizational complexity itself is defined as the degree of diversification the firm undertakes in implementing its growth strategy, relative to dependency. Diversification can take place in both related and unrelated areas, each with its own degree of symmetry and dependency. In the case of WorldCom, Inc., although the overall degree of symmetry was high, there should have been a low degree of complexity (the firm had a high degree of related diversification) as a result of good integration and information sharing. They became an increasingly complex organization because of the issue of information dependency. The more the individual business units became information independent, the more asymmetric and complex the organization became and the more difficult it became to formulate and execute a coherent and comprehensive strategy. A growth strategy of merger and acquisition initially suggests a high degree of asymmetry, independence and complexity. It is through a strategy of integration where we can reduce these levels. This integration takes place at the functional level of the organization. The separate billing systems that existed for different businesses which provided the same service, serves as an example. This, of course, did not happen at WorldCom, Inc.

In order for a firm to execute a strategy effectively several events must occur. First, a good relationship must exist among the various units of an organization at a given level of the firm and there must be some relationship that exists among the levels in the corporate hierarchy. The information generated by these individual units and the extent to which it is shared and used in the decision-making process, can have a great effect on the outcome of a particular course of action. A firms' Executive Information System (EIS) must function both effectively and efficiently for this to happen. Any breakdown in this system, no matter how small, will cause the effect of the EIS to decrease dramatically. This starts out at the most fundamental level of the organization and makes its way up the corporate hierarchy. As we have seen with WorldCom, Inc., this breakdown did occur.

Systems which should have been integrated at the lowest levels were not, and this resulted in some very disastrous effects. Those effects were magnified at the business level where a lack of information sharing (reciprocal dependency) undermined its competitiveness to the point of cannibalization. WorldCom, Inc. was unable to effectively execute at this level. The value-addedness which could have existed through its critical value activities was for the most part non-existent. It was no longer able to deliver high quality service for the lowest price possible. As a result, service renewals were decreasing. The lack of reciprocal dependency and information sharing ensured this. This is somewhat like "shooting yourself in the foot." When this happens organizational silos tend to emerge as these units compete for even more limited resources, each trying to justify their own existence and often times, unknowingly, at the expense of the firm.

As a result, the organization became more asymmetric and increasingly complex. This occurred at such an alarming rate that new dependencies had to be found in order to give the appearance that the EIS and the organization were functioning properly. This occurred at the corporate level when they compiled reports for outside investors and stockholders. Information that was largely negative in nature was being reported as positive. The EIS at the corporate level, gave the impression that everything was operating smoothly, effectively and efficiently.

If the structure of an organization is what gives it its form, then the information system that is in place helps hold that form together. In the context of the universe, solar systems and galaxies and they way they are configured, give the universe its form. This is something we can see, much like an organization chart. However the gravitational pull of these individual systems and the pull that these systems have on one another is what helps hold that shape together. This component is unseen, much like the information system that links (forms a dependency) the various areas together. Here is where we see the true cause and effect of organizational units and their relationships come to bear.

It is not so much the big things that can cause the demise of an organization, even though if unplanned for they will. It is the little things, if not done well (e.g. monitoring the environment, internally and externally; getting systems to talk to each other), that will have a compounding effect in and throughout the firm. Recognizing the benefits of the causal mapping approach and using it to help determine the extent of cause-and-effect relationships in strategy formulation and implementation, can far outweigh the cost associated with not using it. In other words, the ability to be able to see these relationships as we understand them in the proper context is the first part of the process. Then, to be able to use this to determine course(s) of action and monitor their progress to help achieve the desired level of competitiveness at each level of the organization, and as a whole, is what completes the process.

References

Cambell, Bonita J. (1977). *Understanding information systems: Foundations for control.* Cambridge, MA: Winthrop.

Computerworld. (December 15, 2003). *RFID: Smart tags, high costs.*

Computerworld. (March 19, 2001). *Sabre sells IT business to EDS.*

Crockett, F. (1992, Summer). Revisiting executive information systems. *Sloan Management Review*, 39-47.

DeKluyer, C. A. (2000). *Strategic thinking: An executive perspective.* New York: Prentice Hall.

Fransman, M. (1994). *Information, knowledge, vision, and theories of the firm.* Cambridge: Oxford University Press.

Hax, A. C., & Maljuf, N.S. (1996). *The strategy concept and process: A pragmatic approach.* New York: Prentice Hall.

Jenster, P. V. (1986-87, Winter). Firm performance and monitoring of critical success factors in different strategic contexts. *Journal of Management Information Systems*, 17.

Johnson, G. & Scholes, K. (1999). *Exploring corporate strategy: Text and cases*, 5th edition. Prentice Hall Europe.

Marakus, G. M. (1999). *Decision support systems in the 21st century.* New York: Prentice Hall.

Martin, J. (1996). *Cybercorp: The new business revolution.* New York: AMACOM.

Mintzberg, H. (1994, January-February). The rise and fall of strategic planning. *Harvard Business Review*, 107.

Montazeui, A.R., & Dourath, D.W. (1986, March). The use of cognitive mapping for information requirements analysis. *MIS Quarterly*, 45-56.

Nelson, K. M., Nadkaini, S., Narayanam, V.K., & Ghods, M. (2000) Understanding software operations support expertise: A revealed causal mapping approach. *MIS Quarterly*, 24(3), 475-507.

Nelson, K. M., Nelson, H.J., & Armstrong, D. (2000). *Revealed causal mapping as an evocative method for information systems research.* Proceedings of the 33rd Hawaii International Conference on Systems Resources, 2000.

Pagels, H. R. (1985). *Perfect symmetry: The search for the beginning of time.* New York: Simon and Schuster.

Paterson, D. W. (1990). *Introduction to artificial intelligence and expert systems.* London: Prentice-Hall.

Thompson, A. A., & Strickland III, A.J. (1998). *Strategic management: Concept and cases,* 10th Edition. Boston MA: Irwin/McGraw Hill.

Thompson, J. (1967). *Organizations in action.* San Francisco, CA: McGraw-Hill.

Tillquist, J., King, J.L., & Woo, C. (2002, June). A representational scheme for analyzing information technology and organizational dependency. *MIS Quarterly,* 26(2), 91-118.

Trochim, W. M. K. (19). An introduction to concept mapping for planning and evaluation.

Williamson, O.E. (1990). (1990) The firm as a nexus of treaties: An introduction. In M. Aoki, B. Gustafson and O.E. Williamson (Eds.), *The Firm as a Nexus of Treaties* (pp. 1-25). London: Sage.

Case in Point: Worldcom, Inc.

Author's Note: The facts and events portrayed in this case are true. The case, however, is not presented in its entirety, but lists those events necessary for illustrating concept and causal mapping.

Background

In early 1983 in Hattiesberg, Mississippi, the beginnings of what we know as WorldCom, Inc. began to take shape. Bernie Ebbers, along with business associates Bill Fields, David Singleton, and Murray Waldron, began laying the groundwork for the start of LDDS or Long Distance Discount Service. They began their search to locate the firm's headquarters by going from area to area and asking how many long distance companies these communities had in the area. They found their location in this town when they received the answer, "What's that?" when they inquired about the service. In 1984, LDDS opened for business by reselling AT&T services to local people and businesses. The first year of operation proved to be a tough start for them in that they lost money that year and almost went out of business.

In 1985 Bernie Ebbers took the financial reigns of the company and, by applying techniques he used in other businesses he had owned, was able to bring profitability to LDDS. It was soon after that the company began to grow, going through a series of merger and acquisitions over the course of the next 15 years. In June 1999, WorldCom's stock hit its peak at $64.50 per share. The time seemed right for the next deal. In October of that year, WorldCom and Sprint announced a $115 billion merger agreement, with WorldCom, Inc. being the principal. This proposed merger was subsequently called off in June 2000 after objections from U.S. and European regulators. This caused WorldCom's stock to drop and forced the sale of three million shares to pay off their debt. WorldCom's aggressive growth strategy had come to an abrupt end and investment for the future in this manner came to a standstill. In essence, WorldCom moved from being a growth by acquisition company to an operating company and, because of this, a new style of management had to be found.

Corporate Strategy

The corporate strategy was one of growth by merger and acquisition through concentric diversification. This growth would occur at a phenomenal rate and would, according to Ebbers, focus in five areas. These areas were: Voice, Local Service, Internet, Data, and International. The growth strategy was simple. They would build a customer base and then go and merge with or purchase smaller local long distance companies. The subject of integration was never addressed much at this level and the results of this strategy were borne out at the business and functional levels. To many outsiders of WorldCom, such as the investors and stockholders, the company was performing quite well and growth was occurring at a phenomenal rate.

The numbers reported to investors showed that WorldCom was making its earnings expectations, while actual numbers showed them making less. Corporate profits and viability reported at the upper levels did not give a true picture of the firm. The basis for this growth strategy was inadvertently formed at the business level by one of the firm's capacity planners. A model was developed which showed that a sales forecast could be translated into the amount of traffic that could be expected given the value of certain variables in the equation. In the best-case scenario, indications were that Internet traffic would double every 120 days or at 1,000 percent annually. This was slowly disseminated throughout the organization and soon became the model by which they conducted themselves. Industry analysts and the person who developed this model knew that this was not true. Their original strategy of being a reseller of phone lines and growth by merging with smaller firms slowly transformed them into a complex multinational owner of long distance lines.

What was actually occurring was that no formal strategy was adopted for conducting the company's business and no long term plan existed for its business development. In essence, the basic corporate strategy was one of "doing the next deal."

Through the years 1988-1994, LDDS acquired more than one-half dozen communications companies, both large and small and began expanding their reach throughout the United States. In 1989 LDDS became a publicly traded firm through its acquisition of Advantage Companies, Inc. In 1992, they merged in an all-stock deal with long-distance service provider Advanced Telecommunications Corp. The following year saw them acquire long distance providers Resurgent Communications Group, Inc. and Metromedia in a three-way stock and cash transaction. The result of this merger was the formation of the fourth largest long distance network in the United States.

In 1994 growth continued through the acquisition of the domestic and international communication network of IBD Communications Group, Inc. in an all stock deal. The following year they acquired voice and data transmission company Williams Telecommunication Group, Inc. (WilTel) and changed its name to WorldCom, Inc. This name change better reflected the mission and strategy of the organization.

In 1996, WorldCom, Inc. merged with MFS Communications Company, Inc., which owned local network access to facilities via digital fiber optic cable networked in and around major U.S. and European cities. This acquisition played a large part in fulfilling the growth strategy in the area of local service. That same year saw the acquisition of UUNET, which was a large player in the small, but growing segment of the telecommunications industry. It also provided WorldCom with a nationwide Internet backbone, plus local fiber optic networks for businesses in major cities.

WorldCom then went on to complete three mergers two years later. These were some of the largest to be known in history. They were MCI Communications ($40 billion), Brooks Fiber Properties, Inc. ($1.2 billion) and CompuServe ($1.38 billion). The addition of Brooks Fiber provided local telecommunications service in selected cities of the United States. Their services included local exchange carriers, long distance customers, Internet service providers, wireless carriers and business, government and institutional carriers.

Business Level Strategy

With WorldCom's focus on growth through merger and acquisition and with no business model to guide them, the part of their strategy which included integrating the business portfolio soon fell by the wayside. WorldCom wanted to build a competitive advantage by building a large customer base through purchasing and merging with smaller regional companies and being able to offer services at prices lower than the competition in those businesses. For example, the basic marketing plan would be to offer services at a 20 percent discount from AT&T to get local people and businesses to switch. The competitive business arenas were to be in International, Voice, Data and Wholesale. The service they provided was directed toward the small business owner.

They tried to be better than the competition in three separate, but related, areas: price, revenue growth, and cost structure. In the early days when they were known as LDDS, it was fairly easy to do. They would be able to offer subscribers of such competitors as AT&T and Bell South something they did not have previously—a choice. Their main objective was to first establish a customer base and then merge with somebody. This type of competitive strategy mindset continued on even after the company changed its name to WorldCom, Inc.

Because of the extent of mergers and acquisitions, competition became fierce and due to the lack of integration at the corporate level, it began to affect the performance of the business units. Customers would call on a sales force from a number of WorldCom units, such as UUNET, and see what they had to offer. "The real problem came from the fact that you were dealing with different sales forces with different billing systems," as stated by Chris Fouts, a WorldCom pricing analyst. "It was tough to figure out how to set prices. The net effect was that we were writing down our own business, because we were competing with ourselves." When people within the organization tried to get information to get a true picture of the company's position, they were chided as to why they needed that information and told that they really had no need for it because it did not concern them. This type of problem manifested itself from a lack of integration at the functional levels.

Functional Level

As stated earlier, because of the concern and focus on growth of WorldCom, little attention was given to integrating the business units from the business level on down. Little did anyone realize that this would soon contribute to WorldCom's undoing. The focus had shifted from concentrating on the little things in the early days that got them to where they were, to not being able to see the overall big picture. The original goal was to try and get the billing systems to mesh, to get everyone on the same system. While this strategy is initially sound, as a result of the mergers, problems were being experienced with serving their customers, and some of the various issues surrounding the integration at this level were not fully addressed. The systems that were integrated were those that they wanted to integrate. These were in some parts of Voice, Data, International and Wholesale. The problems stemmed from that if they were merging only a customer base, this could be handled. However, if it were more than just a customer base, they would be primarily at a loss because of the complexity involved. For example, in the merger with WilTel, the infrastructure for local service was far more complex than that of long distance. Their failure to manage this aspect properly caused problems at the business level, which eventually made its way to the corporate level. In a sense, they had lost control, and therefore they never made any great attempts at integrating the businesses.

This was reinforced further by Diana Barajon Cole, a former MCI Customer Service Manager. Her job was to keep track of what her customers wanted. She stated, "because the services were not coordinated, you could never tell what the customer was being billed because the systems did not talk to each other. It was a disaster." This was echoed further at the executive level when Richard Hudseth stated, "there was no integration. The situation, (e.g., the discrepancy in performance measures), existed because the numbers compiled for the general public were not going to work. It therefore became evident that you must find a way to make them work." The inefficiencies which existed at the functional level were being covered up by the aggressive growth strategy being evolved/enacted at the corporate level. Clearly, things were not going well. The major question now is: What can be done?

Chapter XIII

Knowledge at Work in Software Development:
A Cognitive Approach for Sharing Knowledge and Creating Decision Support for Life-Cycle Selection

Luca Iandoli
University of Naples Federico II, Italy

Giuseppe Zollo
University of Naples Federico II, Italy

Abstract

Knowledge management practices in software development and engineering have been focused mainly on knowledge sharing and maintenance whereas less attention has been devoted to knowledge elicitation and codification issues. In this chapter we present a methodology based on causal mapping for the investigation and management of knowledge created and elaborated by software development teams in the production of new software applications. The chapter focuses on the early stages of the process when development teams have to make a choice regarding the software life cycle model that best fits, given constraints concerning ambiguity of the requirements, risks, costs evaluation and scheduling. A step-by-step application of the proposed methodology to a case study in a software company is presented to provide the reader with examples drawn from the field analysis and illustrates critical methodological aspects. Implications for knowledge management in software project development are then outlined and discussed.

Introduction

This chapter can be positioned within the research on Knowledge Management in software development (see the special issue IEEE Software, 2002). Typical knowledge management tasks such as knowledge storing, elicitation, codification and re-use have always been relevant issues in the management of projects of new software products. However recent literature explicitly emphasizes the necessity of a systematic approach to knowledge management in software development and engineering through sound methodologies and support tools aimed at facilitating knowledge acquisition, generation, diffusion, exploitation and maintenance, according to the principles of the knowledge value chain (Figure 1).

Managing knowledge within knowledge-intensive organizations such as software firms requires companies to have suitable methodologies and tools for each phase of the knowledge value chain.

Traditionally, knowledge management practices in software development and engineering have been focused mainly on knowledge sharing and maintenance whereas less attention has been devoted to the elicitation issues. Actually, the acquisition step is one of the most critical steps in the knowledge value chain. In particular, this chapter focuses on knowledge acquisition from internal sources such as technicians and managers involved in the development of a new software product. Often being situated, tacit, and idiosyncratic, individual knowledge is not easily captured and transformed into organizational knowledge, which is largely shared and easily accessible to other organizational members (Argyris & Scöhn, 1978; Choo, 1998; Choo & Bontis, 2002; Nonaka & Takeuchi, 1995).

Instead of a software engineering approach to knowledge management, that is rather focused on the management of explicit knowledge, in this chapter we propose the adoption of a knowledge engineering approach, which is usually employed in the design

Figure 1. The knowledge value chain

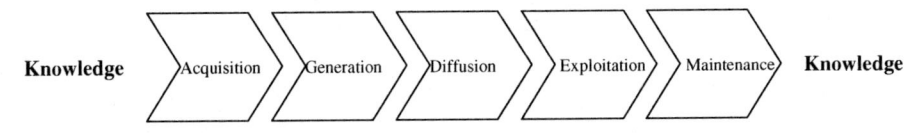

Knowledge ⟩Acquisition⟩ ⟩Generation⟩ ⟩Diffusion⟩ ⟩Exploitation⟩ ⟩Maintenance⟩ **Knowledge**

Adapted/elaborated from Schreiber et al. (2000)

of expert systems for which suitable methodologies are needed to capture and codify highly contextual knowledge possessed by human experts for the execution of specific tasks. In particular the aim of this chapter is to present a methodology based on causal mapping for the investigation and management of knowledge created and elaborated by software development teams in the production of new software applications. The chapter focuses on the early stages of the process when development teams have to make a choice regarding the software life cycle model that best fits, given constraints concerning ambiguity of the requirements, risks, costs evaluation and scheduling.

A causal map is a representation of causal beliefs through a network of causal relations embedded in a collection of individual explicit statements. It can be considered as an explicit representation of the deep-rooted cognitive maps of individuals. (Huff, 1990; Nelson, Nadkarni, Narayanan & Ghods, 2000). Causal mapping allows researchers and practitioners to investigate how people involved in the development process select and attribute meanings to variables influencing the choice of a life cycle model. On the organizational side, information and individual knowledge represented through causal maps can be analyzed and discussed with the developers to increase their level of awareness and participation in the choice process. Once elicited and structured through formal models such as causal maps, individual knowledge can be transformed into organizational knowledge according to the framework of the learning and knowing organization (Argyris & Schön, 1978; Choo, 1998).

By eliciting and mapping individual knowledge, this chapter shows how it is possible to:

a) Identify critical factors that impact the success of new projects as perceived by team members;

b) Compare different individual interpretations represented through causal maps concerning the meaning and the importance of choice variables, to verify the existence of overlapping perceptions and shared beliefs and conflicting interpretations;

c) Analyze individual knowledge and use the results of such analysis for the design of more effective decision support tools for software life cycle selection.

The chapter is structured as follows: Section 2 presents an overview of the critical issues in formal methodology adoption for software development and, in particular of current approaches in software life-cycle selection. Section 3 provides the theoretical background for a cognitive approach to the problem of life-cycle model selection. Section 4 presents the methodology. Section 5 presents the results obtained through the application of the proposed methodology to a case study in a software company. In Section 6 results and implications for decisions support systems deriving from the analysis are illustrated through the description of a support tool designed during the research. Finally implications for practice and lessons learned are discussed in Sections 7 and 8.

Critical Issues in Formal Methodology Adoption for Software Development

Several studies have dealt with the issue of determining suitable methods for the selection of a life-cycle model for software development applications (Boehm, 1988; Bradac, Perry & Votta, 1994; Humphrey, 1989; McConnell, 1996; Putnam, 1992).

The life cycle of a software product begins with the idea formulation and the initial design and ends when the product is no longer available for further use. The life-cycle model of a software product is a formal description of how the product should be developed, usually specifying the development phases, deliverables, guidelines, and evaluation of intermediate and final results.

Examples of life cycle models are the following:

- Waterfall: in this model the development of software products is articulated into a linear sequence of phases usually concerning problem analysis, requirements analysis, development, integration, testing, installation and maintenance. This model requires the definition of intermediate output and deliverables, minimum overlapping between phases and feedback to previous phases in cases of unsatisfying results. The waterfall model is very simple and it can be useful in stable situations when the identification of the requirements is not problematic. The major disadvantages concern the scarce interaction with the user (usually limited at the beginning and at the end of the product development), and the lack of flexibility.

- Prototyping model: in this model the design is carried out to develop a prototype of the product as soon as possible. The realization of the final product is seen as successive refinements of the first prototype to achieve a satisfying degree of convergence between the user's needs and requirements' identification and implementation. This model is particularly useful when the user's needs are ambiguously defined.

- Incremental delivery: incremental models conceive the development of software products as a set of stages, each one organized as a linear sequence of phases (similar to the waterfall model). At the end of each development stage the product presents new characteristics and improvements, i.e., it can be considered an evolution of the previous stage. This model can be used in the case of big projects when the available budget at the beginning of the project may be insufficient to ensure the development of the entire project or when it is important to gain flexibility and adaptation through incremental improvements.

The interest in the definition of suitable life-cycle models is clearly demonstrated by the CMM (Capability Maturity Model) developed by the SEI (Software Engineering Institute, http://www.sei.cmu.edu/) for the evaluation of the maturity level achieved by software companies (Paulk, Curtis, Chrissis &Weber, 1993).

The CMM ranks software development organizations in a hierarchy of five levels, each with a progressively greater capability of producing quality software (Gainer, 2003). Each level is described as a level of maturity. At level one, the "Initial" level, there is little or no formalization of processes. A project's success depends on individual efforts and capabilities, but if this expertise leaves the company there is no guarantee that such knowledge has been incorporated into organizational routines and practice and that it will be re-used effectively in the future.

At the second "repeatable" level, at least basic project management activities are in place, such as configuration management and requirements management. Another step up the scale is the "defined" process level, where basic quality assurance and quality control activities are defined and practiced, such as defined standards, a defined process, structured walkthroughs and formal testing.

To increase their own capability maturity from level two and level three, companies must adequately define the life-cycle of all of their projects. Furthermore, according to the well-known international normative ISO IEC 12207 regarding software process management, in software project planning the project manager must select activities and tasks of the development process and map them onto the appropriate life-cycle model.

The availability in the literature and in professional practice of several life-cycle models implies the problem of selecting the one that best fits the development of a specific software application, given constraints such as requirements, level of perceived risks, and scheduling (Bohem, 1981; Matson, Barret & Mellichamp, 1994; McConnell, 1996; Pressman, 2000; Putnam, 1992).

To support the selection of the best life-cycle model, formal methodologies are often employed to reduce risk, time to market and development costs. Despite these advantages, however, recent literature on software development has investigated why software developers often show resistance to using formal methodologies. Drawing on previous research (Davis, 1989; Riemenshneider, Hardgrave & Davis, 2002; Thompson, Higgins & Howell, 1991), we classify the determinants of resistance to the adoption of formal methodologies in software development into three main categories:

- individual factors related to individual disposition and willingness, as well as capability to employ formal methodologies and tools in software development (e.g., compatibility of the methodology with how developers perform their work, perceived usefulness, ease of use);
- organizational factors related to organizational support and incentives to use formal development methodologies (e.g., management commitment, facilitating conditions and tools, training, career consequences);
- social factors related to the social acceptance of formal methodology adoption (e.g., peer and supervisor opinions, social consensus, image and status).

What seems to emerge from such studies is that developers may perceive formal methodologies as constraining, boring and time-consuming instead of as effective support to software development.

In this chapter it is argued that the adoption of formal methodologies in software development, and in particular in life-cycle selection, should be accompanied by a deep analysis of the context structured into: knowledge elicitation, knowledge coding and mapping through causal maps, and knowledge analysis.

The results of the analysis are obtained by analyzing developers' experience and knowledge embedded in their cognitive constructs (frames, patterns of action, cognitive schemata, beliefs, etc.). Results can then be discussed with the developers to help them achieve deeper knowledge and awareness of the development process. In this way, a cognitive approach to the analysis of life cycle model selection can help to increase the perceived usefulness of formal methodologies at the individual and at the organizational level by transforming them from standard "constraining" tools to learning and knowledge management procedures.

Traditional software development methodologies try to eliminate subjectivity through standardization and usually neglect social and human factors in software engineering (Pfleeger, 1999). In particular their use does not take into account how people frame problems, select clues from the environment, attribute meaning to new events, and leverage knowledge and expertise to deal with ambiguity and novelty rising from new, poorly defined and unexpected situations.

A Cognitive Approach to Life Cycle Model Selection through Causal Maps

In the following we characterize the life-cycle selection as a problem in which developers are expected to choose the best model given information on the project and constraints of time, cost and human resource availability. From a theoretical point of view, such a problem can be investigated by drawing on the literature in organizational decision-making.

It is well known that classical approaches to decision-making are not able to deal with incomplete information and ambiguous definitions in choice problems (March, 1988). In particular, the theory of rational choice (Von Neumann & Morgestern, 1944) assumes that human behavior in choice problems is driven by absolute rationality to the minimization of the cost/benefit ratio. According to this perspective the decision-maker has complete information, is able to process all available information, and expresses consistent preferences and predictions.

Rational choice theory has been criticized by many studies both on theoretical and empirical grounds because it fails in predicting and describing human behavior in most of the choice situations in which the choice itself is not trivial. The main critics of rational theory of choice are the following:

a) Bounded rationality: information is always incomplete and individuals have limited capability to process huge amounts of data (Simon, 1961);

b) Interdependence between choice and evaluation (Cyert & March, 1963): individuals do not evaluate *a priori* the best course of action among several possible ones, but rather their final choice is influenced by intermediate results and by their perception of success;

c) Bounded irrationality: in everyday life individuals solve choice problems through cognitive strategies that do not respect theoretical assumptions and prescriptions of the rational choice theory (Tversky & Kahneman, 1974; Nisbett & Ross, 1980);

d) Knowledge structures: individual tend to activate reasoning schemata and patterns which proved to be effective in past similar situations, thus they do not evaluate all of the possible courses of actions each time (Galambos, Abelson & Black, 1986, Schank & Abelson, 1977);

e) Ex-post rationality (Weick, 1976): individual choices are the result of past actions of which individuals make sense only afterward;

f) Decision making as a decomposable process (Mintzberg, Raisinghani & Theoret, 1976): organizational decision making is the result of a complex and long evaluation processes involving many heterogeneous actors and is only partially analytically investigable;

g) Decision making and power (Allison, 1971; Crozier, 1964): choices are influenced by political variables.

According to many studies, in complex ill-defined situations decision-making problems can be better framed in the "sense-making" perspective (Daft & Weick, 1984; Weick, 1976). In the sense-making perspective, choice is only the final act of an ongoing process in which individuals make sense of the uncertain external environment by drawing on previous knowledge accumulated through past experience, interaction with other people, individual and organizational memory (Walsh & Ungson, 1991).

In the sense-making perspective individuals create knowledge in a three stage process consisting of enactment, selection, and retention (Weick, 1976). In the enactment stage, individuals, on the basis of their pre-existing knowledge, select clues and signals belonging to the ongoing and uninterrupted data flow from the environment. Through enactment people try to reduce the ambiguity of incoming information. In the selection stage, people draw from their mental models of actions (e.g., recipes, scripts, theories, etc.) constructed through experience and learning and that proved to be useful in the past. In the retention phase successful models of action are stored for possible future re-use.

Being influenced by and strictly interrelated with action, cognition is necessarily situated and, as such, influenced by the particular organizational context in which it develops (Blackler, 2002; Brown & Duguid, 1991). This means that enactment, selection and retention may be strongly conditioned by the presence of shared values, roles, organizational procedures, socially and organizationally accepted behaviors, rules, and organizational culture.

By adopting a sense-making perspective to investigate choice and decision-making problems with respect to a specific context of action, one needs to analyze how individual cognition takes place in organizations. For instance, how people frame problems, which values and beliefs influence or draw their actions, how existing models of action influence current and future choices, and how people make and justify their choices. Starting from these considerations, in the following the life-cycle selection, and more in general, choice problems are formulated according to the sense-making approach.

According to this approach, a new fact is interpreted when an individual is able to link the new fact to existing knowledge in a coherent way. Natural language is the most immediate tool to express such knowledge, because it allows individuals to represent nuances, ambiguities, uncertainties and conflicts usually neglected by formal methods to achieve coherence, simplicity and certainty. It is possible to have an idea of the complex contextual knowledge used by an individual when he/she explains the motivations of his/her judgement to other people. Through an explanatory discourse, people introduce hypotheses on the basis of their own background knowledge in an attempt to explain some evidence by relating new facts to known ones. Explanatory discourse means any spoken or written discourse through which an individual tries to make explicit the reasons justifying a choice or an evaluative judgment.

The idea proposed in this chapter is that mapping evaluation through explanations could shed light on how people make their choices in organizations in terms of how they select and relate evaluation criteria. For example, in evaluating different life-cycle models, explanation can be a way to elicit from evaluators' subjective knowledge which project's characteristics play a crucial role in determining his/her preference for one model rather than another, which attributes are evaluated, what is the meaning of those attributes in a specific context, and if and how the attributes are related among them.

Starting from this theoretical background the main assumptions behind the methodology proposed in this chapter and presented in the next section can be summarized as follows:

a) Individual knowledge is incorporated in mental schemata and organizational procedure. Patterns of action, scripts, models of behavior, facts, shared values, and stereotypes resulting from ongoing sense-making activities are stored in both individual and organizational memory (Weick, 1976; Walsh & Ungson, 1991). Organizational and individual memories are socially constructed thanks to an ongoing activity of individual interpretation and collective interaction (Berger & Luckmann, 1966; Nicolini & Meznar, 1995).

b) Ambiguity related to inputs from the environment (e.g., ambiguous requirements in software development) is resolved through interpretation; interpretation occurs when an individual is able to develop an explanatory discourse linking the new fact to existing knowledge in a coherent way (Schanck, 1986; Thagard, 1992; Zollo, 1998). Through explanatory discourses, people relate new facts to known ones by introducing or implicitly assuming hypotheses to explain (enacted) "evidence" on the basis of their own background knowledge.

c) Natural language is the most direct tool to express such knowledge, because it allows the representation of nuances, ambiguities, uncertainties and paradoxical assertions (Quinn & Cameron, 1983).

Following this background one expects that sense-making is deeper and more intense in knowledge-intensive organizations (e.g., software companies) working in an unstable environment, facing new and unexpected situations, and performing non-routine tasks. Consequently, explanations provided by software developers regarding the problem of choosing the best life cycle model in the early stages of a new software product development given information about situational constraints should provide considerable and deep knowledge about how people perceive and frame problems, select and attribute meanings and relevance to critical variables, and eventually make their decisions regarding the development process.

In the following section we propose a methodology based on causal mapping to elicit and represent cognitive constructs that software developers activate when requested to choose a life cycle model given some ambiguous and incoherent information about a product's requirements, customer's need, and constraints about available resources, costs and development time. Following the above assumptions, causal maps represent a suitable methodological approach because:

a) they allow researchers to obtain a formal representation of cognitive constructs activated by developers as a set of causal relationships; this representation is a practical way to elicit and capture, at least partially and in simplified form, the mental schemata and shared beliefs driving individual actions and choice models;

b) explanatory discourse can be easily translated into causal maps; explanations are very often attempts to provide a picture of cause/effect relationships among facts occurring in the real world;

c) causal maps can be constructed from the analysis of natural language information contained in explanatory discourses.

The Methodology: Eliciting and Mapping Developers' Knowlege in the Life Cycle Selection

The idea proposed in this chapter is that causal mapping can be employed to map individual knowledge contained in explanations provided by software developers in the early stages of a new project when a life cycle model has to be selected. Causal maps can be used to model concepts and the relationships between the concepts contained in explanatory discourses. The proposed methodology is articulated according to the following steps:

a) Sample Selection: one or more development teams made up of experienced practitioners in software development are selected according to certain criteria: i) level of expertise, as recognized by other experts or estimated from their position; ii) variety, in terms of roles, organizational positions, background (Calori, 2000).

b) Problem framing: a set of general framing questions concerning the main decision variables involved in the problem of choosing the "right" life cycle model is designed on the basis of the literature analysis and through a first involvement of the developers;

c) Elicitation: framing questions are employed to collect explanatory discourses through interviews;

d) Coding: explanatory discourses are analyzed to elicit concepts and relationships among them (Fletcher & Huff, 1990); relevant concepts are described in detail and reported in an interview dictionary;

e) Mapping: individual causal maps are used to represent concepts and relationships between concepts and analyzed to identify input and output variables, and influential and relevant concepts;

f) Comparison: individual maps are compared to identify similarities and differences in the framing of the life cycle selection problem across different individuals;

g) Data validation is performed through inter-coder reliability and feedback from interviewees;

h) Implication for decision support: once validated, the results emerging from the causal map analysis can be used to improve the design of Decision Support Systems (DSS) for the selection of the "best" life cycle model.

The choice of interviewing people instead of documentation analysis can be justified given the characteristics of the context. First, documentation containing developers' opinions and perceptions about how they frame the problem and make their choices during the development process does not exist.

Second, managing a software development project requires coping with ambiguous requirements, facing unexpected situations and making continuous adjustments to the customer's needs. Developers try to exploit existing knowledge and experience to cope with such novelty. Interviews and explanations try to "force" developers to make sense of an ever changing and unstable environment and to actively reconstruct (*ex post*) the rationale behind their past behaviors and decisions. Linguistic explanation may play a fundamental role in this reconstructing action because the tacit knowledge of informal organization is very often not known and opaque to its same constructors (Schanck, 1986; Weick, 1976). The taken-for-granted world is the world of the "obvious" and its opacity lies in the uncritical and automatic ways which it is enacted and recalled to memory. For these reasons, interviews, which permit direct involvement and interaction, favor the capture of tacit knowledge more than explicit sources such as written speech and documentation.

The proposed methodology was tested through a case study in an Italian software company producing software for accounting, management, office automation, and telecommunication systems. Other activities of the company concern outsourcing management of data elaboration centers. The company belongs to an important group with more than 1,000 employees, half of which are software developers, and a turnover of 80 million euros in 2002.

The activities of a software development team belonging to a specific organizational subunit and involved in the realization of a new product were investigated in depth through the proposed methodology. In the following, a step-by step application of the methodology is presented to provide the reader with practical examples and an overview of the critical issues and results that emerged during and after the field analysis.

Sample Selection

The sample was selected according to the above-mentioned criteria of level of expertise and variety. More specifically, level of expertise was estimated through years of experience in software development, involvement in the development of large projects, and peer and management indication. Through such criteria, it was not difficult to identify an "experienced team." A satisfying degree of variety was ensured by the way the company selects development teams. The team is usually made up of several developers with different roles (system analyst, programmers, network experts, etc.) and by one or more project managers. Of course team composition and duration depend on the characteristics of the project and may change over time. It is worthwhile to note that the number of people involved in the field research may vary as well depending on the research purpose. For example, if one wants to build a very comprehensive collective knowledge base (Calori, 2000), it is necessary to interview a large number of experts to integrate as many different points of view as possible into representative and reliable descriptions. On the other hand, if the research purpose is to investigate in-depth a given organizational aspect through an action research approach (Argyris & Schon, 1978), the number of people involved may be lower than in the previous case. As far as this chapter is concerned, our aim was to use the field analysis primarily to test the proposed methodology and to provide the reader with as many details as possible. Consequently, the presented results are mainly descriptive. However, in the last two sections of this chapter, we outline how the same methodology can be used to develop prescriptive or supportive tools for software project management.

Problem-Framing

The aim of this step was to identify a set of general framing questions needed to structure the interviews performed in the next step. These questions concerned the main decision variables involved in choosing the "right" life cycle model. The framing questions have been designed starting from the literature analysis. On this basis a framework describing variables considered relevant to the final choice of the life-cycle has been constructed. This framework was then presented to some of the company's project managers and developers to be validated and integrated before being employed in the interview phase. Project managers' and developers' suggestions were collected and used to refine the framework, whose final version is depicted in Figure 2. Given the way it has been constructed, one can look at this framework as a sort of collective representation of the problem of choosing the right life-cycle model, though very general, unspecific and approximate.

Framework variables have been grouped into three main clusters:

a) Organizational variables concerning resource availability for the project, investments, manager and team commitment, leadership of the project managers, and organizational culture;
b) Customer-related variables such as requirements, concerns for costs, quality, time, and visibility of changes, i.e., customer perception that his/her requests have been recognized and satisfied through actual changes in the product;
c) Process variables related to production such as team competencies, maintenance, relationships with the customer, and the possibility of further development.

Clusters have been obtained through two steps. In the first step an initial classification was proposed by the authors on the basis of meanings that the considered variables usually assume in the literature. The proposed classification was then refined through developers' observations and suggestions. Moreover, it emerged that each cluster represented a dominant point of view shaping the way each interviewee perceives and looks at the problem. In other words, among the interviewees, some developers empha-

Figure 2. Variables influencing the choice of life cycle model according to team perception

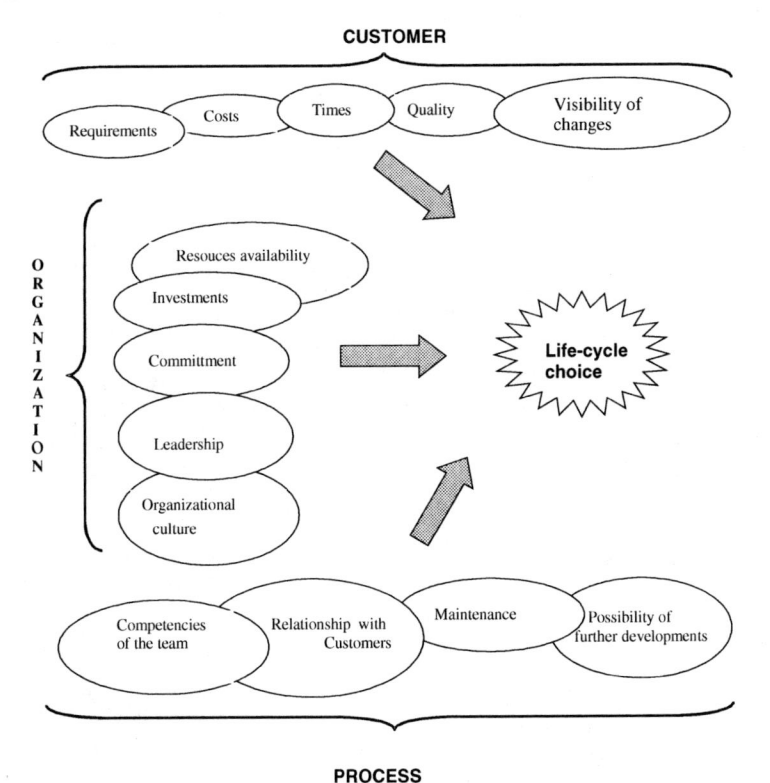

sized more the customer-related cluster, others seemed more concerned about process, while a third group paid more attention to organizational constraints.

Elicitation

The project manager and four team members were separately interviewed in on-site meetings over two months. Framing questions were used to structure the interview. The framework in Figure 2 was presented at the beginning of the interview as a means of stimulating and triggering the discussion. Each interview, whose duration was on average about two hours, was taped and transcribed.

Interviews were aimed at eliciting explanatory relations among concepts provided by software developers such as concepts' explication (e.g., "What does quality mean to you?"), causal relationship: (e.g., "How do individual and team competencies influence project development?"), actions and/or decisions justification (e.g., "How do you cope with high risk when choosing priorities?"), and values and personal beliefs driving actions and choice ("How important is it for you to 'have the control?'"). Interviews developed dynamically through interaction. The interviewer asked participants to explain opinions and beliefs, and to develop arguments until a satisfying level of detail was achieved.

Coding

Interview coding was completed in two steps according to the documentary coding method (Wrightson, 1976), using a concepts dictionary to assemble and identify explanatory relationships between concepts. This method was slightly modified and generalized to code explanatory relationships, which do not express solely causal influence but also justification and concept clarification.

In the first step, relevant concepts were identified and listed; a detailed description of their meaning as emerging from the interview was provided for each concept. Examples of concept descriptions appearing in the dictionary are reported in Table 1.

In the second step the interview text was carefully analyzed to identify and list explanatory relationships linking two or more concepts. For example, in one case, the interviewee underlined the importance of requirements understanding and specifications as follows:

> "Requirements are a fundamental variable: they represent 'what you need to do.' […] If requirements are ambiguous, as often it is the case, you need to create an effective channel to communicate and interact with the client. This usually means spending money and time. A possible outcome of a successful interaction is the reduction of a requirement, that is a reformulation of the customer request that is both able to satisfy his/her needs and is technically clear and feasible. […] A requirement reduction may imply success for a project. Summing up, understanding a customer's needs has a definite contribution on the quality perception of the customer."

Table 1. Part of a Concept Dictionary Drawn From One of the Interviews

Control: set of activities needed to manage project's development. Dimension: can be assessed in terms of project's estimated duration in days/months/years. Flexibility: capability to develop product that are easy to modify and adapt to customer's requests that may arise during project development. Quality: perceived performance, usefulness, measure of "what must be done." Relationship with customers: needed to make ambiguous requirements expressed by customers, as clear as possible. Customers can be more or less easy to manage ... in any case it is necessary to establish a communication channel. Requirements: represent "what you need to do," what the company must deliver to the customer, and this may or not be always made explicit by the customer itself. Requirements reduction: is the possibility to reformulate customer's requests that is both able to satisfy his/her needs and technically clear and feasible. Sometimes reduction means requirements simplification, in other cases it may imply requirements dropping. Risk: risk may arise from an under-qualified team with little or no experience or from huge dimension of a project or from scare familiarity with new technologies. Team: work group and its competencies. Technology: tools for development. Time: it can be a requirement for the customer or time to market. Visibility of change: represents the possibility to customize the product on the basis of customer's request.

It is easy to recognize in this quotation the definition of some concepts such as "requirements," "requirement reduction," as well as several explanatory relationships that were coded in the following format A -> ex -> B, where ex stands for "explain" and can be read as A explains B, B because A, A is a reason for B to occur, A is (a better) way to say B, A (may) influence B, A (may) cause B. Examples contained in the quotation above are as follows:

Ambiguous requirements –ex–> Create a channel with the client

Create a channel with the client –ex–> Spending time and money

Successful interaction –ex–> requirement reduction

A list of explanatory relationships can be reported on the coding sheet where additional information can be added concerning the location in the text, additional notes aimed at further describing the relationships or reporting emphasis added by the interviewee, and links to other items in the list, as shown in Table 2.

Results

The mapping step may be carried out in a direct way from the results of the coding step whenever text analysis and synthesis have been extensively and carefully performed. Given the coding results, mapping means essentially to assemble the several explanatory relationships that emerged from the coding through the well-known graphical representation of causal maps. It is important to remark that mapping concerns relationships such as A causes B, A influences, B, A has an impact on B, and so on. Explanatory relationships state influence between two concepts.

In Figure 3 an example of a causal map elicited from the interviews is presented. The minus sign on the arches between two concepts represents negative influence.

Table 2. Example of coding sheet

Location	Explanatory relationship	Note	Links
P1r3	Ambiguous requirements –ex–> Create a channel with the client	Provide justification for action Channel as a metaphor for finding a possible way of interaction	P1r5
P1r5	Create a channel with the client –ex–> Spending time and money	Customer may be "hard", i.e., it may be difficult to interact and work with them, to speak their same language	P1r3

Observing the map in Figure 3, it is possible to recognize as input variables project dimension, skilled team (competencies), degree of access to technology, standardization (versus customization) and ambiguous requirements. These variables are perceived as sort of basic ingredients for the project success and as constraints usually beyond the scope of developers' control. On the other hand, control procedures and relationships with the customer are considered the variables developers can actually have a certain degree of control over, to have a positive impact on final results such as delivery time, costs, and product's performance.

Through a software tool (Decision Explorer), a quantitative analysis of the concepts' relevance contained in the map of Figure 3 was performed. Relevance was evaluated through domain and centrality analysis.

The domain analysis gives an indication of the complexity of the linkages around concepts. The centrality analysis gives an indication of the influence of a concept in the wider context of the map. The rationale behind domain analysis is that concepts representing "key issues" will be highly elaborated, and consequently the algorithm assigns to key concept a high domain score equal to the number of incoming and outgoing links.

Centrality analysis is complementary to domain analysis in that it looks beyond the immediate environment around the concept and examines the complexity of links at a

Figure 3. Causal map example

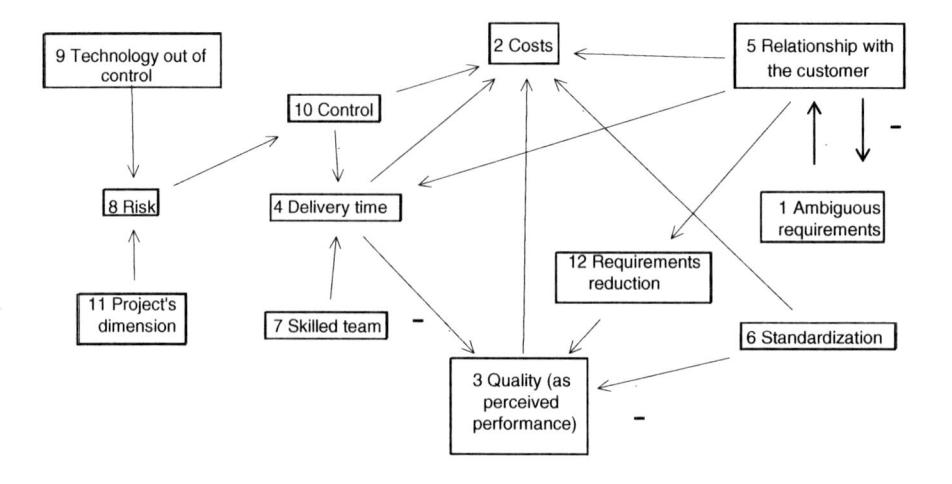

number of levels away from the center. The centrality analysis evaluates the capability of a given concept "C" to influence other concepts belonging to the same map by calculating a score increasing with the number of other concepts directly and indirectly influenced by "C." Table 3 contains the results of domain and centrality analysis.

Individual Map Comparison

The same procedure of coding and mapping was applied to each interview collected in the field analysis. Centrality and domain analysis were performed for each map. The aim of this step was to compare individual perceptions of the problem to identify the consensus level among developers belonging to the same team. Consensus can be assessed with respect to three main aspects: problem framing, meaning, and concept relevance.

a) Problem framing: By examining the structure of the collected maps, a high degree of homogeneity appeared, in terms of map overall structure, input and output variables, and connections among concepts (see Figures 3 and 4). Dominant and recurring issues are: ambiguity of the requirements, team competencies, concerns about scheduling and delivery time, and project dimensions. Other concepts such as the customer's role and the need to manage customer relationships appeared only in two maps out of five. The project manager's map appeared to be slightly more complex and rich in feedback and the relationships between concepts. Customer-related concepts play a major role only in the project manager map, whereas the developers' maps appear to be more concerned with scheduling, project dimensions, and delivery time.

b) Concept meaning: By analyzing the concept dictionary attached to each map it is possible to identify convergence and discrepancies in the meaning attached to each concept by different developers. In the considered case, though a high level of consensus has been achieved in defining the overall framework of Figure 2, there were differences across the team members' concept meanings in some cases.

Table 3. Results of domain and centrality analysis of the causal map depicted in Figure 3

Top 4 concepts importance according to the priority declared by the interviewee	Top 4 concepts obtained from the domain analysis	Top 4 concepts obtained from the centrality analysis
Requirements Costs Delivery time Quality	Costs (5 links around) Delivery time (5 links around) Relationship with customer (4 links around) Quality (as perceived performance)	Delivery time (7 of 11 concepts) Costs (7 of 11 concepts) Control (6 of 11 concepts) Relationship with customer (6 of 9 concepts)

Figure 4. Causal maps from interviews with two software developers

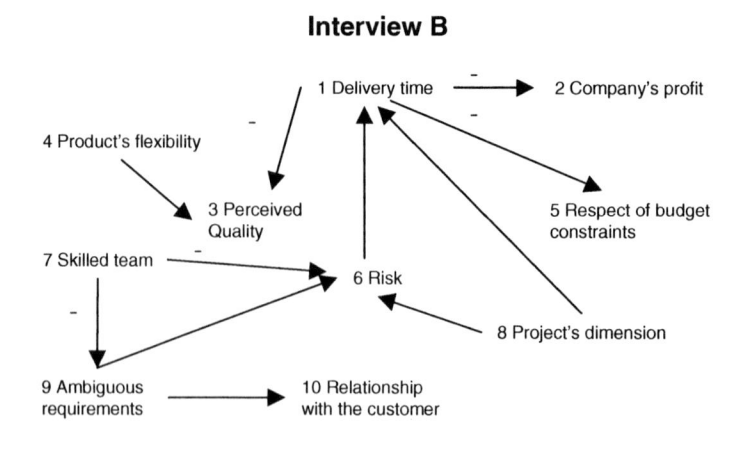

Interview B

Interview C

Table 4 contains a description of the meanings attributed by each interviewee to the main concepts. Summing up, the main discrepancies in meaning that emerged from the explanation analysis involve the following concepts: quality (for the customers), relationships with the customers, and requirements.

c) Concept relevance. The main differences in the importance of variables, that emerged from the centrality and domain analysis concern delivery time and, again, quality. Table 5 reports a comparison between the five interviewees concerning concept relevance as obtained from interviewee's declaration, domain and centrality analysis. Note that Table 5 shows a certain degree of homogeneity for concept relevance.

Numeric weights were assigned to concepts through an importance indicator calculated on the basis of the domain and centrality analysis according to the following rule: the

Table 4. Differences and similarities in concept meaning as emerged from interviews analysis

Concepts	Interview A	Interview B	Interview C	Interview D	Interview E
Requirement	What has to be done to accomplish customer's request	Client's desire or intention both formally and informally expressed	Customer's request	Customer's request	How the customer formalizes the request
Quality	- performance - usefulness	- faultiness level (quality measures, imperfections) - quality manual, software documentation - quality of the organization and of the development process	- easy to maintain software, - easy to read software - few errors, well documented - easy to use product - customer care	- delivery time - software robustness	- availability of all product's functions for the customers, - well documented software for each development phase - adequate level of technological sophistication - optimization - durable quality
Time	- completion time as a performance parameter for the customer - time to market	- delivery time	- delivery time	- delivery time	- delivery time
Relationship with the customer	- level of interaction, communication channel, - keep into account of interaction on the level of trust in the company perceived by the customer	NA	NA	NA	- Requirements identification and refinement
Visibility of changes	possibility to customize the product on the basis of customer's request, also customer care	NA	NA	NA	NA
Team	Competencies	NA	NA	Team working	Competencies Conflict
Risk	- inadequate skills - tight scheduling - available budget	- inexperienced team - project dimensions - new activities - new technologies	- ambiguous requirements - project dimensions	- low quality product - inadequate skills	- tight budget - underestimation of resources and time

importance of a given concept increases with: i) the score in centrality analysis, ii) the score in domain analysis, and iii) the number of interviewees that consider the given concept relevant. By applying such a rule, the weights contained in Table 6 were obtained. The procedure to calculate importance weights contained in Table 6 is the following:

1) calculate domain and centrality scores, respectively d_{ij} and c_{ij} for the i-th concept in the j-th interview;
2) calculate normalized domain and centrality scores d'_{ij} and c'_{ij};
3) calculate the concept weights w_i through the following equation

$$w_i = 1/2 \sum_{j=1,...,n} d'_{ij} + 1/2 \sum_{j=1,...,n} c'_{ij}$$

where n is the number of interviews and $c'_{ij}, d'_{ij} = 0$ if concept i-th does not appear in the interview j-th;
4) normalize the w_i to obtain concept importance.

Table 5. Differences and similarities in concept relevance

	Interview A	Interview B	Interview C	Interview D	Interview E
Top four relevant concepts as declared in the interview	-Requirements -Costs -Time -Quality	-Requirements -Time -Competencies -Costs -Quality	-Requirements -Time -Costs	-Requirements -Time	-Requirements -Time -Costs -Relationship with the customer -Competencies -Quality
Top four relevant concepts as emerged from domain analysis	- Costs - Time - Quality (perceived performance) - Relationship with the customer - Control - Risk	-Time -Risk -Requirements -Quality -Competencies	- Budget flexibility - Risk - Team - Requirements - Time	-Requirements -Quality	-Requirements -Time -Costs -Quality -Project fragmentation -Competencies
Top four relevant concepts as emerged from centrality analysis	- Time - Risk - Costs - Control	- Risk - Time - Requirements - Dimension - Competencies	- Budget flexibility - Risk - Requirements	-Requirements -Time	- Project fragmentation -Quality -Budget -Time -Requirements -Competencies

Table 6. Concept importance calculation

Requirements	21%
Costs	17%
Time	20%
Quality	10%
Risk	17%
Relationship with the customers	2%
Competencies	8%
Dimension	5%

Data Validation

Validation of the results was carried out in two steps. First, the coding and mapping steps were performed independently by each member of the research team for the same interview. Coding and mapping results were then compared, discussed and homogenized with the research team. A research report containing the results was sent to the interviewees and discussed with each of them separately. The aim of the discussion was to verify if the interviewees recognized in the map an adequate representation of their ideas. The concepts dictionary was validated in the same way.

Furthermore, a subsequent group discussion of the results was organized to construct a shared dictionary of the concepts in which each concept was defined as trying to include or improve individual contributions.

Implications for Decision Support

A Simple DSS For Life-Cycle Selection

In this section we examine the issue of how to employ the results obtained from the analysis presented in the previous section to develop a simple DSS for the problem of life-cycle selection. In particular results emerging from the analysis were integrated into a DSS for life-cycle selection adapted from McConnell's approach (McConnell, 1996). McConnell's approach is based on the definition of a selection matrix $S = [s_{ij}]$ reported in the Appendix.

The table allows software project managers to compare a set of alternative development models reported in the matrix columns with respect to a set of evaluation criteria reported on the rows. Life-cycle models that are reported in the table can be well-known models drawn from the literature or customized models developed by a company thanks to its know-how and past experience. The same applies for evaluation criteria whose list can be modified and integrated depending on the context of the application.

The value s_{ij} is a verbal evaluation assessing the capability of the model j-th to satisfy the i-th criterion. Such evaluations are the result of the analysis of the strengths and weaknesses of each model. The set of judgments contained in each column can be considered the description of the ideal case in which the corresponding life-cycle model should be used. For example, one should use the spiral model if: a) requirements and architecture are very ambiguously defined, b) excellence in reliability, large growth envelope, and capability to manage risks is requested, c) respect for an extremely tight predefined schedule is not required, d) overhead is low, and e) the customer needs excellent visibility on progress.

McConnell suggests that decision-makers evaluate a given project according to the criteria contained in the table and then select the alternative that best fits the characteristics of the specific project.

Starting from the Appendix table and using the results obtained from the field analysis, a simple tool to support decision-makers in the selection of the most suitable life cycle was built. The developed tool allows its users to define a selection matrix, to add life-cycle models and evaluation criteria, and to establish weights for evaluation criteria. The input and output interface of the DSS are illustrated in Figure 5.

To identify the best life cycle for a given project, users are asked to evaluate each criterion by assessing the characteristics of the project through a Likert scale ranging from one to five. In the example shown in Figure 5 the evaluator is saying that for the given project, the capability of the life-cycle model to cope with a poor definition of requirements and architecture should be poor to average, the capability to ensure high reliability should be excellent, etc. The user is also required to assign weights representing criteria importance expressed as a percentage and then normalized. The algorithm then calculates a score for each model stored in the selection matrix representing the distance between the profile of the considered project described in terms of the evaluated criteria and the ideal profile corresponding to each model. Consequently, the model to which the lowest score is assigned should be selected as the best one for the given project. In the example

Figure 5. Input output interface of a DSS for life cycle selection

Evaluation criterion	Evaluation	Weights
Works with poorly understood requirements	2	20%
Works with poorly understood architecture	2	5%
Produces highly reliable systems	5	15%
Produces system with large growth envelope	5	5%
Manages risks	5	8,0%
Can be constrained to a predefined schedule	5	2%
Has low overhead	4	14,0%
Allows for midcourse corrections	4	15,0%
Requires little manager or developer	4	12,0%
Provides customer with progress	5	3%
Provides management with progress	5	1%

1= poor 2= poor to average 3= average 4= average to excellent
5= excellent

100%

Waterfall	Evolutionary	Spiral
1,92	1,65	1,24

On the basis of your judgements, the best life cycle model For your project is	Spiral model

shown in Figure 5 the numbers 1.92, 1.65 and 1.24 represent the distances between the profile of the given project described in the column "evaluation" and the profiles of, respectively, the waterfall the evolutionary prototyping and the spiral model as contained in the selection matrix. On the basis of such results the best choice is the spiral model.

Causal Map Analysis For DSS Improvement

The analysis of causal maps helps in improving the meaningfulness and the reliability of the DSS presented above. The in-depth analysis performed through causal maps can help companies to elicit unshared knowledge at the individual- as well as at the team-level that may be potentially useful. Such knowledge can be discussed and analyzed through the methodology presented in this chapter. Eventually, outputs of the analysis can be integrated into decision support tools described above in the following way:

a) construction of a better (i.e., richer and more complete) definition of evaluation criteria: concept dictionary analysis and group discussion can help researchers identify evaluation criteria on the basis of the experience of developers through the integration of different points of view; existing criteria can be updated and new criteria can be added as new experience is gained;

b) reduction of ambiguity of evaluation criteria meaning: comparison of individual maps and the dictionary can be used to identify possible discrepancies in meaning attribution to a same evaluation criterion by different developers; as shown in the examples presented in the fifth section, this situation can occur frequently. Through the methodology presented in the fourth and fifth sections, those discrepancies can be elicited; different interpretation can be integrated into more comprehensive ones, while incoherence and conflicts can be analyzed and discussed in depth. Analysis through discussion and self-reflection increases knowledge sharing, people's involvement, and the participation of team members in the decision-making process concerning project development;

c) assessment of criteria relevance through calculation of weights representing criteria importance: quantitative analysis of causal maps permits the estimation of criteria importance through weights that are more reliable than weights expressed in a direct way since they take into account concept relevance in the considered domain of analysis and causal patterns between them.

Evaluations can be expressed by the project manager or through a group discussion. It is also possible to implement multi-person aggregation algorithms to collect separately and aggregate opinions of different experts. Evaluation sessions can be stored in a database and re-used in similar situation according to a case-based reasoning approach (Schanck, 1986; Kolodner, 1991), with *ex post* comments about the validity of the choice made. Through time the conjoint application of causal mapping and DSS can allow companies to store knowledge and past experiences that can be continuously revised and updated.

Conclusions and Implications: Knowledge Management through a Cognitive Approach

The adoption of formal methodologies for software development contributes to substantially improve software development projects in terms of both efficiency and effectiveness. Nevertheless, such methodologies are often perceived as constraining and limiting developers' knowledge and capabilities. As a consequence, promised benefits are not achieved if developers resist their adoption. This chapter shows that an investigation of the development process in its early stage from a cognitive point of view can:

a) reduce the degree of resistance through involvement and consensus policy in the choice phase;
b) help to identify in advance multiple meanings and interpretations used by team members and possible conflicts arising from such differences;
c) enrich team knowledge and competencies through multiple interpretations;

d) resolve differences and possible divergences through internal discussions or through training initiatives;

e) provide team members a deeper knowledge, higher visibility of the process and a higher level of awareness of the problems in a specific development process.

As outlined in the introduction of this chapter, by eliciting and mapping individual knowledge, the methodology shows how it is possible to:

a) Identify critical factors that impact the success of new projects;

b) Compare different individual interpretations represented through causal maps concerning the meaning and the importance of choice variables, to verify the existence of overlapping perceptions, shared beliefs and conflicting interpretations;

c) Analyze individual knowledge and use the results of such analysis for the design of more effective decision support tools for software life cycle selection.

Critical factors are elicited through interviews and then represented through causal maps.

The concept dictionary contains the description of the meaning of each variable. Centrality and domain analysis help to identify the most critical and recurring issues as perceived by team members. Finally, individual map comparisons permit us to identify those factors that have different and divergent meanings according to different individuals. Therefore one may say that critical factors are such because of their relevance, and because of the presence of several, multifaceted and/or conflicting individual interpretations.

Representing developers' discourse through causal maps provides analysts with an immediate tool to compare how individuals frame a same problem, and how complex and articulated is the structure of their reasoning in the given context of analysis. The number of concepts, number and kind of connections, and low or high presence of feedback are structural characteristics that are easy to identify in causal maps. Difference in relevance of a concept can be calculated through centrality and domain analysis. The comparison of different concept dictionaries can help to identify differences in meaning.

Finally, the analysis of individual knowledge obtained through causal maps can be used to improve the design of DSS in software development as shown in this chapter. The basic idea is to integrate the formal and explicit knowledge contained in a DSS with human expert knowledge, which is usually situated, highly contextualized, unshared and tacit. Through the proposed approach this could be done in several ways (e.g., by adding new evaluation criteria, new life-cycle models, by redefining criteria weights, or by merging different individual interpretations into more complete and richer definition of criteria's meaning).

At a first level of intervention, the in-depth analysis carried out using causal mapping can be used to improve the reliability and meaningfulness of the system, as shown in the case of McConnell's approach. At a more sophisticated level, the use of causal mapping can be considered as a fundamental step in the cognitive approach to knowledge management in software development. Actually, what causal mapping can help to do is to elicit and model expert knowledge to construct formal and manageable representations of individual knowledge. Such representations can be used for descriptive purposes and analyzed to improve the design of formal decision support tools. What really matters is that from this perspective decision support tools can be conceived as open platforms which can be continuously revised, updated and enlarged through knowledge elicitation and mapping, as individual and organizational knowledge gradually increase thanks to new experience and know-how. For instance, a simple tool like McConnell's table could be transformed into a knowledge base for a DSS by storing knowledge over time (e.g., adding new evaluation criteria, new development models, by revising weights and reformulating meaning of evaluation criteria).

A remarkable advantage offered by causal mapping is that knowledge elicitation and mapping is actually obtained through a strong involvement of employees and managers. This brings about many advantages not strictly related to decision support issues such as:

a) people's involvement may increase employee motivation;
b) companies gaining more knowledge about how things go on in their organization, i.e., they can investigate the theory-in–use and detect possible discrepancies with the organizational espoused theory contained in formal procedures, documentation and organizational charts (Argyris & Schon, 1978);
c) divergent or conflicting interpretations can be elicited and analyzed;
d) group discussions can allow team members to have an occasion to reflect on their problem framing and to compare their opinions and cognitive schemata and attitude with other team members;
e) improvements in training and learning can be obtained.

Lessons Learned

The methodology and the case study presented above can be further discussed to highlight both conceptual and theoretical implications for knowledge management and learning in knowledge-intensive organizations, as well as in terms of practical implications for the management of software projects.

Theoretical Contribution: Causal Maps as Tools To Investigate Organizational Learning

In the proposed approach, the emphasis is on the problem-setting stage in the decision-making process when managers must identify key issues and alternative evaluation approaches for the development of a new software project.

This stage can be investigated through the analysis of formal processes used by the organization for life-cycle selection (espoused theory following Argyris and Schön's terminology) and the actual way in which the selection is implemented (theory in use). The espoused theory and the theory-in-use do not always coincide and it is important to understand the reasons for such a discrepancy. Describing the espoused theory, explicit by definition, and the theory-in-use, very often tacit and not easy to formalize, means to map the organizational knowledge employed by the organization in the life-cycle selection process.

Knowledge engineering approaches (Schreiber et al., 2000), causal mappings and studies on organizational cognition (Weick, 1976, Huff, 1990, Eden & Ackermann, 1996) can offer theoretical as well as methodological contributions to support organizational knowledge mapping.

From this perspective, life cycle selection, as any organizational evaluation, is a product of the organizational knowledge, here intended as the combination of formal espoused theories and idiosyncratic situated theories in use. If the analysis of official organizational procedures can shed light on the espoused theory, causal mapping can help to elicit the theory in use and, at least to certain extent, to evaluate how and in which sense it differs form the espoused theory.

An in-depth analysis through causal maps can help to elicit the theory in use, very often only partially shared and more or less tacit, to compare different theories in use, and to incorporate such knowledge into formal tools, such as DSS, and procedures, in other words into the espoused theory.

When this occurs one might accept that an organization has updated its knowledge, i.e., organizational learning has occurred. Even if issues such as what is organizational learning, how and if it actually happens, etc., are largely debated and questioned in the literature, the contribution to such a debate advanced in this chapter and offered as reflection for the reader is that causal maps can be a methodological tool to investigate organizational learning, especially in knowledge-intensive organizations such as software companies.

In particular, the process of software development, involving an intense level of decision-making activity both at the individual as well as at the organizational level, can be investigated within this framework. For instance, the selection of a life-cycle model and the way through which such choice occurs is actually influenced by the existing theory-in-use and the espoused theory about "how to develop the project given certain constraints."

Summing up, the methodological implications deriving from such a theoretical perspective can be condensed in terms of the following recommendations:

a) both the theory-in-use and the espoused theory about how the organization makes a decision should be analyzed;

b) theory-in-use can be elicited and analyzed through causal maps by asking people to explain how they usually make a decision, which variables influence their choice, what is the meaning of these variables, etc.;

c) useful implications for the design of the "right" selection method can be drawn from such an analysis.

Managerial Implications

Increased reliability/meaningfulness for decision support tools and organizational analysis, and self-reflection can be considered as the added value obtainable through a cognitive approach to knowledge management in software development. It is quite straightforward to maintain that the methodology proposed in this chapter, by combining a cognitive approach with a decision-support system orientation, can help organizations in facilitating or enabling knowledge elaboration and creation. With reference to the well-known Nonaka and Takeuchi terminology (1995), the proposed methodology can contribute to achieve this result through the following mechanisms:

a) Knowledge socialization through group discussion;
b) Knowledge externalization through causal maps;
c) Combination of implicit knowledge contained in interviews and explicit knowledge contained in manual, procedures and DSS;
d) Internalization, through self-reflection.

Group discussion for data validation and comparison facilitate individual knowledge sharing and hence knowledge socialization (causal maps can also be constructed through a group interview — an approach not tempted in this chapter). Interview coding and mapping help knowledge externalization through the formal representation obtained with coding sheets, concept dictionaries, and above all causal maps. Combination can be favored by integrating results from different sources of explicit knowledge such as existing DSS, formal methodologies for software development and new explicit knowledge contained in individual causal maps, and group maps could also be constructed by combining individual knowledge. Finally, causal maps facilitate internalization in two ways. First, by allowing an individual to analyze formal representations of their problem-framing and problem-solving strategies, maps play a reflexive function inducing individuals to actively reflect and re-evaluate their ways of thinking with respect to a specific context of action. Second, once elicited knowledge is integrated into a new DSS, it is then critically reviewed and applied by individuals in everyday practice.

Acknowledgements

The authors wish to thank Valerio Teta and Mario Capaccio for their support in the field analysis and for their suggestions and collaborations during analysis of the results, and Vincenzo D'Angelo who participated in the field research. The authors also wish to thank the anonymous reviewers for their valuable suggestions and contributions.

Copyright © 2005, Idea Group Inc. Copying or distributing in print or electronic forms without written permission of Idea Group Inc. is prohibited.

Notes

Even though the paper is the fruit of the collaboration of the authors, in this version, Sections 2, 4, 5 and 6 are by Luca Iandoli, Sections 1 and 3 are by G. Zollo, and the rest is work common to both the authors.

References

Allison, G. (1971). *Essence of decision explaining the Cuban Missile Crisis.* Boston, MA: Little Brown.

Argyris C., & Schon D.A. (1978). *Organizational learning. A theory of action perspective.* Reading, MA: Addison-Wesley.

Axelrod, R. (Ed.) (1976). *Structure of decision: The cognitive maps of political elites.* Princeton, NJ: Princeton University Press.

Blackler, F. (2002). Knowledge, knowledge work and organizations. In C.W. Choo and N. Bontis (Eds.), *The strategic management of intellectual capital and organizational knowledge.* Oxford: Oxford University Press.

Boar, B. (1984). *Application prototyping.* New York: Wiley and Sons.

Boehm, B. (1988). A spiral model for software development and enhancement. *Computer*, 5, 61-72.

Boehm, B. (1981), *Software engineering economics.* Englewood Cliffs, NJ: Prentice Hall.

Boehm, B., & Basili, V. (2000, May). Gaining intellectual control of software development. *IEEE Computer*, 27-33.

Booch, G., Jacobson, I., & Rumbaugh, J. (1999). *The unified software development process.* Reading, MA: Addison-Wesley.

Bradac, M., Perry D., & Votta, L. (1994). Prototyping a process monitoring experiment, *IEEE Transactions on Software Engineering*, 10, 774-784.

Brown, J., & Duguid, P. (1991). Organizational learning and communities-of-practices: Toward a unified view of working, learning, and innovation. *Organization Science*, 2(1), 40-57.

Calori, R. (2000). Ordinary theorists in mixed industries. *Organizational Studies*, 6, 1031-1057.

Capaldo G., & Zollo, G. (2001). Applying fuzzy logic to personnel assessment: a case study. *Omega*, 29, 585-597.

Choo, C.W. (1998). *The knowing organization.* Oxford: Oxford University Press.

Choo, C.W., & Bontis, N. (2002). *The strategic management of intellectual capital and organizational knowledge.* Oxford: Oxford University Press.

Crozier, M. (1964). *The bureaucratic phenomenon.* London: Tavistock.

Cyert, R., & March, J.G. (1963). *A behavioral theory of the firm.* Englewood Cliffs, NJ: Prentice Hall.

Daft, R.L., & Weick, K. (1984). Toward a model of organization as interpretation systems. *Academy of Management Review*, 2, 284 - 295.

Davis, F. (1989). Perceived usefulness, perceived ease of use and user acceptance of information technology. *Management Information Systems Quarterly*, 13, 318-339.

Eden, C., & Ackermann, F. (1992). The analysis of causal map. *International Journal of Management Studies*, 29, 310-324.

Fletcher, K.E., & Huff, A.S. (1990). Argument Mapping. In A.S. Huff (Ed.), *Mapping strategic thought*. Chichester: Wiley and Sons.

Gainer, J. (2003). *Process improvement: The capability maturity model.* Retrieved from the World Wide Web at: http://www.itmweb.com/f051098.htm

Galambos, J.A., Abelson, R.P., & Black, J.B. (1986). *Knowledge structures.* Hillsdale, NJ: Lawrence Earlbaum.

Huff, A.S. (Ed.) (1990). *Mapping strategic thought.* Chichester: Wiley.

Humphrey, W.S. (1989). *Managing the software process.* Reading, MA: Addison-Wesley.

Jones, C. (1991). *Applied software measurements.* New York: McGraw Hill.

Kosko, B. (1992). *Neural networks and fuzzy systems.* Englewood Cliffs, NJ: Prentice Hall.

March, J.B. (1988). *Decisions and organizations.* Oxford: Blackwell.

Matson, J., Barret B., & Mellichamp, J. (1994). Software development cost estimation using function point. *IEEE Transactions on Software Engineering*, 4, 275-287.

McClure, C. (1989). *CASE is software automation.* Englewood Cliffs, NJ: Prentice-Hall.

McConnell, S. C. (1996). *Rapid development: Taming wild software schedules.* Redmond, WA: Microsoft Press.

Mintzberg, H., Raisinghani, D., & Theoret, A. (1976). The structure of "unstructured" decision processes. *Administrative Science Quarterly*, 21, 246-274.

Nelson, K. M., Nadkarni, S., Narayanan, V. K., & Ghods, M. (2000). Understanding software operations support expertise: A causal mapping approach. *Management Information Systems Quarterly*, 24, 475-507.

Nicolini D., & Meznar, M.B. (1995). The social construction of organizational learning: conceptual and practical issues in the field. *Human Relations*, 7, 727-746.

Nisbett, R., & Ross, L. (1980). *Human inference: Strategies and shortcomings of social judgement.* Englewood Cliffs, NJ: Prentice Hall.

Nonaka, I., & Takeuchi, H. (1995). *The knowledge creating company.* Oxford: Oxford University Press.

Paulk, M.C., Curtis, B, Chrissis, M.B., & Weber, C.V. (1993). Capability *maturity model for software version 1.1,* Report CMU/SEI-93-TR-24, Software Engineering Institute, Carnegie Mellon University, Pittsburgh, PA.

Pfleeger, S.L. (1999). Understanding and improving technology transfer in software engineering. *Journal of Systems and Software*, 47, 11-124.

Pressman, R.S. (2000). *Software engineering: A practitioner's approach*, 5th edition. New York: McGraw-Hill.

Putnam, L., & Myers, W. (1992). *Measures for excellence*. New York: Yourdon Press.

Quinn, R.E., and Cameron, K.S. (1983). Organizational life cycles and shifting criteria and effectiveness. *Management Science*, 9, 33-51.

Riemenshneider C.K., Hardgrave, B.C., & Davis, F.D. (2002). Explaining software developer acceptance of methodologies: a comparison of five theoretical models. *IEEE Transactions on Software engineering*, 12, 1135-1145.

Schank, R.C. (1986). *Explanation patterns: Understanding mechanically and creatively*. Hillsdale, NJ: Lawrence Erlbaum.

Schank, R.C., & Abelson, R.P. (1977). *Scripts, plans, goals and understanding, an inquiry into human knowledge structures*. Hillsdale, NJ: Lawrence Erlbaum.

Schreiber et al. (2000). *Knowledge engineering and management. The CommonKADS methodology*. Cambridge, MA: MIT Press.

Simon, H.A. (1961). *Administrative behavior* (2nd ed.). New York: Macmillan.

Thagard, P. (1992). *Conceptual revolution*. Princeton, NJ: University Press.

Thompson, R.W., Higgins, C.A., & Howell, J.M. (1991). Personal computing: Toward a conceptual model of utilization. *Management Information Systems Quarterly*, 15(1), 125-134.

Tversky, A., & Kahneman, D. (1974). Judgement under uncertainty. *Heuristics and Biases, Science*, 185, 1124-1131.

Von Neumann, J., & Morgestern, O. (1953). *Theory of games and economic behavior*, Princeton, NJ: Princeton University Press.

Walsh J.P., & Ungson, G.R. (1991). Organizational memory. *Academy of Management Review*, 1, 57-91.

Weick, K.E. (1976). *The social psychology of organization*, 2nd edition. Reading, MA: Addison Wesley.

Wrightson, M.T. (1976). Documentary coding method. In Axelrod, R. (Ed.), *Structure of decisions: The cognitive maps of political elites*. Princeton, NJ: Princeton University Press.

Yourdon, E. (1988). *Managing the system life cycle*. Englewood Cliffs, NJ: Prentice-Hall.

Zadeh, L. (1973). Outline of a new approach to the analysis of complex systems and decision processes. *IEEE Transactions on Systems, Man and Cybernetics*, 35-48.

Zollo, G. (1998). Cognition, words and logic: How fuzzy logic can help us to design new organizational procedures. Accepted for presentation at the *Academy of Management Meeting*, San Diego, August.

Appendix

Table for the Selection of Life-Cycle

Lifecycle model capability	Pure Waterfall	Code & fix	Spiral model	Modified Waterfall	Evolutionary Prototyping	Staged Delivery	Evolutionary Delivery	Design-to-Schedule	Design-to-Tools	Commercial Off the Shelf Software
Works with poorly understood requirements	Poor	Poor	Excellent	Fair to Excellent	Excellent	Poor	Fair to Excellent	Poor to Fair	Fair	Excellent
Works with poorly understood architecture	Poor	Poor	Excellent	Fair to Excellent	Poor to Fair	Poor	Poor	Poor	Poor to Excellent	Poor to Excellent
Produces highly reliable systems	Excellent	Poor	Excellent	Excellent	Fair	Excellent	Fair to Excellent	Fair	Poor to Excellent	Poor to Excellent
Produces system with large growth envelope	Excellent	Poor to Fair	Excellent	Excellent	Excellent	Excellent	Excellent	Fair to Excellent	Poor	N/A
Manages risks	Poor	Poor	Excellent	Fair	Fair	Fair	Fair	Fair to Excellent	Poor to Fair	N/A
Can be constrained to a predefined schedule	Fair	Poor	Fair	Fair	Poor	Fair	Fair	Excellent	Excellent	Excellent
Has low overhead	Poor	Excellent	Fair	Excellent	Fair	Fair	Fair	Fair	Fair to Excellent	Excellent
Allows for midcourse corrections	Poor	Poor to Excellent	Fair	Fair	Excellent	Poor	Fair to Excellent	Poor to Fair	Excellent	Poor
Provides customer with progress visibility	Poor	Fair	Excellent	Fair	Excellent	Fair	Excellent	Fair	Excellent	N/A
Provides management with progress visibility	Fair	Poor	Excellent	Fair to Excellent	Fair	Excellent	Excellent	Excellent	Excellent	N/A
Requires little manager or developer sophistication	Fair	Excellent	Poor	Poor to Fair	Poor	Fair	Fair	Poor	Fair	Fair

Adapted from McConnell (1996)

Section IV

Potential Directions

Chapter XIV

Object-Oriented Approaches to Causal Mapping:
A Proposal

Robert F. Otondo
The University of Memphis, USA

Abstract

Comparing, contrasting, and collectivizing causal maps provides a useful way for extending representations of individual-level cognitions to an organization-level of analysis. Carrying out these processes can be tricky, however, because the terms used to denote nodes within causal maps are often so terse that important nuances and meanings critical to linking or distinguishing the espoused beliefs of multiple individuals may not be faithfully represented. Previous efforts in causal map research are extended by representing these linguistic and semantic nuances in associative, categorical, or other cognitive maps, then using those maps to link related elements of causal maps. These multiple types of cognitive maps are then integrated in a logical view (i.e., class and object structures) of a graph-theoretic, object-oriented design.

Introduction

Causal maps represent the network of causal relations embedded in an individual's explicit statements, and as such provide an explicit representation of the deep-rooted cognitive maps of individuals (Huff, 1990; Nelson, Nadkarni, Narayanan & Ghods, 2000).

While causal maps provide a concise representation of an individual's beliefs and assumptions about causality, that conciseness often fails to represent important nuances in complex beliefs and assumptions that are crucial to extending individual causal maps to an organization-level of analysis. These nuances in word use can lead to the same term being used to represent different ideas, different terms being used to represent similar ideas, or a host of words changing and emerging within a vocabulary over time as individuals share beliefs. These patterns of word use create difficulties in the comparison of individual causal maps, and suggest that while a causal map may be sufficiently "rich" to represent causal beliefs at the individual level of analysis, collections of individual causal maps do not adequately represent the richness of the problem space of social causal cognition.

The purpose of this chapter is to provide frameworks for representing important nuances in language use during social causal cognition, and to embed those frameworks in group- and organization-level causal maps. These goals will be accomplished through two objectives. First, an overall strategy for mitigating the representational limitations of causal maps will be presented. This strategy augments collections of causal maps with other representations of the cognitive, communicative, and behavioral aspects of knowledge sharing. This family of representations, collectively called cognitive maps, is a general class of physical representations of thoughts and beliefs that can represent individual assertions, or those elicited from a group (Huff, 1990; Montazemi & Conrath, 1986). Cognitive maps can provide a rich resource for comparing, contrasting, or collectivizing large numbers of causal maps. Causal maps are only one sub-class of cognitive maps. Other sub-classes of cognitive maps include such representations as categorical maps that focus on relationships of similarity and associative maps that represent frequencies and changes in word use (Huff, 1990).

The second objective of the chapter is to provide a design for a tool that can seamlessly acquire, store, and manipulate multiple cognitive maps. This is a tall order because augmenting causal maps with various types of cognitive maps would significantly increase the computational complexity of processing causal maps. Computer-based information systems are a likely candidate for this tool because they have been successfully used in the past for problem spaces of similar complexity.

The chapter is organized as follows. First, difficulties of using causal maps at the social level of analysis are examined. Second, alternative high-level designs for a computer-based tool that are commensurate to the characteristics of cognitive mapping are proposed and discussed. This discussion is then extended to a more detailed description of data and functional elements necessary for the proposed computer-based tool. Finally, conclusions, limitations, and potential applications are discussed.

Representing Causal Beliefs at Social Levels of Analysis

Causal maps were originally designed to represent an individual's beliefs about causal relationships between entities in the real world. There are several reasons why these representations of individual cognition might contribute to our understanding of social cognition. Perhaps the simplest reason is that a comparison of causal maps from different individuals is useful for identifying similarities and differences in causal beliefs from across an organization, thus providing measures of an organization's cognitive homogeneity (Laukkanen, 1994). Causal maps are also useful for documenting changes in co-workers' causal beliefs over time, therefore providing a means for analyzing the processes of belief sharing and organizational learning (Langfield-Smith, 1992). A third reason lies in the hope of identifying feedback loops and organization-wide effects, which could help mitigate "vicious circles" and unintended effects (Morecroft, 1988; Senge, 1990; Senge & Sterman, 1992; Eden, Ackermann & Cropper, 1992). These various processes for using individual causal maps to represent and understand social causal cognition are called, for the purposes of this chapter, social causal mapping.

Social Causal Mapping Across Diverse Vocabularies

While comparing, contrasting, and collectivizing causal maps can play important roles in understanding social cognition, these processes are often problematic because the terms, words, and phrases elicited from subjects revealing their causal beliefs can be difficult to match. Unlike the systems dynamics models of engineered physical systems that reflect modules interconnected via well-defined interfaces described in more-or-less standardized nomenclatures (e.g., Forrester, 1961), collections of causal maps are representations of individual cognitive belief systems that typically reflect a wide variety of experiential, cultural, contextual, and procedural knowledge domains and related vocabularies. This complexity is especially evident in knowledge management systems, and is embodied within Davenport and Prusak's (1998) differentiation of knowledge (i.e., "a fluid mix of framed experience, values, contextual information, and expert insight that provides a framework for evaluating and incorporating new experiences and information" from data (i.e., "a set of discrete, objective facts about events") and information (i.e., data that "informs," that "makes a difference"). These differences, Davenport and Prusak argue, require that knowledge management projects encompass a wider set of behavioral factors, including the motivation of trust, communication, encouragement, and rewards.

Comparing, contrasting, and collectivizing diverse causal maps under these circumstances is typically complex, especially when the terms used in the nodes of causal maps are terse distillations of complex beliefs. Past research has usually addressed this complexity in one of two ways. One approach unifies the interpretations and terms embedded within causal maps into a "standard" vocabulary in which one word is chosen to represent a group or category of synonyms. An example of this approach is displayed in Figure 1. That example is based on the ways an organization can mitigate risk, and expanded into how those perceptions might be conceptualized and asserted by two individuals. Such mental concepts are represented as nodes, which typically bear the name of that item or concept (e.g., "risk" and "loss of data"). Causal relationships between nodes are represented by solid arcs in which the node at the "tail" of the arc is a determinant of the node at the "head" of the arc. Arcs representing causal relationships are typically valued as "+" or "-" to denote whether the arc represents a directly or inversely proportional relationship, respectively. Arcs representing categorical relation-

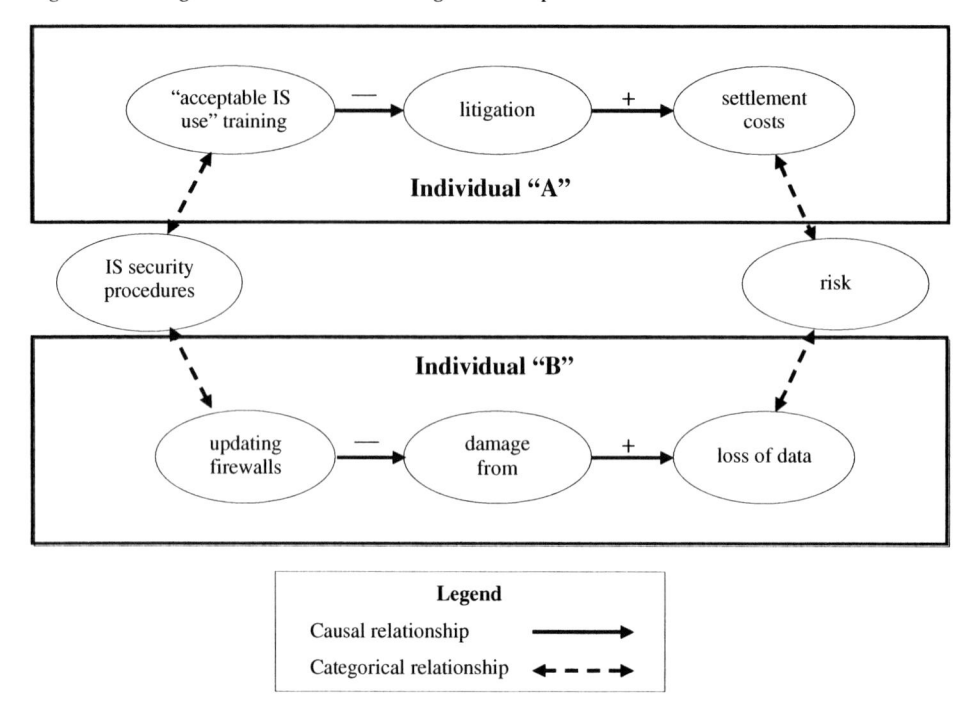

Figure 1. Integrated causal and categorial maps

ships do not need plus and minus signs. For the purposes of this chapter, categorical relationships are represented by two-headed dashed arcs (←--→) that signify the nodes so linked are co-members of a set of synonyms. Figure 1 contains two sets of synonymous terms: one set refers to hazards of organizational life (i.e., risk, settlement costs, and loss of data), while the other refers to the protection of information systems (IS) (i.e., IS security procedures, "acceptable IS use" training, and updating firewalls).

Another method for comparing, contrasting, and collectivizing diverse causal beliefs relies on multiple group interview sessions. In this approach, all participants meet together at one or more times, and one or more collective causal maps are drawn up to represent the "products of [their] collective cognitions" (Langfield-Smith, 1992). Thus, a collective causal map can document single or multiple group interviews. The degree of shared beliefs is often represented with dotted and hatched areas (Figure 2). Causal beliefs elicited from individuals within these group meetings can be conceptualized as sets, in which each individual's causal map is represented as a distinct set. Each individual causal map is then represented within a circle of a Venn diagram. Shared beliefs among group participants are represented as intersections between the circles of individual causal map sets (Figure 2). Multiple collective causal maps, each documenting one group session, can show changes in the use and understanding of specific terms as well as in general levels of shared beliefs. This approach to collective causal mapping places the responsibility of establishing word meanings on participants, not researchers.

Another approach to collectivizing raw individual maps relies upon generalized terms, typically drawn from academic theory or disciplines, as a basis for interpreting and/or translating idiosyncratic causal assertions into a common language (e.g., Narayanan & Fahey, 1990; Laukkanen, 1994). While useful, such references and interpretations should be recorded to maintain the integrity of the original causal assertions and to document interpretation, translation, and learning processes over time.

Representing Diverse Vocabularies in Social Causal Mapping

Unfortunately, these approaches have suffered from shortcomings in the representational powers of causal maps. That is, causal maps may be "good enough" to represent causal beliefs at the individual level of analysis, but they have significant limitations in representing the linguistic and temporal aspects of the underlying beliefs, knowledge, and learning processes that play important roles in collectivizing large numbers of causal

Figure 2. Collective beliefs (extended from Langfield-Smith, 1994:328)

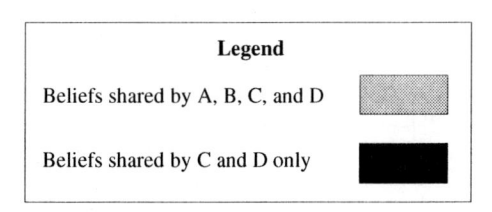

maps at the group and organization levels of analysis. One limitation results from individuals who use different terms for the same concept (i.e., synonyms). Another limitation results from the use of the same term for different concepts (i.e., connotations). Such differences have been found to lead to disagreements over appropriate descriptions of particular ideas. Similar difficulties arise when individuals have not developed "a sufficiently comprehensive body of shared language" or cannot agree on "the most appropriate language with which to describe a particular idea" (Langfield-Smith, 1992). Moreover, these concepts and word uses may change over time as the individuals learn about the environment around them, presenting additional difficulties in relating causal maps elicited across long periods of time. The nuances of human language and thought and the idiosyncrasies in the styles and rates of individual learning make it difficult to compare the causal assertions of multiple individuals over time and thus construct collective causal maps (Langfield-Smith, 1992).

Linguistic, learning, and other social phenomena may not be properly considered when causal maps are simply linked together. That approach treats node and arc elements as (in the words of Boland, Tenkasi & Te'eni, 1994) "unproblematic, predefined, and prepackaged" rather than "subjective" and "interpretive," and ignores the need to "provide the conditions for surfacing and challenging important assumptions..., for complicating their thinking...and for enabling significant change when it is required." To adequately represent the linguistic and learning dimensions of the social causal reasoning problem space, collections of causal maps should exhibit characteristics of "good" representations. "Good" representations exhibit the following characteristics (Winston, 1984):

1. "make the important things explicit"
2. "expose natural constraints, facilitating some class of computations"
3. "are complete...[they] say all that needs to be said [about the problem space at hand]"
4. "are concise"
5. "are transparent" (i.e., easy for users to understand)
6. "facilitate computation...[they] can store and retrieve information rapidly"
7. "suppress details" unless requested
8. "are computable by an existing process"

Causal maps exhibit many of these aspects in representing individual causal reasoning. They are explicit, concise, and relatively transparent. However, they are not so good at representing social causal reasoning. They do not explicitly reveal nuances in human language and cognition, which are important considerations in the social construction of meaning. It is also difficult to represent opposing views of causality within a single causal map. This means that a single causal map cannot represent this important feature of social learning. This limitation also limits the computational power of causal maps in understanding multiple node-arc-node segments or feedback loops (i.e., multiple node-arc-node segments that form a chain that returns to the point of origin, thus creating a "loop").

Fortunately, there are other types of cognitive maps that more fully represent the linguistic, temporal, and conceptual dimensions of the problem space of social causal cognition. Again, the term cognitive map refers to a general class of maps that represent cognition, understanding, and beliefs, of which causal maps are only one type. Other types of cognitive maps that can assist in social causal mapping include categorical cognitive maps showing how concepts and words are related linguistically across vocabularies and knowledge domains. Associative maps describe patterns of word use, such as those found through content analysis. Argument cognitive maps represent an individual's assumptions, evidence, and reasons that underlie beliefs. Collections of cognitive maps are thus better able to meet the requirements of "good" representations.

Long-term collections of categorical, associative, and other cognitive maps can facilitate deeper insight into how organization members reason and develop patterns of causal belief over time, and provide important tools for making the representation of social causal thinking more complete. Thus, collections of cognitive maps are better though nonetheless imperfect representations of the problem space of social causal cognition. Descriptions of cognitive maps and related terms are summarized in Table 1.

Representing Social Causal Cognition with Information Technology

The use of multiple types of cognitive maps can address issues of representational completeness in social causal cognition, but unfortunately that approach exacerbates the already challenging problem of analyzing large numbers of causal maps. Processing large numbers of causal maps is difficult enough. For example, Axelrod (1976) found that

Table 1. Definitions

Term	Definition	Source
Argument Map	Represents assumptions, evidence, and reasons that underlie beliefs.	Huff (1990).
Assertion	An individual's statement concerning their thoughts or beliefs about the world, environment, etc.	Axelrod (1976).
Associative Map	Inventories concepts and their complexities, and describes patterns of word use.	Huff (1990).
Cognitive map	A general class of physical representations of thoughts or beliefs. These maps can represent individual assertions, or those elicited from a group.	Huff (1990); Montazemi and Conrath (1986).
Causal map	A sub-class of cognitive maps that focuses on the representation of causal beliefs; a network of causal relations embedded in an individual's explicit statements, an explicit representation of the deep-rooted cognitive maps of individuals.	Huff (1990); Nelson, Nadkarni, Narayanan, and Ghods (2000).
Categorical map	A sub-class of cognitive maps that focuses on relationships of similarity (e.g., a map linking word synonyms).	Huff (1990).

elite foreign policy decision makers "employ rather large structures in presenting their images of their policy environment," citing three maps whose sizes were 31 nodes and 43 arcs, 53 nodes and 84 arcs, and 73 nodes and 116 arcs. Analyzing dozens of similarly sized causal maps is a daunting task. This problem would be exacerbated by including association, categorical, argument, and other cognitive maps into such analyses.

Set-Theoretic Representations of Causal Mapping

The increased computational complexity of the social causal mapping problem space requires a concurrent increase in the representational power of the corresponding information system. Accordingly, Winston's (1984) characteristics of "good" representations (i.e., make important things explicit, expose natural constraints, completeness, etc.) can be applied to information systems representing cognitive maps, just as they have been applied to cognitive maps representing human cognition.

While computer programs have been available for some time to create and evaluate individual causal maps, most of those systems store individual maps in separate files whose contents are not easily integrated. This shortcoming severely restricts their use for social causal mapping. Other information systems that have been used to represent cognitive maps are set-theoretic relational databases, i.e., those based on the axioms and mathematical theories about sets (Codd, 1970). Such databases exhibit many of the characteristics of "good" representations: they are explicit about their important features (e.g., the membership relationship between an element and a set) and clear about their constraints (e.g., they cannot express operations that produce transitive closure over binary relations) (Ullman, 1988). They are also concise, transparent, efficient, and abstract (i.e., details can be hidden unless requested). Some processes (e.g., inventorying organizational knowledge) can be addressed efficiently via set-theoretic algorithms similar to those now employed in some knowledge management systems, e.g., "knowledge Yellow Pages" (Davenport & Prusak, 1998).

Unfortunately, set-theoretic approaches do not fully reflect the graph-theoretic nature of causal and other cognitive maps. That is, the relationships between elements in set-theoretic approaches correspond to membership in a set, while those in graph-theoretic approaches correspond to one element "pointing to" another. For example, determining the shortest path between two non-adjacent nodes in a causal map cannot be done with set-theoretic approaches because set theory does not represent the logic necessary to travel across—or traverse—multiple node-arc-node segments. This limitation is important because it restricts the types of analysis that can be performed (i.e., it contradicts the representational requirement for the existence of computational procedures). These analyses include: tracing paths along multiple nod-arc-node segments, summing the effects of a series of direct and inverse relationships, and identifying feedback loops. These graph-theoretic procedures cannot be performed efficiently—if at all—by set-theoretic relational databases on long series of node-arc-node segments. Differences between set and graph theories are summarized in Table 2.

Table 2. Set theory versus graph theory

Characteristic	Set Theory	Graph Theory
Relationships between elements	Based on membership in a set	Based on one element "pointing to" another
Pictorial representations	Venn diagrams	Directed graphs, workflow diagrams

Examples of computer programs	Relational databases
	  Oracle®,
	  Microsoft® Access)
	Query languages such as SQL
		Work-flow simulation programs
		  Vensim®
		  Arena®
		Object-oriented languages
		  Java
		  C++
		Some object-oriented languages (e.g., Java) can be written to draw data from relational databases.

Graph-Theoretic Representations of Causal Mapping

Computer-based systems designed upon graph-theoretic representations and algorithms (Smith & Smith, 1977a, 1977b; Ullman, 1988) are a more promising approach. The cognitive maps in Figure 1 can again serve as an example. The map in Figure 1 represents assertions from two individuals about their conceptualizations and perceptions of risk. Since it contains the causal assertions of multiple individuals, it can be considered as a social causal map. Consider the problem of identifying and comparing the individuals' causal assertions between IS security procedures and risk. The traversal algorithm must identify two and only two paths of node-arc-node chains:

1. IS security procedures ←--→ "acceptable IS use" training ──⁻→ litigation ──⁺→ settlement costs ←--→ risk

2. IS security procedures ←--→ updating firewalls ──⁻→ damage from virus attacks loss of data ←--→ risk

where ←--→ represents synonymous (i.e., categorical) relationships, ──⁺→ and ──⁻→ represent causal relationships of direct and inverse proportionality, respectively.

Graph theory facilitates the analysis of cognitive maps because it has long supported the development of algorithms that can efficiently and effectively travel across the repetitive "node-arc-node" structures of graphs (i.e., node-arc-node-arc-node-arc-node-etc.). Other programs can build upon these traversal algorithms to assess the total effects of chains of node-arc-node segments. For example, a computer program can be developed to support the query whether two individuals agree if IS security procedures and risk are directly or inversely proportional (e.g., the parallel paths 1 and 2 above). The program can be conceptualized as follows: 1) use a traversal algorithm to identify parallel node-arc-node chains between IS security procedures and risk, regardless of whether the arcs are causal and linguistic (i.e., word categorical); 2) sum the "+" and "-" values of the causal arcs in iterative fashion during traversal; and 3) compare the sums of causal values of the two paths. If the two final sums are equal, the individuals share the same belief. If the final two sums are unequal, the individuals have contradictory beliefs.

The previous discussions about social causal reasoning and mapping in Sections 2 and 3 can be summarized in the three following design criteria:

1. Social causal mapping systems must represent the multiple types of cognitive maps that reflect social causal cognition.
2. Social causal mapping system must integrate and process large numbers and many types of cognitive maps that will result from working with large numbers of organization members.
3. Social causal mapping system should retain the maps in such a way that incompatibility problems within and between long-term storage units are eliminated.

These three design criteria should be met in the context of providing "the conditions for surfacing and challenging important assumptions..., for complicating their thinking...and for enabling significant change when it is required" (Boland et al., 1994).

Enhanced Representation of Cognitive Maps: An Object-Oriented Approach

The directed cause-and-effect structure of causal maps is more consistent with graph-theory than with set theory. Relational databases, being based on set theory (Codd, 1970), are thus ill-suited to the task of representing the complexity of causal mapping. Object-oriented systems, on the other hand, are better suited because of four major elements of object-oriented modeling: abstraction, encapsulation, modularization, and hierarchy.

Abstraction

Abstraction is perhaps the most important element in object-oriented development. Abstraction has been defined in many ways, but perhaps the most succinct is a "selective emphasis on detail" (Shaw, 1984). Abstraction is particularly useful in IS analysis and design because many of the problem spaces faced by IS professionals are complex and messy, and abstraction allows the analyst to subdivide a complex problem into workable segments. Abstraction facilitates this strategy by permitting the analyst to focus on those facets of the problem segment that are important, and ignore those that are not. In the domain of social causal mapping, abstraction permits the designer to focus on one type of cognition at a time (e.g., causal assertions or linguistic relationships between words) and to derive specifications based on that type of reasoning for its corresponding cognitive map. One particular form of abstraction, called aggregation, is particularly useful in social causal mapping because it supports compositional views of nested objects (i.e., nodes and arcs are nested within feedback loops, which in turn may be nested within a collection of individual causal maps).

Encapsulation

The second element of object-oriented modeling, encapsulation, refers to "the process of compartmentalizing the elements of an abstraction that constitute its structure and behavior" (Booch, 1994). The notion of "compartmentalization" means that only those details that are necessary to interact with the "compartment" are visible to outside entities. Non-essential details are hidden from view. In this way, encapsulation not only facilitates representational conciseness, transparency, and efficiency, it also enhances data integrity within the program because objects can interact only according to strictly enforced rules and interfaces, and cannot access variables and values that are internal to (i.e., encapsulated within) another object. In addition, encapsulation is not bound to any particular sort of processing theory. Unlike relational databases that are limited to set-theoretic algorithms, object-oriented programs are free to incorporate a variety of algorithms that correspond to the processing requirements of causal mapping. One set of algorithms that are particularly important for cognitive map analysis is graph-theoretic algorithms. Encapsulating these algorithms within an object supports many processes relying upon the traversal of node-arc-node segments, a process that is exceedingly difficult—if not impossible—with set-theoretic algorithms.

Modularization

The third element of object-oriented modeling is modularization. Modules serve as "the physical containers" in which the abstractions and encapsulated compartments are stored (Booch, 1994). This concept directly impacts designers and implementers of IS-based social causal mapping systems because it gives them a useful means for partitioning the data and information into an orderly, integrated fashion. This element is particularly important to causal mapping, because in the past causal maps of individuals and groups have been stored in separate physical files that were difficult to integrate. These physical limitations have created significant barriers to understanding social causal cognition over large numbers of individuals and long time frames. The design and implementation of compatible modules can overcome these past barriers, thus facilitating research in social causal cognition.

Hierarchy

The fourth element is hierarchy, "the ranking or ordering of abstractions" (Booch, 1994). Hierarchies of abstractions—whether they concern structure, behavior, or both—facilitate transparency and conciseness by allowing the user or designer to focus on one level of abstraction at a time. For example, all cognitive maps are directed graphs made from nodes and arcs. A hierarchy of abstractions permits the designer to focus on one of many levels of the representation problem (e.g., designing representations for nodes and arcs versus designing algorithms that trace node-arc-node chains across the causal maps from multiple individuals). Hierarchy, like encapsulation, facilitates the orderly development of representational complexity. This orderly development not only assists in the design, implementation, and maintenance of software tools for causal mapping, it also allows designers to integrate the various types of cognitive maps. Integration can be achieved because the causal, categorical, and other cognitive maps share a common structure (i.e., node-arc-node segments) that allow them to be linked together in a unified and analyzable fashion (e.g., as in the example IS security procedures $\leftrightarrow$ updating firewalls $\xrightarrow{-}$ damage from virus attacks loss of data $\leftrightarrow$ risk, where $\leftrightarrow$ represents synonymous (i.e., categorical) relationships, and $\xrightarrow{+}$ and $\xrightarrow{-}$ represent causal relationships of direct and inverse proportionality, respectively).

The four elements of abstraction, encapsulation, modularization, and hierarchy will now be used to describe the abstract problem space (i.e., the logical model) for a social causal mapping system. In object-oriented analysis and design, those elements involve abstractions and their interrelationships which are then described in terms of object and class structures. A summary of descriptions of abstraction, encapsulation, modularization, and hierarchy is provided in Table 3 for convenience. Readers desiring more in-depth descriptions of those elements are referred to works such as Booch (1994).

Table 3. Object-oriented concepts for social causal mapping

Concept	Definition	Application to Causal Mapping
Abstraction	The emphasis of details that are relevant and the suppression of those that are not (Shaw, 1984:10). "The essential characteristics of an object that distinguish it from all other kinds of objects" (Booch, 1994:511)	Common characteristics of causal, categorical, and other maps can be generalized within a common framework (a "super-class" such as CognitiveMap); aids design and implementation of software for multiple kinds of cognitive maps.
Encapsulation	The separation of an object's interface from its implementation (Booch, 1994:513).	Provides independence of cognitive map types.
Hierarchy	"A ranking or ordering of abstractions" (Booch, 1994:514).	Hierarchies exist in the several ways. Aggregations form hierarchies based on fundamental objects used to construct higher-order objects (e.g., maps built from nodes and arcs). Taxonomies of classes can be formed from sub-class and super-classes (e.g., cognitive maps are subdivided into causal, categorical, and other maps).
Inheritance	The ability of super-classes to impart their data and method structures to their sub-classes	Promotes re-use of design structures, thus enhancing efficient program coding and consistency of design across the software and information system; helps ensure that important general structures and methods are not forgotten in the implementation of specialized sub-classes.
Modularization	"A unit of code that serves as a building block for the physical structure of a system" (Booch, 1994:516).	Modules describing individual or collective causal maps should be compatible; that is, data and information from one module should be easily accessed by another module.

Object Structures for Social Causal Mapping

The problem space of social causal mapping centers on the use of individual causal maps to represent and understand social causal cognition. Representing this problem space involves a variety of abstractions, ranging from lower-level views of the constituent components of cognitive maps (e.g., nodes and arcs) to higher-level aggregations of individual maps (e.g., a chain of node-arc-node segments describing a chain of causality drawn from the assertions of multiple individuals). These abstract structures and their behaviors constitute examples of object structures of a logical model.

Object structures are often based on a compositional, or "part of" architecture, such as that found in an automobile composed of an electrical system, a power system, an air conditioning system, and so forth. In turn, the electrical system is composed of a fuse system, a wiring system, and a battery system. The power system is composed of an engine, a fuel system, a lubrication system, and a cooling system. This compositional architecture also applies to causal and other cognitive maps. Like an automobile, a causal map can be viewed as a single object and as an integrated system of component parts. Just as automobiles can be envisioned as a composition of an engine, brakes, wheels, headlights, etc., so too can causal maps be envisioned as a composition of nodes and arcs. Social causal maps can be envisioned as a composition of individual causal maps (e.g., Figure 2), or as a composition of cognitive maps (Figure 1).

This compositional view is called aggregation, "an abstraction which allows a relationship between named objects to be thought of as a (higher-level) named object" (Smith & Smith, 1977a). Compositional views of object structure are typically designed according to varying levels of granularity within the problem space of social causal mapping. At the fundamental level, "fine-grained" objects representing nodes and arcs are aggregated into higher-level "coarse-grained" objects (e.g., causal, categorical, or associative maps) that represent an integration of the individual's assertions about his or her thoughts and beliefs. In turn, these individual cognitive maps can be organized into still higher-level aggregations, such as the linking of segments of cognitive maps from multiple individuals, where "relevant" may encompass entire cognitive maps, or if need be, only those portions that meet a specific characteristic (e.g., those that form a path between two nodes of interest). The object's granularity (i.e., its breadth and scope) is determined largely by the issue at hand and the way the users have framed that issue within the problem space.

Object structures can be described in terms of their data structure and methods. These two descriptions will now be explored in greater detail, particularly in regard to the way in which they support information technologies for social causal mapping.

Data Structures for Social Causal Mapping

Data structures provide the means for storing information about critical elements of a problem space. In causal maps, nodes represent such things as physical items or mental concepts, and are typically described with the name of that item or concept. Arcs represent assertions about causal relationships between nodes. They have a distinct "head" and "tail," wherein the "head" of the arc points to the node that is influenced by the node at the "tail" of the arc. Arcs are typically valued as "+" or "-" to denote whether the arc represents a directly or inversely proportional relationship, respectively. These various characteristics (e.g., node names, arc directions, arc "+" or "-" values) are outlined in data structures, in that the data structures provide blueprints for the construction of data storage.

Data structures should also contain information to help users of social causal mapping systems obtain deeper understandings of causal assertions. This information could include the contributors' names, contact information (e.g., e-mail address and phone number) and their departments. It may even include references to simulations or other decision models that contributors used to develop or justify their beliefs, or to diverse media files such as text, graphs, pictures, audio, and/or video (Boland et al., 1994). Such information, when contained in or referenced by the object data structures within a social causal mapping system, can facilitate organizational learning and knowledge management when they are designed to link concise abstract knowledge elements embodied in causal maps to the rich "fluid mix of framed experience, values, contextual information, and expert insight" of their organizational participants. The addition of data structures storing contributors' names or identification numbers can implement this linkage, thus allowing collections of causal maps to "map" the organizational knowledge "terrain." The use of such labels requires that members within that terrain must be allowed to contribute knowledge freely and with sufficient confidence so that they will willingly attach their names or employee identification numbers to their contributions. Then and only then can the chain of cognitive patterns, contributing individuals, and their rich tacit knowledge be reliably forged into a useful knowledge management tool.

For social causal maps to be an effective organizational learning tool, the information about those maps and their contributors must be available for long-term use. In object-oriented modeling, this concern is called object persistence (i.e., how the objects are stored over time). Most cognitive mapping tools available today typically store this information in modularized but non-integratable files (usually graphic). This approach creates difficulties in analyzing large numbers of social causal maps and the social cognitions they represent. The proposed social causal mapping system differs from other mapping approaches by stipulating an inclusive, comprehensive system of storage whose components can be integrated regardless of the time, place, or individuals from whom they were elicited. This goal of comprehensive storage can be achieved with a design that enforces the way new cognitive maps are added to the system. Objects can be stored in one or more long-term structures and media as long as the data and information within those structures and media are integratable with the rest of the proposed system.[1]

Methods for Cognitive Mapping Systems

Causal maps, and the other cognitive maps that can augment their collectivization, represent important organizational knowledge. This knowledge can be quite useful in addressing a variety of organizational problems, including those associated with the analysis, design, implementation, and maintenance of information systems (e.g., improving customer service, reducing costs, or streamlining business processes). The causal assertions of organizational members thus form an important but complex part of organizational memory.

The potential size and complexity of creating, manipulating, storing, and retrieving large numbers of cognitive maps demands the use of a computer-based information system. Software components within such a computer-based information system can be employed by the user to manipulate object structures in a variety of social causal mapping activities. These components, called methods, can be used to construct and destroy nodes and arcs, update and maintain data within data structures, traverse chains of node-arc-nodes, calculate the total effects of node-arc-node chains (e.g., $xyz = x\ z$), and retain cognitive maps in long-term storage. A more generalized collection of functions for organizational memory information systems (OMIS) has been identified by Stein and Zwass (1995). Their collection contains five sets of functions that should be applicable to social causal mapping systems because such systems are a form of organizational memory. These five sets will now be described and adapted to the design of methods providing similar functionalities for social causal mapping.

Mnemonic Functions

Mnemonic functions address the "acquisition, retention, maintenance, search, and retrieval of information" and knowledge (Stein & Zwass, 1995). These functions are typical of most kinds of information systems. However, retention warrants some discussion here because of problems that have resulted from the way in which causal maps have been retained in the past. Retention refers to the way in which nodes, arcs, and related data should be placed in long-term storage. In the past, individual cognitive maps have been stored primarily through segregated graphic files. Such files have been difficult to merge, and often require extensive use of "copy and paste" procedures. Retention design also affects the design of maintenance functions: in a multi-user system, maintenance functions must be secure so that contributors are prevented from modifying the maps of others. A maintenance function would have to be designed so that contributors could update and modify their cognitive maps while mitigating data inconsistencies (e.g., if a user changes the name of a node, that change would be reflected in all cognitive maps using that node). Search and retrieval should be non-problematic.

Integrative Functions

Integrative functions are designed "to ensure that the internal knowledge of the organization regarding technical issues, past decisions, projects, designs, and so on is made explicit and available for future use, complete with contexts, rationales, and outcomes" (Stein & Zwass, 1995). Internal knowledge within organizational memory can be made available by integrative functions that build chains of contiguous node-arc-node segments across the causal maps of individuals (e.g., the path $g \rightarrow m \rightarrow n \rightarrow e$ in Figure

2). When those paths contain information that can identify the individuals who have contributed their causal maps to the database, the user is given the option of locating those individuals and engaging them in rich social dialogue. Such individuals are more complete sources of knowledge than the terse nodes contained in their causal maps, and may offer more insight and flexibility than the textual, graphic, or other repositories in the organization's knowledge base.

Adaptive Functions

Adaptive functions support "boundary spanning activities to recognize, capture, organize, and distribute" environmental knowledge to organizational participants (Stein & Zwass, 1995). Examples of "boundary spanning" information that would be useful to a social causal mapping system would be external data that confirms or rejects a causal assertion (e.g., the assertion $x \xrightarrow{+} y$ is contradicted by external data showing $x \xrightarrow{-} y$). Here, "external" is a relative term, in that data could be "external" to the organization or to the department in which the contributor works.

Goal Attainment Functions

Goal attainment functions support planning and control. Goal attainment functions "help organizational actors frame and identify goal states in the context of the organizational past, store goal states, formulate strategies for achieving goal states, evaluate progress in the direction of goal states, suggest alternatives based on the evaluations, update goal states based on new information, and store annotated histories" (Stein & Zwass, 1995). Planning and control methods address relationships between the strategic, tactical, and operational variables that constitute the organization's vertical and horizontal dimensions. Accordingly, planning and control methods would match the objects and relationships among the cognitive maps of individuals of differing organizational levels. Such patterns link managerial knowledge with multiple operational domains, thus facilitating planning and control over a broad spectrum of organizational activities. As with adaptive functions, graph-theoretic databases are more capable of constructing these transitive vertical associations than relational databases.

Pattern Maintenance Functions

Pattern maintenance functions refer to those functions that help preserve and develop human resources over time (Stein & Zwass, 1995). Accordingly, these methods can generate a variety of inputs to the firm's human resources system. Perhaps some of the most important pattern maintenance functions would be those that track the added value of an individual's contributions. These functions could help answer such questions as how often the individual's cognitive maps have been accessed, how many times contributors have met with other employees to elaborate upon their contributions, and the extent to which an individual's causal maps have influenced organizational decision-making and sense-making activities. In this way, the social causal mapping system could help ensure that contributors are fairly rewarded. These reports would also be beneficial in identifying important causal maps that could be incorporated into the firm's employee training activities. Since the causal maps would be drawn from both IS personnel and their clients, the pattern maintenance functions within a social causal mapping system could help support the careers of both sets of employees.

Mnemonic, integrative, adaptive, goal attainment, and pattern maintenance functions go beyond the simple mechanistic linking of cognitive maps, i.e., the "aggregation" of causal maps (Bougon, 1992). When embedded with suggestions, rules, and procedures for understanding distributed and social cognition—such as those that ask questions challenging assumptions, or treating "human meaning" as subjective and interpretive rather than as unproblematic, predefined, and prepackaged (Boland et al., 1994)—these OMIS functions support the continuous social negotiation and enactment of the organization's social system (i.e., Bougon's 1992 concept of "congregation"). In this way, a computer-based social causal mapping system can serve as an important tool for research, practice, and organizational policy making.

Constituent Processes of OMIS Functions

Stein and Zwass' OMIS functions give a high-level description of some of the methods required of a causal mapping system. These methods can be decomposed into more fundamental processes. Research in organizational learning has long relied upon graph theory as a means of analyzing such phenomena as the cumulative effects of paths and feedback cycles and the emergent properties of causal maps (Forrester, 1961; Axelrod, 1976). These include the relationship between changes in individual cognitive maps and changes in organizational stability (Axelrod, 1976; Fiol & Lyles, 1985), and how reorganization or reengineering changes cognitive maps within the organization (Fiol & Lyles, 1985; Huber, 1991).

Concatenations of node-arc-node segments should be processable in such a way as to identify salient features of the organization's knowledge terrain. One such process is traversal. Traversal requires that elementary node-arc-node components be assembled into transitive "paths." Here, "transitive" is used in its mathematical sense (i.e., a→b→c), not in its temporal sense. The transitive nature of organizational knowledge cannot be easily represented in set theory. However, rules taking the form "if A_1 and A_2 and ... A_n are true, then B is true" (Ullman, 1988) can be used to calculate transitive closures. Such statements, called Horn clauses, can be applied when organizational memory is represented in a logical rather than a relational form. This logical form, called predicates, allows the representation of knowledge as functions mapping arguments to TRUE and FALSE values. This representation permits the identification of paths between nodes, and can identify relevant data for computing overall effects of the paths (e.g., $x \xrightarrow{+} y \xrightarrow{+} z = x \xrightarrow{+} z; x \xrightarrow{+} y \xrightarrow{-} z = x \xrightarrow{-} z$).

Traversal is often accomplished via iterative functions that typically use a relatively simple algorithm to step repetitively across node-arc-node segments. Iterative traversal functions can discover long chains of node-arc-node segments—something that is virtually impossible for causal beliefs represented in set-theoretic relational databases. However, care must be taken in the analysis of cyclic paths to avoid infinite loops. Therefore, more sophisticated algorithms—such as those that identify the existence of cyclic paths, or the shortest available path (e.g., Dijkstra, 1959)—should be applied.

Traversing a collection of causal maps can help a user identify characteristics of concatenated causal relationships between important organizational variables. For example, locating and resolving equivocalities—the existence of contradictory beliefs—is an important form of organizational learning (Weick, 1979). Equivocalities may exist in a number of forms. The simplest involves a direct contradiction between two causal beliefs (e.g., $x \xrightarrow{+} y, x \xrightarrow{-} y$). Another more complex example involves contradictory paths of concatenated causal beliefs (e.g., $x \xrightarrow{+} u \xrightarrow{+} y, x \xrightarrow{+} v \xrightarrow{-} y$). A third example can use categorical maps to locate equivocalities: the causal beliefs $x \xrightarrow{+} y$ and $x \xrightarrow{-} z$ are equivocal if there exists a categorical relation between y and z such that y = z.

Methods that encode traversal algorithms offer a means for integrating causal knowledge (represented by causal maps) with multiple vocabularies, patterns of word use, assumptions, decision models, and other aspects of reasoning represented by categorical, associative, and other cognitive maps. This integration of multiple types of representations thus increases the depth of knowledge and semantic richness of a social causal mapping system. This increased depth of knowledge may also allow users to compare their causal beliefs to information contained in other organizational knowledge repositories. The usefulness of this last approach can be demonstrated in the following comparison of individual beliefs and empirical reports. Suppose that a particular belief $x \xrightarrow{+} y$ is held by a wide number of organization members. Suppose also that the opposing belief $x \xrightarrow{-} y$ is not held by any organization member, but that an empirical report generated from the organization's data mining programs supports the interpretation $x \xrightarrow{-} y$. The contradictory interpretation $x \xrightarrow{-} y$ embodied within the empirical report is an example of causal associations generated from non-human, organizational memory.

The creation of these molecular organizational knowledge structures composed of human- and computer-generated components does not guarantee organizational learning will occur. However, it can help support organizational learning in at least two ways. First, it supplies useful raw materials for organizational learning processes, such as conflicting causal beliefs (i.e., equivocalities), undesirable feedback loops (e.g. "vicious circles"), and unintended effects (e.g., a change in one node may lead to an unwanted change in another). Second, it identifies individuals who can participate in social processes in which they may elaborate upon the richer context of that knowledge. That is, individuals who have contributed to the causal mapping system can be called upon at a later date to explain or elaborate their causal assertions.

Class Structures for Social Causal Mapping

Class structures describe the structure of the objects representing concepts, abstractions, and other items within a problem space. In other words, class structures provide blueprints for building the data structures and scripting the behaviors of objects within an object-oriented system. Class structures in the cognitive mapping domain would describe a variety of objects spanning a range of granularity. Class structures describing "fine-grained" objects serving as fundamental building blocks of a social causal mapping system would represent an individual's concepts and assertions of causality (i.e., nodes and arcs, respectively). Those fundamental class structures must also describe methods to create, store, link, dispose of, and otherwise process nodes and arcs. Higher-level class structures would describe the building of "coarse-grained" objects from "fine-grained" fundamental objects (e.g., aggregating nodes and arcs into causal maps). Methods associated with these higher-order objects would prescribe processes for analyzing large numbers of maps, such as identifying equivocalities and feedback loops within and between individual causal maps.

A thoughtful, coherent set of class structures can facilitate efficient software design and coding in many ways. Perhaps the most useful way to do so is by designing the class structures so that they integrate and cooperate with each other. This can be achieved in object-oriented design through hierarchies of interrelated classes in which commonly-used data and method structures are encoded in high-order "super-classes" that allow related lower-order "sub-classes" to re-use, or inherit, those structures. This and other applications of hierarchical classes structures will now be explored in the context of social causal mapping.

Hierarchies of Classes in Object-Oriented Design

Class hierarchies are based on what's commonly called an "is-a" relationship. Objects exhibit an "is-a" relationship with their classes, just as someone's pet dog "is-a" member of the canine family. Likewise, two classes can also be linked through an "is-a" relationship, just as a canine "is-a" type of mammal and a mammal "is-a" type of animal. "Is-a" relationships are transitive, so it can be said that a particular dog "is-an" animal.

Hierarchies of sub-classes and super-classes facilitate the creation and encoding of object-oriented software by allowing designers to conceptualize the given problem space at various levels of abstraction. This approach is similar to—but not exactly like—the common example of the taxonomies of animal species. For example, the generalized notion of "mammal" arises from the abstraction of common characteristics of groups such as lions, dogs, weasels, and humans: all are mobile, have seven vertebrae in their necks, nurse their young, and have hair. In turn, the term "animal" is a more abstract concept encompassing fish, birds, reptiles, mammals, and other mobile life forms. The abstract notions of "mammal" and "animal" are useful because they help biologists construct taxonomies that succinctly structure knowledge about related forms of life. A diagram

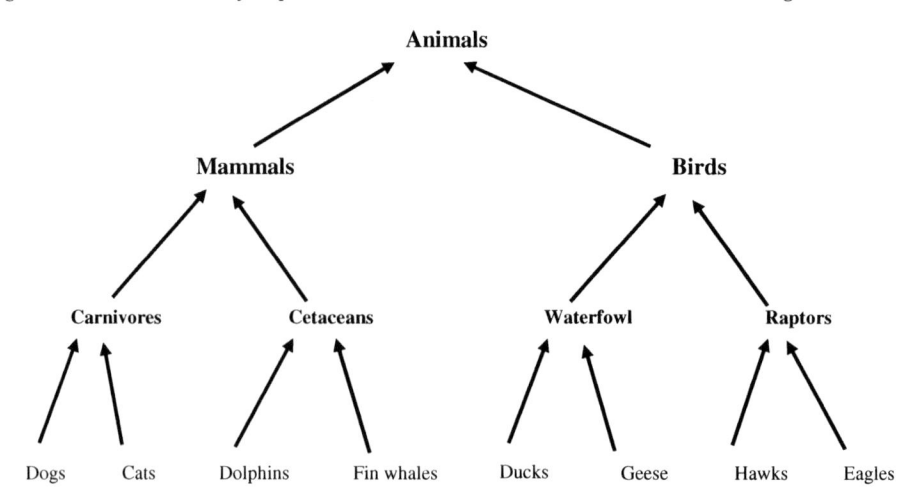

Figure 3. Hierarchies of super-classes and sub-classes in the animal kingdom

depicting a hierarchical, taxonomic structure of animal classifications is displayed in Figure 3.

Object-oriented design extends the notion of taxonomy beyond the hierarchical positioning of related groups and objects into an efficient approach to designing information systems. This approach relies upon inheritance, in which the characteristics of higher-level classes are imparted to—or inherited by—their lower-level counterparts. Inheritance is particularly helpful in object-oriented design. It promotes the re-use of design structures, thus enhancing efficient program coding and consistency of design across the software and information system. It also helps ensure that important general structures and methods are not forgotten in the implementation of specialized sub-classes.

Inheritance typically takes two steps. The first step involves grouping data structures and methods that are common to a set of classes within one class (e.g., the super-class CognitiveMap). Data structures and methods that are particular to one or more but not all members of that group are relegated to unique sub-class structures (e.g., the sub-classes CausalMap, CategoricalMap, and AssociativeMap). The second step involves identifying the relationships between a super-class and its sub-classes. This step is typically accomplished with a software statement. The Java clause "class CausalMap extends CognitiveMap" is an example of how a super-class/sub-class relationship could be identified by a software statement.

Hierarchies of Classes for Social Causal Mapping

The similarities among the data structures and methods among causal, categorical, and other cognitive maps suggest that these classes can be arranged in one or more hierarchies of sub-classes and super-classes. Three hierarchies are of immediate interest: one concerns the maps themselves (i.e., a hierarchy of cognitive maps), while two concern their constituent components (i.e., nodes and arcs).

A Hierarchy of Cognitive Maps for Social Causal Mapping

The general notion of cognitive maps can be abstracted from causal, categorical, and other similar types of representations. All are directed graphs composed of nodes and arcs, and all exhibit functionalities (i.e., encoded in their methods) that can contribute to the five OMIS functions conceptualized in Stein and Zwass (1995). It is these elements and characteristics that are common to and drawn from causal, categorical, and other related maps that are used to construct the super-class of cognitive maps (i.e., Class CognitiveMap). A diagram of these hierarchical relationships is displayed in Figure 4.

Cognitive map sub-classes (e.g., CausalMap, CategoricalMap) would inherit data and method structures delineated in Class CognitiveMap, but would also contain unique characteristics as well. For example, the Class CausalMap would contain a method to sum the "+" and "-" values in a chain of causal node-arc-node segments. Class CategoricalMap would not need that function because categorical arcs do not exhibit "+ or "-" values. Indeed, the differing natures of the nodes and arcs within the causal and categorical maps suggest that separate class hierarchies are needed for nodes and arcs. These two hierarchies are explored next.

Figure 4. Hierarchies of super-classes and sub-classes for social causal mapping

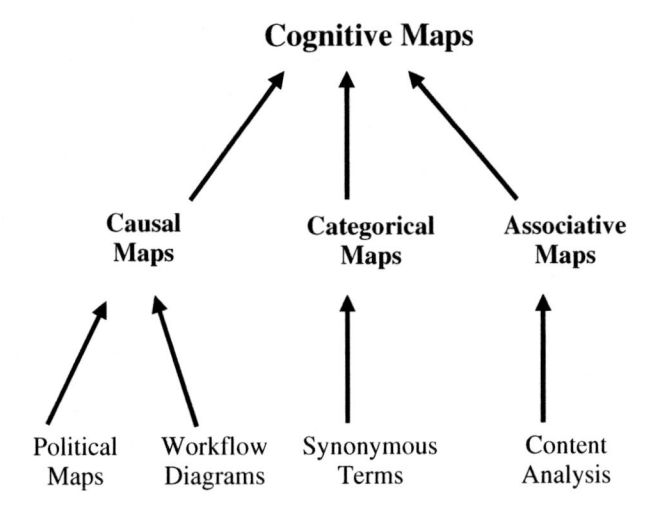

Cognitive Maps
- Causal Maps
  - Political Maps
  - Workflow Diagrams
- Categorical Maps
  - Synonymous Terms
- Associative Maps
  - Content Analysis

Hierarchies of Node and Arc Classes for Building Cognitive Maps

Hierarchies of super- and sub-classes for nodes and arcs are based on several observations about their use in cognitive mapping. One observation is that object data structures and methods of nodes tend to be quite similar in cognitive maps, but those of arcs typically differ in important ways from each other. These differences require that class structures representing the various arcs must differ accordingly. For example, the arcs used in causal maps require a value to signify whether the relationship between the head and tail nodes is directly or inversely proportional (e.g., "+" and "-"). Arcs used in categorical maps represent similarities in linguistic meaning, so no variable exhibiting "+" or "-" values is required. These differences between causal and categorical arcs require differences in their data structures and methods. Class CausalArc would require a data element for the proportionality variable and a constructor method incorporating a proportionality variable as input. Class CategoricalArc would not have these requirements.

As with cognitive maps, the use of a super-class would offer the advantages of abstraction: common data elements (e.g., variables referencing the nodes at the ends of the arc) and methods would be embedded in a super-class (e.g., Class Arc). In turn, Classes CausalArc and CategoricalArc would inherit those common characteristics.

Conclusion

Causal maps are useful but limited representations of human causal reasoning. Those limitations constrain the usefulness of collections of causal maps in understanding and promoting social causal cognition. The chapter addresses those limitations in several ways.

First, an approach based on supplementing causal maps with other types of cognitive maps was described. These cognitive maps represent many of the processes in social causal reasoning that are not represented by causal maps, such as overcoming nuances of human language and thought, surfacing and challenging the participants' assumptions, and documenting evidence from internal and external information repositories that supports or contradicts causal assertions. Simply linking individual causal maps together does not adequately represent these processes or their effects. Collections of causal, associative, categorical, and other types of cognitive maps can better represent the social processes of social causal reasoning than can causal maps alone.

The second lesson is that the information system representing the complex problem space of social causal mapping must itself be sufficiently complex. A logical model for a graph-theoretic, object-oriented social causal mapping system that is compatible with the directed graph structure of causal maps was presented. Class models were described that facilitate the incorporation of multiple, distributed types of organizational knowledge maps into complementary, coherent representations. The use of classes and encapsulated iterative traversal functions were shown to provide more complete, more complex, derivable representations of knowledge at the organizational level. These enriched representations can assist in identifying interesting patterns of variables and relationships within the organization. These traversals were shown to assist in the inventorying of organizational knowledge, as well as assist in addressing such traditional organizational learning issues as equivocality reduction. These traversals can be recorded, permitting the construction of molecular components for organizational knowledge structure representation. Traditional relational databases that rely upon set theory are not sufficiently powerful to represent social causal mapping (e.g., multiple node-arc-node traversals).

The proposed social causal mapping system can be used to support an organization's learning and knowledge management capabilities by facilitating the efficient and effective representation, construction, and integration of molecular components of organizational knowledge for the identification of interesting organization-level knowledge structures. These knowledge structures can then be used to identify contributing individuals and records that can provide the "fluid mix of framed experience, values, contextual information, and expert insight that provides a framework for evaluating and incorporating new experiences and information" (Davenport & Prusak, 1998). The proposed system may have other uses as well. For example, it could be used as a human resources tool to measure the extent to which employees contribute to learning and knowledge across the organization. This objective could be achieved by monitoring who contributes to the social causal mapping system, how often those contributions are used by others, and to what extent the contributions play a part in strategic, tactical, or operational improvements, product or service innovations, or increased organizational competitiveness.

Future work is needed before the proposed approach can be fully implemented. Classes of heuristics for the identification and manipulation of interesting components of organizational memory remain to be identified. Suitable applications of graph-theoretic algorithms remain to be tested. Object and class models for organizational knowledge structure representation must still be implemented.

References

Axelrod, R. (1976). *Structure of decision: The cognitive maps of political elites*. Princeton, NJ: Princeton University Press.

Boland, R. J., Tenkasi, R.V., & Te'eni, D. (1994). Designing information technology to support distributed cognition. *Organization Science*, 5, 456-475.

Booch, G. (1994). *Object-oriented analysis and design with applications*. 2nd edition. Reading, MA: Addison-Wesley.

Bougon, M. G. (1992). Congregate cognitive maps: A unified dynamic theory of organization and strategy. *Journal of Management Studies*, 29, 369-389.

Codd, E. F. (1970). A relational model of data for large shared data banks. *Communications of the ACM*, 13, 377-387.

Davenport, T. H., & Prusak, L. (1998). *Working knowledge: How organizations manage what they know.* Boston: Harvard Business School Press.

Dijkstra, E. W. (1959). A note on two problems in connexion with graphs. *Numerische Mathematik*, 1, 269-271.

Eden, C. S., Ackermann, F., & Cropper, C. (1992). The analysis of cause maps. *Journal of Management Studies*, 29, 309-324.

Fiol, C. M., & Huff, A.S. (1992). Maps for managers. *Journal of Management Studies*, 29, 267-285.

Forrester, J. W. (1961). *Industrial dynamics.* Cambridge, MA: MIT Press.

Huber, G. P. (1991). Organizational learning: The contributing processes and the literatures. *Organization Science*, 2, 88-115.

Huff, A. S. (1990). Mapping strategic thought. In A. S. Huff (Ed.), *Mapping strategic thought* (pp. 11-49). Chichester: John Wiley & Sons.

Langfield-Smith, K. (1992). Exploring the need for a shared cognitive map. *Journal of Management Studies*, 29, 349-368.

Laukkanen, M. (1994). Comparative cause mapping of organizational cognitions. *Organization Science*, 5, 322-343.

Lyles, M.A. (1985). Organizational learning. *Academy of Management Review*, 10, 803-813.

Montazemi, A. R., and Conrath, D. W. (1986). The use of cognitive mapping for information requirements. *Management Information Systems Quarterly*, 19(1), 44-57.

Morecroft, J. D. W. (1988). System dynamics and microworlds for policymakers. *European Journal of Operational Research*, 35, 301-320.

Narayanan, V. K., & Fahey, L. (1990). Evolution of revealed causal maps during decline: A case study of Admiral. In A. S. Huff (Ed.), *Mapping strategic thought* (pp.109-134). Chichester: John Wiley & Sons.

Nelson, K. M., Nadkarni, S., Narayanan, V. K., and Ghods, M. (2000). Understanding software operations support expertise: A causal mapping approach. *Management Information Systems Quarterly*, 24, 475-507.

Senge, P. M. (1990). *The fifth discipline.* New York: Doubleday.

Shaw, M. (1984, October). Abstraction techniques in modern programming languages. *IEEE Software*, 10-26.

Smith, D.C.P. (1977b). Database abstractions: Aggregation and generalization. *ACM Transactions on Database Systems*, 2, 105-133.

Smith, J. M., & Smith, D.C.P. (1977a). Database abstractions: Aggregation. *Communications of the ACM*, 20, 405-413.

Stein, E. W., & Zwass, V. (1995). Actualizing organizational memory with information systems. *Information Systems Research*, 6, 85-117.

Sterman, J.D. (1992). Systems thinking and organizational learning: Acting locally and thinking globally in the organization of the future. *European Journal of Operational Research*, 59, 137-150.

Ullman, J. D. (1988). *Principles of database and knowledge-base systems.* Rockville, MD: Computer Science Press.

Weick, K. E. (1979). *The social psychology of organizing*, 2nd edition. Reading, MA: Addison-Wesley.

Winston, P. H. (1984). *Artificial intelligence.* Reading, MA: Addison-Wesley.

Endnotes

[1] The details of this storage design are beyond the scope of the present chapter, and are left for future work.

Chapter XV

An Outline of Approaches to Analyzing the Behavior of Causal Maps[1]

V.K. Narayanan
Drexel University, USA

Jiali Liao
Drexel University, USA

Abstract

Analysis of the behavior of casual maps is not as well developed as the analysis of their content and structure. In this chapter, we propose a set of approaches to examine the behavior of causal maps. Simulation approaches that invoke computer simulations, influence diagrams and fuzzy causal maps are eminently suitable to examine the intrinsic behavior of causal maps. Empirical approaches attempt to build a theory of cognition-behavior linkages from the ground up, by unearthing stable linkages between cognition and behavior. Both approaches could be combined in major programs of research.

Introduction

In empirical works employing causal maps, researchers usually address the content, structure or behavior of causal maps (a point that was elaborated in Chapter I). Content-based studies typically focus on the specific concepts in a causal map or the differences among concepts across maps. Structure refers to the pattern of relationships, or the differences among patterns in comparative studies. Indeed most of the studies reported in this book have chosen to focus on content or structure.

By the term, "the behavior of causal maps" we mean the *prediction* or *analysis* of decisions or actions that one can make, based on a given causal map. Some examples will illustrate the meaning of this definition. For example, if a firm constructed a competitor's causal map with industry conditions as a set of causes and strategic actions as consequences, the firm may be interested in using the causal map to predict the behavior of its competitor, i.e., predicting its competitor's strategic actions. This is of great interest in competitive intelligence systems. In another sense, behavior could refer to the analysis of the consequences of specific policy actions initiated by a firm. As an example, in Information System (IS) design work, if a causal map of the implementation process is constructed (that embraces relevant stakeholders), then designers can assess the consequences of various managerial alternatives in order to identify satisfactory actions that can be initiated by the management during implementation.

The analysis of the behavior of causal maps remains the Holy Grail in research using causal mapping. Although the analysis of behavior is much more prevalent in intervention contexts, empirical research on the behavior of causal maps is almost non-existent. This has been partly due to the absence of easily accessible methodological tools and theoretical lenses. Thus, the primary goal of this chapter is to invite future research in causal map theory focusing on behavior, not merely the content and structure of the maps. Specifically, the chapter aims to: 1) review and summarize promising avenues to connect causal maps and behavior; and 2) enumerate some specific tools to deploy in each avenue.

The scheme of this chapter is as follows: In the next section, we will provide an overview of the fruitful approaches to examining the behavior of causal maps. Following that, we will deal with three simulation approaches. Next we will sketch the empirical approach that we are beginning to witness in some disciplines. We will conclude with a comparative analysis of these approaches.

At the outset, we want to make one observation to place our discussion in perspective: Our approach is to identify fruitful, but not yet tested techniques for the analysis of the behavior of causal maps. Only as these techniques are put to use, will we know their relative merits or applicability. Thus, this chapter represents a preliminary guide to the uncharted territories that remain in the methodology of causal mapping.

Review of Approaches for Studying Behavior

Broadly, we may identify two approaches to the behavioral analysis of causal maps:

1. The first approach relies on computer simulation of causal maps. In both cases — prediction and analysis — it is assumed that since a causal map represents a system of cause-effect linkages, once the values of the causes change, *logically* the effects should change. Here the focus is on logical connections, i.e., what can the intrinsic patterns of relationships within a causal map tell us about future behavior of the unit (e.g., a competitor), without recourse to additional observations.

2. The second approach, which we will call empirical, tries to link the causal maps of any social unit to the actual behavior of the unit itself. Advocated primarily by students of the organization science school, this approach seeks to isolate empirically the behaviors that can be linked to causal maps. The key assumption is that under many conditions these linkages are stable. Hence, once the linkages are empirically established, the behaviors can be predicted from the knowledge of causal maps.

Figure 1 sketches the plan of our review of the approaches to the study of the behavior of causal maps.

Figure 1. A schematic of approaches

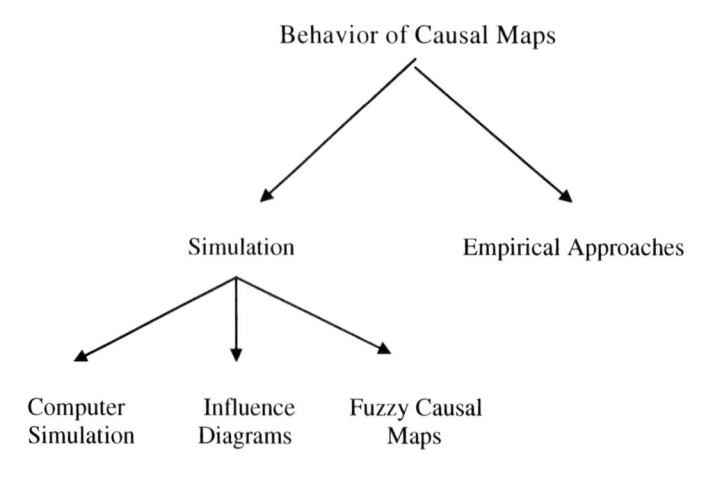

```
                 Behavior of Causal Maps
                   /              \
             Simulation         Empirical Approaches
          /      |      \
  Computer   Influence   Fuzzy Causal
  Simulation Diagrams    Maps
```

Simulation Approaches

Three simulation approaches have been proposed or employed to study the behavior of causal maps:

1. Nozcika, Bonham and Shapiro (1976) have proposed an approach to the computer simulation of individual belief systems.
2. As noted in Chapter I, the affinity of causal maps to system dynamics modeling has prompted some to advocate influence diagrams as a way to analyze the behavior of causal maps.
3. A third approach is based on fuzzy logic and the use of neural networks. Fuzzy logic has been advocated and demonstrated in many IS designs, whereas the possibility of linking fuzzy logic to neural networks has been demonstrated but not widely adopted in the literature.

We will briefly sketch the main ideas in each approach.

Computer Simulation

As reported in Axelrod (1976), Bonham and Shapiro used a computer simulation approach to analyze the cognitive map of a Middle East expert and to predict three years later his explanation of the Syrian Intervention in Jordan in 1970. The authors found a striking resemblance between the predicted explanation and the explanation the expert gave when asked about the actual crisis three years later.

Nozcika et al. (1976) detailed the computer simulation approach Bonham and Shapiro used to generate the predictions. Representing the causal map in matrix form, they derived the reachability matrix (see Chapter II), before generating the predictions. The

Box 1. Nozchika, Bonham and Shapiro's six step process

The six steps employed by Nozcika et al. (1976) were:
1. *Search for antecedent paths*: Involves the identification of the various linear sequences of concepts leading to the concepts highlighted. From the full set of antecedent paths identified, a set of plausible set is derived based on the degree to which relationships on the path are historically supported.
2. *Search for consequent paths*: This step is similar to the previous one but the focus is on the value concepts.
3. *Formulation of alternative explanations*: Explanation selection is based on a path balance matrix, under the axiom that the explanation that will be preferred by the decision maker will be the one with the highest cognitive centrality.
4. *Selection of preferred explanation*: The cognitive centrality of each path is computed and using the preferred explanation search algorithm, explanations are identified.
5. *Search for relevant policy options*: This involves the examination of reachability matrix to determine if for each policy concept, one or more concepts that are part of the explanation are reachable.
6. *Evaluation and ranking of relevant policy options*. Here again a policy impact index is calculated to evaluate and rank policy options.

The authors constructed a simulation model in FORTRAN IVH for the IBM 370/135 system available at the American University Computer Center.

authors chose some concepts for their policy relevance, and once the concepts were established, they employed a six-step process of deriving the predictions (See Box 1).

Bonham and Shapiro argued that this mode of analysis of behavior is very useful in inductive efforts to build a theoretical model of decision making in specific domains. We may add that this approach may also have great value in predicting behavior (e.g., competitors) as well.

Influence Diagrams

In the Roos and Hall (1980) example cited in Chapter I, the authors analyzed the causal map they derived qualitatively to discover the cycles of cause-effect links that explained the behavior of the director of the emergency care unit they studied. The authors acknowledged the limitations of their approach:

It ignores the more complex dynamic properties of feedback, such as dampened or sustained oscillations arising from multi-order negative feedback loops.

To identify the critical feedback loops, Roos and Hall redrew the complex causal map they obtained, by identifying as a starting point variables characterized by a large number of inflows and outflows and by tracing paths through the original causal map that were recursive, i.e., led back to the starting point. This was repeated until every possible path through the system was accounted for. The loops thus identified were analyzed by summing the signs of correlation around each loop in the direction of causality. Roos and Hall noted that they could infer the polarity of a loop since an odd number of negative signs results in a negative feedback loop while no negative signs or an even number of negative signs generates a positive feedback loop. Of course, a negative feedback loop will tend to restore the system to some equilibrium by constraining changes, whereas a positive feedback loop will amplify the changes in the variables in that loop.

Roos and Hall thus illustrated that a complex causal map may not only incorporate direct linkages between variables, but also a set of *indirect* linkages to both virtuous and vicious cycles as represented by the feedback loops. According to them, each loop presented policy choices to accelerate or dampen changes in the emergency care unit under study, and the director of the unit could enact some, but not all of these policy choices.

Roos and Hall (1980) noted that the use of influence diagrams derived from larger causal maps may be a particularly valuable tool for consultants in conflict-laden situations. Stated in our terms, this approach may be useful primarily for intervention contexts.

Fuzzy Causal Map

The connection between Axelrod's causal mapping and fuzzy logic was originally made by Bart Kosko. Kosko's Ph.D. advisor, Lofti Zadeh, then a professor at the University of California Berkeley, had introduced the term "Fuzzy Set," to a set or groups of objects whose elements belonged to the set to different degrees. A technical treatment of fuzzy logic and its application is beyond the scope of this chapter. The interested reader is urged to consult the references given in this chapter as a starting point.

When introduced, fuzzy logic was a controversial idea, but Kosko applied it to the study of causal maps, calling them fuzzy cognitive maps. In his words, "A *fuzzy cognitive map* or FCM draws a causal picture. It ties facts and things and processes to values and policies and objectives. And it lets you predict how complex events interact and play out."

The connection of the causal maps to fuzzy logic occurs in two ways. First, causal arrows in the maps can be weighted with any number between 0 and 1, and with a s + or – sign specified. Second, each node can be fuzzy also by "firing" to some degree from 0% to 100%.

In *Fuzzy Thinking,* Kosko illustrated his ideas with three examples:

1. An example of the first kind was based on an article by Henry Kissinger, "Starting Out in the Direction of Middle East Peace," that appeared in *Los Angeles Times* in 1982. Kosko represented Kissinger's reasoning by means of an FCM, and showed that this FCM had no feedback loops.
2. A second example was an FCM that showed how bad weather could affect the speed with which someone drives on a Los Angeles highway. This had two feedback loops built into them, which made the FCM more complex than the earlier one.
3. A third example was the economic logic behind Walter Williams' article, "South Africa is Changing," that appeared in the *San Diego Union*, which detailed the relationship between foreign investment and apartheid in South Africa.

Kosko made the intriguing connection between the behavior of fuzzy causal maps and dynamic systems, thus opening up the possibility of empirically examining the behavior of causal maps, with predictions grounded in complexity theory. Thus when simulated, FCMs may settle down on one of the three attractors: a fixed-point attractor, a limit-cycle attractor, or chaotic attractor. Kosko argued that FCMs can be simulated by neural nets to discover the behavior of the dynamical system represented by the FCM.

Kosko emphasized that his approach dealt with the intrinsic logic of the causal map, i.e., it can not establish if the predictions are correct but can give insight into the dynamics if the map were accurate. Nonetheless, in all the above examples, he argued that FCMs yielded predictions that on a common sense basis were acceptable.

In recent years, many have advocated the use of fuzzy causal logic for the analysis of causal maps. An illustrative set of papers is listed in Table 1. Yet empirical works using FCMs are still rare, both in organization sciences and in IT. This may partly be due to the lack of awareness of the technique by the empirically minded research community. Given the increasing interest in complexity theory on the part of organizational science scholars, this technique may provide a valuable avenue to move the empirical research onto a solid theoretical foundation.

Table 1. Illustrative examples of papers in IS using fuzzy causal maps (FCM)

Author	Focus	Type	Technique	Software
David Brubaker	Introduction of Fuzzy Cognitive Maps	Theoretical	N/A	N/A
Alex Chong	Establishing and evaluating a framework for DSSG based on FCM	Empirical	Expert opinions	FuzzyGen Self-developed
D.Kardaras, B.Karakostas	Application of FCM in Strategic Planning of IS	Applied	Simulation	Not mentioned
Alberto Vazquez Huerga	Balanced Differential Algorithm to learn Fuzzy Conceptual Maps from data	Theoretical	N/A	N/A
Zahir Irani, Amir Sharif	Use FCM as a technique to model each IT/IS evaluation factor	Applied	N/A	N/A

Empirical Approaches

A conceptual framework for the empirical approach was suggested by Walsh (1995) in his review of work on managerial cognition. The framework incorporated three major themes:

1. Under many conditions, we should expect direct linkages between cognition and behaviors, however,
2. Behaviors mediate the relationship between cognition and outcomes such as grades or profits, and
3. Cognition, in turn, may change due to the feedback of outcomes from behaviors.

The framework is sketched in Figure 2. The figure summarizes the thought-action-outcome linkage as a system of variables, which incorporates both *strategic behavior* (i.e., behavior as the consequence of thought) to realize outcomes, and *learning*

Figure 2. A framework for analyzing behavior

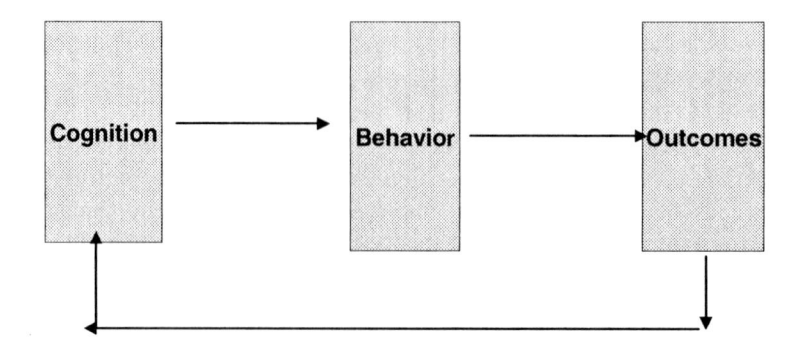

(outcomes leading to change in thought).

Walsh was interested in managerial cognition, broadly conceived. Others, building upon his work, have built up more complex frameworks, appropriate to their disciplinary domains. For example, Rajagopalan and Spreitzer (1997), in their review of research in strategic management, constructed a model that incorporated antecedent conditions, strategies, and both economic and non-economic outcomes. It is outside the purview of this chapter to review different models. Suffice to say, as the work in IS progresses, we expect researchers to develop more complex models in their specific domains.

For our purpose, the utility of the framework is to highlight the empirical approach to establishing the relationship between cognition and behavior. Stable relationships, once established, could become the basis of predictions. We illustrate this approach with a couple of examples:

1. Calori, Johnson and Sarnin (1994) linked the degree of diversification and the complexity of the causal maps of decision makers. They argued that complex maps are needed to manage diversified corporations, since these companies are more complex than non-diversified corporations.
2. Nadkarni and Narayanan (2004) argued that both complexity and centrality of causal maps are drivers of strategic flexibility. Complexity will be reflected in a broad strategic repertoire (resources and competitive actions) and more frequent shifts in both resources and competitive actions, whereas centrality constrains both behaviors.

These relationships are among the easier to hypothesize, and hence it is not surprising that researchers initially paid attention to them. Nonetheless, both these approaches suggest stable relationships between causal maps and certain behaviors. The empirical approach focuses on accumulating these predictions to generate a theory of cognition-induced behavior. Once accomplished, such a theory could become the basis of predictions.

Concluding Thoughts

Although many of the above listed approaches have multiple uses, there may be differential advantages:

1. Computer-based simulations and influence diagrams appear to be eminently suited for intervention contexts, sine they require judgment about the specific alternatives to explore.
2. Fuzzy causal maps appear useful for investigations that attempt to link causal maps and complexity theory.
3. Domain specific empirical approaches may be useful in hypothesis testing studies or in studies attempting to build an empirically grounded theory.

Also there are advantages to combining simulation and behavioral approaches. Simulation approaches that explore the intrinsic behavior of causal maps, may be used to predict behavior which then may be compared to actual behavior (as in Shapiro and Bonham study). In this sense, unexpected behaviors or counter examples can be unearthed which become the foci of theory expansion or modification.

As we have noted, the analysis of behavior of causal maps is in its infancy. We urge researchers interested in advancing causal mapping methodology to give serious attention to this facet of causal maps.

References

Axelrod, R. (1976). *Structure of decision: The cognitive maps of political elites.* Princeton, NJ: Princeton University Press.

Brubaker, D. (1996a). Fuzzy cognitive maps, *EDN Magazine,* 41(8), 209-211.

Brubaker, D. (1996b). More on fuzzy cognitive maps, *EDN Magazine,* 41(9), 213-215.

Calori, R., Johnson, G., & Sarnin, P. (1994). CEOs' cognitive maps and the scope of the organization. *Strategic Management Journal,* 15(6), 437-457.

Chong, A. (2001). Development of a fuzzy cognitive map based decision support system generator, Department of Information Technology, Murdoch University, *Fourth Western Australian Workshop on Information Systems Research.* Retrieved from the World Wide Web at: http://wawisr01.uwa.edu.au/2001/Chong2.pdf

Irani, Z. Sharif, A. Love P.E., & Kahraman, C. (2002). Applying concepts of fuzzy cognitive mapping to model: The IT/IS investment evaluation process. *International Journal of Production Economics,* 75, 199-211.

Kardaras, D., & Karakostas, B. (1999). The use of fuzzy cognitive maps to simulate information systems strategic planning process. *Information and Software Technology,* 41(4), 197-210.

Khan, M.S. Chong, A., & Quaddus, M. (1999). Fuzzy cognitive maps and intelligent decision support-a review, *Proceedings of the 2nd Western Australian Workshop on Information Systems Research, WAWISR 1999,* Murdoch University, Murdoch, Western Australia. Retrieved from the World Wide Web at: http://wawisr01.uwa.edu.au/1999/KhanChongQuaddus.pdf

Kosko, B. (1993). *Fuzzy thinking: The new science of fuzzy logic.* New York: Hyperion.

Liu, Z. (1999). Contextual fuzzy cognitive map for decision support in geographic information systems. *IEEE Transactions on Fuzzy Systems,* 7(5), 495-507.

Marchant, T. (1999). Cognitive maps and fuzzy implications, *European Journal of Operational Research,* 114(3), 626-637.

Miao, Y., & Liu, Z.Q. (2000). On causal inference in fuzzy cognitive map, *IEEE Transac-*

tions on Fuzzy Systems, 8, 107-119.

Nadkarni, S., & Narayanan, V.K. (2004). Strategy frames, strategic flexibility and firm performance: The moderating role of industry clockspeed. *Best Paper Proceedings of the Academy of Management Conference 2004,* New Orleans, LA (in press).

Nozcika, G.J., Bonham, G.M., & Shapiro, M.J. (1976). Simulation techniques. In R. Axelrod (Ed.), *Structure of decision: the cognitive maps of political elites* (pp. 349-359). Princeton, NJ: Princeton University Press.

Rajagopalan, N., & Spreitzer, G. (1997). Toward a theory of strategic change: A multi-lens perspective and integrative framework. *Academy of Management Review*, 22(1), 48-80.

Roos, L.L., & Hall, R.I. (1980). Influence diagrams and organizational power. *Administrative Science Quarterly,* 25(1), 57–71.

Vazquez, A. (2002). A balanced differential learning algorithm in fuzzy cognitive maps. Technical Report, Departament de Llenguatges i Sistemes Informatics, Universitat Politecnica de Catalunya (UPC), C\Jordi Girona 1–3, E0834, Barcelona, Spain. Retrieved from the World Wide Web at: *http://www.upc.es/web/QR2002/Papers/QR2002%20-%20Vazquez.pdf*

Walsh, J.P. (1995). Managerial and organizational cognition: Notes from a trip down memory lane. *Organization Science*, 6, 280-321.

Zhang, J.Y., Liu, Q., & Zhou, S. (2003). Quotient FCMs-A decomposition theory for fuzzy cognitive maps. *IEEE Transactions on Fuzzy Systems*, 11(5), 593-604.

Endnotes

[1] The authors thank Paige Rutner, University of Arkansas for her comments on an earlier draft of this chapter.

About the Authors

V.K. Narayanan is currently the Stubbs professor of strategy and entrepreneurship at Drexel University, Philadelphia, Pennsylvania (USA) and Associate Dean for Research in the LeBow College of Business. He holds a Ph.D. in business from the Graduate School of Business at the University of Pittsburgh, Pennsylvania. Since 1988, he has been on the editorial board of *Organization Science*. He has authored (or co-authored) more than 60 papers and four books. His articles have appeared in leading professional journals such as *Academy of Management Journal, Academy of Management Review, Management Information Systems Quarterly, R&D Management* and *Strategic Management Journal*.

Deborah J. Armstrong is an assistant professor of information systems at the University of Arkansas (USA). She received her Ph.D. from the University of Kansas (2001) with a concentration in information systems and supporting emphasis in organizational communications. Dr. Armstrong's research interests cover a variety of issues at the intersection of IS personnel and mental models involving the human aspects of technology, change, learning and cognition.

****

Fran Ackermann is a professor of strategy and information systems. Her main research areas include investigating how information systems can enhance the process of modeling complex qualitative data (in areas such as strategy making, problem solving and project failure). Through using a combination of cause mapping and information systems she is interested in exploring how the processes of eliciting, structuring, analyzing and enabling the group to directly interact with the resultant model can be supported and enhanced. With Colin Eden she has developed both Decision Explorer and Group Explorer, group decision support packages enabling groups to manage such complexity. She has written widely in the fields of management science, strategic management and information systems.

Mari W. Buche is an assistant professor of information systems at Michigan Technological University (USA). She earned her Ph.D. in business administration/management information systems from the University of Kansas. She investigates issues related to the impact and management of technology change on employees within the business environment. Her research interests include software engineering, change management, information security, and work force issues in IS. Her current work focuses on the changing work identity of information technology professionals.

Kathleen M. Carley is a professor of computation, organizations and society at the Institute for Software Research International at Carnegie Mellon University (USA). She received her Ph.D. from Harvard University. Her research combines cognitive science, social networks and computer science. Her specific research areas are computational social and organization theory, group, organizational and social adaptation and evolution, dynamic network analysis, computational text analysis, and the impact of telecommunication technologies and policy on communication, information diffusion, disease contagion and response within and among groups particularly in disaster or crisis situations. She has co-edited several books including: *Computational Organization Theory, Simulating Organizations, and Dynamic Network Analysis*.

Gail P. Clarkson earned her Ph.D. at Leeds University Business School, The University of Leeds (UK) where she is currently employed as a post-doctoral researcher, under the auspices of the UK Advanced Institute of Management Research (AIM). A recent entrant to the academic profession, following a successful career as a university administrator, Dr. Clarkson has particular expertise in the application of causal mapping techniques in organizational field settings. In collaboration with Gerard P. Hodgkinson, she is currently investigating sensemaking and other socio-cognitive processes among frontline workers, with a view to developing new insights that will ultimately enhance employee effectiveness and well being.

James F. Courtney is a professor of management information systems at the University of Central Florida in Orlando (USA). He received his Ph.D. in Business Administration with a major in management science from the University of Texas at Austin. His papers have appeared in several journals, including *Management Science, MIS Quarterly, Communications of the ACM, IEEE Transactions on Systems, Man and Cybernetics, Decision Sciences, Decision Support Systems, the Journal of Management Information Systems, Database, Interfaces, the Journal of Applied Systems Analysis*, and the *Journal of Experiential Learning and Simulation*. His present research interests are knowledge-based decision support systems, knowledge management, inquiring (learning) organizations and sustainable economic systems.

Copyright © 2005, Idea Group Inc. Copying or distributing in print or electronic forms without written permission of Idea Group Inc. is prohibited.

About the Authors

Jana Diesner is a research associate and linguistic programmer at the Center for Computational Analysis of Social and Organizational Systems (CASOS) at the Institute for Software Research International, School of Computer Science, Carnegie Mellon University (USA). She received her master's degree in communication science from the Dresden University of Technology (Germany). Her research combines communication science, linguistics, social networks, and computer science. Her specific research area is computational text analysis. She investigates new approaches towards the effective and efficient analysis of the network structure of large-scale collections of textual data and methodological aspects of the technique.

Colin Eden is director of the University of Strathclyde Graduate School of Business and Professor of Strategic Management and Management Science (UK). His major research interests are the relationship between operational decision making practices and their strategic consequences; the processes of strategy making in management teams; the use of group decision support in the analysis and making of strategy; and managerial and organizational cognition. He is the author of seven books and over 150 scholarly articles in management science and strategic management.

Gerard P. Hodgkinson (Ph.D., University of Sheffield) is a professor of organizational behaviour and strategic management at Leeds University Business School, The University of Leeds (UK). His principal research interests center on the analysis of psychological factors in individual and organizational decision making, effectiveness and wellbeing (especially the nature and significance of actors' mental models and the development and validation of methodological techniques for the investigation of managerial and organizational cognition). His work on these and other topics has appeared in a number of major journals and other prestigious outlets including *Human Relations, Organizational Research Methods, Organization Studies* and *Strategic Management Journal*.

Luca Iandoli received his degree in electronics engineering. Currently he is a researcher with the Department of Business and Managerial Engineering, University of Naples Federico II (Italy). In 1998 he received a graduation award from Fiat Research Center; in 1999 he worked at the Department of Computer Science of University of Naples within the European research project Compete. His current research interests include application of soft computing techniques to business and management, human resource management and decision making support systems. His papers have been published in *Small Business Economics, Journal of Global Information Technology and Management, Journal of Information Science and Technology,* and *Fuzzy Economic Review*.

Jiali Liao received a B.E. (Industrial Management Engineering) from Xi'an Jiaotong University and Master of Management from Xi'an Jiaotong University (1999). She is currently a doctoral student at the department of decision sciences, Drexel University (USA). Her research interests include financial engineering and risk management.

Tor J. Larsen earned a Ph.D. in management information systems from the University of Minnesota. Since then he has worked as associate professor at the Norwegian School of Management (Norway), Department of Leadership and Organizational Management. From 2001-2002, he was visiting professor at the John Cook School of Business, Saint Louis University. In addition to reviewing for many central conferences and journals, he has acted as associate editor for the *Journal of Global Information Management, Computing Personnel*, and *MIS Quarterly*. Dr. Larsen's publications are found in publications such as *Information & Management* and the *Journal of MIS*. His present research interests include innovation, diffusion, innovation outcome specification, management information systems, and systems development.

Douglas L. Micklich is an instructional assistant professor of management at Illinois State University in Normal, Illinois (USA). He holds an M.B.A. from Illinois State University and undergraduate degrees in management information systems and organizational behavior from The University of Tulsa. Doug's research interests include the role of information systems in strategy formulation and implementation, corporate and competitive strategy, concept/causal mapping in strategy, and leadership in strategy development and implementation. He is published in *The Journal of Private Enterprise* and has articles in the proceedings of professional organizations such as *The Association of Private Enterprise Education, The Association for Business Simulation and Experiential Learning* and *The Small Business Director's Association*.

Kay Nelson is an associate professor of MIS and director of The Center for Information Technologies in Management at the Fisher College of Business, The Ohio State University (USA). She holds a Ph.D. from the University of Texas at Austin in information systems. Dr. Nelson has published articles about IT strategy issues, software engineering, and IT/Business partnership in publications such as *MIS Quarterly, European Journal of Information Systems* and *Decision Support Systems*. Her research awards include the ICIS best paper award and the WITS best paper award. Dr. Nelson is a National Science Foundation Career Scholar.

Fred Niederman serves as the Shaughnessy Endowed Professor of MIS at Saint Louis University (USA). His doctoral degree is from the University of Minnesota. His primary research areas pertain to using information technology to support teams and groups, global information technology, and information technology personnel. He has published more than 20 refereed journal articles include several in top MIS journals including *MIS Quarterly, Communications of the ACM*, and *Decision Sciences*; has presented papers at several major conferences; serves as associate editor of the *Journal of Global Information Systems*.

Robert F. Otondo is an assistant professor of management information systems at The University of Memphis (USA). He received his Ph.D. in computer information systems from the School of Accountancy and Information Management at Arizona State University. Dr. Otondo's research interests include organizational learning, knowledge management, and system dynamics, and their associations with emerging technologies such as Radio Frequency IDentification (RFID). His research has been published or accepted by *Decision Support Systems, Personnel Psychology, Best Paper Proceedings of the Academy of Management Conference, Cycle Time Research*, the *Society for Industrial and Organizational Psychology Conference*, and academic books.

Marshall Scott Poole (Ph.D., University of Wisconsin) is a professor of information and operations management and of communication at Texas A&M University (USA). He has conducted research and published extensively on the topics of group and organizational communication, computer-mediated communication systems, information systems impacts on organizations, conflict management, and organizational innovation. He has co-authored or edited eight books including *A Manual for Group Facilitation, Communication and Group Decision-Making, Research on the Management of Innovation*, and *Organizational Change and Innovation Processes: Theory and Methods for Research*.

Tom L. Roberts is an assistant professor in the Accounting and Information Systems Department in the School of Business at the University of Kansas (USA). His current research interests include project management, collaborative technology, and the behavioral aspects of the information technology profession. His publications have appeared in variety of IS journals.

Steven D. Sheetz is an associate professor of accounting and information systems at the Pamplin College of Business at Virginia Tech (USA). He received his Ph.D. in information systems from the University of Colorado. His research interests include the cognitive complexity of developing information systems, learning and use of object-oriented development techniques, medical information systems, and the application of group support systems technology. He has published articles in *Decision Support Systems, International Journal of Human-Computer Studies, Journal of Management Information Systems, Journal of Systems and Software, Decision Support Systems*, and *Object-Oriented Systems*.

Rajendra P. Srivastava is the Ernst & Young professor of accounting and Director of the Ernst & Young Center for Auditing Research and Advanced Technology at the School of Business, University of Kansas (USA). He holds a Ph.D. in accounting from the University of Oklahoma, Norman and a Ph.D. in physics from Oregon State University, Corvallis. Professor Srivastava's publications have appeared in *The Accounting Review, Journal of Accounting Research, Auditing: A Journal of Practice and Theory, Journal of Management Information Systems* and many other accounting and AI journals. He is currently associate editor of *Journal of Emerging Technologies in Accounting*, and has been a member of the editorial and review board of several journals.

David P. Tegarden received his Ph.D. from the University of Colorado at Boulder. He is an associate professor of information systems and a research fellow in the Center for Human-Computer Interaction at Virginia Tech (USA). His current research areas include object-oriented software engineering, collaborative cognitive and concept mapping, continuous assurance, and information visualization. He has published in the *Communications of the AIS, Decision Support Systems, International Journal of Accounting Information Systems, International Journal of Human Computer Studies, Journal of Information Systems, Journal of Management Information Systems, Journal of Systems and Software, Object-Oriented Systems, Omega,* and *Software Quality Journal.*

Linda F. Tegarden received her Ph.D. from University of Colorado at Boulder and is an associate professor of management at Virginia Tech (USA). Her areas include strategy, entrepreneurship and innovation management. In addition to causal mapping research in the strategic management area, she also studies performance implications of innovation and technological change on both incumbents and startups and strategic planning processes in high technology environments. Her articles are published in *Strategic Management Journal, Journal of Management Studies, Journal of High Technology Management, Entrepreneurship Theory and Practice, Journal of Managerial Issues* and *Journal of Business Research.*

Huy V. Vo is an assistant professor of management information systems at Ho Chi Minh City University of Technology (Vietnam). He received his Ph.D. in business administration (management information systems) from Texas A&M University. He has published articles focusing on organizational problem formulation, IS curriculum development for developing countries, and decision support systems in journals like *International Journal of Information Technology and Decision Making* and *Electronic Journal of Information Systems on Developing Countries.* His present research interests are system dynamics organizational problem formulation, multiple perspective approach to IS development, and IS issues (ERP implementation, e-commerce acceptance, etc.) in developing countries.

Giuseppe Zollo is a professor of business and management at the Faculty of Engineering of the University of Naples Federico II (Italy). During the years 1985-86 he was visiting research associate at the Department of Economics of Northeastern University. He published many articles in the area of technological innovation, small innovative enterprises, information technology management, competencies management, software industry, fuzzy sets, and evaluation systems. His papers have been published in *International Contributions to Labour Studies, Journal of Systems and Software, International Journal of Technology Management, International Journal of Manufacturing Technology and Management, Omega, Small Business, Information Resources Management Journal, Fuzzy Economic Review,* and *R&D Management.*

Index

A

abstraction 352
aggregate mapping approach 144
aggregating 145
aggregation 352
analysis and design 236
applicative cycle 178
argument 350
argument cognitive maps 349
association 350
AutoMap 88

B

basic probability assignment function 113
behavioral simulation 295
belief function approach 109
belief functions 110
benchmarking 31

C

categorical 350
categories 198
causal assertions 20
causal inference 5
causal map(s) 2, 22, 47, 109, 206, 343
causal map elicitation 208
causal mapping 143, 206
causal mapping (CM) 1, 20, 47, 110, 233, 285, 314
causal statements 27, 196
cause-effect relationships 4
class structures 354
cluster analysis 205
coding 6
coding guidelines 267
coding scheme 30, 196
cognitive diversity 204, 205
cognitive factions 205
cognitive map 6, 21
cognitive mapping 47
cognitive maps 2, 48, 144, 350
collective belief systems 50
collective cause maps 205
collective maps 143
comparison of causal maps 56
comprehensiveness 176
concept classification 87
concept identification 87
concept/cognitive mapping 285
concepts 198
conceptual underpinnings 178
congregate mapping 144
constructs 176, 198
content 3, 22, 189
corporate strategy 285
covert networks 89
critical success factors 285
critical value activities 285

D

data flow diagrams 234
decision analysis 127
decision theory 5
Dempster-Shafer 110
Dempster-Shafer (D-S) theory 109
Dempster's rule of combination 111, 114
dependence 285
descriptive modeling 111
diagram 35
discovery 195
discovery contexts 14
diversity 177

E

empirical approaches 374
encapsulation 352
entity identification 87
evaluative assertion analysis 5
evidential diagram 110
evidential nework 116
evidential reasoning 110
evocative contexts 15
expert-anchored 13

F

four-stage process 180
fuzzy causal map 372
fuzzy logic 371

G

graph and analyze data 87
graph theory 5, 351
group mapping 265
group support systems 208

H

hierarchy 352
human behavior 2
hypothesis testing 9

I

ideographic 54
in information systems 143
industrial dynamics 3
influence diagrams 8, 371
information asymmetry 292
information silos 292
information symmetry 285
information systems (IS) 46, 263, 264
information technology (IT) 1, 46, 109
inheritance 362
interactively elicited causal maps 22, 196
interrelated information 144
intervention contexts 16
interview execution 240
interview transcripts 196
interviews 179
IS developers 275
IS research 12

J

job satisfaction 110

K

knowledge 84
knowledge elicitation 48
knowledge engineering 313
knowledge management 313
knowledge management practices 312

L

level of agreement 197
level of granularity 198
life cycle 314
links-to-nodes ratio 145

M

map analysis 84
map density 145
map structure 55
matrix 35
mental models 88
meta-matrix model 81
meta-matrix text analysis 88
methods 355
modularization 352

N

neural networks 371
nomothetic 54

O

object structures 355
object-oriented (OO) software 174
object-oriented modeling 352
objectivist 13
ontological status 48
OO software development 175
open-ended questions 196
organizational context 234
organizational memory 318, 357

P

perform map analysis 87
probability theory 112
probes 196
project outcomes 235
propagation of beliefs 118
psycho-logic 5
psychometric proprieties 60

Q

qualitative 4, 40

R

RCMs 175
reachability 183
reliability 30, 60
research contexts 22
revealed causal map 22
revealed causal mapping (RCM) 110, 111, 180, 195
revealed causal maps 50, 110, 175

S

semantic networks 83
sensitivity analysis 127
shared meaning 51
simulation 369
social causal mapping 345
social constructionist 13

social network analysis (SNA) 85
soft systems methodology (SSM) 264
software development 313
stakeholders 263
standard vocabularies 9
strategic business units (SBU) 291
strategic planning 204
strategy development 266
structure 21, 177
structure of arguments 3
structured interviews 238
structured systems analysis and design method (SSA 264
survey 186
system dynamics 371
systems development projects 238

T

text based causal maps 22
theoretical cycle 178
theoretical frameworks 176
theory-driven 31
top management team 204
Toulmin framework 3
traversal 351

U

unified modeling language (UML) 233, 234
users 275

V

validity 60

W

workshop 270

Instant access to the latest offerings of Idea Group, Inc. in the fields of
INFORMATION SCIENCE, TECHNOLOGY AND MANAGEMENT!

InfoSci-Online Database

- BOOK CHAPTERS
- JOURNAL ARTICLES
- CONFERENCE PROCEEDINGS
- CASE STUDIES

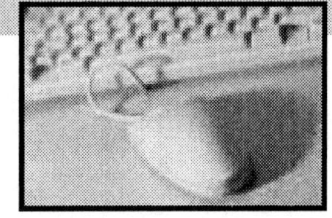

"The Bottom Line: With easy to use access to solid, current and in-demand information, InfoSci-Online, reasonably priced, is recommended for academic libraries."

- Excerpted with permission from Library Journal, July 2003 Issue, Page 140

The InfoSci-Online database is the most comprehensive collection of full-text literature published by Idea Group, Inc. in:

- Distance Learning
- Knowledge Management
- Global Information Technology
- Data Mining & Warehousing
- E-Commerce & E-Government
- IT Engineering & Modeling
- Human Side of IT
- Multimedia Networking
- IT Virtual Organizations

BENEFITS
- Instant Access
- Full-Text
- Affordable
- Continuously Updated
- Advanced Searching Capabilities

Start exploring at www.infosci-online.com

Recommend to your Library Today!
Complimentary 30-Day Trial Access Available!

A product of:
Information Science Publishing*
Enhancing knowledge through information science

*A company of Idea Group, Inc.
www.idea-group.com

BROADEN YOUR IT COLLECTION WITH IGP JOURNALS

Idea Group Publishing is an innovative international publishing company, founded in 1987, specializing in information science, technology and management books, journals and teaching cases. As a leading academic/scholarly publisher, IGP is pleased to announce the introduction of 14 new technology-based research journals, in addition to its existing 11 journals published since 1987, which began with its renowned Information Resources Management Journal.

Free Sample Journal Copy

Should you be interested in receiving a **free sample copy** of any of IGP's existing or upcoming journals please mark the list below and provide your mailing information in the space provided, attach a business card, or email IGP at journals@idea-group.com.

Upcoming IGP Journals
January 2005

- ☐ Int. Journal of Data Warehousing & Mining
- ☐ Int. Journal of Business Data Comm. & Networking
- ☐ International Journal of Cases on E-Commerce
- ☐ International Journal of E-Business Research
- ☐ International Journal of E-Collaboration
- ☐ Int. Journal of Electronic Government Research
- ☐ Int. Journal of Enterprise Information Systems
- ☐ Int. Journal of Intelligent Information Technologies
- ☐ Int. Journal of Knowledge Management
- ☐ Int. Journal of Info. & Comm. Technology Education
- ☐ Int. Journal of Technology & Human Interaction
- ☐ Int. J. of Web-Based Learning & Teaching Tech.'s

Established IGP Journals

- ☐ Annals of Cases on Information Technology
- ☐ Information Management
- ☐ Information Resources Management Journal
- ☐ Information Technology Newsletter
- ☐ Int. Journal of Distance Education Technologies
- ☐ Int. Journal of IT Standards and Standardization Research
- ☐ International Journal of Web Services Research
- ☐ Journal of Database Management
- ☐ Journal of Electronic Commerce in Organizations
- ☐ Journal of Global Information Management
- ☐ Journal of Organizational and End User Computing

Name: _____ Affiliation: _____

Address: _____

_____

E-mail: _____ Fax: _____

Visit the IGI website for more information on these journals at www.idea-group.com/journals/

IDEA GROUP PUBLISHING
A company of Idea Group Inc.
701 East Chocolate Avenue, Hershey, PA 17033-1240, USA
Tel: 717-533-8845; 866-342-6657 • 717-533-8661 (fax)

Journals@idea-group.com   www.idea-group.com

NEW RELEASE

Web Information Systems

David Taniar, PhD, Monash University, Australia
Johanna Wenny Rahayu, PhD, La Trobe University, Australia

The Internet is already more widely deployed than any other computing system in history and continues to grow rapidly. New technologies, including high speed wide area network and improved software support for distribution, promise to make the Internet much more useful for general purpose distributed computing in the future. ***Web Information Systems*** is dedicated to the new era of information systems on web environments, due to not only the growing popularity of the web technology but also the roles that web technology play in modern information systems. The major elements of web information systems include web semantics, XML technologies, web mining and querying, web-based information systems, information extraction, and web semantics.

ISBN 1-59140-208-5 (h/c) • US$79.95 • ISBN 1-59140-283-2 (s/c) • US$64.95
• 388 pages • Copyright © 2004

"*The uniqueness of this book is not only due to the fact that it is dedicated to important issues in Web information systems but also due to the solid mixture of both theoretical aspects as well as practical aspects of web information system development.*"

- David Taniar, PhD &
Johanna Wenny Rahayu, PhD

**It's Easy to Order! Order online at www.idea-group.com or
call 717/533-8845 x10
Mon-Fri 8:30 am-5:00 pm (est) or fax 24 hours a day 717/533-8661**

Idea Group Publishing

Hershey • London • Melbourne • Singapore

An excellent addition to your library

2004 RELEASE

Business Intelligence in the Digital Economy:
Opportunities, Limitations and Risks

Mahesh Raisinghani, PhD, University of Dallas, USA

Business Intelligence in the Digital Economy: Opportunities, Limitations and Risks describes what Business Intelligence (BI) is, how it is being conducted and managed and its major opportunities, limitations, issues and risks. This book takes an in-depth look at the scope of global technological change and BI. During this transition to BI, information does not merely add efficiency to the transaction, it adds value. Companies that are able to leverage the speed and ubiquity of digital communications are going to have the advantage over those who are late-adopters in the years to come. The book brings together high quality expository discussions from experts in this field to identify, define, and explore BI methodologies, systems, and approaches in order to understand the opportunities, limitations and risks.

ISBN 1-59140-206-9 (h/c) • US$79.95 • ISBN 1-59140-280-8 (s/c) • US$64.95
• 304 pages • Copyright © 2004

"*Business Intelligence in the Digital Economy: Opportunities, Limitations and Risks* discusses current state-of-the-art best practices and future directions/trends in Business Intelligence technologies and applications as well as Business Intelligence in next generation enterprises and virtual organizations."

– Mahesh Raisinghani, PhD
University of Dallas, USA

**It's Easy to Order! Order online at www.idea-group.com or
call 717/533-8845 x10
Mon-Fri 8:30 am-5:00 pm (est) or fax 24 hours a day 717/533-8661**

Idea Group Publishing
Hershey • London • Melbourne • Singapore

An excellent addition to your library